WOMEN, WAR, AND THE MAKING OF BANGLADESH

WOMEN, WAR, AND THE MAKING OF BANGLADESH

Remembering 1971

YASMIN SAIKIA

DUKE UNIVERSITY PRESS

DURHAM AND LONDON

2011

ORIGINALLY PUBLISHED IN INDIA IN 2011
BY WOMEN UNLIMITED, K-36, HAUZ KHAS ENCLAVE,
NEW DELHI-110016, INDIA
PUBLISHED OUTSIDE OF THE
SOUTH ASIAN MARKET BY DUKE UNIVERSITY PRESS
ALL RIGHTS RESERVED
PRINTED IN THE UNITED STATES OF AMERICA
ON ACID-FREE PAPER ∞
DESIGNED BY KATY CLOVE
TYPESET IN HOEFLER TEXT BY ACHORN INTERNATIONAL
LIBRARY OF CONGRESS CATALOGING-IN-
PUBLICATION DATA APPEAR ON THE LAST
PRINTED PAGE OF THIS BOOK.

For

JAHANARA RAHMAN-SAIKIA (1936–2009)

Philosopher, teacher, social worker, friend, mother

CONTENTS

Preface ix

Acknowledgments xv

Glossary of Terms xix

PART I

INTRODUCING 1971

———

1. THE TOLD AND UNTOLD STORIES OF 1971 3

2. CREATING THE HISTORY OF 1971 34

PART II

SURVIVORS SPEAK

———

3. VICTIMS' MEMORIES 109

4. WOMEN'S SERVICES 158

5. WOMEN'S WAR 186

PART III

A NEW BEGINNING

———

POSTSCRIPT: LESSONS OF VIOLENCE 215

Notes 243

References 279

Index 299

South Asia, a term coined by the United States government in the post–cold war era, was quickly adopted in academic circles. In 1964 the Centre of South Asian Studies opened at Cambridge University. Today, academics use the terms *South Asia* and *Indian subcontinent* interchangeably with the emphasis, of course, on Indian Studies, which is the primary focus of most of the scholarly research and writing. In 1999 when I was selected to hold the first appointment in South Asian history at the University of North Carolina, Chapel Hill, I suddenly acquired the title of assistant professor of South Asian history. No one asked me nor did I understand the implication of this newfound responsibility, but I knew that South Asian history is much more than Indian history, a field I had studied for several years in India and the United States. Since I had taken up the position to teach South Asian history, I had to deliver on my commitment. This meant learning and studying South Asia on my own in order to teach it to my students once I had some grasp of the region and its multilayered, multifaceted history. And what better way to learn about the people and places of South Asia than traveling and listening to these people tell their history from their very own experiences?

As a person of Indian origin, for me travel to Pakistan was a little tricky and the outbreak of the Kargil war in 1999 made any person-to-person interactions even more complicated and difficult. Bangladesh, on the other hand, was a little less threatening. Being close to my home state of Assam, I was somewhat familiar with the Bengali language and people with whom we share a love-hate relationship, but beyond this acquired politics of identity I had a personal connection to Dhaka. My father had studied at Dhaka University for several years, and the memories that he shared with me were the basis of my curiosity and fueled my desire to travel there. Also, because the relations between India and Bangladesh were semi-friendly, it enabled me to get a visa and travel to Dhaka in the summer of 1999 before I started my teaching job at Chapel Hill.

Once in Dhaka I decided that my first visit would be to the Dhaka University in memory of my father. Though instead of going to the university, I was taken to a "forbidden" place called Camp Geneva where the "stateless" Bihari community lives. In Camp Geneva people were very curious about me, why I was there, what I wanted, and some were even hostile. Once they heard me speak in Urdu (their mother tongue), they recognized I was not a Bengali woman and many welcomed me to listen to their saga of misery after the war of 1971 and their present status as people without identity. While I was speaking with two middle-aged women outside their shack, a young man approached us. One of the women was his mother. When his mother went inside her hut to fetch a picture of her parents who were killed in the war, he told me, "My parents will go to their graves without anyone knowing their story. Why must we suffer for the crimes of another generation?" This question stunned me.

Instantly, I realized that for a community living under the negative power of history's politics it is not a subject of research and study; it is a burdensome inheritance filled with hidden memories. This chance encounter motivated me to find and write a history of South Asia, and not a history of its made-up glorious past or its rich legacy of semi-mythical heroes. I would instead look for heroes in the people who experienced history in their lives and would be willing to share it. Also, it became clear to me that 1971 is a very appropriate beginning point to investigate such a history of South Asia because it is a distinctive moment; this was the only instance after the end of British colonialism when the people and governments of the Indian subcontinent—India, Pakistan, and Bangladesh—encountered each other. This encounter was not friendly or nostalgic, but it was designed and expressed in violence and terror. Since then the three nation-states of the subcontinent have never shared a common moment together. Thus my journey to explore and probe the history of South Asia began in 1971.

For several years thereafter, I spent extended periods of time in Bangladesh, Pakistan, and India meeting and talking, listening and sharing with people their stories of the war. It was a journey into deep pain and unforgettable memories of loss for survivors, but I also saw the face of incredible resilience and heartening human compassion. Every time I despaired about the South Asian human community, I was immediately reminded of the inexhaustible source of human endurance and respect for fellow human beings, and I became intimately aware of the capacity of good and evil within us. History was no longer someone else's story or a project for teaching, research, and getting tenure; it was a personal encounter to know and become implicated in the shared story of the past and present and learn to share the space with one another. Refracting from the moment and memories of 1971 I have tried to convey the message of a common human narrative that survivors share with us.

My focus is on the story of gender violence in the war of 1971 in Bangladesh, concentrating on the relationships between nation, history, and women—one of the most vulnerable groups in postcolonial South Asia. Moving beyond the external story of the war as a clash of ideologies and struggle for power between rivals India and Pakistan and East and West Pakistan, I tell the story of the war as a human event of individual losses and personal tragedies suffered by both women and men. Their individual stories articulate a collective loss of humanity (*insāniyat*) that transcends the politics of history and nation. Combining oral testimony with archival research in India, Pakistan, and Bangladesh, I weave together the social, political, and cultural history of the subcontinent after the partition of India and Pakistan in 1947 to show the gaps between people and their governments, memories, and history. By privileging oral testimonies of the survivors of 1971, a spotlight shines on unfamiliar heroes and on their suppressed and hidden memories, essentially recovering a people's history. My goal is to demonstrate the importance of studying violence, and by knowing it ethically and personally we move toward developing a human language for reconciliation between victims and perpetrators—women and men, as well as nations like India, Pakistan, and Bangladesh.

I have divided the book into three parts. In part I, I engage the theoretical and methodological issues of writing about violence from a South Asian viewpoint. I tell the story of 1971 as people experienced it, decolonizing the narrative of postcolonial history and claiming agency that enables "us" to accept the good and bad within "our" history. By using a cultural methodology to write the story of violence, I emphasize the forgotten, premodern exchanges and dialogues between the Sufi and Bhakti traditions that had generated a vocabulary of insāniyat and a shared responsiveness that enabled humanization, which was undermined by violence in 1971. It is women who invoke the capacity to remember and enable a new narrative, highlighting women's humanity despite the violence they suffered.

From a theoretical standpoint, I privilege the investigation of the partition of 1947 and its representation by South Asian scholars, and I weave my story of 1971 with theirs to continue the conversation on how to write a history of violence in South Asia within its shared cultural and historical experiences. To show that the South Asian case is neither unique nor exclusive, I have drawn upon the literature of the Holocaust, the Truth and Reconciliation Commission in South Africa, and the genocides in Rwanda and Darfur that make evident the widespread nature of violence and connect multiple stories by people in many different parts of the world. In chapter 2, I draw on the concept of forgiveness by presenting the Islamic concept of *huquq al-ibād* (rights of humans) and individual responsibility to suggest closure for the traumatic violence of 1971.

The heart of the book is part II, where women share their stories of the war. Women's stories are rich and varied, and they tell their experiences in polyversal narratives that continuously make us aware of the feminine self that was under siege during the war but could not be destroyed.[1] In part II, I tell the stories not only of victims, *birangonas* (a term coined in 1972 to recognize the rape survivors of the war), but I also include the voices of women who worked in multiple capacities during the war, as active participants giving care and support to victims and survivors, and, in addition, as soldiers that joined the war. Chapter 5 focuses on women as warriors and is particularly useful because it shows women as aggressors capable of doing the same violent acts as men did in the war, with the exception of rape.

The narratives of part II consist of testimonies produced verbatim, with only slight modifications to eliminate repetition and some redundancies when necessary. The names of the women are pseudonyms unless someone explicitly requested I use her real name. Even then, I have tried not to give details about individuals because of the sensitive nature of the testimonies that may lead to women's further marginalization for speaking out against the established official narrative and due to social and religious backlash in a conservative Muslim society such as Bangladesh.

Chapter 3, "Victims' Memories," consists of five testimonies focusing on rape and its impact. It begins with the first interview I had with a victim, Nur Begum, and her daughter Beauty, who was born of the violence of rape. Beauty is our most important interlocutor because it is her generation born out of the war that asks us to face the true consequences of suffering a violent history. Choosing these five narratives of rape from a vast collection of more than fifty that I recorded in Bangladesh was a difficult decision. These narratives are not unusual compared to the others that are not recounted here. In fact, they are just like the others, and it was their representational characteristics that helped me make the decision to share them. They span the concerns of the individual alongside the collective and raise critical questions about witnessing.

Chapter 4, "Women's Services," includes three narratives of women who served in the war efforts as social workers and in the government abortion program after liberation. The social workers and medical professionals in Bangladesh belonged to both the Hindu and Muslim Bengali communities. As such, their communal affinities restricted and confined their work to their own communities, thereby making the healing process after the war a limited Bengali experience. Nonetheless, women's direct intervention in the postwar efforts enabled Bengali women to re-create and reconvene somewhat normalized lives. Women's work as social healers and caregivers is crucial in understanding the postwar period and women's role in enabling the new and independent nation of Bangladesh.

Chapter 5, "Women's War," constitutes the memories of women as soldiers. The two narratives included in this section shift our focus from women as victims and healers to the more active role that women played in the war as combatants. This is an important issue to consider when we revisit 1971 and the experiences of Bengali women, who were both victims and agents of violence, acted on by others as well as acting on their own volition to fight on behalf of the nation. With these two narratives, we learn of the passion and determination of two women that motivated them to jump into the thick of the battle, and we are made painfully aware of the subsequent discrimination that they suffered because of their gender in the male-dominated turf of war, so much so that neither of them has received official recognition as *mukti joud-dha*.[2] Their stories are not uncommon; the vast majority of women who fought for the freedom of Bangladesh have been silenced and remain unrecognized.

In short, the narratives of part II bring to light the experiences of violence that women suffered and their resilience that make it possible to write a new history of 1971 after the war. Women's resilience and refusal to forget combine to serve the most useful function, making the illegible, legible and generating a new register of memory that is able to address the pain of violence and war and the possibility of hope for a new and different beginning. This is, in my estimation, women's particular strength, to not become fixed in their "victim" status but to represent themselves as creators and architects of family, society, and community.

Women's experiences of 1971 are not limited to their condition in isolation, as they make us aware of sexual violence as a crime committed by men's abuse of power, which, in turn, enabled me to see the horizon of my own research. Rather than arriving at a conclusion, the research expanded to include another new angle: the exploration of men's memories.

With the postscript, I begin to contextualize men's memories in brief excerpts to evaluate what happened to Pakistani soldiers, Bengali Mukti Bahini guerillas, and ordinary militia men who learned crucial lessons of their fragile human status in committing acts of violence. By highlighting the changes in men, from being perpetrators to turning the narrative back to their humanity, I do not seek to exonerate men for committing crime. Instead I present their stories to show how personal encounters with violence taught perpetrators lessons that made them reconsider the contingent nature of external identities informed by religion, nation, and ethnicity, and it brings into focus the unmarked ground of humanity in the subcontinent. This momentary unmarking enables the interrogation of structures like nation, state, and national identity and creates a language of acknowledgment to reach toward the closure of a violent history. The perpetrators' ability to acknowledge the violence committed against another human being is the most powerful statement they can make, and it is capable of delivering a justice to their victims that no court of law or state can. And ultimately we need to listen to this language of acknowledgment in order to move forward in the subcontinent and develop understanding among the people for a just and better future in the region.

ACKNOWLEDGMENTS

I owe this book to my mother, Jahanara Rahman-Saikia, who gave me the first lessons on humanism and feminism. My mother, a professor of philosophy, made it a mission in her life to speak and work for the vulnerable and marginal in Assam, India. In turn these men and women became her friends, and together they enriched each others' lives with care and concern. We used to tease my mother of her "morning durbars." Everyday, my mother welcomed anyone who came seeking her help, fed and talked to them, provided them with monetary help, and represented their grievances to the highest authorities in the state for redress. She truly believed "service to mankind is service to God." Her humanism was exemplary and her love for destitute women and children was special. My intellectual and personal journey into the lives of the survivors of 1971 is a product of the early lessons of empathy for others that my mother instilled in me.

In Bangladesh, Jahanara Karim provided me a place in her home in Dhaka and her friendship and love sustained me through the initial stage of the research project. There were times I could not bear the stories of violence; it shook the very foundation of my humanity. Jahanara Karim's warm welcome with food and talk at the end of the day gave me the capacity to endure and move forward. A whole host of men and women in Bangladesh facilitated and enabled my research. I cannot name each one of them individually, the list would be unending. I would like to personally acknowledge Akku Chowdhury, Shahriar Kabir, Mizanur Rahman Shelly and the office staff at the American Institute of Bangladesh

Studies, the late Enayatur Rahim, the late Jamal Warris, Sofia Warris, Kader Siddique and his family, Gazi Salehuddin, Muntassir Mamoon, Habibul Alam, Ferdousi Priyabhasini and Ahmed Ilias for support in undertaking my research. To my research assistants Rafiuz Zaman, Taslima Mizziboni, and Kabir Chowdhury I owe a very special thank you for their companionship and unstinting dedication to enable my exploration of war memories. This book could not have been written without the women, the survivors of 1971, who told me their experiences and shared their deepest and darkest secrets with the expectations that I would share them with others. Each one of them is a very special person and I was privileged to have met and listened to them.

In Pakistan, I was singularly fortunate to have started my discussion on the war with Colonel Nadir Ali, a veteran of 1971. Colonel Ali's trust and invaluable support enabled me to have access to people and materials in Pakistan that otherwise would have been unobtainable. My heartfelt appreciation goes to him and his family, who opened their home and hearts to me. I am also indebted to Brigadier Talat Saeed Khan of Fauji Foundation University, Brigadier Shafi of the Sir Syed Memorial Society, and Ikram Seghal for their contacts and invaluable insights about the war and its hidden memories in Pakistan. I am gratefully indebted to Iqbal Chawla, Saba Khattak, Scheherzade Asdar, Omar Suheyl, Salimullah Khan and the staff at the National Documentation Center in Islamabad, especially Jaffar Mohammad, Nasira and Javed Iqbal, Tariq Rahman, Kishwar Naheed, Ghazala Irfan, Tahira Mahzar Ali, Masud Mufti, Dr. Mubashir, Rashad Rahman, Ahmed Rashid, the Orangi Pilot Project office staff, especially Javed Akhtar and Shamsuddin, Gulbaz Afaqi, Nadeem Akbar, Saeed Shafqat, Karamat Ali, Ahmed Salim Javed Shah, and Tahira Saeed and Manzhar Mohammad at the Pakistan National Archives in Islamabad for their generous guidance and assistance in undertaking the research. I cannot offer enough thanks to my research assistant, Mubasshira, as well as Mushtaq and Razzak at the American Institute of Pakistan Studies in Lahore, and our "Pakistan family"— Bibi, Ismat, Mavra, Guddu, and Riaz for their generosity and kindness. Above all, my deepest gratitude is due to the survivors and the men who told me what they had not dared to tell anyone before, their crimes in the war and their deep regret of their banal actions. These truly brave souls made me realize the immense potential of being human, which they have nurtured with incredible pain and deep struggle.

In India, Aditi Sen, Ashok Mitra, Major General Lakshman Singh Lehl, Major General Jack Jacob, Squadron Leader Rana Chhima, Sukendu Dev Barma, Bikash Choudhury, Heramba Bora, Amalendu De and Naseema Banu, Mohini Giri, Kuldip Nayar, and Ashis Nandy enriched this study immensely. I am immensely thankful to my two young assistants, Zoheb Ahmed and Nida Ali, who worked long hours with me in the summer heat of Delhi digging through the archive and libraries for the political story of 1971.

From the beginning of this project, a few teachers guided and provided me with incredible knowledge, without which this book would not have taken shape. Cemalnur Sargut and Bruce Lawrence encouraged me to think beyond history as an event and to engage it as an experience, and Sheikh Nizamuddin Auliya and Maulana Jalaluddin Rumi have been the source of my inspiration.

My family consisting of Chad, Anne and Guni, Gini, Javed, Zoheb, and Shahveer have been my anchor and comfort. I could not imagine undertaking such an endeavor without the home they have provided me and always kept open to return to, and this was particularly appreciated after traumatic research trips. To my friends David Ludden, Willem van Schendel, Lamia Karim, Kamran Asdar Ali, Jean Quatraet, Don Raleigh, Naveeda Khan, Urvashi Butalia, James Lancaster, Andrew Withehead, Nila Chaterjee, Jerma Jackson, Lolita Guitrez Brockington, and Jeri van Goethem, I am immensely grateful for the innumerable joys of conversation and patient listening. I owe a huge debt to my editor Valerie Millholland for her trust, continuous support, and encouragement, as well as to Miriam Angress who inherited the book and took on the responsibility of publication after Valerie suddenly fell ill. I wish to thank the anonymous readers of Duke University Press whose critical comments, sharp observations, and theoretical insights helped me to improve and expand on ideas that I was initially hesitant to address. They gave me the fortitude to "go there" and weave together personal, political, and scholarly issues. To Doann Houghton Alico, my mother-in-law, I am especially indebted for doing the initial editing of the text as well as providing wonderful sailing trips on her boat in the Mediterranean Sea.

Finally, the book became possible due to the generous support of many organizations and institutions. I am deeply thankful to the University of North Carolina, Chapel Hill, for multiple summer fellowships and granting me two years of leave from teaching to undertake research in Bangladesh, Pakistan, and India. The financial support of the American Institute of Bangladesh Studies, American Institute of Pakistan Studies, and Harry Frank Guggenheim Foundation made it possible for me to complete the research and write this book. I am also immensely grateful for the efficient and helpful staff of the Liberation War Museum at Dhaka; the National Archives, Dhaka; the Bangladesh Radio Archive, Dhaka; Ain-o-Salish Kendra, Dhaka; the Tripura State Archive, Agartala; the Asiatic Society Library, Kolkata; Nehru Memorial Museum and Library, New Delhi; Centre for Armed Forces Historical Research, New Delhi; the Assam State Archive, Guwahati; National Defense College Library, Islamabad; Iqbal Academy, Lahore; Human Rights Commission Library, Lahore; National Documentation Center, Islamabad; Pakistan National Archive, Islamabad; and the International Red Cross Archive and Library, Geneva.

I discussed some of the themes of this book with colleagues at the Lahore University of Management Studies, the Indian Institute of Technology (Assam), the History Department of Delhi University, the Kroc Peace Institute at Notre Dame, the University of Iowa, Rice University, the University of Oregon, the University of Nottingham, the University of Southampton, the Centre for the Study of Social Science at Kolkata, and Johns Hopkins University, and I benefited immensely from all of these discussions. For the shortcomings of this book, however, I alone am responsible. My husband and partner, Chad Haines, is the best critic and my strongest advocate. Without him, I cannot imagine my life and work. If this book has worth, then it is because of the people mentioned here and those who remain unmentioned who gave me their only possession, the memories of their experiences. Their stories allow us to recognize our humanity because we are human, like them.

GLOSSARY OF TERMS

Al-Badr	paramilitary force constituted by Bengalis who supported the Pakistan Army
Al-Shams	paramilitary force of Urdu speakers who supported the Pakistan Army
apa	sister, also referred to as *baji*
ashram	Hindu devotional spaces
barangona	penetrated, used for prostitute
bhajan	Hindu devotional music
Bhakti	Hindu devotional practice
birangona	rape survivors of 1971; term coined in 1972 by Sheikh Mujibur Rahman
diya	compensation
dharshan	rape
Eid ul-Fitr	Muslim festival at the end of Ramadan
gham	suffering
gunah	sin, fault, or misconduct
hanadar	refers to the Pakistan Army; a term commonly used in the tenures of the President Ziaur Rhaman (1977–81) and General Ershad (1986–91)
haqq	rights, truth, plural *haquq*
huquq-al-ibad	rights of humans
insān	human being
insāniyat	humanity
izzat	honor

kanqah	Sufi spiritual center where the *pir* or saint lives
karkhana	factory
maner manus	man of the heart
Muhajir	the name of Indian Muslims who migrated to Pakistan at the time of the partition of India in 1947; or generally a refugee, one who has left his country and friends for the cause of religion and to seek refuge from oppression
Mukti Bahini	Bengali militia created with Indian support to fight against the Pakistan Army in 1971
mukti jouddha	freedom or liberation fighter
Mukti Juddho	liberation struggle
namaz	the five daily ritual prayers; also called *salat* (Arabic term)
nirjatika	brutalized or violated
pir	Sufi guide
qawwali	Sufi utterances, also Sufi musical composition
quam	nation
rajakar	Bihari volunteers of the Pakistan Army
Rakhi Bahini	special armed forces created by Mujibur Rahman for his protection after 1972
Shari'a	Islamic law derived from the Quran and Hadith
Sufi	Muslim mystic; a follower of spiritual discipline
tauba	repentance
wali-al-dam	authority to demand compensation on behalf of a victim
zameer	conscience
zulm	atrocity, violence of a sexual nature

PART I  INTRODUCING 1971

I

❧

THE TOLD AND
UNTOLD STORIES OF 1971

HISTORY AND MEMORY

In 1971 multiple wars broke out in East Pakistan (later known as Bangladesh): one was a civil war fought between East and West Pakistan; another was an international war fought between India and Pakistan; a third war erupted between the Bengalis and Urdu-speaking groups, the so-called Biharis;[1] and finally, a rampant gender war broke out against vulnerable women within East Pakistan. Men representing the armies of Pakistan and India, as well as the Mukti Bahini (a Bengali militia created with Indian support) and pro-Pakistani Bengali and Bihari civilians who volunteered in the paramilitary forces of Al-Badr and Al-Shams, raped, looted, killed, and terrorized noncombatants in East Pakistan. At the end of the civil war the Pakistan government lost legitimacy in its eastern province; the international war resulted in the partitioning of Pakistan and the creation of an independent nation-state of Bangladesh; the ethnic war transformed the Biharis from citizens into stateless refugees; and the gender violence destroyed the very fabric of society, creating multiple marginal communities of absent subjects in postliberated Bangladesh.

Today the war of 1971 is remembered in various ways in history books in Bangladesh, India, and Pakistan. In Bangladesh it is celebrated as the War of Liberation from Pakistan, and it is certainly the most important event in the history of Bangladesh. The war ended West Pakistan's "colonialism" in the east, and Bangladesh came into being.[2] In Indian history, 1971 is enshrined as the Indo-Pak conflict, and India's triumphant success is viewed as a settling of scores for the partition of 1947 and the founding of Pakistan. In Pakistan there were many attempts to forget the events of 1971, and as a result, today very few people remember that East Pakistan was once an integral part of a united Pakistan. The war is generally viewed as an act of "betrayal" by the Bengalis.[3] The tendency of national histories in Bangladesh, India, and Pakistan is to partition the memories of 1971, allowing for blame to be relegated to the Other; nearly four decades later the binary memories of "us" as good versus the Other as evil produces simplistic narratives without addressing the complexities of the conditions and circumstances that produced horrific outcomes in the war and the impact of violence and terror on people's lives.

The disproportionate allocation of resources in favor of West Pakistan; the political ambition of the West Pakistani elite; the rabid demands of political Islam in the public sphere accompanied by further marginalization of minority communities, such as the Hindus in East Pakistan; the ethnic tensions between the Bengalis and the Punjabis; and the interference and support of India in motivating the Bengalis to secede from Pakistan all lie at the heart of the clashes leading to the outbreak of war. The violence did not, however, remain confined to confrontations between armed groups of men. The violence harmed and destroyed unarmed, unresisting civilians of all ages, particularly women, who had done no injury to their aggressors. Ultimately the war of 1971 was not simply a war that men fought; it was a crime against vulnerable groups of the elderly, women, and children.

By using a "multi-sited" ethnographic research methodology that combines oral history with archival, literary, and visual materials and keeping in mind that the diverse memories of 1971 produce polyversal narratives, I explore an inner history of the war that is not in circulation in the public sphere.[4] The forgotten, hidden memories belong to women who were terrorized, brutally sexualized, and marginalized in the war. Their stories provide a human voice that illuminates the experiences of the majority who were not directly involved in the war, yet became the site on which violence and power were inscribed. The disengagement with women's trauma in the existing official histories creates a yawning gap that makes 1971 almost impossible to understand. What is submerged in this official history is also forgotten in the public collective memory, and the awareness of the violent past is lost. In turn, a peculiarly skewed, officially backed representation of the war as a nationalistic life-and-death struggle (between the Bengalis and the Pakistanis) is produced both in the site of history and public accounts. An official narrative is constructed that focuses on the events and actions happening at an external level. Therefore, combat operations, tactics, strategies, leaders, and campaigns are privileged and become the stuff of memory and history.[5]

As a South Asian person I understand the conflicting passions in the subcontinent regarding gendered memory and the public uneasiness with such a project as this one. Recalling this hidden and forgotten past unearths complexities that are moral, political, social, religious, and psychological. As such, on the one hand there is a need to remember, and, on the other hand, there is the desire to forget the episodes of violence in the war. The exploration promises an exciting possibility to access history and the actors who made it. Simultaneously, it is frightening because the investigation will reveal the story of our times and that of our parents. We do not want to ask an entire generation to bear witness to the activities and crimes of a "minority" (Arendt 1945). More so, perhaps we are afraid we may find ourselves as both victims and perpetrators. Hence, we push violence away "like someone else's history—or even, *not* history at all" (Pandey 2001, 6). Can we continue to live in this state of denial and exclusion? My aim is not to arrive at a transcendental truth and create a knowable, documented, archived "history" that would stand in as testimony for what happened in 1971. Instead, I offer a narrative of the hidden memories to make sense of gendered violence in the war, to understand the human cost, and to move beyond it to explore how people process violence and the lessons they learn from it. In particular I pay attention to the human voice of women and men, survivors of 1971, emerging from the abyss of violence and teaching us new lessons of humanity that are not in conflict but resonate with common themes. With the shift in focus from the external story of the war to the internal dimensions of people's memories, I highlight the internal capacity for developing an ethical memory that I hope will initiate multiple tellings of 1971, and through repetition and new probing we can grasp and understand the forgotten, as well cultivate a site for the divided people of South Asia, in India, Pakistan, and Bangladesh, to contemplate a different self and Other relationship.

Coming to terms with the past and voicing the memories of ordinary people, particularly noncombatants who experienced extraordinary violence from combatants during wars and conflicts, have become the most important concerns of memory projects in the twentieth and early twenty-first centuries. It has been suggested that telling the past will enable survivors to recognize what they had experienced and create public awareness, allowing individuals and societies to move beyond the legacy of trauma. Individuals and nations are seeking survivors' memories to develop a collective spirit of bonding in the public sphere and build community and identity through belonging. A well-known example is the Truth and Reconciliation Commission (TRC) in South Africa that was instituted from 1996 to 1998 to examine in the public space the gross human rights abuses committed against individual victims during the apartheid regime. The hope was that all South Africans could come to terms with the past and move on. In other words, the pursuit of truth and reconciliation in this case was a search for justice and a common ground between victims and perpetrators to redeem the past and create a new beginning in South Africa.

The revisiting of violence in public accounts of victims' sufferings and perpetrators' violence was meant to create a record to enable a final closure of a traumatic period. Individual "victims" were encouraged to tell their experiences under the glare of the public media to seek restorative justice and reparations for the violence they suffered, and "perpetrators" were promised amnesty for "truth telling." The TRC's privileging of individual stories placed the location and site of traumatic history at the personal level; thus its hope for "imagining" a "new rainbow nation" based on individual reconciliation did not do enough to account for the institutional context of apartheid that organized power and enabled structural violence, which the critiques of TRC point out was its most glaring shortcoming (Bundy 2000; Mamdani 2002; Wilson 2001). The memory project for seeking justice initiated by the TRC was limited to a narrow purpose of admitting the horrific crimes committed by individuals, which may have served as a cathartic process, but the emphasis on remembering and revealing personal experiences was not enough to answer the larger questions of how a state can resort to making up laws to violate people's rights. There was no forum to speak about or bear witness to the violence of an apartheid regime.

Particularly, the TRC failed to address the location of conflict, which was everywhere, and that it was not individuals but entire communities marked on the grounds of race and ethnicity who were subjected to routine violence. Even more significant, the relative absence of women's voices throughout the "truth collection" process led to serious gaps in the collective memory and dislocated women's experiences from the historical context that produced everyday gendered violence. The hierarchy of men's truth and women's silence persisted. The pursuit of healing through forgiveness based on the public exposure of certain kinds of "truth" within the national context, which was a "political compromise" (Mamdani 2002, 33), obscured the multiple ways vulnerable constituencies of people, especially women who were not state agents or political or national actors, experienced regular violations in the apartheid state.

When the public telling of traumatic memories becomes a challenge for victims due to the intense suffering of violence, and when social, cultural, and political structures discourage the voices of victims before even a murmur develops, then a project like the TRC is not enough. Devalued survivors excluded from the moral universe of the new regime of truth and justice cannot find voice to reconcile and heal. The juridical notion of truth is not a substitute for what happened and cannot reconcile victims and perpetrators based on a selective representation of suffering. The truth that people know cannot be imposed or extracted by coercion or persuasion, and the promise of reconciliation engineered by institutional engagements is not the way out of a turbulent past.

At a certain point it becomes clear that the "new politics of truth" (Foucault 1979) have an essential lacuna: instituted truth obscures the history that produces the conditions for making victims and perpetrators. And this instituted truth and its resultant history cannot explain how victims and perpetrators experience the violence and deal with their memories. Thus, the engineered history can only bear witness to a narrow definition of the truth, and, in turn, it defines the boundaries of what is permissible, what can be spoken and consumed by an audience coached to forget the rest. The troublesome memories that produce unease and even a sense of guilt do not become part of the "truth collection," and at times the sheer power of violence is such that it can devastate survivors' ability to speak, according to Holocaust scholars (Felman 1992; Agamben 1991, 1999). What kind of memory inhabits the site of pain that has never been resolved or visited? How does forgetting and remembering enable the semblance of continuity for victims who experience gendered violence carried out with the aim of destroying their humanity? How can we integrate the voices of women who are suffering violence? These are all questions that have received amazingly little attention in memory projects such as the TRC.

The memories of the survivors of 1971 are brought to center stage not to debunk the existing histories or annul national identities that are important to the citizens of the respective countries but to confront the project of history that has forgotten and deleted what the anonymous survivors, particularly the women of Bangladesh—Bengali and Bihari, Muslim, Hindu, Christian, Buddhist, and others—suffered and endured. Survivors' memories are added to the existing histories and memories to offer another way of engaging with the violence of 1971 and to question the dominant constructions of official national histories. The result is the creation of a new narrative that humanizes victims and perpetrators, the people of South Asia, and reclaims a people's history. Writing a people's history of 1971, I suggest, is a way of developing a shared responsiveness for allowing transformation within the self while simultaneously acknowledging interconnectedness with others.

Retrieving survivors' memories is, of course, not an easy, straightforward process. The memories of violence are inchoate; there is nothing coherent about the violence that has left survivors asking how to tell the experiences, and this reality is at the heart of this book. The forgotten, suppressed memories of survivors are hard to grasp and fashion into a narrative because survivors are often not aware of their shared experiences of loss, and they continue to fragment their memories based on gender and class, religious, ethnic, and national divides and continue to think of their experiences as unique and exceptional. Because we lack a narrative structure to accommodate the people's history of 1971, we have to make sense of survivors' memories, both women's and men's, on our own and make it our common goal to understand the trauma of violence and dehumanization within a single frame of reference. Interrogating the restricted site of history made in the halls of power is the beginning step, as we can examine the limitations of the national history and the official memory project and see a vacant place for the forgotten memories of survivors.

By history I do not mean the past or the narrative we tell about ourselves in the light of the present. By history I mean the artifact that is the product of a systematic construction, the development of a corpus of knowledge produced in the sites of power and revised and deliberately woven into a murky mess to generate a confused collective memory about the past. History in this sense is an institutional tool and must be engaged with as a character in the national plot with strategic use.

The writing of history as official knowledge to give and create identity in South Asia developed with the entry of the British colonials and was inaugurated in the late eighteenth century by Warren Hastings, who was determined to find the ancient past of the Hindus as separate from the Muslims. Through active circulation and repetition of the divided history—*Hindu* and *Muslim*—the colonial agents (James Mill, Mounstuart Elphinstone, and Vincent Smith, to name a few early British administrators and historians) created believability about the Indian past they produced, while other forms of remembering and knowing were undermined in the official story.[6] To assert its power, official history in South Asia since the colonial times and even now depends on people forgetting much of the lived past. We cannot afford this kind of history any longer. The different, possible narratives preserved in people's memories must be explored and acknowledged if we in South Asia are to confront what decolonization really means.

We have to recognize that "the perpetrator is history," that this perpetrator polarized individuals and groups and made them enemies of each other (Mamdani 2002, 56). In East and West Pakistan, the two groups fought with each other to correct the history inherited from the British, and they sought to create an identity for ensuring the future and, in consequence, transformed themselves into victims and perpetrators. As Primo Levi has said in the context of Holocaust, no one was more human than the other during the violence and war (Levi 1986). This complex reality is not acknowledged by official history, although it passes sentence on the past that is 1971. The collective memory that transcends the limited official history must be more than a site of remembrance for creating identity in the present; it must have what James Booth calls an "ethical dimension" (Booth 2006) and dare to remember the lofty successes as well as the sordid misdeeds of a community. The absence of the ethical in South Asian history has become an urgent concern for many scholars, including Ashis Nandy, Martha Nussbaum, Veena Das, and Gyanendra Pandey, to name a few.

The connection between ethics and history in the subcontinent, however, is not new. In the confluence of premodern historical encounters between Sufi Islam, which was the main channel through which Islam spread in the region, and Hindu Bhakti mysticism, the discourses of "humanization" (Dallmayr 2002) and its importance took root and became part of everyday language, combining culture with historical processes.[7] The Sufi and Bhakti encounters created new humanistic vocabularies and vernacular concepts such as *insāniyat* (in Urdu), *manushyata* (in Bengali), and *manabata* (in Assamese), facilitating linkages between multiple religious communities.[8] The effort was to make connections and develop a web of relationships and interdependence between the populace. The process was not authored or directed by state efforts, but rather it was facilitated by the diversity of neighbors that lived side-by-side without ignoring or trying to eliminate differences. The memory of a shared sense of humanity in the subcontinent offers a space for dialogue even among those separated by hate and national politics in India, Pakistan, and Bangladesh. People's memories and their ability to use them to generate their own narratives can work as resistance against the limitations of official history and present different ways of knowing the past.

To overcome the amnesia of official history, I turn to the silent testimonies of the women of Bangladesh. Their memories provide an opportunity to engage the debates about what 1971 means to people in the subcontinent and how memory can serve the more useful and important function of generating a better future in the region. Women's previously (unspoken) testimonies make us aware of the lacuna in the official history of 1971, or they most certainly bear witness to gendered silencing in the sites of history. In the process of telling the missing part of history, women remind us in their voice that they are agents and can create a new beginning. This human act, this telling, is the first step toward developing a people's history of 1971. Women's creativity is set in sharp contrast to their dehumanization through violence, when they were deemed as objects to be destroyed. Women's memories are situated in this paradox, to claim their humanity and become agents of change they have to tell about their dehumanization and form a bridge between the internal and personal and the external and public spheres of the war. In so doing they enable our understanding of the experiences of the collective and show the scars that individual woman endure. More importantly, women's memories make us deeply aware of their resilience, to come to terms with the past, to move forward, and to engender a new future. Women's truth telling questions our own culpability in enforcing a dehumanizing silence upon them, and we need to know their stories in order to know ourselves in postcolonial South Asia, especially if we hope to change any part of the region.

The current history of 1971 that leaves out women's experiences should not mislead us into believing that traumatic memories of the collective have been overcome or erased. Forgetting is imposed as a strategy to hide the haunting memories that cannot be revealed without destroying our romance with nationalism. The trauma of gendered violence lurks in the background, in women's private lives. In other words, forgetting the traumatic memories of the war requires a deliberate effort by survivors to try and not remember that which is unforgettable and is inscribed in memory. The memories of gendered violence haven't died; they occasionally surface in speech and sudden silence at the threshold of the inner and outer experiences of the war. For the victim and survivor the account is not a content-based narrative for contextualizing the received history, but it is a story of an event with multilayered moments overlapping one another. In Bangladesh women's personal experiences of horrific violence simultaneously constituted a public act of nationalism for men as well as "shame" for the nation that is hidden. In retelling this multilayered moment as women understand it, the victim and survivor draws her listeners into her world of memories and experiences, creating trust by revealing the ruin she experienced and the subsequent vacant place within society that is now hers. The delicate balance of women's testimony rests on a complex duality of the potentiality to tell the "unthinkable" (Bourdieu 1980) through an impossibility of telling it in a coherent narrative. This makes their stories incredibly important and reveals the human condition in violence. Women's memories cannot be subsumed within categories and reduced to analytical frames, but we have to learn to engage them as voices capable of excavating an embedded story of the past.

In the testimonies shared in this book, women express their trust and recount the moments of violence, but the details that marked and made her a victim are not the emphasis; rather what is remembered are situations that ruptured the known and made it unknown, unfamiliar, and frightful for which there is no speech. The trust that was undone and destroyed is of greater concern to them. Women tell about the events of loss, loss of established relationships with neighbors and friends who became the enemy during the war. In their testimonies women remind us that they do not feel ideologically driven to adopt the male self-image of the fighter, the *mukti jouddha* (war hero), even when they performed heroic acts. For women the war was a period of brutality and loss of honor, family, and community. The sexual violence that destroyed them is unspeakable in the public sphere dominated by a male patriarchy; they resort to silence to tell this betrayal of trust.

Women's recognition of loss during the war is simultaneously voiced with a tentative understanding that they have survived the destructive violence. They are also proud that the war freed their country, and they cherish it despite their personal losses.[9] They tell of the ways they forged new relationships in the thick of battle and cut through the grid of divisions—national, ethnic, and religious—to offer a more elastic understanding of the events and actors, telling a story without trying to locate it on a preexisting map provided by polarized history. Their narratives of survival make us appreciate the meager resources they drew upon to press ahead to the site of hope. This is a heartening message that women convey. The incredible resilience of women reveals a self that lies buried under the debris of destruction, no longer whole, but a human self nonetheless—one that shines through in its refusal to forget.

Women's memories thus stir us to probe and search for the answer to the fundamental question of what was lost and regained in the war. Through their halting speech women reveal the most important lesson learned from violence—the loss of humanity when they were reduced into objects by powerful men. Violence, women tell us, destroyed everyone, particularly the men who in trying to exert manly power destroyed themselves and their humanity in their heinous acts against the vulnerable. They remind us in their penetrating speech that the problem must be evaluated using the larger conceptual framework of the loss of humanity (Urdu speakers often referred to it as insāniyat) due to men's inability to accept and tolerate difference, which allowed institutions to reduce people into categories and labels to be attacked and destroyed. The cost of violence had to be borne by the people whose lives were dramatically changed thereafter. In women's speech the first philosophy of any society must be the capacity to accept difference and not reduce the Other to fit the classifications created from the location of self. The basis of this ethical humanism that survivors of 1971 teach us is a transformative space where we can begin a new narrative in the subcontinent, empowering ourselves with a regained sense of our humanity after violence.

Our relation to the Other is the foundation of our developing subjectivity. Emmanuel Levinas asserts that human responsibility toward others has to develop prior to any knowledge or emotional connection, and this capacity belongs in us, as thinking and feeling human beings, and not in institutions (Levinas 1972 and 1981).[10] Every person carries the potential to achieve this ideal status of humanness that is discerned in relation to others. Levinas's injunction of the ideal human stands in sharp contrast to the empirical human that we are or have become and is represented in the activities of the states we have created. Reaching out beyond the masculine nationalism that relegates empathy and emotional identification to devalued females, Levinas's philosophy seeks a source of ethical life in the voice, the face, the very presence of the Other. It is this injunction to live with ethics for the Other—the stranger, the vulnerable, and the unknown—and refuse to take sides in the drama that we have not authored that comes through as a demand in Bangladeshi women's testimonies. We were not there in East Pakistan in 1971, why should we assume to know what happened and take sides? Accepting survivors' silence as testimony of a shared condition and refusing to play our assigned role in the theater of violence is an ethical obligation. The unknown survivors humanize us because in their survival we survive as humans without the flag of nationalism as our crutch. This guides my witnessing of 1971.

A slight caveat is necessary to briefly address the popular local expression of insāniyat that survivors of 1971, men and women, use and that we will hear throughout the text. Although Bangla speakers did not use the term *insāniyat*, or its equivalent *manushyata*, in general conversation, almost all survivors, particularly women, expressed deep anxiety that violence undermined people's humanity and must be avoided to make a humane society. Insāniyat is not a learned concept in schools in South Asia, yet it has great cultural currency and encompasses the responsibility entailed in being human. The moral source of insāniyat is in lived experiences that teach us the ethical obligations we owe to another. Being human in this sense is a contingent and fluctuating condition, and its expression is evident in the choices one makes, for example, choosing to do good rather than evil acts. As Mohammad Iqbal, the poet laureate of Pakistan, asserts, it is the capacity of choice that makes people human. Iqbal invokes this concept from the Quran, which distinguishes between the state of *bashar* (primeval humans) and *insān* (the evolved person who exercises choice).[11] The journey toward one's humanity, becoming insān, and gaining a repository of insāniyat are concomitant and evolving processes. Insān in this conceptual form understandably has a deep etymology. Men choosing to commit violence, women remind us, led to the loss of insāniyat.

How can a subject give an account of its ruin? The telling of violence beyond the experiences of the survivors rests on the listeners. The inseparable intimacy between women's silence and speech and the listener's engagement with an internal and gendered story of violence brings into being a testimony that remains outside written histories (Agamben

1999; Behar 1993; Ofer and Weitzman 1998). Listening transforms the empty subject position of survivors and fills it with the potential of "bearing witness" to shaping an ethical memory.[12] Bangladeshi survivors' (incomplete) speech places their listeners in a special position to see how in the name of war and nation making power was exercised, how human values were undermined and overlooked, and why the powerful attacked the powerless with the intention of destroying them. The act of listening to the unspeakable memories of 1971 gives access to women's subjectification as victims and simultaneously enables their desubjectification as human beings. Thus the listeners and survivors are joined in a common project of producing testimony of the unarchived interiority that escapes both memory and the forgetfulness of history. The transformed listeners become living reminders of the violence and carry with them the knowledge of survivors' experiences and can share them with others.

Listening is a responsible as well as a political act (Enloe 1990). We are obliged to tell the unspeakable and invite the community of listeners to grasp the intimate and gendered human interiority, and we can take what is said and heard and use it to scrutinize the events and make connections between the individuals and the collective, the personal and the political, and the sacred and the profane ideals that fueled violence in the war and have since silenced their exposure. I engage women's speech on 1971 both conceptually and methodologically to highlight that "the humanist is a speaker" (Davies 2008), grounding their understanding of humanity not in the language of theoreticians but in the utterances of the lived experiences of violence.[13] I contend that listening exorcises these experiences of violence, making the memories meaningful for both the teller and listener. It educates beyond the present, confronting what was done that is now forgotten. Listening to the stories of 1971 as told by women makes it possible to focus on the human issues and explore a larger story—of war, of the struggle for freedom, nationalism, and nation building, which are vexed and passionate concerns for people in the subcontinent. Thus, we enter into a pact for understanding and developing tools to represent the traumatic experiences for purposes of accountability. Transformed as a result of listening to the speaker and teacher and then endowed with memories of the event, we can speak the words of the humanist teacher and a new narrative emerges.[14] This humanist approach is at the center of survivors' speech and thus at the center of this book.

The glimpses into the violence of 1971 lead us into looking at other wars and at the concept and process of war itself in terms of its total cost. Bangladeshi women's memories, no doubt, plunge us into an abyss of darkness, but from within rises a human voice enlightening the contours of lived reality, allowing for a reassessment of a historical moment. Rather than generating a politics of hate, women's silence and (disjointed) narratives bear witness and fully verify the missing testimony in history. It completes the project of knowing what otherwise would not be known and marks the threshold for the destroyed to claim human dignity once again. It makes it clear that violence destroys but it cannot obliterate; humans are resilient and can have the last word.

This book is about women's memories as told by women. Feminist scholars like Ruth Behar (1993) and Laila Abu-Lughod (1993) and Holocaust studies scholars like Dalia Ofer and Lenore Weitzman (1998) and Carol Rittner (1993), as well as Partition studies scholars like Urvashi Butalia (1998) and Ritu Menon and Kamla Bhasin (1998), maintain that the study of women's experiences is not only valid but necessary to redress the absence of women's lives in social documentation and for preserving the memory of their experiences during violent events. Women's memories deserve our undivided attention as they constitute a new text of historical memory on 1971. Taken as a whole the book engages and addresses three main themes that weave into and interact with one another: women's voices are not restricted to *birangonas* (victims) but include women's resilient assertion of their role in contributing to the liberation and making of Bangladesh; the power of oral narratives of the silenced to generate a new story located in people's experiences of their humanization in violence; and the revelation of the gaps in official history in order to offer in its stead a richer and more nuanced text of people's memories spanning the divided nations of India, Pakistan, and Bangladesh to tell a story of connection between the region and people.

LOCATING THE SCHOLARSHIP

The use of personal narrative and memory for speaking about trauma is not new or peculiar to the subcontinent or the study of 1971.[15] In South Asian history specifically, there has been substantial discussion on issues of oral history and fieldwork (Amin 1996, 2005; Singer 1997; Butalia 1998); the limitations of national history (Chakrabarty 1992a; Kumar

2001; Mayaram 2003; Saikia 2004a, 2004b); of violence, pain, and endurance (Pandey 1992, 1995, 1999; Mookherjee 2006); and of the variety of ways to organize the past using myths, memory, and forgetting (Nandy 1995; Skaria 1999; Chatterjee 2002). Methodologically, however, the effort and outcome of oral history are unusual in that they allow for asking questions that were, perhaps, ignored or not imagined in the past and evoke recollections and understandings that were previously silenced or overlooked (Thomson 1998; Perks and Thomson 1998; Mamdani 2001; Herzfeld 2005). The process of oral history creates conditions for face-to-face encounters with the agents of history and challenges us to move beyond the limited world of conventional history and to engage in human interaction (Sereny 1983; Butalia 1998; Menon and Bhasin 1998; Redlich 2002). These interactions seep into and penetrate the research project, requiring oral historians to account for human relationships generated in the field, to contextualize the research method and narrative to answer larger questions about overcoming stigmatized history, and to create a more sensitive interaction with the silenced subjects for democratizing history and memory.[16]

The connection between violence and narrative has attracted much attention, contributing to multiple oral history projects bringing together different disciplines. Silence is the language of trauma that history cannot recall without undermining its own project of power, Trouillot contends in his reading of the Haitian Revolution (Trouillot 1995). The gap between traumatic experience and speech has been explored in some detail, providing coverage to the experiences of the Holocaust (Langer 1991; Felman 1992; LaCapra 1994; Santner 1992; Caruth 1996), the Vietnam War (Lifton 1979; Tal 1996), and feminist readings on pain (Scarry 1985; Taylor 1997; Yaeger 1997; Brison 2002). The Holocaust literature, in particular, has brought sharp focus to the "crisis of witnessing" (Felman 1992). Giorgio Agamben, Theodor Adorno, and Ellie Weisel maintain that the enormity of the events precludes describing and language fails in representing the Holocaust. The ones who survived the "atrocity" cannot tell the pain of the ones who truly suffered, "the ones who touched the bottom," the Mussalman who perished in the violence (Agamben 1999, 34). In the absence of the "true witnesses," Primo Levi writes, "survivors speak in their stead" (Levi 1986, 83). The testimonial struggle to tell what cannot be told or comprehended, Maurice Blanchot paradoxically describes as "the wish of all, in the camps, the last wish: know what has happened, and do not forget, and at the same time never will you know" (Blanchot 1986). The witness who returns speechless is a recurrent theme in the Holocaust literature.

Curiously, even while one speaks of the Holocaust as "proofless," it is amply "witnessed" more than six decades after the event. In fact, it is the most well-documented event in historical memory (Horowitz 1992). We have to accept that "those who were there can tell, at least most of it, if not all" (Berenbaum 1995, 91). This is evidently clear in Lawrence Langer's *Holocaust Testimonies* (1991) where he peals layer after layer of memory to face the core experience. It brings us close to understanding what it was like there, but the reenactment of memory, endlessly repeated in the fourteen hundred testimonies collected by Langer, does not result in healing: "the injury cannot be healed, it extends through time" (Levi 1986, 24). How to respond to this "witness-less" but unending suffering? To become a producer of history or art, Horowitz argues, is no longer witnessing. The work cannot be done from the "outside," but rather it must be done from the "inside" by sharing the contagion (Horowitz 1992, 62). Giving up the "outsideness," Emmanuel Levinas posits, is an ethical response in which good surpasses "objective experience" and history, "calling of consciousness into question" (Levinas 1986).

While the Holocaust literature offers a rich language and scholarship to engage the issues of violence, trauma, and silence, its location and context is within a Western world that has a specific idiom of cultural, political, and social power. Nonetheless, the Holocaust was not a unique event that defies our understanding (Browning 1992; Clandinnen 1999)—it continues to serve as a very important learning site to know the inhumanity of our times. For people in South Asia it is not the Holocaust, but events and violence that happened within their own midst that have the power to shock.

The partition of 1947 that created the nation-states of India and Pakistan is at the center of contemporary scholarship on violence and trauma in the subcontinent. It is deemed *the* moment of rupture that scarred the region, forever disabling a continuous telling of the past. Driven by the anxiety of partition and not certain who to blame, for more than forty years after the event the story of partition remained a silent episode unremembered and unrecalled in public historical space. But recent events of violence in India, particularly the Delhi riots of

1984 in which nearly three thousand Sikhs were killed by Hindu mobs (Das 1995); the 1992 destruction of Babri Mosque and an attack on the minority Muslim population of India by the supporters of the Bharatiya Janata Party (BJP) (Gopal 1993; Nandy 1995); and the Bombay riots of January 1993 against the Muslims (Hansen 1999 and 2001; Appadurai 1993 and 1995) created an urgent need to revisit the deep divisions between the religious communities of Hindus and Muslims and probe the intercommunity violence during and after partition.

Since the 1990s, in various sites of discourse and representations, including academic history, literature, media and films, and memoirs and biographies, the traumatic events and silence of partition experiences have been scrutinized and interrogated to create a provisional story of the moment so that people can begin to understand what happened at the juncture of a massive political change.[17] A market is emerging that is packaging and delivering the trauma of partition to the respective national communities in Pakistan, India, and Bangladesh. These histories provide limited and partial accounts because the past (before 1947) can no longer be told as a story that was once shared between the divided nations of the present. The national histories produced in India, Pakistan, and Bangladesh today are testimonies of the loss of collective memory, and despite the explosion of interest to document partition, an authentic story is nearly impossible.[18] All history after the event, one can contend, is spurious.

With partition being deemed the definitive catastrophic moment, history in the subcontinent is divided into two time frames: before and after partition.[19] Before 1947, we have a long history of a semi-mythical "united India" that is divided into classical, medieval, and modern periods, a formula developed by the colonial British historians and administrators. After 1947, the unity of British India being undone in partition, divided and separate histories of postcolonial and post-independent India, Pakistan, and Bangladesh emerged. But is this neat demarcation and division really the history of the people living in the subcontinent? Vazira Zamindar (2007) argues that partition is not a moment, it is a process that was ongoing for several years after the haphazard demarcation of territory into India and Pakistan; people continued to negotiate the place they would call home through protracted arrangements and careful planning. By connecting the various moments in this long history of partition and by maintaining a constant awareness of the dramatic changes that ruptured the collective memory of the region, we get a better sense of how history then and now is affected and manifested in national institutions, as well as in the lives of ordinary people living across the divide. Overcoming partition by silencing the memory of the past is not the way out of the mess of history. Rather a return to the repressed, unspoken, incoherent pain of those who suffered the division and working with them from the "inside" is what is needed. The partition of 1947 is not over and done with, but in the abyss of contemporary national history created by the complex entanglements of personal memories, political manipulations, collective amnesia, and national lies the traumatic moment of partition and the shared past are dispersed, and the entanglements become evident in different sites triggering violence over and over again (Tambiah 1990; Tarlo 2003; Pandey 2006). The vexed relationship between the partition of 1947 and the contemporary violence that reenacts the traumatic memories of the past is an obvious concern to many scholars; my focus is on the 1971 war, one of its devastating manifestations.[20]

I contend that the shocking violence of 1947 was not total and final. In fact the haphazard division of territory creating India and Pakistan, forcing people to choose one or the other country based on their religion, did not solve the problems on the ground, but it incubated the seed for further fragmentation that became evident when language and ethnicity and not religion became the site for violence between the Muslim Bengalis and the Muslim Punjabis and Urdu-speaking groups. The ferocity of the violence in 1971 leads us not only to question the 1947 partition and history writing in South Asia but also puts under scrutiny the fiction of our human identity. Revisiting the capacity and incapacity of our human actions and developing an awareness of the Other is not an annulling of our national identities. Faiz Ahmed Faiz, the famed dissident poet of Pakistan, succinctly describes this in the poem "Dhaka se waapsi par" (On returning from Dhaka) (1974) written as a tribute in memory of the place and relationship that was lost in the violence of the war.[21] Here I quote a small section that sums up the anguish and emotions of loss but also speaks of hope for a better future for the people of the subcontinent:

> ham ke thehre ajnabi itni mulaaqaaton ke baad
> phir banein ge aashna kitni mulaaqaaton ke baad
> kab nazar mein aaye gi be daagh sabze ki bahaar
> khoon ke dhabe dhulein ge kitni barsaaton ke baad

[We have become strangers after so many meetings
How many meetings will it take for us to become friends again
When shall we see the beauty of the verdant green, once again
How many monsoons will it take to wash away its patches of blood]

Like Faiz and many others, I am calling into question what we can make of ourselves as human beings, people who live side-by-side in South Asia in India, Pakistan, and Bangladesh. With this shift in focus the emphasis is centered elsewhere from the national to the capacity to humanize ourselves, which must be an ongoing practice to enable us to contemplate a different self and other relationship than what we have at present as divided citizens.[22] Moving away from nation to the human is a goal to work toward, but this path is not etched in official historical scholarship. It is in the space of a sociocultural vocabulary of Indo-Islamic Sufism and Hindu Bhakti tradition that the ethical concerns for the human are evident and can be explored.

The presence of Sufi and Bhakti literature in South Asia is immense and inspiring. Conventionally, the history of Sufism in the subcontinent began in the early eleventh century as individual Sufi masters settled in the region. The most well known of the early settlers is Abul Hassan Ali Hajwiri or Data Sahib, the patron saint of Lahore and Khwaja Muinuddin Chisti in Ajmer-sharif, India, who started the famed line of the Chistiyas in the subcontinent. Likewise, a variety of Bhakti saints are revered throughout the subcontinent—Kabir, Ramdas, Mira bai, and Guru Nanak, who founded a separate religion called Sikhism. Poetry and music accompanied by the establishment of new and inclusive community centers called *kanqahs* and ashrams, where local men and women congregated and learned religious precepts and moral values alongside new and improved methods of agriculture, animal husbandry, livelihood skills like weaving and carpentry, were the main tools for disseminating the Sufi and Bhakti message in premodern South Asia (Eaton 1994). In this environment a new ethos of the self and other interaction, a process of humanization, developed and took shape and survived. At the time of partition of India and Pakistan curious dilemmas and obstacles emerged when people had to leave the shrines of their Sufi and Bhakti masters for the new national spaces of Pakistan and India that suppressed the ongoing dialogues between multiple religious groups.[23]

To me the Sufi and Bhakti message that shuns the fiction of enclosed and fixed identities and emphasizes dialogue for linking humans and enabling their humanization (that is, we learn to be human through human interactions and shared responsiveness) is most eloquently explained by Maulana Jalaluddin Rumi, a poet and scholar of Islam in the thirteenth century (he lived and wrote in the Seljuk kingdom of Konya, Turkey) and Lalon Fakir, a mystic of rural East Bengal (later known as East Pakistan in 1947 and then Bangladesh after 1971) in the nineteenth century. The human journey for realizing humane attributes is not limited to the mundane settings of human societies, but it is ultimately transgressive and self-transcending to reach the Divine, according to Rumi's message.

Departing from the traditional mold of a teacher delivering a scripted message, Rumi's discourses and poems were impromptu and from the heart. Instead of adhering to a rational framework of ontology, his utterances talked about opening up to the possibility of intrusion from the outside, a stranger, the unknown, which interrupts the project of ego and creates a new possibility for a different kind of knowing. Rumi begins his famous book of poems, *The Masnavi*, by reminding listeners that in telling stories of others, we begin to understand our secrets.[24] The blurring of distinctions between self and other is a repeated theme in Rumi's discourses and poems.

Without denying the varieties of identities that we adopt—ethnic, religious, linguistic, economic, social, and cultural—Rumi urges his listeners not to confine themselves to these markers but continue the search for something within them that can be shared by others; in other words, find the common ground that makes one a human being like another. In this message, Rumi delivers a powerful concept of humanity that overcomes the distinction between self and other.

Rumi's call for the end of individual ego and submission for unison should not be read in line with the Hegelian ontology of sameness or likeness. Rather, his point is to unsettle human subjectivity, permitting us to talk about the human relation or nonrelation to other humans and God—in short, to overcome the process that is fixated on destroying the other so that the self or ego can triumph. This elevated intellect, which Rumi calls "heart-knowledge," makes us human and enables transcendence to see self in another. Of course the state of being and nonbeing and becoming part of a collective whole, Rumi suggests, is not a platform for making common goals and experiencing monolithic humanity. He urges people to fulfill the role required of us as human beings because the creative possibility and potential of being human is a gift and a promise to humankind.

Rumi's call to unmask individual ego and embark on a shared human journey is an active process blending the sensory and the spiritual worlds that enables continuous change and transformation within self while simultaneously acknowledging the interconnectedness with a variety of others. The significance of this webbed relationship between self and others undoes the totalizing and stifling hegemony of individualism and makes room for exploring new meanings. I read this message within a historical framework, taking it up to revisit the question of violent nationalism in 1971 and draw attention to the substratum of connections shared by people in the subcontinent, even those separated by hate and national politics in India and Pakistan and the newly emerging Bangladesh as well. In other words, I draw upon Rumi's message to ask: can we write a people's history of the subcontinent using the language of humanity?

The linkage between humaneness and the process of recognizing our shared humanity was most eloquently sung by Lalon Fakir in the nineteenth century. Lalon's focus was on the concrete human experiences in the world, and he was concerned with cultivating the ability to recognize one's humanity and the capacity of one's humaneness, which is a lifelong undertaking. Calling upon his listeners to move beyond structures of caste and sects and the crudest division of hierarchy manifested in demarcating people based on geography, he yearned for the *maner manus* (man of the heart). Like Rumi, Lalon urged that ego has to make way for real human experiences:

> Watch out for blunders, my heart,
> when engaged with this world.
> You choose to renounce it,
> yet fly your loincloth as a glorious flag. (Bhattacharya 1999, 133)

Lalon communicated his teachings in the religious idiom of his audiences but reached a human message:

> Learn about *namaj* [prayer] before you do it.
> Keep your eyes on the human Mecca.
> Fulfill man's desires
> Here and now, through man.

Handsome Kala [time] plays in the world
Of the human body. (Salomon 1991, 279–80)

For Lalon the potential of being human is the most privileged gift. He prays:

Can I ever again be born as a man?
Hurry up, my heart,
and act as you wish
in this world.
God has created man
in immortal form,
wishing to be human.
Nothing is better than man
. . .
man can pray
only by loving. (Bhattacharya 1999, 136)

Rumi and Lalon both narrate the story of humankind, evolving and learning new meanings of being human. The progressive endeavor is not an individual effort, though each person must enable the process, instead the human journey is a shared undertaking. As such, it is an interactive process. Rumi teaches this anecdotally in telling the story of a man preparing to travel to a foreign country despite being discouraged by his well-wishers. When asked why he wanted to go to a strange land where no one there was like him or spoke his language or shared his religious beliefs, the man replied that the last time he was there he spoke at a public gathering and they (the strangers) cried. Despite the lack of a common language of communication the people understood the man's message that came from his heart and responded to him.

Survivors of 1971 learned the lesson of dehumanization in violence and in recalling that memory today both men and women urge us to recognize our and their humanity too. Against this background they tell their story of violence to teach us a new language of agency, and they appeal to us to undergo a mutual learning process for overcoming binaries that blind people within encumbered structures of differences. They also make us realize that the individual encounter can be understood as a collective experience if we shed our attitude of extreme individualism and make space for shared responsiveness. Above all, they raise critical questions about the easy acceptance of external identities and enable us to see the internal dimensions of being human, oscillating between the local and universal and the historical and timeless, an ongoing process of humanization.

The language of insāniyat or *manushyata* that survivors draw upon can serve as the cultural and conceptual term to interpret this demand for humanization. Insāniyat has a wide range of meanings. The terms and concepts encompassed by humanity, humaneness, and humanism are often used to convey in a simple sense the meaning of insāniyat, although they represent only a small fraction of the varied connotations. To some modern humanists, particularly in the West, humanism is self-evidently secular and Western in origin (see Headley 2008). Humanism to people in the subcontinent, though, is inseparable to theological roots, and its source of inspiration is religion that dignifies human behavior. As I had mentioned earlier, generally speaking the development of a humanistic philosophy in the subcontinent is seen as a conversation between Sufi Islam and Hindu Bhakti ideas and philosophies that nurtured tolerance of diversity and difference.[25] In esoteric Sufi usage, insāniyat is love within a human being that transcends ego, enabling one to see and recognize the shared human condition that brings one closer to the Divine. It is this understanding as interconnected with others (and transgressing self and ego to reach closeness with the Divine) that Rumi reminds us is necessary to embark on the human journey, making individuals realize that they are inescapably part of a larger whole.

This shared language of insāniyat resonates even today throughout the Urdu-, Hindi-, and Punjabi-speaking regions of north India and Pakistan, particularly in the genres of music called *qawwali* (Sufi utterances) and *bhajan* (Bhakti devotional composition).[26] In Assam, where I am from, *manabata* (insāniyat) is a proudly used idiom that Assamese claim is a local ethical philosophy.[27] When people in the subcontinent refer to insāniyat they usually mean it as the capacity for recognizing the shared human status, which informs their actions and promotes understanding and facilitates relationships with others. Human beings, in order to retain their insāniyat, have to develop a vigilant outlook not to lose awareness of the Other, because it is in the other's well-being that the survival of the self is possible. In contrast the loss of insāniyat destroys human relationships and is the pathway for self-destruction. This loss manifested in the partition of India and Pakistan was one such devastating moment, and it shocked the witnesses and storytellers of

1947, particularly Hasan Manto, Intizar Hussain, Kuldip Nayar, and Govind Nihalini among others.[28] The shocking violence of 1971 has also provided a limited vocabulary to some commentators to conceptualize the loss.[29] In their reminiscences we hear the frightful recollections of human degradation and the loss of insāniyat in men's banal crimes of passion, greed, and anger.

The theoretical position of humanism that survivors of 1971 urge us to consider can be particularly useful for the people in the subcontinent given that the majority live within and also beyond the boundaries of given identities and divided histories; they enact tension using religious and political fundamentalisms while simultaneously showing an incredible capacity for tolerance toward difference and a willingness to live with others. This complex duality breed's violence and, simultaneously, nurtures humanization. Again, this is not to suggest that the heterogeneity of South Asia should be negated and collapsed into one homogenous syncretic identity. Rather, as Rumi, Lalon, and survivors of 1971 suggest, it is a site for engaging and developing humane concerns while accepting the tensions between the groups and the subsequent dialogical process. This space enables a renewed interrogation aimed at understanding the relationship between men and women—Indian, Pakistani, and Bangladeshi, Hindu and Muslim—and facilitates multiple narratives of people capable of altering the received narratives of history in South Asia.

The critical challenge I see in telling the story of women's experiences in 1971 is not to reproduce the spectacle of violence or reduce the violence into a text for analysis and critique. Veena Das (2000) and Ashis Nandy (1995), among others, have cautioned academics against overemphasis on theory and preoccupation with critique that can lead to devaluing empirical research. The Gorgon-like effect of gender violence in the war of 1971 that stuns and stupefies us cannot frighten us into silence, and the Nandian outlook would be to look at the face of violence to grasp its meaning to produce a narrative beyond the one already enclosed by history (Nandy 1995, 2008). In maintaining this line of investigation, I follow Nandy's injunction that history must address and engage memories of violence to reveal the losses that people suffer and to promote an understanding of violent events in all their complexities. I would like to push this inquiry a step further toward investigating history's forgetfulness, because at the point of forgetting the past, violence becomes possible in the present.

Again, one of the fundamental questions arises: what was forgotten in 1971? There can be multiple responses to this question. The women-centered approach that I have adopted focuses on the forgotten that women in Bangladesh drew my attention to. Paying attention to women's representations of their own reality during and after the war as dehumanized, we begin to grasp how power works for destroying and marking Others. Telling personal stories serves as a meaning-constructing activity and an affirmation by women toward reclaiming their humanity. The capacity to recall these memories reconvenes women's agency, or at the very least, it is a beginning step.

Bangladeshi women's narratives are personal stories that are also political and this makes women's narratives inherently valuable. In telling their memories, their stories force an interrogation of the nation-building process, and they simultaneously pose a challenge to post-1971 historiography, highlighting the silences in the official histories offered to date. Women's lived experiences of violence challenge us to engage and work through the losses they suffered and their resilience in making meaning beyond it, so that we can begin to see what happened in the war and start a process of understanding the historical conditions and intersections that connect 1971 with other violent episodes of postcolonial history. I argue that violence must be studied not only historically and theoretically, but we need to think about violence ethically and politically to make sense of its meaning and impact in people's lives.

HISTORY WRITING IN SOUTH ASIA

The growing interest in investigating the history of violence in South Asia has produced many schools of history writing in consequence. For example, the secular nationalist historians in India assert that the project of colonialism and colonial production of history should be blamed for creating and making violence possible before and after 1947 (Chatterjee 1992; Panikar 1995; Hasan 1995; Thapar 1992, 2002; Datta 1999; Sarkar 2001). They emphasize that the syncretic relationships between plural and diverse communities of subjects were written out of the text of subcontinental lives when colonial officialdom codified and tabulated Hindu and Muslim, majority and minority, "civilized" and "tribal," and marked people with identities who had not developed them on their own. The "epistemic violence" of colonialism, they argue, is the site for exploring and explaining religious conflict in the subcontinent.[30]

Pakistani historians, on the other hand, do not emphasize the mutu-ally developed culture of the Indus and Gangetic communities; some even denounce the Muslim kings of Delhi as un-Islamic for supporting Hindu and Muslim interaction.[31] They go a step further to claim that the Hindus were more hostile to the Muslims than the British colonial administration. Thus they justify the creation of Pakistan as a victory against the Hindus.

Not unlike the rabid fundamentalist historians of Pakistan, in India too, the Hindu fundamentalist school of Hindutva blames the Mus-lims—the Other—for violence in India. They claim that violence was the doing of Muslim occupiers and therefore the Muslim minorities within India must be made accountable for the "original" violence com-mitted by their ancestors.[32] Interestingly, this rhetorical construction of the history of Muslims as conquerors and occupiers is accomplished by glossing over the variety of Muslim groups and their different trajec-tories of settlement by reducing them into one monolithic and artificial category.[33]

Muslims constitute a variety in the subcontinent, and they came in different periods of time. In the early seventh century, a group of trad-ers established a nascent Muslim community in Makran, Sind (Sindh), in present-day Pakistan (Richards 1994; Wink 1990, 13; Hodgson 1974). Today, Pakistani historians claim this initial commercial establishment as the beginning of Pakistan's history and situate Sind as the doorway of Islam. In the ninth century, a group of Arab traders settled in South India, creating the first Muslim settlement in the peninsula (Dale 1990; Moore 2006). Muslim groups of various ethnicities and from different geographical locations in Central and West Asia also came to the sub-continent through various channels as conquerors, traders, itinerant preachers, scholars, poets, soldiers, Sufis, refugees, and others. The dif-ferences among these Muslim groups were many, and they often battled against each other. In fact, Babur, a Central Asian princeling, who later became the founder of the Mughal dynasty (1526 CE), was invited to oc-cupy Delhi by Sikander Lodi, an Afghan Muslim who was fighting a fel-low Afghan Muslim, Ibrahim Lodi, who was his contender to the throne of Delhi. Not surprisingly the complex histories of tensions between the different Muslim groups and their settlement in the subcontinent are suppressed both in the Indian version as well as in Pakistani narra-tive history because they are not useful for either the Hindutva or Is-lamization projects of history writing.

In turn, historians who support the Hindutva ideology of making India an exclusively Hindu land begin the story of Muslims in India from the period of the Mughal rule, shortening the temporal length of Muslim presence in India by several hundred years and declaring the Muslims as aggressive conquerors (Chatterjee 1997; Guha 1995). Curiously in this abridged version of history, events and characters are shortchanged, and in the popular version (told to me by an automatic rickshaw driver in Delhi who claimed everyone knows the story), Babur is said to have fought against Prithviraj Chauhan, a Rajput king, and thus the contestation is represented as a struggle between the invading Muslim conqueror and an indigenous Hindu king and his subjects. Identifying the foundational moment of Muslim occupation to Babur's conquest of Delhi makes it possible to cast present-day Muslims of North India as *Babur ka santan* (the scions of Babur) and transform them into a community of occupiers who must be forcibly removed from India (Amin 2005). The Mumbai riots after the demolition of the Babri Mosque was a case in making this point. In Pakistan, on the other hand, the history of Muslims and the teleology of Pakistan are conveniently combined and this length is stressed as much as possible, some even "imaginatively [reclaim the] pre-Islamic Muslim world" (Jalal 1995, 78).

The Marxist school of historians in India (dominated by the Aligarh group) as well the Subaltern Studies Collective have paid scant attention to the issue of violence between the different religious communities in premodern and colonial British India. An exception to the case, however, is Gyan Pandey's study of communal riots in colonial North India (Pandey 1990). In the scholarship of the Marxist and subaltern historians the emphasis has been on the structural violence that was cultivated and maintained by the institutions of the state to exert power and coerce the subject communities into submission. Not unlike the secular school of historians, both the Marxist and the subaltern historians focus on the process of exploitation and oppression during colonialism to understand the rift between the different local communities, but they do not push for an exploration of the consequences of the divide among the weak and disempowered Hindu and Muslim masses of the subcontinent.

In Pakistan today a complicated and made-up history of the national past is in circulation. Although no defined school of history on Pakistan's past is evident, as early as 1948 the government of Pakistan constituted a committee to rewrite a history of the nation that privileged the

Muslim past.[34] Ayesha Jalal writes, "Pakistan, with its artificially demarcated frontiers and desperate quest for an officially sanctioned Islamic identity . . . the struggle for formal self-definition has been conducted in pitched battles between a vocal Islamic lobby and their 'secular' and 'modernist' opponents" (Jalal 1995, 74). The rewriting of history from an Islamic standpoint was given a high priority with the creation of the Islamic Research Institute in 1956. The institute was given the responsibility to "research in order to identify and bring out the achievements of Muslims in the world of philosophy, science, religion and culture." The institute started with the premise that "Islamic civilization and culture have been great forces in world history," and to substantiate this claim devised a research agenda to prove it.[35] The historian Ishtiaq Hussain Qureshi, who was appointed as the director of the institute, claimed an exclusive heritage for the Muslims for which he invoked the politically constructed "two-nation theory" that developed in the nineteenth and twentieth centuries and read it back into the past for writing a Muslim history. Driven to undo the history of Hindu and Muslim interaction in the precolonial period, he asked "if the Muslims were to forget their uniqueness and come to absorb, as Akbar [the Mughal emperor known for his secular and tolerant attitude toward non-Muslims in India] did, contradictory tendencies and beliefs from other religions, could the Muslim nation continue to exist as a separate nation?" (quoted in Ali 2002, 4530).

In 1961 history as a subject was discontinued in Pakistan and was incorporated into textbooks on social science (Ali 2002, 4531). As such, the development of debates and different schools of history was not even given a chance. The state bureaucracy and the government-appointed historians colluded to write a history, presented as "Pakistan Studies" from an Islamic standpoint and negated all other influences on Pakistan's people and culture. The privileged position of West Pakistan dominated in this representation.

The obvious problem that faced the scholars of Pakistan studies is where and when to start Pakistan's history. Including the ancient past of the subcontinent would mean including the influences of different non-Muslim communities and locate Pakistan's history within the Indus and Gangetic milieu, perhaps even focusing on East Pakistan because that region had established a sultanate independent of Delhi as early as the thirteenth century. To overcome this unnecessary fact of history, Ahmad Hasan Dani, a reputed Pakistani archaeologist and historian, suggested that Pakistan had closer and stronger cultural links with Central Asia than with India and that should be the focus of Pakistan's past before Islam. Later, Aitzaz Ahsan, a lawyer turned historian, claimed in his book the *Indus Saga* (1997) that Pakistan's past was more deeply connected with Central and West Asia than with the Gangetic valley.

The general tendency was to overlook the history before the advent of Muslims in the region, and the starting point of Muslim history was identified with the invasion of Mohammad bin Qasim in the seventh century, which in Indian historiography (created by the British colonials as well as the BJP historians) is also represented as a shattering moment of warfare that destroyed peace in the region. In Pakistan, however, this event is a matter of pride as it inaugurated the establishment of Muslim power in the subcontinent. M. D. Zafar writes in his *A Text Book of Pakistan Studies* that "Pakistan had spread to include the whole of Northern India and Bengal," then under the Khilji dynasty "Pakistan moved further southward to include a greater part of Central India and the Deccan," and finally under the rule of Aurangzeb the "Pakistan spirit gathered in strength" but waned again with his death (quoted in Jalal 1995, 79). But of course, the Pakistan spirit revived once again under the leadership of Mohammad Ali Jinnah and the Muslim League, who led the Muslim Pakistanis to their independent destiny.

But it was not enough to claim an exclusive Muslim past for the Pakistani people in history. Pakistani historians also had to train the public to be "true Muslims," particularly the people of East Pakistan. Besides importing to East Pakistan the Urdu language and compelling people to learn it, the more important change was directed at creating a new historical memory by reminding the East Pakistani Bengalis of the "great privations they had undergone at the hands of the Hindus over a long period of their history."[36] The orientation to renew the study of history of East Pakistan as Muslim history was a directive that came from President Ayub Khan in 1965. By government mandate a committee was appointed to write the "History of Pakistan." In this new state-written history that was to be taught to East Pakistani children and the public, the successes of the Muslims were emphasized and the weaknesses of the Hindus were highlighted. The Bangla Academy that was created in Dhaka, alongside the Islamic Research Institute in Lahore, was established to research and write about the contributions of the Muslims. It was admonished for increasing its pro-Tagore activities, which were deemed "anti-national" and a symbol of Bengali Hindus in East Pakistan.[37]

In 1966, by order of the Cabinet Division working under the direct supervision of President Ayub Khan, the term *partition* was dropped from the official lexicon of Pakistan's administration because it "gave the impression that Pakistan was an artificially created country which is far from the truth. In fact, Pakistan is a different country than India bound together by the British rule for a period of only two centuries." In lieu of using partition, the words *achievement for independence* were mandated and history was divided as "Pre-independence" and "Post-Independence" history.[38] Evidently, Pakistan had fully internalized the colonial history of Hindus and Muslims and accepted that they were totally separate communities with little or no interaction in the past. The rhetoric of Hindu as an "enemy" of Muslims that the colonials had endowed became the language and ethos of independent Pakistan. It would be unfair to blame Pakistan alone for keeping alive the inherited history of divided communities. In India, too, the enemy narrative is active and gaining ground every day.

Bangladesh's history before the war of 1971 is more or less silent about the Pakistan period, except for occasional reminders of the economic exploitation by West Pakistani business interests and civil bureaucrats.[39] This problem creates a totally skewed history and the only language that survives about the Pakistan era is "colonization." Bangladeshis can no longer determine who the real colonial masters were—the British or the West Pakistanis. The intimacy with the Other (Pakistan and Pakistanis) as well as the fear of remembering so engulfs the Bangladeshis today that they have willfully lost the segment of the pre-1971 history.[40] After Bangladesh emerged as a "liberated" nation, a narrative of the war took shape and provided the beginning for writing a "true history."

I have argued elsewhere that the colonial violence of identity making in history is something we cannot forget (Saikia 2004a). Neither can we overlook the frequent and violent outbreak of tensions based on this history, mostly directed against the Muslims in India after partition (after the Babri Mosque issue there have been many riots, the most bloody was the post-Godhra violence in Gujarat in 2002 which marked the tenth anniversary of the demolition of the mosque). Whatever the reasons for the claim of "originary" violence, my concern is to focus on the realities on the ground and inquire how we have incorporated received histories—secular or fundamentalist, Marxist or subaltern, colonial and postcolonial, Indian, Pakistani, or Bangladeshi—into our present political lives and transformed them into tools to enact violence for national pride, disabling people to see the destructive force of their own violence. It is this void of locating violence and putting it into perspective that allows forgetting and creates a crisis of memory, which survivors of 1971 are urging us to take stock of and to make it pivotal in the study of critical events in our time.

To tell the past, one must remember it, which involves a struggle for the survivors and the social and political life of the nation. Remembering, as Gyan Pandey (1992) argues, may force us to address issues and open wounds that a nation does not want to deal with. But the project of remembering the traumatic past has to be more than coming to terms with the bad and ugly that national history wants to silence. Moreover, remembering need not be directed at creating an oppositional story, as Ranabir Samadar (2001) argues.[41] The cognitive structure of writing a people's history in South Asia today has matured enough to move beyond and outside the control of already produced state history learned from the colonials, which is a self-selective process determined to control the outcome by creating *included* and *excluded*, *us* and *them* (Trouillot 1995).

It is true that not all the episodes within the state history remain externally placed, outside people's lives and their memories. Some memories do interact with history and produce interesting outcomes, as Gyan Pandey (1995 and 1999) and Shahid Amin (1995) have evocatively argued. An example of this is the story of the rickshaw driver who told me his version of Indian history that Prithiviraj Chauhan fought against Babur, in which the native hero is posed against the foreign invader. This popular version of the past that resides in collective memory in contemporary India is not different from the "bad" official history produced during the tenure of the BJP in India and Ayub Khan in Pakistan. In both versions of history—the official and the popular—one group is represented as the defenders of the motherland or homeland and the other group as the invading aggressors. We have to remember that this kind of polarized history is not totally contrived, either by the people or the state, but involves a careful sifting process undertaken by select groups of agents—official historians, government officials, vested parties, including the public looking for identity in history. Curiously, the outcome of this kind of history is to flatten the multivocal experiences and produce a simplified narrative for consumption that spawns and penetrates people's knowing of the past.[42] The process that excises some episodes and people out of history is concerning because it decides what is acceptable about the past in the present.

The silences within history and memory are produced and reaffirmed at many sites: there is a silencing in the selection of sources and there is silencing in the creation of archives, the repositories of historical records. Choices are deliberately made in the official process of collection, some accidents occur, and some of the recorded past is intentionally removed. The corpus called *history* thus produced is only a partial record of the past, but it becomes the final product backed by the official power of the state and is memorialized. The official history that is an engineered product must be questioned, or otherwise the silenced and unnarrated will remain unthinkable and unknowable. History's privileged claim to know the "truth" must be evaluated and analyzed and the gaps created by colonial knowledge production, postcolonial nationalism, and religious politics in the subcontinent have to be fully addressed. Above all, history's spurious currency that circulates so easily in the region should be questioned, and this is possible if we listen to the people who are the agents and subjects of history.

2

CREATING THE HISTORY OF 1971

THE POLITICS OF PAKISTAN AND INDIA

In 1947, at the end of British colonial rule, the subcontinent was partitioned, creating India and Pakistan. India was founded on the ethos of a secular republic but soon became mired in majoritarian politics expressed in communal and religious violence that has bloodied the landscape of postcolonial history.[1] Pakistan, on the other hand, was founded on the rhetoric of religious nationalism popularized by a variety of Muslim organizations and campaigns throughout the early twentieth century that emboldened the Muslim League party under the leadership of Mohammad Ali Jinnah to make an assertive demand for Pakistan. Immediately on the birth of Pakistan, Jinnah downplayed the exclusive Muslim identity and a somewhat tempered rhetoric of inclusion was publicly announced. In Jinnah's inaugural speech to the members of the Constituent Assembly of Pakistan on August 11, 1947, he declared,

> You are free; you are free to go to your temples, you are free to go to your mosques or to any other place of worship in this State of Pakistan. You may belong to any religion or caste or creed—that has nothing to do with the business of the State. . . . We are starting with this fundamental principle that we are all citizens and equal citizens of one State. . . . I think we should keep that in front of us as our ideal, and you will find that in due course Hindus would cease to be Hindus and Muslims would cease to be Muslims, not in the religious sense, because that is the personal faith of each individual, but in the political sense as citizens of the State.[2]

The collective consciousness of the Muslims that led to the creation of Pakistan, it seems from Jinnah's speech, ceased to be the state's focus in independent Pakistan, and the state decided against publicly flaunting a Muslim identity.[3] During this initial period, the Muslim did not deem the Other—Hindu—as its enemy; at least this was not publicly announced. The inaugural speech of Mohammad Ali Jinnah made on the floor of the Constituent Assembly stands as testimony to the equality of all citizens, irrespective of their religious beliefs, in the newly founded nation-state of Pakistan. It was not religion but ethnicity that became the site of conflict between East and West Pakistan even at the early stages of building the new nation.

The multiple ethnic and linguistic communities of Punjabi, Bengali, Sindhi, Pathan, Baluchi, and the Urdu-speaking groups from Bihar and Uttar Pradesh (émigrés from India—Muhajirs) that made up the Pakistani nation were divided physically, emotionally, politically, and culturally. Territorially the nation was divided into two wings—East and West Pakistan. The Punjabis who dominated in the West vied for power against the Bengalis in the East, who constituted the majority population in Pakistan. Supported by the Urdu-speaking immigrants from Bihar and Uttar Pradesh, who spread and established themselves in West and East Pakistan, the Punjabis slowly established their prominence in Pakistan's identity and politics.

The state's attitude of favoritism toward groups in West Pakistan, particularly toward the Punjabi and the Urdu-speaking émigré community created public tensions in Pakistan. It was suggested that Urdu would be the national language of Pakistan, although the majority population of Pakistan, the Bengalis, refused to accept it. Language riots marked the 1950s with violence. Fluency in the state's officially recognized language meant access to power, and the state's attitude of discriminating against non-Urdu speakers (constituting the Bengali majority) proved very costly to the Pakistani state.[4]

Throughout the 1960s, Bengali ethnonationalism found expression in a variety of public activities and unrest, and their demands became strident. The major grievances that motivated the Bengalis to fight to separate themselves from the Punjabi-dominated Pakistani state were the inequitable distribution of national resources, economic exploitation, restrictions on Bengali speech in the public sphere, and a lack of political representation in Pakistan's national parliament. The military

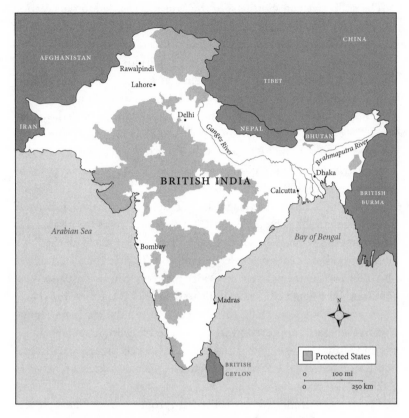

British India, 1947.

dictators who ruled Pakistan from 1958 to 1971 refused to accommodate the demands made by the Bengalis.

The emphasis on ethnic superiority of West Pakistani Punjabis and Urdu speakers was particularly evident during Ayub Khan's military dictatorship (1958–1969). Ayub Khan's constitution in 1962 even attempted to drop the term *Islamic* in describing Pakistan but was forced to rescind due to the religious backlash within the country.[5] He succeeded in making a very important change on the register of ethnicity, which had far-reaching effects on the Pakistani people's psyche and shaped the politics to come. By establishing West Pakistan as "One Unit," rather than maintaining the ethos of a federated union of the constituent regions, which was the original agreement, the division of West and East Pakistan was administratively sanctioned. This policy established "parity" between the two wings and gave equal electoral weight to East

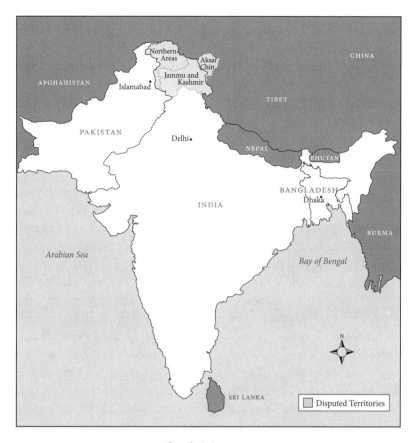

South Asia, 1971.

and West Pakistan, although the West, 40 percent of the total population of Pakistan, constituted a minority. In turn, the Bengali majority of Pakistan was reduced into secondary players in the polity, and the Punjabi and Urdu-speaking minority in the West established their position to become the power brokers.

The establishment of the two-wing state and the toning down of the Muslim political rhetoric within the nation facilitated the creation of a new enemy. The construction of *Hindu* as Pakistan's enemy developed in the military and political sites as fractured narratives. Within the realm of national politics by the mid-1960s, the term *Hindu* was invoked to mobilize Pakistan's struggle against the enemy nation—India—and after 1965 the categories *India* and *Hindu* were interchangeably used.

India became Hindu in the view of the Pakistani state, and this impression was widely publicized in the public sphere through political rhetoric and discourse, particularly by Zulfikar Ali Bhutto who used the idea of Musawat Muhammadiya or Islamic Socialism to reconstruct a Pakistani identity. The Pakistan Army continued to maintain its public persona as a secular institution for a while, within which the ethnic politics of the superiority of the Punjabis took precedence, as many veterans of 1971 admitted to me. But as the conditions and politics in Pakistan changed and the demand of the Bengalis became more vocal, the rhetoric of Hindu as the enemy of Muslim became a tool for the army to use against the people of East Pakistan, who were increasingly viewed as "Hindu-like." The racially tinted outlook of Punjabi superiority and Bengali inferiority motivated the military dictators' policies and produced decisions that became evident after the 1970 general election.

Sheikh Mujibur Rahman, the Bengali leader of the Awami League (AL), won a landslide victory in the 1970 general election, gaining 160 of the 162 seats in East Pakistan; while his rival Zulfikar Ali Bhutto, the founder of the Pakistan Peoples Party (PPP), won the majority in West Pakistan with 81 of the 138 seats. The results of the election were unexpected by the military junta and the political parties in West Pakistan.[6] Several of the political parities of West Pakistan, most importantly Zulfikar Ali Bhutto's PPP, refused to attend the inaugural session of the National Assembly in Dhaka scheduled to be held on March 3, 1971, to sort out the political stalemate. Failing to reach a consensus among the AL and the PPP to share power or accept Sheikh Mujibur Rahman, a Bengali, as the prime minister of Pakistan, Yahya Khan, the president and martial law administrator, deployed the Pakistan Army against the Bengali people to stifle the growing unrest and political instability in East Pakistan.[7] Added to the deployment of the Pakistan Army were the steady and intrusive incursions of the Indian security forces, Indian spies, and troublemakers into East Pakistan, which obviously worsened the situation for people in East Pakistan.[8] Increasingly, the Pakistan Army and politicians began to view the Bengalis as rebels and anti-Pakistan. The military solution of Yahya Khan found easy acceptance among the political leaders of West Pakistan, and it was fully backed by Zulfikar Ali Bhutto. In a nationally broadcast radio speech on March 26, 1971, Yahya Khan told his "fellow countrymen," meaning West Pakistanis, that military action "over there" was necessary "because of Mujib's obstinacy, obduracy, and absolute refusal to talk sense . . . [which]

leads but to one conclusion that the man and his party are enemies of Pakistan, and they want East Pakistan to break away completely from the country." He also announced that he was "proud of [the Pakistan Army]" and asked "the nation to appreciate the gravity of the situation for which the blame rests entirely on anti-Pakistan and secessionist elements and to act as reasonable citizens of the country because therein lies the security and salvation of Pakistan."[9] Sheikh Mujibur Rahman and AL party leaders were declared rebels, the Bengali units in the Pakistan Army were disarmed along with the police, and efforts were made to arrest the leaders of the student organizations and eliminate the intellectuals of Dhaka University.

The state declared war against the people of East Pakistan on March 25, 1971. In showing support to the military decision, Zulfikar Ali Bhutto publicly announced "Thank God, Pakistan has been saved."[10] Many think this single statement summed up the attitude of the West Pakistanis toward East Pakistan, that for West Pakistanis the people of East Pakistan did not matter at all; they were the Other, Hindu-like, and deserved destruction. Pakistan resided in the western wing and the rule of the elite of this region had to be guaranteed by all means, even if it meant whipping up a sentimental, but unfounded, rhetoric of "saving Islam from the Hindus" by brutalizing the people of East Pakistan. For nine months, a reign of terror and violence took over East Pakistan and resulted in the killing of many nationalist Bengalis. The war was not confined to Pakistan, but its long-standing enemy and neighbor, India, became embroiled in the conflict and lent its support to the Bengalis to fight and break away from what they saw as Muslim West Pakistan. Thus, alongside a civil war between East and West Pakistan, an international war between Pakistan and India also broke out.

Just as Pakistan used religion to separate *us* from *the enemy*, so too did India. When assessing the damage done by the West Pakistanis against the East Pakistani Bengalis through belligerent and armed violence, the Indian government found the opportunity to use religion to add to the sense of panic and horror in East Pakistan. Indian agents, who were working in East Pakistan from January 1971 as is evident from visual accounts of the time, encouraged the East Pakistanis, especially the Hindu minority, to migrate to India.[11] The migration of large numbers of Hindus from East Pakistan to India achieved its purpose of confirming that religious persecution was driving the violence in the war, and this was highlighted in the Indian press.

In turn, the minority Urdu-speaking community in East Pakistan, commonly referred to as Bihari, turned to the Pakistan Army for protection of their Muslim identity.[12] They provided assistance to the West Pakistan soldiers to carry out violence against the Bengalis struggling for liberation in East Pakistan. The Bengalis were deemed the enemies of Pakistan and, because of their support from India, were now increasingly and readily accepted as Hindu-like, which justified violence against them. The ethnic war between Bengalis and Biharis thus became the third war in East Pakistan.

In the civil and ethnic wars, West Pakistani troops along with the support of Al-Badr and Al-Shams, constituted by local Bengali and Bihari militias, committed widespread violence against the nationalist Bengalis, who were deemed "Hindu turncoats," to justify Muslim (Pakistani) violence against them (Mascarenhas 1971; Sisson and Rose 1990).[13] In turn, the nationalist Bengalis, with the assistance of the Indian Army, created a local militia called Mukti Bahini (Liberation Army) and wreaked havoc in communities deemed enemies of the nationalist Bengalis.[14]

In particular, during the civil war the Biharis were targeted as the supposed enemy of the Bengalis. This was partly economic as much as it was ethnic hatred, and the easy accessibility to this group, rather than the Pakistani soldiers who lived within their protected barracks, made them vulnerable. Because the Biharis were Urdu speakers, they had an edge in the Pakistani administration and were employed in the public sector as well as in the privately owned West Pakistani businesses in the East. Being émigrés from India they were not landed people and, unlike the Bengalis, were not agriculturalists and did not spread out to the villages. The livelihood options of the Bihari were confined to the industrial and business sectors, resulting in their formation of compact communities living in ghetto-like conditions in the urban spaces. The cleavages between the Bengalis and the Biharis in speech, livelihood, and living arrangements enabled the transformation of the Biharis into an outcast group by the Bengali nationalists, who targeted Biharis for violence. The majority of the ethnic attacks happened in towns where the Bengalis and Biharis worked and lived side-by-side as neighbors before the violence broke out.[15] Most Biharis did not have an armed presence to protect them. Their vulnerability made them easy targets, and fearing for their lives, the majority relinquished home and property. After the war, the Biharis were transformed into "stateless refugees" (Withaker,

Soldiers and devastation. *(Source withheld)*

Guest, and Ennals 1975; Aziz 1974).[16] Today, more than 250,000 Biharis still live in refugee camps in Bangladesh without basic human rights.[17] It was in one of these camps, Camp Geneva, where I first encountered the stateless Biharis in Bangladesh. Neither Pakistan nor Bangladesh recognizes them as citizens, and they have nowhere else to go.

Rampant violence also took place against innocent and helpless Bengali civilians, mostly vulnerable groups of religious minorities and women, during the nine months of war. The Pakistan Army and their helpers, the Bihari and Bengali loyalists, often attacked villages and razed them to the ground. The intensity of these attacks on Bengali villages was at its highest immediately after March 25, 1971, and it lasted until early May. There was a short lull thereafter, but the spark caught fire once again when the Mukti Bahini guerillas started placing landmines indiscriminately and destroying the Pakistan Army tanks in large numbers with the help of Indian intelligence gathering. The Pakistan Army's reactive strategy was to punish the local rebels in the villages and towns and randomly pick up people for interrogation followed by brush firing (firing a gun on anyone indiscriminately). Few survived to tell their tales.[18] Pakistani attackers also murdered the old and young in the villages and raped women. Sexual violence was widespread at this time. The Pakistanis hoped that the tactics of fear and extreme punishment and humiliation of Bengali honor would prevent future rebel recruitment by the Mukti Bahini. But that was not the case. The rank of Mukti Bahinis swelled and eleven sector commands were established, of which only one was located within East Pakistan. The rest of the sectors were established and functioned from the India and East Pakistan border. The Mukti Bahinis with the direct help of the Indian government made it into an all out civil war. In turn, the Pakistan Army's violence increased exponentially.

The violence compelled both Hindu and Muslim Bengalis, mostly women, children, and the elderly, to migrate across the border to India. The Bihari women, children, and their elderly had nowhere to escape to. The Bengali refugees went to West Bengal, Tripura, and Assam because these places were already etched into the path of migration from East Pakistan to India. The refugee pressure on the resources of the host communities became acute, leading to intense questioning in the national parliamentary debates as to whether India should continue to assist the Bengalis in their struggle.[19] In support of the Hindu Bengali refugees (who formed 60 percent of the East Pakistani refugee population) arguments were made that in the future they would become "good Indian citizens" and hence their migration to India from East Pakistan was not discouraged but deemed legitimate. On the other hand, the Muslim refugees were pushed into a liminal category of "illegal immigrants," and vociferous demands were made to remove them from the body politic of India.[20]

The international war that broke out in 1971 between India and Pakistan was part of the long, drawn-out series of battles that started soon after 1947. In 1948 and 1965, the two countries went to war over Kashmir but could not resolve the problem. From early 1970, the government of India became actively involved in destabilizing East Pakistan. Using intelligence agents and the Border Security Force for creating panic, India lured the Hindu Bengalis to leave East Pakistan. Rumors of forcible

Families destroyed.
*(Courtesy of Shahriar Kabir/Forum for
Secular Bangladesh and Trial of War Criminals of 1971)*

What is there to live for?
*(Courtesy of Shahriar Kabir/Forum for
Secular Bangladesh and Trial of War Criminals of 1971)*

occupation of Hindu properties and conversion to Islam, disrespect of religious places, molestation of women, robberies, and similar harassment and crimes were circulated. Propaganda that refugees would be given land in West Bengal (approximately two hectares for each family) was used for enticing landless cultivators to cross over. The active support of the Indian relief agencies, such as the Omega Team, and the special rehabilitation offices that were set up at the border proved great encouragement and assisted a variety of Bengali people to leave East Pakistan (Prasad 1992).[21] The violence of the Pakistan Army added further impetus to migrate to a safe haven.

Initially, the number of refugees to India did not seem to be an impressive count. The minister of labor and rehabilitation, R. K. Khadilkar, informed the Parliament of India on May 27, 1971, that between March 26 and March 31 only three hundred refugees had crossed over into India. By April 17, however, 119,566 persons had crossed into the Indian border states of West Bengal, Assam, Meghalaya, and Tripura. From the middle of April, the refugee influx started increasing rapidly. The steady stream of Bengali refugees to India justified Indira Gandhi's ambition for seeking international involvement (Prasad 1992, 81–82, 90–92).

Furthermore, Pakistan's belligerence and use of armed forces against the civilian population enabled India to argue for a humanitarian crisis in East Pakistan.[22] After months of deliberation and fighting a proxy war on behalf of the East Pakistan Bengalis, on November 26, 1971, India launched a frontal attack against the Pakistan Army in East Pakistan.[23] The Pakistan Army responded on December 3 by attacking India's western front, on the border of Punjab. Within twelve days, the Indian Army assumed the upper hand in the war in East Pakistan with the help of the Mukti Bahini. On December 16, 1971, the war was over. Pakistan surrendered to India.

With the direct help of India, the new nation-state of Bangladesh was created in the former territory of East Pakistan. The United States, Pakistan's traditional ally, did not interfere with the outcome. Pakistan was broken up, and the Bengalis won their independence. Behind the story of the proud beginning of Bangladesh was a terribly dark human story of loss and destruction. Bangladesh claims that in the nine months of war nearly a million Bengalis were killed by the Pakistani military, several million were rendered homeless, and several thousand women were

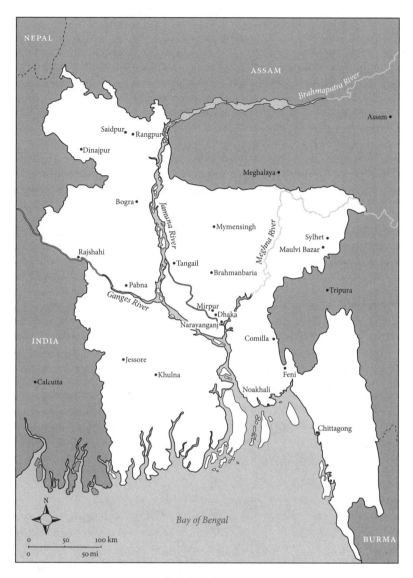

Bangladesh, 1971.

raped. Although the loss of Bihari lives was never accounted for by the Bangladeshi authorities, independent sources, such as the International Red Cross, documented that over 250,000 Biharis were displaced after the war. The stateless Biharis were quarantined in internment camps where the vast majority is still languishing in the hope of a settlement of their status.[24]

VIOLENCE ON THE SIDE: WAR ON NONCOMBATANTS

The multiple levels of victimization in the war are little known. Instead, triumphant narratives of "success" and "liberation" are written and re-written in Bangladesh and India, and they are consumed as the one and only history of the war. In Pakistan, there is a general uneasiness when talking about the war, and the long silences of memory in the public space have crystallized into a kind of amnesia. The constructed histories in India and Bangladesh and the silencing of memories in Pakistan have created a great deal of confusion, and there is an ongoing quarrel about who to blame for the violence and differing claims of victimhood. The debatable nature of the past allows for new narratives to be produced that suit the purposes of remembering or forgetting. Few can deny, however, that in the wars of 1971 state violence combined with ethnic and religious hatred to target the vulnerable; all the groups involved in the wars were complicit in the violence.

When civil war broke out in East Pakistan, the Pakistan Army supplied arms to Al-Badr and Al-Shams to eradicate the Bengali nationalist rebels. In turn, the Indian political authorities sanctioned the establishment of local cells to arm the Bengali Mukti Bahini guerillas to fight the Pakistanis and their supporters. The divided groups of armed men did just that; they went on a house-to-house rampage against each other, the Bengalis against the Biharis and vice versa even before the civil war broke out.[25] In this volatile scene of ethnic warfare the direct intervention of the Pakistan Army complicated matters even further. The military administration motivated their Punjabi soldiers to annihilate nationalist Bengalis. Indian politicians and their supporters also used the war as an opportunity to cut Muslim Pakistan down to size and neutralize the eastern border. Leaders and followers thus reduced their enemies into abstract numbers and demographic units, categorizing *us* and *them*. The abstraction of humans to fit ethnic, religious, and national labels opened the space for a cold, inhuman purpose for one human being to violate another human being. Bounded communities saw themselves as enemies of other bounded communities. Instigated by their leaders, men elevated violence to the level of duty for furthering the sovereign power of the nation. The vulnerable humans, the victims, who were used and exploited by the system, were not accounted for, and their lived experiences were obscured and erased from the national registers. Women who were brutally attacked and exploited were annulled from national historical memory; their experiences were a site of shame.

The human tragedy of 1971 is overwhelming. What is most shocking in exploring the violence is that those responsible for the killings and brutalities were often common people, who took sides with their ethnic or political groups, and were armed by the Pakistan and Indian armies to act out their wills. The multiple actors and perpetrators complicate the picture, and it is almost impossible to distinguish victims and perpetrators. We know that the majority that died in the war of 1971 were not combatants and they were not involved in the making of violence. They were victims, innocent or guilty, only of being Bengali, Hindu, or Muslim, or Urdu speaking or Bihari. They were killed because they were there in East Pakistan in 1971. Some among them supported Sheikh Mujibur Rahman, the Bengali leader who aspired to become the prime minister of Pakistan and, in fact, had the votes for at least a power-sharing role, which went against the wishes of the military junta and the politicians of West Pakistan. Most of those who were killed in East Pakistan during the war had no hope of escaping. But can we read the violence as genocide?[26] Genocide scholars agree it is a contested concept; there is a great deal of disagreement about what qualifies for the term (Straus 2005; Staub 2000).

Genocide is strategically used by perpetrators to accomplish their mission of establishing their power. They define the event through their motivation to willfully destroy and annihilate the victim community that they identify as different from them. The processing required for committing genocide can be an "industrial" production that occurred in Nazi Germany, or genocidal violence can occur within communities that share intimate and passionate relationships, as in the case of Rwanda and Bosnia. Genocidal violence is part of a cold and rational plan and not irrational, random acts of killing (Newbury 1998; Herzfeld 2005). The number of dead bodies is not the determinant issue in the labeling of the event. In Nazi Germany, Rwanda, Bosnia, and now Darfur, which are recognized as genocides, a common thread links them together.[27] The violence in all these events was engineered by a group within the country to produce the death of others, over whom they had power. The Nazi activities of creating and using concentration and labor camps, gas chambers, and other inhumane means to remove all traces of the Jewish population from the body politic of Europe is the most cited example of genocide in the twentieth century.[28] In Rwanda genocide was not a single, spontaneous event but happened in five phases involving calculated designs and plans. It started in the mass killings beginning in Kigali on April 6, 1994, and lasted for three months spreading to the northeast, south central Rwanda, and then extended to the south and west. These were not war zones but killing fields where the slaughter of the Tutsis by the Hutus was carried out with knife and machete, as well as by guns and grenades (Herzfeld 2005). International involvement, particularly the abusive power of the French authorities, is a much debated issue in understanding the Rwandan genocide.

In East Pakistan death was not produced in a factory-like environment nor was there one group of perpetrators. Violence was a passionate outburst staged in intervals as a reaction to previous episodes. The violence happened between and within communities of people who knew each other and lived alongside each other, as neighbors, as teachers and students, as colleagues and co-workers, as strangers and friends. These people were driven by the passion of their group interest, politics, personal vendettas, and even material greed. Violence was also carried out by outsiders—the Pakistan Army and the Indian Army. No single group had a monopoly on committing violence, nor did one single group control the production of death in East Pakistan. Pakistani Punjabi soldiers, nationalist Bengali militias, Bengali supporters of West Pakistan, Bihari civil armed guards, and Indian Army men, along with other less identifiable groups, killed, tortured, and destroyed those who opposed them and their politics.[29] It is true that the West Pakistani soldiers and their supporters killed large numbers and that they were supported by the institution of the army, a state apparatus, to carry out violence against the people of East Pakistan. What motivated the Pakistani soldiers to kill nationalist Bengalis who were until then a part of Pakistan and were citizens of the same country? Did the Pakistani soldiers think they were committing genocide?

Many veterans in Pakistan recall that they were ordered by their superiors to teach the Bengalis a lesson, and they obeyed the command of their superiors and performed their duty.[30] They viewed the Bengali uprising as a rebellion and were determined to crush it.[31] Some reveal that they killed noncombatant Bengalis because they feared their own deaths. Also, they hoped the example of corporeal punishment would deter the Bengalis from continuing their freedom struggle and that the terror of death would compel them to accept defeat. They tortured Bengali women because they wanted to humiliate and dishonor Bengali men and reduce their women into objects. Sometimes, they raped women because they lusted after them and no one punished them for their lack of discipline on the war front. Ultimately, the violence of the Pakistan Army was driven by the desire and motivation to save Pakistan and make the Bengalis submit. Women were attacked in their homes; they were stripped naked in front of their family members; they were raped and thrown into drains; women were imprisoned in sex camps that were set up with or without the knowledge of the higher-ups in the West Pakistani administration; their hair was chopped off; they were tied down and repeatedly raped, forced to take off their sari and wear rags or men's shirts; and they were even denied the food they were accustomed to and many starved and died. Imprisoned women were forced to do the physical work of digging graves to bury the dead.[32] The Bengalis, too, killed members of their own community as well as Biharis and West Pakistani families living in East Pakistan who did not support their struggle for freedom. They, too, raped and terrorized Bihari and West Pakistani women and drove the entire population of Biharis out of their homes and imprisoned them in internment camps.[33]

Much public debate has focused on what label to give to the events of 1971. Before the war was over and the Pakistan Army surrendered to the Indian Army, the term *genocide* crept into the lexicon for naming the event. On June 13, 1971, in the *Sunday Times*, journalist Anthony Mascarenhas published an article called "Genocide" that appeared on page one. His graphic descriptions and personalized style of narrating the stories of crimes committed by the Pakistan Army that he witnessed during his ten day visit to East Pakistan brought international attention to the event.[34] Immediately, in the Indian newspapers, radio broadcasts, and public political rallies, the term *genocide* began to appear, and assertive claims were made to expose the inhuman nature of the Pakistan Army. The Indian press extended this understanding to label the Pakistanis as a whole and pathologized them as criminals and inhuman, which served the Indian government's interest and plans for an armed attack in East

Pakistan. But the Indians did not come out publicly to the rescue of the people in East Pakistan, not until late November. In the interim period, violence had spread all over and was executed by overt and covert means by multiple perpetrator groups. The violence was definitely not confined to the ten days witnessed by Mascarenhas. It lasted beyond June and did not end with the war on December 16, 1971. Routine violence against the Biharis continued and persists even today as they remain confined to their camps in the condition of statelessness.

Another viewpoint for naming the violence comes from scholars of genocide studies who focus on empirical findings to refer to this event as "politicide," whereby political issues lead to mass murder of communal victims (Harff 2003; Staub 2000).[35] Unlike genocide, which is defined by the perpetrators based on their differences with the victim community, in politicide groups are defined by political terms, and victims oppose the regime and dominant groups. West Pakistani soldiers performed the task they were told to do, which included killing and destroying the Bengalis, because they believed the enemy group was working with the Indians and that the Indian government's political interest was to destroy Pakistan. These men fought and killed to save their nation, which was in their political interest. The Bengalis' demand of freedom was oppositional politics, and they carried out armed violence against the West Pakistan government in support of their cause of liberation. This is distinct from the violence committed by the Nazis against Jews. Jews were not a political or military threat to Germany. They were killed solely because of their ethnoreligious identity.

The story of violence committed by the Bengalis is less well known and is poorly represented in the news media, except the Pakistani Urdu news press, which obviously toed the line of their leaders to vilify the Bengalis. Although people in Bangladesh were reluctant to talk about the violence committed by the Mukti Bahini or disparate Bengali groups and individuals, many recalled specific incidences of local violence in which the Mukti Bahini volunteers and local Bengalis were the perpetrators. The local incidences of violence, many believed, were a cause of grave concern, and peace committees were set up to create normalcy in the region, but they failed. Sometimes, members of the peace committees themselves became involved in committing violence.

According to a report from the Bangladesh newspaper the *Daily Star* on April 4, 2008, the War Crimes Fact Finding Committee (wcffc) has created a list of 1,597 war criminals responsible for the mass killings, rapes, and other atrocities during the war. Of those on the list, 369 were from the Pakistani military; 1,150 were local collaborators including *rajakars,* members of the Al-Badr and peace committees; and 78 were Biharis.[36] There is, of course, no mention of the violence that the Mukti Bahini or Indian Army committed because it does not suit the purposes of the committee to remember their crimes. The obvious slant of the document undermines its credibility and leaves the complex nature of violence in the nine months of war in East Pakistan open for investigation.

Obviously the misguided ethnocentric and political interests of the participants—Pakistani, Bengali, Bihari, and even Indian—led to mass violence. There was no fixed group of perpetrators or victims in this story to tell of the inhumanity of the other. Should we conclude that there were multiple genocides within the nine months of war? Or, for that matter, can the application of the term *genocide* really provide us with a better understanding of what happened in 1971 in East Pakistan? The indeterminacy of the term and the lack of an ability to identify a clear-cut perpetrator community leave us puzzled.

Rather than confining ourselves to the debate surrounding the naming of this event, I agree with scholars of mass violence and genocide studies that the focus should be on what lessons we learn from the violence. The mass graves that have been unearthed in many sites in Bangladesh stand as grim reminders of the dead. Among them are many unsung heroes and heroines of the war. As well, there are many innocent victims who were not involved in politics. They were bystanders who died simply because they were in the scene of the battle, in East Pakistan, and suffered its consequences. These victims did not label themselves for posterity, to later be claimed as belonging to one ethnic group or another (although the attempt is to identify all the exhumed skeletons, bones, and other human remains as belonging to Bengali martyrs). A new remembering of the war is urgent in South Asia. Otherwise, we will continue to remain willfully ignorant and refuse to learn how genocide, politicide, or mass killings originate and perpetuate painful experiences for the self and others.

The other vexing issue of the war's violence is the mass rape of women. The rape of women during the war of 1971 is not unique; it is part of a familiar, though horrible, feature of wars, including the more recent examples in Bosnia, Kosovo, Croatia, and Rwanda. In these and other wars, women were targeted for male violence and dehumanized as part of the war effort to reduce enemies into submission. Why did men rape women in the war of Bangladesh is a question rarely asked and there are no definitive answers. Were there state directives given to men to rape women? One thing is quite obvious, rape was about power: raping women in Bangladesh asserted the power of men to destroy the vulnerable and make it impossible for a woman to find a whole self after the war. Rape was also a tool to destroy women's link with the past. The women in Bangladesh were doomed to live without their collective memory; their personal history became a secret that could not be disclosed. The voicelessness of women's position offers a lens to understand their dehumanization.

West Pakistani men who were, in turn, motivated to fit the state's "pattern" of overlooking the capacity or incapacity for individual functioning in the warfront (this resonates with the "pattern" of dehumanizing highlighted in Kay 1994) were nominated as masculine agents, and they acted as the state to force their idea of Pakistan onto the people in the East. The vulnerable communities of women were the easiest targets. The imagination of a pure Pakistan demanded a cleansing of the body politic, which was allegedly made corrupt by the Hindu presence. Muslim Pakistani (read: pure) men assumed that the sacrifice of the Hindu women was necessary to undo the national malaise. In 1971, one can argue the plans to purify as well as destroy were given shape simultaneously. In turn, men and pattern, individuals and state became deeply enmeshed, and women, who were already reduced in Pakistan to second-class citizens, were annulled as Bengali and Hindu or Hindu-like, marginal and excluded from the rank of humanity. The militarization of Pakistani men and the destruction of Bengali women went hand in hand in imagining a new nation.[37] This was, however, not unique to Pakistan. After the war the Bangladeshi government mandated an abortion program to get rid of the "bastard Pakistanis,"[38] and women were compelled to accept the state's intervention if they wanted inclusion within the newly liberated country and to live a normal life, at least at an external level. A clinic for rape victims was set up in the heart of Dhaka city called Sada Bahar on February 18, 1972, and it functioned for six months thereafter. A rehabilitation center called Nari Punarbashon was also established to assist victims. The violence of rape was responded to with more violence by the Bangladeshi state represented by the liberators, Bengali men. Ideals of purity and impurity, belonging and exclusion, were worked out and physically enacted on the body of women—the site of alleged national dishonor, and the site where men could display their power to control the imagining of a new "liberated" nation.

Discussion of rape by women continues to be a difficult subject in Bangladesh. Shame and fear of the accusation of complicity and collusion prevents women from publicly discussing the sexual violence that is privately discussed. In Muslim Bangladesh (which is showing a rising trend of fundamentalism) discussion of sexual violence is ultimately a taboo subject. The obstacles placed by society and religion inhibit speech and compel survivors to forget the experiences of gendered violence.[39] Furthermore, speaking is not easy or important to many survivors. For them the moment of violence is total, also it is multiple, fractured, and dispersed. Women cannot retrieve this memory in its entirety because they know it is not possible to recapture their loss and dehumanization. There is no going there, no point of access to the unforgettable iconic memory that lingers in the background but is not spoken.[40] The struggle for women is to try to make sense of the incomprehensible experience. Both Bengali and Bihari women have therefore pushed these memories into a remote site, to silence, forcing forgetfulness. The lack of a serious demand to probe the circumstances and agents of gender violence has enabled the internalized oppression within Bangladesh to continue, where rumors, gossip, and slander abound.

The community of feminist scholars within and outside Bangladesh has committed very little emancipatory labor toward dismantling patriarchal domination in producing new knowledge about the war and events of 1971. As such, although 1971 is considered to be one of the most intense cases of the brutalization of women in twentieth-century conflicts, the story has been largely unacknowledged, especially by the scholarly community in the West. Susan Brownmiller's pioneering book, *Against Our Will: Men, Women, and Rape* (1975) is the only exception. As yet, no full-length monograph on the subject has appeared for a renewed engagement with the subject.[41] Without a scholarly discourse of the oppression that Bangladeshi women suffered in the war, alongside the stories of other oppressed groups of women who are not white and Western, we will continue to promote a two-tiered world for women, differentiating and excluding some from human knowledge while continuing with the hypocritical rhetoric to address women's experiences.

Added to scholarly neglect that has not yet configured a way to tell a women's narrative of 1971, rape continues to be an uneasy topic of discussion whether speaking or writing within the culturally and socially

Raped and left to die.
*(Courtesy of Shahriar Kabir/Forum for
Secular Bangladesh and Trial of
War Criminals of 1971)*

scripted practices of normative knowledge in South Asia. Cultural unease is expressed in the lack of an equivalent word for rape in Urdu, and
in Bangla although there is a word for rape, *dharshan*, it is never used in
women's testimony of war experiences.[42] The problem of naming the
violence that women suffered creates a real problem for historical accountability. There is no language or vocabulary for survivors to tell us
what they experienced in that moment.

Alongside the dominant establishment of patriarchy that controls
and limits women's language and speech, the religious cultures of Islam
and Hinduism also circumscribe the enunciation of gendered memories
in the public domain and make discussion of rape a dishonorable matter. The community cultures of South Asia have also determined the
limits of acceptable and unacceptable speech and have found ways to
hide the embarrassing traces of women's experiences in the war from
public and social memory. Women's memories survive, it seems, only in
the private sphere and are dealt with as private matters by the victims'
families and often solely by the victim who hides in shame.

Immediately after the war, women's experiences were not just ignored, but they were discounted as an absent subject in public history.
Clearly, the hierarchy of gendered identity in post-liberated Bangladesh
became evident in the dismissal of women's voices. In the Bangladeshi

media and official memory only men's experiences were eulogized. The vast majority of the published memoirs of the war are personal accounts written after the event (for example, Alam 2006; Khan 1998; Shafiullah 1995; Siddiqui 1985; Islam 1981; Bhuianh 1972). The memories of male *mukti jouddhas*, the liberation heroes, dominate, and they are narratives of euphoria. Between 1992 and 2001, over twelve hundred books on the "War of Liberation" have been published in Bangladesh.[43] Over and over again in these accounts, we hear about the sacrifices that men made during the war, their fighting abilities, strategies of guerilla warfare, and triumph despite the betrayal by rajakars, the Pakistani supporters living in East Pakistan. A second genre of writing that has emerged is the compiled *thana* (district) reports that are of interest to local historians of Bangladesh but do not develop a larger picture of the actors and their impact on the war efforts (Hussain 2007). A third type of writing about the war is presented as documents of war crimes with names and pictures of the war criminals. It is focused on identifying and describing the rajakars (see Kabir 1999; publications by the Liberation War Museum 1987, 1994). Finally, there is a variety of writing on the issues of civil society and politics during 1971 (for example, Imam 1986, 1991; Firdousi 1996; Mamoon 2000) and a variety of novels and juvenile writings. In short, the war of 1971 is a well-told tale of *liberation* in Bangladesh.

There has been very little effort to bring together these multiple personal stories and genres of narratives for compiling a history of the Liberation War so that people can grasp and understand the genesis of the war, the violent events and their impact, and thus develop a social memory based on people's experiences. The fifteen volumes of the Liberation War documents published by the Bangladeshi Ministry of Information and edited by Hasan Hafizur Rahman (1982–1985) is probably the only effort, although incomplete, in this direction. Within this fifteen-volume compendium, the unpleasant events that happened in the war are submerged and pushed to the margin. The apparent hope is that people will overlook those stories and forget them soon.

The only memory about women that emerged soon after the liberation of Bangladesh is about *birangonas* (brave women) or, in other words, victims of sexual violence. Women did not give themselves this label nor present themselves as birangonas. The term *birangona* was coined after the war in 1972 by the first prime minister of Bangladesh, Sheikh Mujibur Rahman, to officially acknowledge the women who were violated during the war. He hoped that through this recognition a space

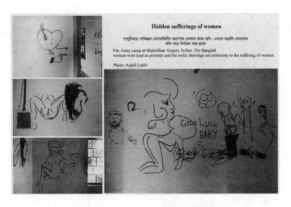

Grafitti from 1971.
(Courtesy of the Liberation War Museum)

would be created for women to claim their contribution in the war. The label was backed by a concrete policy of redress to enable the women to reconvene a normal life in society. Men who agreed to marry birangonas were rewarded with jobs and land. The effort was to re-create a semblance of normality and family life for women who suffered sexual violence. Sheikh Mujib's efforts at recognizing and rehabilitating women were well founded, one would assume, but the outcome was counterproductive. The labeling of some women as birangonas also marked them, and they were increasingly seen by society as "fallen," or "loose" women. Thus they were reduced to the level of corrupt women, equivalent to prostitutes. Very few women associated with the label of birangona, not even after it became widely used in the official and activists circles. For them to have survived rape was a life-changing event. To have to confront a new social stigma was far from what they envisaged would be their fate thereafter.

The social discrimination and neglect of women who were transformed into birangonas due to the violence in the war is lucidly addressed in a semi-fictionalized narrative by Nilima Ibrahim in her book *Ami Birangona Bolchi* (1998). Ibrahim's narrators are birangonas that offer scathing criticisms of the post-liberated Bangladeshi society's inability to deal with them as human beings that deserve human understanding of their experiences and the chance to reintegrate into society to create normal lives. The seven women who tell their stories conclude that there is no place for them "at home," in Bangladesh, any longer.

উত্তরের এক জেলা শহরের কলেজ-ছাত্রীর ছবিটি তুলেছিলেন নাইবউদ্দিন আহমদ ।
পাকিস্তানি ক্যাম্প থেকে উদ্ধারের পর তোলা এই ছবি অপালিত দুঃখিনী নারীর অবস্থান
ও প্রতায় দুইয়ের প্রকাশ ঘটিয়েছে

Naibuddin Ahmed has photographed this college girl after
she was freed by the Freedom Fighter from a Pak Army camp

Making women invisible.
(Courtesy of the Liberation War Museum)

They preferred to leave the country and migrate to Europe or Pakistan, to make their lives there.

From Ibrahim's account of birangonas' lives and my own conversation with many birangonas in Bangladesh, it is clear that those who found a house and a husband to settle down with were rarely treated well. A vast majority of men who married birangonas did not stay in the marriage after they received the financial benefits from the government. The compensatory justice that the government implemented benefited men and their families rather than the women who continued to suffer social neglect. Thus, the government's policy inadvertently created a situation for some unscrupulous men to exploit vulnerable women and did not empower women on their own terms. The policy also produced an opposite effect. Instead of love and respect from the public, birangonas received very little in the way of people's understanding, and the social stigma of rape compelled most birangonas to hide their experiences in order to resume a normal life. Women did not want to be heroes in this sense, as rape survivors, because in newly liberated Bangladesh there was no place for them.[44]

Not unsurprisingly, birangonas were rarely allowed to speak for themselves. Their experiences were spoken of by others who were powerful

পাকবাহিনীর পাশবিকতার শিকার নারী অ-কোনো একজন : ১৩ বছরের এই মেয়েটিকে নকেক মাস আটক রাখা হয়েছিল সিপাহীদের কামে। নিহতের ঘর বাবা যৌদ্ধ যাতে করে চলে আসে নিয়ে আসে নারী পুরুষসব ছেলে, সোখানে এদিকে সেব শত্রু সৈন্য তর করার লক্ষ্য। বর্বর বাংলাদেশে প্রতীক এই ভঙ্গী ছাপা হামিনি নারানো জিগৌবিক পরিবার। (আগালাইড ছিল ছুরিতা)
Women were the worst victims of Pakistan army led atrocities. While the male members of the household went off to fight the enemy, the "women" became easy targets. Over 250000 women were tortured and raped by the barbarian Pakistani soldiers. This 13 year old girl was kept for months in a millitary camp to satisfy the Pakistani soldiers lust.

Displaying *birangona*: where is the perpetrator? *(Source withheld)*

actors in the newly formed Bangladesh government. The way other people's agency is exercised on the victims of 1971 became explicit during a mock trial that was organized in 1996 in Dhaka. Four very poor survivors were encouraged by a women's group at Dhaka to give testimony about their experiences in the war. The victims were assured state protection and assistance as part of their reward for testifying. Immediately after they went public with their testimonies, the village community boycotted the four women, branded them prostitutes, and denied them access to the commons. Threatened by further backlash, their children disowned them. In the end, the women were duped to participate in the trial, but they did not get what they were promised—houses, jobs, and social dignity. The fiasco of the public encounter with the traumatic past discouraged other women from disclosing their memories of violence. Even today only doctored narratives of birangonas are available, and when they "speak" in public they generally adhere to the lines given to them by their sponsors. The engineered narratives do not enable us to understand women's sacrifices and their contributions in the war. They become external, almost pornographic, stories about women's loss of honor (see Islam 1991). Not surprisingly birangonas, although projected as female heroes, are also viewed as being complicit in the crime of rape. Women's multiple individual experiences have been and are being reduced to a label without a history, so there is no explanation of what they actually experienced in the war.[45]

It did not take long for the term *birangona* to be folded into another level of men's speech, *barangona*, which refers to penetration and penetrated; women obviously were deemed as promiscuous and prostitutes. Women's corporeal experiences in the war thus were reduced into a site of shame in newly liberated Bangladesh, and in an effort to make the supposedly fallen women honorable and to domesticate them, the government provided these women rehabilitation in the form of teaching them sewing, weaving, and training to be midwives. Instead of enabling women to be their own agents for change, the government's rehabilitation program rewarded men with jobs and land for their willingness to marry and transform birangonas (read: barangonas) into obedient wives. In the governmental and familial remake, women's rape experiences were made into a homogenized stereotype of victimization. In consequence, although people were willing to hear the stories of male heroes and laud them for their glorious feats of victory and sacrifices in war, they did not wish to hear about the sufferings of birangonas. Reduced to the level of prostitutes, these women were made guilty of the crime of rape. The denial of their voice was thus justified, and the nation and society received sanction to forget women's experiences and suppress their memories from the historical narrative.

Added to the social and collective loss of memory, the government of Bangladesh created another new problem. The chilling mandate of the government headed by Sheikh Mujibur Rahman was to implement abortion for women impregnated during the war. As was mentioned earlier, the idea was to rid the nation of the "bastard Pakistanis." A massive emergency abortion program was implemented and doctors from Australia and India alongside Bangladeshi doctors performed abortions to surgically remove the odious Pakistani presence. It is said that since then the family planning program in Bangladesh has been a major success, and it continues to thrive despite Bangladesh's Islamic orientation, which frowns on government intervention to restrict reproduction. Women who continued to defy the government injunction to be aborted and delivered their babies took a huge risk. Most of them could not keep their babies, though. Fortuitously for Bangladesh, Mother Teresa and the Sisters of Charity, who had been working throughout the war in the refugee camps of West Bengal providing succor to the displaced and traumatized Bengali women and children, stepped in to "rescue" the "war babies" (see D'Costa 2005).[46] A massive adoption scheme was devised and most of the war babies were exported to the Netherlands, Canada, and other European countries through the contacts established by Mother Teresa's foundation.[47] Indeed, Bangladesh got rid of the "bastard Pakistanis," and Mother Teresa was hailed for her humanitarian intervention during and after the war. The women who were raped and lost their babies due to abortion and adoption were made invisible, and their children became objects for others to rescue. The stories of women's and children's losses were never publicly acknowledged, lest the gendered shame wrought by the war become a national shame.

The strategic claim that the enemy Pakistanis had raped two hundred thousand Bengali women transformed real women into an abstract number of bodies. Reduced into objects, survivors could not tell who had raped them, but the omnipotent government decided that rape of women was done by the Pakistani enemy. The revenge rhetoric that followed made the rape of women during the war of 1971 a spectacle without the backing of an investigation and allowed for continued gendered subjectivity. The fantasy of retribution against the Pakistani enemy was given new life after a list was prepared. The initial list prepared in 1972 contained the names of 195 Pakistani "war criminals." Since then new lists have been prepared. The most recently published list contains the names of several thousand men. In the new list the number of local rajakars, particularly representing the pro-Pakistani Bengali groups who are identified as war criminals, is much larger than the numbers of Pakistani perpetrators. One can deduce that the fluctuating list is a political tool rather than a real attempt to identify and locate the perpetrators. From the beginning, the show of concern on the part of the government enabled it to further its own image in the eyes of the aggrieved Bangladeshi public without really providing a solution to remedy victims' lives. In turn, this suited the national agenda for continuing the writing of a limited, official history.

In Bangladesh, women were made complicit in the plot created by a government run by Bengali men (see Mookherjee 2006, 2004). After three decades of silence, a limited and partial memory of Bengali women's experiences in the war has started to appear, but they do not adequately address the multiple experiences of the variety of women in Bangladesh (for example, see Begum 2001; Akhtar et al. 2001; Ibrahim

1998; Lahiri 1999). Also, the voices and experiences of minority women, such as the Biharis, are not included within the women's efforts to remember. Bengali women have co-opted the Bengali men's will to construct meanings of nationalism and feminism within culturally and ethnically specific contexts today. The construction of the Bihari women as the Other makes it possible to imagine such an identity. Hence instead of challenging the patriarchal values and authority, Bengali women have become subjects and accomplices in dehumanizing others.

The construction of desire is the language that is used to achieve the effect of dehumanizing the Bihari and humanizing the Bengali women. In Bengali women's reminiscences of the war, especially those presented as third-person narratives, not once is a Bihari woman represented as beautiful, intelligent, or even as a *known* person, school mate, or perhaps even a neighbor. Bihari women are an invisible nothing, without name, face, place, or association. They were *them*, without subjectivity. In turn, many Bengali women explained sexual violence against their "sisters"—Bengali women because they were beautiful, "she had lovely hair that everyone noticed," or that "her big eyes attracted everyone." What they convey is two metanarratives—one about selective victimization of women and the other about ethnicity. They perform stereotyping and totalizing discourses, denying other people subjectivities and human faces.

Through some mystic unity Bengali women claim they are part of the land, nation, and Bengali identity; while Others—the Bihari women—are outsiders, the enemy, hateful occupiers of their Sonar Bangla (Golden Bengal). In this gendered construction a woman is reduced into an inaccessible category, her pain is made irrelevant, her lack of home is of no concern for she cannot belong to the society of human women that is only limited to Bengali womanhood in Bangladesh. The subhuman Other, the Bihari women, in Bengali women's representations are undeserving of a human language of understanding.[48] The politics of gendered memory in Bangladesh thus must be viewed and evaluated through the lens of men's will to exercise power and enforce forgetting by using the tools of ethnicity, religion, and language.

Three decades after the war, the entrenched national history has become the accepted story and people believe without questioning and demanding evidence. Like the Truth and Reconciliation Commission (TRC) report that rewrote the story of apartheid by creating "reconciliation" between the colonizer and colonized communities based on moral

and political considerations that overlooked lived history, the nationalist framing of 1971 generates through strategic efforts a history that is
different rather than truly reflective of the experiences of the people
of Bangladesh, particularly the experiences of women. The national
policy of erasing and forgetting women's trauma and training people to
only believe in the official history has, in turn, forced traumatized survivors, both Bengali and Bihari women, to erase, blot out, and silence the
details they know about their victimizers; it is a survival strategy. The
human witness who can tell the history of the violence in Bangladesh
is silenced and destroyed. Fear of new subjugation for speaking against
the established story relegates them into inaccessible isolation. At the
heart of the official memory and the memory of survivors is forgetting.
The loss of the event of trauma and the loss generated by active national
forgetting, in turn, create an acceptable history that is consumed by the
public in Bangladesh.[49]

A challenge to this history of 1971 that was created and recreated since
1972 by different political actors in Bangladesh came from the Mukti
Juddho Jadughar (Liberation War Museum) situated in Dhaka.[50] The
museum was opened nearly three decades after the war in 1996 and was
founded by a consortium of businessmen whose aim is to perpetuate
the memory of the Liberation War so that future generations can "know
our rich heritage, . . . and pay homage to the great martyrs, the freedom fighters and people all over the world, who supported the Liberation War in 1971."[51] The purpose, though grand and well meaning, is to
construct another "new" history to remember the war in a specific way
rather than tell the events of the violence with all its complexities. The
displays and exhibits allow viewers to see the sights of horror that im-
passions the audience to demand accountability for the atrocities suffered by the Bengalis. The suffering of 1971 is, once again, packaged and
delivered as a Bengali trauma. Nonetheless, it is worth noting the effort
of the Mukti Juddho Jadughar in reviving the debate of the multiple
sites and actors, particularly common peoples' contribution to the war,
and making the experience a far more personal and immediate visual
encounter offers another possible way the event of 1971 can be told.

The endorsement of forgetfulness in an official history and a failure
to include the history of the Others' experiences in the war is not confined to Bangladesh. Both Pakistan and India have created their own
heroic narratives, forgetting their violent activities in East Pakistan. In
Pakistan, immediately after the war ended in December 1971, the gov-

ernment headed by Zulfikar Ali Bhutto made a show of interest to learn about the events and the reason for the dismal failure of the Pakistan Army in the war. The Hamoodur Rahman Commission constituted by a single person, Justice Hamoodur Rahman, was appointed to ascertain the facts of the war. The commission interviewed 213 persons, including General Yahya, Zulfikar Ali Bhutto, senior commanders and officers of the armed forces, and various political leaders. The commission submitted its first report in July 1972 to twelve individuals. Immediately all the reports were destroyed; except the one that was handed over to Zulfikar Ali Bhutto, but the findings were never made public. The public in Pakistan were never informed what had happened in East Pakistan and about the violence that the armed personnel had committed against unarmed combatants in the war. Neither did people learn why the war turned out to be a debacle or why the state lost more than half of its population and a large national territory.

In 1974 the inquiry was reopened, once again. This time the commission interviewed seventy-three bureaucrats and top military officers and submitted its supplementary report in November 1974. Once again, the report established that the Pakistan Army had carried out senseless and wanton arson, killing Bengali intellectuals, professionals, officers, soldiers (on the pretence of quelling their rebellion), civilian officers, businessmen, and industrialists (particularly members of the Hindu minority), and raping a large number of East Pakistani women as a deliberate act of revenge, retaliation, and torture. The commission recommended that these grave allegations should be dealt with seriously so that Pakistan did not repeat the mistakes of the war of 1971 in the future and so the country and its people were not exposed to these brutalities again. The report and its findings were not disclosed and years later, on August 21, 2000, when people had nearly forgotten about the events of 1971, the supplementary report of 1974 was published by an Indian magazine called *India Today*.

By this time the public in Pakistan had come to accept that the loss of East Pakistan was inevitable and were no longer interested in interrogating the armed forces for their brutal actions in the war. They believed that the publicizing of the report by the Indian media was a diversion to shift attention from the international pressure that was demanding a solution to the Kashmir issue, an ongoing tussle between India and Pakistan. Immense human rights violations were being reported by international organizations such as Amnesty International and Asia Watch with reference to the role of Indian security forces in Kashmir. Few in Pakistan took into account the report's allegations against the Pakistan Army and its activities in the war. The war of 1971 and the violence committed against the people of East Pakistan had become a forgotten memory, even among scholars and students.[52]

In the Pakistani military academy, too, the war of 1971 was largely forgotten and when remembered appeared to be a lesson for teaching strategy, battle plans, and operations. One issue that continues to linger and haunt the army men is the revolt of the Bengali officers in the East Bengal Regiment (EBR) in March 1971.[53] The Pakistani officers continue to talk about the civil war, of "brothers killing brothers," and seemed unable to understand why and how that could have happened.[54] The confusing memory of 1971 as a story of "betrayal" within a "family saga" depoliticizes the issue and makes it easy for the military administration to only recall it as an event for tactical study rather than address the violent event for its destruction of the people and country, both East and West Pakistan.

The dilemma of public memory of the war in Pakistan is fully evident in the literary circles. In contrast to the reflections in literature on the 1947 partition, in Pakistan the war of 1971 has not been investigated in any great depth. As Muhammad Memon writes, "Pakistani men of letters, otherwise known for their strident espousal of social and political issues at home and abroad, have been less than forthcoming on the meaning and consequence of their own national disintegration" (Memon 1983, 107).

Likewise, in India the war of 1971 has not been investigated, and India's role in the violence remains curiously unscrutinized. Notwithstanding the lack of research and deep excavation of the event, two dominant genres have gained currency in Pakistan and India. Both address the external issues of the war—politics and military strategies. The military and political history of 1971 focuses on diplomacy and war maneuvers, operations, strategies, tactics, and conventional issues of local politics, and it is written by political scientists and journalists in Pakistan and India (for example, Choudhury 1974; Siddiq 1977; Dasgupta 1978; Dixit 1999; Bose 2005). The second emerging genre glorifies soldiers' personal memories of valor and bravado, and it has created a semi-fictionalized narrative of the war and the men involved in it (for example, Jacob 1997; Niazi 1998; Singh 1979; Matinuddin 1993; Qureshi 2003).

In the Indian retelling the violence committed by Indian Army men is overlooked. They present the war as a game of brilliant strategies, tactics, operations, and diplomacy, totally obliterating people's experiences within East Pakistan. To this day, the Indian state has continued to deny its active role in creating the war of 1971, its forced engagement with political issues inside East Pakistan, its blatant use of the humanitarian crisis to justify its armed intervention against the Pakistan Army, and the looting and plunder of moveable properties, including heavy machineries, cars, iron and steel, factory equipment, and so on. There is no mention of the small acts of violence committed by Indian soldiers of stealing from people who were poorer than them and depriving them of their household goods like radios, watches, and televisions after the end of the war. India treated Bangladesh as its new colony to loot and has failed to recognize its imperialist attitude.[55] The lust and greed of Indian soldiers is completely forgotten and even the recorded stories of local town councils' complaints against the lewd behavior of Indian soldiers stationed there are erased.[56] Thus the national memorializing in India and what is written presents a superficial recounting of the war, representing it as a charitable act that freed the East Pakistani people from their tyrannical West Pakistani masters, and the refusal of both Pakistan and India to bear witness to the violence against women is a willful forgetting that indelibly marks their national histories as spurious.

National histories in the subcontinent fail to question the silence surrounding women. Silence, one can productively argue, is a vehicle of witnessing what lies at the heart of trauma and is a form of testimony (Felman and Laub 1992; Caruth 1996; Agamben 1999). The problem, I contend, resides in the location of historical production. History is used by the official sites of power as a tool for national celebration, and these sites of power have created a realm of forgetting where the memories of what happened are lost. The silence that pervades in the subcontinent negates the gender violence that occurred in the war of 1971. But where does this silent past reside, though? If history produced through the state's engineering of the past serves to confuse and fix the story, what other resources are available to us to move beyond the statist account of history and wake up from its "nightmare," as James Joyce might call it (1922, 24)? One answer is to explore the memories of the people and communities in South Asia and to pursue a depoliticization of their experiences and the concepts of history shaped by forgetting traumatic experiences.

In Bangladesh, India, and Pakistan the current production of history or lack of memory reveals traces of the play of power that deserve our attention. The making of history, however, is a public act and begins with bodies and artifacts—including people, texts, documents, fossils, and social and physical architecture. In 1971 a history was made. Then and now, the powerful players follow the colonial model of history writing, telling the external story to demarcate the "good" from the "bad" guys, while using the narrative to establish their power to make some of the parts they do not like disappear, but it is not that easy to delete what happened. The unpleasant reminders of the past keep interrupting and making appearances at the interstices of silences in the public and private domain. The disjointed, often silent, testimonies act as a voice of liberation, opening the wounds of history for reevaluation, but, of course, it is not a totally free voice. It is inscribed by culture and economy and is situated within the limited, hierarchical world of Bangladeshi and Bihari women's lives. It is also a partial voice. Nevertheless this voice creates a picture that provides enormous hope for leverage against the epistemic violence of history that mystifies and silences women's experiences.

BECOMING AWARE

Often times, I have been asked how I started the project and why the events of 1971 should matter to me. It is considered to be a national event that belongs to the people of Bangladesh and Pakistan, and since I am not from either place my interest should be moot. The intimate connection that is assumed between a nation, its history, and its citizens in South Asia is very problematic because it suggests ownership and makes the past an object that one has a claim to based on shared nationality. The general assumption is that the national boundaries constitute the terminus of history and those outside this sphere cannot tell the story because it is not their experience and the history doesn't belong to them. To overcome the divisive nature of history in South Asia and move beyond the demarcated national stories, I decided to search for women's memories of the war of 1971 and move from a state of forgetting to an active memory about these women's experiences of violence.

The focus is not on the prism of nationalistic history but rather on the universality of violence against women during war. I do not believe the lack of enunciation about women's experiences in the national histories of South Asia should limit our ability to understand what women suffered because it is not language but ethics that should direct us to grasp the experiences of others and create access to the moment of suffering by developing and encouraging speech within the silence in the hope of seeking redress for survivors now.

The war of 1971, however, was not part of our generation's historical memory when I was growing up in Assam, in northeastern India. Like everyone else in Assam, I absorbed the social and collective fear of Bangladeshis that was integrated into the politics of Assamese identity through the public discourse of the All Assam Students Union (AASU). We became afraid that the Bangladeshi settlers would take over our land and turn us into a minority group in our homeland. To drive out the Bangladeshis living in our midst, the AASU led the Assamese people into a long drawn-out struggle against the central government in Delhi and demanded a revision of the immigration laws and electoral process in Assam. For several years, the Bangladeshi issue continued to dominate politics in Assam, although, by and large, people remained unenlightened about the genesis and root cause of the so-called Bangladeshi problem.

The "Assam movement" that was discussed in newspapers, books, and magazines never made a connection between the Assamese struggle for identity and the war of 1971 that led to the exodus of people from Bangladesh. There was no mention of the catastrophic human tragedy that the war had entailed. A kind of amnesia about India's role in the war had set in, and very few people remembered that the migration of refugees from East Pakistan to the east Indian states of Assam, West Bengal, and Tripura was facilitated by the Indian government during the prime ministership of Indira Gandhi.[57] The surge of refugees to the eastern provinces of India had allowed Indira Gandhi to justify to the world the need for overt military intervention in East Pakistan in November 1971. This history was forgotten during the Assamese identity movement; rather the drumbeat was that through an orchestrated policy (of external agencies and internal Muslim agents) Assam was on the verge of becoming a "mini Bangladesh."[58] Like most Assamese, I believed this rhetoric and was determined to not ever let this happen.

The lack of empathy for Others, that is in this case, Bangladeshis, was accepted as a requirement for being a good Assamese.[59] And no one felt guilty.

In 1985 when Rajiv Gandhi signed a peace accord with the leaders of AASU (turned politicians under the banner of Assam Gana Parishad or AGP), we heaved a sigh of relief. In Assam, normal life slowly reconvened and there was hope that the Bangladeshi problem would be solved. We believed we would, once again, be happy in our predictable Assamese familiarity of each other and have the freedom to elect Assamese representatives to head the legislative and administrative bodies without the Bangladeshi settlers influencing the electoral process. Of course, the politics that followed did not deliver the promise of Assamese autonomy.

Several years later, after I started researching Assam's history and identity, I became increasingly aware that I could not continue to be indifferent to the story of our neighbors and settlers. Assam borders Bangladesh in the south and Bhutan in the north. As such, there are many so-called Bangladeshis living in our midst in Assam. It was clear that the Assamese identity question was intrinsically connected with the issue of identifying *ethnic* from *nonethnic* and *real* from *spurious* Assamese, and violence was justified in the name of finding the supposedly authentic Assamese (much to my dismay). My interest in the war of 1971 and Bangladesh, however, did not emerge from these political and intellectual concerns alone. Three separate and personal episodes instigated my studies. I share these stories because they highlight the essential themes and driving forces of this book. Each episode stands alone, independent of the other, but they are also connected because they are stories from and about Bangladesh.

Saji, or Abdul's Mother: The Inheritance of Memory   Abdul's mother, as she is referred to by her family, worked for me while I was living in Assam in 1996 and working on my doctoral dissertation. Since her personal name was Saji, I called her so. Saji was an unusually quiet person, and she generally kept a very low profile. Toward the end of my stay, Saji expressed an interest to tell me the story of how her family came to Assam. Her story centered on a memory that she had inherited from her mother. Saji told me she was born in Assam, but her grandmother's village was on the Bangladeshi side of the border. "When *gondagul* (unrest) broke out in grandmother's village a long time ago during the war [of

1971], most of the women fled for their safety and migrated across the border," she confided in me. Over time, it appears they did not return to their native villages but settled down and reformulated their lives in their newly adopted homeland, in Assam. In response to why she wanted to tell me about her family's settlement process in Assam, which could be an invitation to trouble for being a Bangladeshi in Assam, Saji explained that she needed to share this unforgettable memory. How could she have a memory of an event that she did not experience? It appeared as if she identified so deeply with her grandmother's loss of a homeland that it became part of her own identity and the memory perpetuated in her own consciousness. It perplexed me, but on reflection I understood that survivors cannot forget the tragedy of losing their home (in Bangladesh), even though it happened a long time ago, because only by dwelling on their people's history of loss can they make sense of the persecution they were now suffering in Assam, which threatened them with displacement again.

My Father, a Personal Story   Like Saji, I too have a personal memory of Bangladesh that I inherited from my father. Like many in his generation in Assam my father traveled outside the state (this was toward the end of British colonial rule in the late 1940s) for higher education, and he chose to go to Dhaka University in erstwhile East Bengal of British India for his undergraduate and postgraduate studies. At Dhaka he was a resident of Samilullah Muslim Hall, which was a place of intense educational and literary activities at that time. On completing his education in 1952, my father returned to Assam never again to travel to Dhaka, but he treasured the fond memories of his experiences there. The memories of Samilullah Muslim Hall, the friendship with his peers, the inspiration of his professors, and the taste of Dhakaya biryani[60] were always alive for him. In 1997, when my father suddenly passed away, I decided to visit Dhaka as a tribute to his memory. I was able to actualize this plan in the summer of 1999.

I arrived in Dhaka with no preparation, except the memories of Samilullah Muslim Hall conveyed to me by my father. After being in Dhaka for a couple of days, one afternoon, I decided to visit the university and see firsthand the famed Samilullah Muslim Hall. I engaged a rickshaw to take me to Dhaka *vishwa-vidyalay*. My use of a chaste Bangla word in lieu of the generally used English word *university* confused the rickshaw driver, I later realized. He took me to a place that was by no stretch of the imagination a university. Instead, I found myself in a chaotic bazaar, and I was frightened. The sounds and sights in the bazaar were unlike anything I had experienced in Dhaka during my brief stay. Shopkeepers were yelling and beckoning toward me, simultaneously speaking in Bangla and Urdu: "Appa, eikhane asho, idhar aiye (sister, come here)." I was stupefied. The rickshaw driver realized that he had made a mistake and decided to take me back to the guest house. As we were leaving, I saw what looked like a flag of Pakistan fluttering in the wind. "Where am I?" I wondered.

Back in the guest house, on inquiring with the manager, he casually told me that "the place is called Camp Geneva and is a Bihari colony." "What is Camp Geneva and who are the Biharis?" I pressed for an answer and learned a sad story of history that is totally hidden from us. Camp Geneva is the place where the so-called Biharis, a rather inexact label for the enemies of the Bengalis who also happen to be Urdu speakers, live as stranded and stateless" subjects.[61] These people live in a state of exclusion without any rights or representation, desperately waiting for a solution or repatriation to Pakistan, which, of course, is unlikely nearly four decades after the war.[62]

I had come to Dhaka to celebrate a memory of a place that my father loved dearly. When I left Dhaka after one month, I had the opportunity to see Samilullah Muslim Hall and Dhaka University, no doubt, but I also became acquainted with the traumatic stories of the camp dwellers. They had been living in a hopeless and helpless world in Camp Geneva where they were taken to by the aid workers of the Red Cross International soon after the war ended in December 1971. Since then they have been living there because history has forgotten them after wreaking violence in their lives. I felt the burden of suppressed violent history that is continuous and has become part of everyday life in Bangladesh now.

Fatima, Wounded Memory Outside Dhaka in Mirpur Camp, another ghetto where the Biharis live, I met Fatima. Fatima is a young woman with four children. Her husband, an old man, is sick and bedridden, and this has forced Fatima and her two oldest children to work in a *karkhana* (a workshop where they weave saris) to support the family. In 1971 Fatima was six years old. Her family lived outside Dhaka, near Mirpur, where her father owned a small shop. "Toward the end of the *shadi-nota andolan* (liberation struggle)," Fatima recalled, "my family was destroyed, the house was pillaged, and everyone was killed." Her voice rose to a screech and her hand gesticulated toward her forehead, showing me a deep gash running from her hairline to the middle of her head. She recalled that "they hit me with an axe. I was hiding under the dead body of my father. I became unconscious. Three days later, the Red Cross volunteers found me and brought me to the camp. I have lived here since. This will be my grave," she said sadly and withdrew within herself, leaving a trail of deeply wounded memories for us to access and begin to understand—what had Fatima, only a child in 1971, suffered and cannot forget as an adult? For a family that was so poor to be under attack and to mark a child as an enemy seemed illogical to me. But at the time of war, the distinction between groups and the passion of hate drove people into committing irrational, desperate acts of violence that survivors now report.

Nearly four decades after the war, it is embarrassing that we haven't begun to seek information and do the work of history, even though it may be conflicting and confusing. What happened in 1971? We created a bloody path with violence and now we hide behind forgetfulness, over-looking a traumatic episode in which we are all implicated. Rather, in South Asia we chant slogans of identity in multifarious voices and resort to more violence to solve our problems. My location as an Assamese but, more importantly, my commitment to the study of South Asia within a regional framework, has compelled me to research the history of the war so that we can make sense of it in our time and make it *our* concern to gain a better understanding of people's experiences and memories.

The war of 1971 was a tragedy that the people of Bangladesh, whether they were young or old, Bengali or Bihari, Muslim, Hindu, Christian, or Buddhist suffered. It is also a history of violence that the armies of Pakistan and India and the Bangladeshi militias and their uniformed and un-uniformed supporters committed. To understand the impact of the violence, we must listen to the people, the multitude who experienced the moment and became victims and perpetrators in consequence. Some of them survived and carry with them stories of their experiences that are neither shapely narratives nor easy to hear. But we have to try and listen because survivors have saved this memory from total oblivion. The task of regional history in South Asia is to seek to understand what these witnesses tell or do not tell in order to comprehend the process of postcolonial nation building and the production of history and memory, both remembering and forgetting, revealing the complex combinations within events.[63] If we listen to them, a new language for dialogue among the people of Assam, Bangladesh, Pakistan, and India seems possible. It would be a language that facilitates the processing of their grievances and the resolution of political battles, as well as allowing a comparison of real people's lives in the subcontinent.[64]

In bringing women's stories of the war into perspective, my role is that of a "middle voice" (White 1992) creating immediacy and intimacy with a distant event and urging my readers to become active agents in making the obscured history of 1971 an engaging subject for understanding and envisioning new relationships in the subcontinent.

EXCAVATING THE RUINS OF MEMORY

My first visit to Dhaka in the summer of 1999 had made me aware that the war of 1971 was an unfinished business, and it was poignantly visible in the Bihari refugee camps that remained even three decades after the war. The haunting silence about women's experiences during the war also revealed the continuation of the victimhood of women in Bangladesh. But there was no written text to present the details and discover why the war had failed to deliver its promise of liberation to so many people. In its place was a national myth that said that Bangladesh was a nation born due to the hard work and sacrifices of freedom loving, proud, and honorable Bengalis, who were represented as "a people." Those who opposed the liberation of Bangladesh were differentiated as *rajakars*, supporters of Pakistan and thus people who did not belong to the body politic of the Bengali nation. The assumption that Bengalis constituted "a people" allowed them to cast the rajakars as outsiders, and they were transformed into the Other.[65] Thus the narrative of the war was constructed in the national memory as a product of the organic unity of people who belonged to the same ethnicity, religion, territory, and had led a popular uprising with nationalist aspirations.

The telling and retelling of the populist myth has molded history to fit the presentism of nationalist memory that is controlled by a small ruling elite based in Bangladesh's capital city, Dhaka. From the perspective of this group they can assume the role of spokesmen because they view themselves as the main architects of Bangladesh's freedom movement. Not surprisingly, the experiences and political aspirations of this group are repeatedly mentioned in the official narrative to remind the public of the particular role this group played in enabling the freedom of Bangladesh, and, in contrast, the threat posed by the pro-Pakistani elements within the Bangladesh state, the rajakars, is sensationalized through public shaming.

The rajakar Other is not an easily identifiable category but generally pro-Pakistan Bengalis and ordinary Urdu-speaking people, who are commonly referred to as Bihari due to their affinity with the Urdu-speaking Pakistanis, are, by and large, deemed rajakars. Since after the war the Bengali people as a whole were liberated, the Bengali rajakars among them mingled with the populace and shed their previous political affinities, publicly at least. The Biharis, on the other hand, whether they were involved in the war or indifferent to politics were identified as the Other (read: potential rajakars) and were targeted for everyday Bengali violence to overcome the trauma of the war. My visits to the Bihari refugee camps and subsequent interest in the condition of these people were viewed with suspicion by the Bengali elite of Dhaka. The bitter calculative approach to other ethnic groups limits the capacity of the powerful Bengalis to communicate the stories of violence as it had happened in the war—to men and especially to women, Bengalis, and different groups of others, including the Biharis. The collective memory of Bangladesh's urban elite is skewed, and because the constructed history is incomplete and lacking, the gap between what happened in 1971 and what is said to have happened is widening. History, state, and elite interests continue to serve each other for a limited purpose: the control of political power (see Nandy 2006).

These impediments make it even more compelling to investigate what happened, particularly to vulnerable groups of women during the war, and find out what is hidden and submerged behind the celebratory national story. With this objective in mind, I returned to Bangladesh in 2001 and spent a year there. As a research fellow of the American Institute of Bangladesh Studies (AIBS), I had at my disposal several privileges that would not have been available to me without institutional affiliation. In particular, Mizanur Rahman Shelly, the AIBS field director in Dhaka, had personal friendships with a number of mukti jouddhas and veterans based in Dhaka, which enabled me to enter into conversations with them and piece together the events of the war and their impact on Bengali society. This was an important entry point. For all the valuable information that these men shared with me, I am most grateful, but being a historian, I wanted to find their backing in the archive to put them into context. Although I am well aware that the written archive is not always a reliable source for exploring the intimate stories of people, I continued to search for written records to put the first source, the oral tradition on the war of 1971, into perspective.

Historians know that archival research is a process and an exercise in endurance. In South Asia, the archive is a formidable space and is marked as a site accessible to only those who are powerful or can display power. Knowledge and particularly its production is tightly guarded and controlled. Also in South Asia the archive is thought of as a storehouse of national memory and claims to this memory are an inheritance of the national citizens. My institutional affiliation with AIBS and identification as a historian were not sufficient proof of evidence to gain access to the documents of the war of 1971 in Bangladesh. Rather, my identity or what was seen as my identity, a non-Bangladeshi person, constituted a problem, and although the officers and staff in the libraries and archives were welcoming, I did not get access to the prized documents of 1971, that is, if any exist. What little I saw was not sufficient to write a "thick description" of violence in the war of 1971 in the Geertzian (1973) sense, locating the individual within the collective society to make connections between an individual's distinctive peculiarities and routine patterns of society that drove violence.

The National Archive in Dhaka is an arid place to search for a people's history of 1971. My repeated visits bore some results, and I was able to do preliminary research on political history leading to the war. The recorded historical evidence mainly focused on political parties and student organizations and their activities. Additionally, some material was available in the National Museum Library, but, they are mostly standard documents about political organizations focusing on the Awami League Party (AL) and Sheikh Mujibur Rahman, who was presented as the "father of the nation." The patrimony of Bengali history and community are the focus of the state documents.

War stories are generally only available in newspapers, and they were produced after the liberation of Bangladesh, since during the war the Pakistani state controlled the news channels within East Pakistan and restricted the flow of information with strict censorship. The headline news for the first year after liberation, throughout 1972, was about male fighters and the battles they fought and won, and accompanying these heroic stories were images of wounded soldiers and guerilla fighters. Very few women were mentioned as participants in the war, and they mostly appeared within generic war stories. There are several visual representations of women, the focus being on their physical exercise train-ing, but the stock images were of destitute and homeless women on the long march to some unknown destination as refugees.

My continuous visits to the director's office of Bangladesh Radio in Dhaka office and my research assistant Kabir's unrelenting reminder to them produced a few recorded oral stories of women's experiences. These narratives recollected the desperate losses that women suffered due to the death of a child or a spouse. A vast collection of uncataloged letters in the Radio Archives was available for random search. The di-rector read to me parts of some of the letters lying on his desk. The letters that I had the privilege to hear recounted individual loses that women suffered, although some were more reflective and addressed is-sues of nationalism, freedom, and the outcome of the war and violence within a larger context. Although they asserted agency and wrote to inform the unknown and unseen listener in their self-representation, women reinforced the male norm of women as subjects: mothers, wives, and sisters, and the losses suffered within their status as subjects were their main concerns. Women did not claim to be individual actors, nor did they tell their experiences in a comprehensive manner. The method of collection in the various archives, the impossibility of access to the material, and their dispersed locations, comically or tragically conveyed the message that women's experiences could not be integrated within the national story. There was no effort in the halls of history-making institutions to move beyond an established position of casual indiffer-ence to these women. The scattered archive contributed in creating for-getfulness; forgetfulness regarding the experiences of women, as well as common people and minorities.

The failure of the archives was not replicated in the public sphere where a new public memory about the war of 1971 had been actively growing and circulating since 1996. In the media and public campaigns in 2001, an election year, politicians invoked with shrill voices the vio-lence of 1971 and demanded redress. In this political public discourse, every man from Pakistan was reduced to one generic label: perpetrator. Bengali men, on the other hand, emerged as war heroes, and rajakars were deemed as traitors. Within this bounded discourse, the support-ers of both the AL and the Bangladesh National Party (BNP) fought over many issues, but the most banal argument was whether their respective leaders, Sheikh Mujibur Rahman or Ziaur Rahman, was the first among the heroes of 1971. Each group upheld their leader as the undisputed and true hero of the war. This national political memorializing was creating a text of 1971 without a serious investigation of the historical events and outcomes. In this seemingly fluid stage of historical production, women were tellingly absent and whenever inserted appeared as victims. The memory of sexual violence done to Bengali women was used by politicians to mobilize anger against Pakistani enemies and rajakars several decades later.

The obvious memory of women as victims had a hidden and pernicious subtext. The rhetoric of sexual violence against Bengali women now stood for the rape of Bangladesh. Preposterous as it may sound, these narratives enabled a mystic unity between woman, land, and nation.[66] A powerful continuity between the land and nation was made and emphasis was shifted to the violation of Bangladesh by Pakistan. A unique human being with a unique experience of suffering disappeared and was turned into a symbol, a story for justifying the vendetta against the Pakistanis and their rajakar supporters, who are still at large in Bangladesh and were identified as belonging to the political party called Jama'at-e-Islami and labeled as Muslim fundamentalists.

The representational images in the politicized public sphere in the election year of 2001 generated two powerful narratives: one was that *our* (Bengali) women were victimized, and the other was that of a secular Bengali ethnicity.[67] The two narratives were entangled and merged, and the claim of the violated Bengali nation was strident and powerful. The raped woman, on the other hand, was reduced to a nonentity. There was no available voice for this woman, and in conspiratorial tones of secrecy and gossip people discussed the victim as a *doshto* or fallen woman. It was ironic that the symbol of the raped and victimized was a powerful tool used to call for revenge in the public sphere, but the real victims, the women, were subjected to more violence in speech and action. The national male heroes were using rape as a weapon, once again so it seemed, to make gains for themselves.

This understanding was not lost on women in Bangladesh. A well-known activist and business woman, who had suffered firsthand the indignity of violence in the war, told me, "Why should I tell anyone my story of victimization? Will it make my husband love me anymore, or will my son respect me because of what I had endured? Instead, they will ridicule me. Miss, you are asking a Western question. Pack your bags and go back to America. Here women will not speak to you about these private matters." I was disturbed by her admonition and emotive outburst, but the point she made was clear. It is not her shame that forbids her to talk about what she suffered; it is the fear of reprisal from the men who dominate her life—her husband and her son—that silences her. Added to this is the fact that in Muslim Bangladesh the power of orthodox Islam has made women's gendered speech of violence into a matter of shame, forcing them into silence to hide their embarrassment. Her invocation of the cultural differences between us drove home the point of the different worlds that she and I inhabit. In my world, discussion of rape has become a classroom topic, whereas in her world there is no space to name the violence and claim the experience. It became an essential issue for me to bear in mind during my research. An understanding of power, the sites where it is created and kept alive, along with an evaluation of how power works as a gendering tool became critical concerns in evaluating the silencing of the sources of knowledge and the production of a conventional history in the service of a patriarchal Bengali nationalism. I also became keenly aware that the Western academic objectification of the study of rape is in sharp contrast to the cultural and religious normative world of Bangladeshi women in which rape is objectified too, but it is the women who are under scrutiny in Bangladesh, not the act of rape. To deny and delete that objectification, women have to resort to silence and forget the violence.

In post-liberated Bangladesh, silence is not simply cultural and political, it is epistemic. Documents of survivors, case histories of birangonas, pictures, police reports, medical records, family documents, letters, and similar materials have been destroyed, erased, lost, and removed from the archival storehouses. In Dhaka, at the Ministry of Women's Affairs, they told me that the records were lost in the process of three moves to different buildings. In the Women's Rehabilitation Center in Dhaka, the board members told me that due to reasons of maintaining confidentiality, access to women's case histories was not permitted. In Dinajpur, a border town in northern Bangladesh that was known for intense ethnic and communal violence during the war, the staff in the Women's Affairs Office declined to dig out the files because they supposedly were too dusty and messy. In the regional offices, I was told often that they had sent the documents to Dhaka. In turn, in Dhaka they told me that I was misinformed. When I tried to meet the chairperson of the Women's Rehabilitation Commission, Rahman Sobhan, who spearheaded the commission in 1972, I could not get a date for an interview. Important sources closely associated to him and the rehabilitation process confided that the documents and case histories of women were destroyed and discussion with Sobhan would not yield results. The ludicrous rhetoric of protecting women's honor by making them invisible and refusing to give access to government reports and documents exposed a deep social and cultural misogyny, evidence that the state controlled by men could not interact with the survivors of rape as human beings but had to hide, disperse, and dismember their memory and speech to regain manly honor for Bangladesh. Mishandling, willful neglect, loss, and theft of files are ways to discourage research on the subject.

In rare cases when documents are available, they are suppressed, neglected, and glossed over. In a regional office in the town of Sylhet, in northeast Bangladesh, I found a moth-eaten list after going through a number of unmarked files hastily dumped in the "to be cleared" section of the office. Initially, I was not permitted access to this section. On repeatedly requesting, the director reluctantly let me speak with the clerk warning me that my effort to search for traces of institutional memory would not produce positive results. The clerk showed me the files "to be cleared" repeating the same warning as the director that I wouldn't find anything there. The important records were destroyed, he reminded me. One file in the pile surprisingly produced an enormous wealth of material. It contained the names of over five hundred Hindu and Muslim women, ranging between the ages of twelve to forty-seven, who were victims of sexual violence in the war. Some were married women, others were single, and some were widows. They were Muslim, Hindu, and Manipuri women from the Kamalganj Thana, Maulvi Bazaar, and Sylhet districts. Interestingly in the survey that these women returned, not one of them used the word *dharshan* (rape) but used terms like *osohay* (helpless), *bhoi* (fear), and *nirjatika* (brutalized) to explain their reasons for seeking help from the government. When I inquired why the office had not taken better care of such an important historical document, the director apologized that "probably no one thought it would be useful." I also found two confidential letters written to the office of the district family planning board in Sylhet requesting medical assistance for women who were "dishonored" and had abortions performed on them despite late-term pregnancy. They had run into serious complications as a result of it and needed immediate medical attention in Dhaka, but we do not know if sufficient medical attention was ever provided.

Even more telling was another document I found by chance in Dhaka. It was a First Investigation Report on rape filed by twelve survivors from Mymensingh in central Bangladesh. Today this priceless document is hidden from public view in the storeroom of a museum in Dhaka. I cannot comment on why it is hidden, but the archivist confided that "such documents will never be made public." Why? Taken as a whole, silence and forgetting what women endured in the war is a policy, and the masculine Bengali identity obscures women's silence and makes it an instrument specifically used by powerful actors for limited political purposes, reducing survivors to dehumanized objects without agency.

Bangladeshi men continue to blame the Pakistanis for the brutality against women in the war. They assume the moral high ground of being the liberators and defenders of freedom. In a casual conversation at the Dhaka Club, when I asked a prominent freedom fighter and decorated soldier if he had done anything to save one woman from sexual violence during the war, he replied, "I did not join the Mukti Bahini to save women. I joined the Liberation War to save my country." When I reminded him that women, too, were part of his country and questioned why he did not do anything to save one person from sexual atrocity, he rebuked me that "this is not a subject of history." Further he added, "This talk about women and rape is okay to an extent. But the kind of history that should be written about the war is the glorious victory of the Bangladeshis against the Pakistanis. Rape happened in the war. But that is not something to tell the future generation."[68] The conviction that the history of Bangladesh should serve the purpose of creating a myth of glory and pride is not unique or shocking. It is now well established that the archival story of history almost everywhere involves tales constructed by powerful actors to service their version of the truth. The Bangladeshi elite actors, too, want a history that tells about their power and greatness, rather than one that reveals the dreadful secret of the Bengali-self as vulnerable and fragile; there is no place for such truths to be admitted as the decorated mukti jouddha reminded me.

It is not just a matter of shame that restricts speech concerning gender violence in the war in Bangladesh, but at the deepest level these stories stir up disturbing memories of the breakdown of family and community; the Bengali-self finds itself haunted by its own shadow. In the mirror of memories today, Bengalis see a distorted image. Their speech is jarring, and silence hides the pain of torturous realizations. Gender violence has been neglected and pushed to the margins. To date in Bangladesh, only one woman, Firdousi Priyabhasani, has publicly acknowledged her corporeal experiences. Transcripts of her testimony are available in the Ain-o-Salish Kendra's library, an NGO that advocates on behalf of women and vulnerable groups.

After several weeks in Dhaka and daily visits to the archives, museums, and libraries that wielded little information about what had happened in 1971, I was demoralized. As an outsider in Bangladesh, I could only interact with the history at an external level. No one was willing to let me enter into the inner world of memories because despite the talk of 1971 as history and a collection of facts, I understood there were many charged emotions, images, sentiments, and reminiscences. For Bangladeshis, the war of 1971 constitutes memories about "ourselves." These memories refer to their self-images and emotions within which they find themselves as both victims and perpetrators. This complex knowledge stored in memories was not yet my privilege, but I did not stop the search. Rather, I met with several scholars and local activists involved in a variety of women's organizations, and while many listened to me attentively, almost all of them told me it was a hopeless project because women would not reveal to me what they experienced in the war, particularly not the stories of sexual violence. Many even said that "people have forgotten what happened after so many years," or "women have created normal lives since then, and they don't want to return to those horrific days of the war." They reasoned that talk about rape is socially inadmissible and hence survivors hide their experiences to continue living a "normal" life.[69]

Almost all the women activists I met with asserted that it was Bengali women who suffered and actively discouraged me from talking and meeting with Bihari women. The issue of who controlled power to remember or forget the violence and, further, interrogate those structures of power, I realized, was crucial if I wanted to continue the research. I was convinced that survivors could tell me a history on their terms if I asked. Nevertheless, I was conscious that in searching for an alternative women's story of the war, it was crucial not to trespass and transgress women's personal boundaries, making public what they have guardedly hidden for many decades. I was also fully aware of the asymmetries that would mark our interactions: as a researcher I wanted to hear their stories because I believed this would contribute to the knowledge on 1971. Survivors, on the other hand, preferred to remember in silence and make the private act of remembering their very own. Survivors' silence is not equivalent to the silence of society. Survivors' silence is an issue of trust and functions like an embrace that speaks volumes when one encounters it. It brings one nearer rather than creating distance between the victim and researcher.

What, in turn, did I have to offer to the women? Did the women also want to seize the initiative and play an active role in the interpretative process of writing a new history? Did they want to become their own historians? Was I being naïve in my approach? I knew that I could not assume to know the answers to these questions. I had to reach out to women in Bangladesh and engage them in order to grasp what the war has meant to them and how they want to represent their experiences. This had to be tested on the ground since there were no ready-made answers.

Where was I to begin? I shared this concern with Akku Chowdhury, then the director of the Mukti Juddho Jadughar. Akku Chowdhury encouraged me to pursue my research on women's experiences but advised me from being too optimistic, warning me that it would be a delicate and difficult task to undertake. As an initial step, he introduced me to Asaduz Zaman Noor, a cultural and political activist (who was serving as the minister of health in the AL government) and, in turn, he provided me a letter of introduction to a cultural group in Rangpur. This was the most fortunate break for me. The cultural group, an active and lively collective of street theater actors, journalists, singers, social workers, doctors, and businessmen warmly welcomed me to undertake research in their area. Mizanur Rahman Shelly's personal request for my accommodation in the government circuit house enabled my research assistant, Rafiuz (Rafi) Zaman, and me to set out to Rangpur in northern Bangladesh and live there. We started our oral history work in Rangpur in February 2001. For the next several months, on and off, we traveled throughout Bangladesh meeting and talking to a variety of women who allowed us into their inner world of memories and emotions and revealed multiple stories that undid the learned narrative of 1971 and produced another history.

But why tell the story of 1971, one of the most violent events in postcolonial South Asia and, perhaps, the least studied by historians, using personal narratives of individual women? How can individual experiences illuminate for us the larger historical canvas of the war and its effects? In other words, one may ask about the logic of this narrative form. The war of 1971 is a site of many histories and retellings that cannot be enclosed by assertions of definitive truth and fact-finding missions. With no established and authentic site to tell the polyversal story, I have decided to pay attention to the memories of women I encountered in the course of my research in Bangladesh. It is not an exhaustive source, but I cannot dismiss women's narratives as sentimentality or individual affect and start with a premise of disbelief. They are experiences that matter to the individual person who wants to be heard. Notwithstanding the limitations of personal accounts, without the individual taking us to that moment of trauma with their stories, we cannot comprehend the incomprehensible violence. It is their stories that make the "high history" of nationalism and nation building accessible, and we can begin to understand the ordinary actors of history, who, in turn, provide us "imaginative access" (Brison 2002) to a "devastating moment." Without their voices and memories that moment of loss would be rendered mute in the grand story of history. My effort is thus not to fix the historical memory of 1971, but to engage the different versions and their fluctuating memories as a resource to understand how the war is remembered in different sites and what these memories mean to survivors today.[70]

TRACKING 1971 WITH THE MEMORIES OF WOMEN

Rafi and I started our work in Rangpur, in northern Bangladesh, a remote, agricultural region not far from the Indian border. In Rangpur our first interlocutor was Beauty, a war baby. Beauty requested me to use her real name because she wants "the world to know her story and, if possible, enable her to reconvene a human life as a person." She "does not want to hide behind anonymity," she said, because she is "tired of [her] invisibility." She wants "acknowledgement as a survivor and [to] regain [her] dignity." Her mother's name, Nur Begum, on the other hand, is a pseudonym. Although, soon after the war Nur Begum was publicly identified as a birangona and her story was made public, now she wants to suppress the public memory of her victimization and avoid more suffering because of it. A few years back, Nur Begum married a Bihari man. She says that she does not want to bring dishonor to him, although he is well aware that she was sexually victimized during the war.

On Beauty's request and suggestion, I met with her mother, Nur Begum, and we had a long discussion about her experiences in 1971. Beauty's mission is to find the truth concerning her conception and birth, and she adopted a method of interrogation to achieve her objective. Nur Begum, however, claimed that she had lost her mind after the war for which she was incarcerated in a mental asylum for several years. As such she had forgotten what had really happened. I have reproduced the narratives of Beauty and Nur Begum in their own words in the next chapter.

Suffice it to say that both Beauty and her mother have very difficult lives, not only socially and economically but because of the basic issue of their identity—what they can reveal and have to hide destabilizes and dislocates them. They have become "nomadic subjects" without the choice to claim the disjunctures that make their lives (Braidotti 1994). The nomadic self of survivors (like Beauty and her mother) is not a politically conscious self, but a person reduced to living like a shadow because both community and culture refuse them admission and accommodation in their ranks.

Beauty's tormented identity as a war baby has led her to find and identify many survivors of the sex camp in which her mother was held captive in 1971. Beauty led me to some of these women, and with her help I entered the hidden world of survivors and was able to embark on the research project. Besides Beauty's direct help, several journalists and members of the Projonmo Committee (translated as the New Generation and constituted by children who had lost their parents in the war) provided me assistance in Rangpur. Women told me multiple stories of loss—about sexual violence and loss of family members, spouses, and children—that have devastated them. Many told me about their first-hand experiences of witnessing rape and their helplessness when not being able to do anything for the victim. They told horrific stories about finding dead bodies of women in the town hall, abandoned bunkers, in graveyards outside government rest houses, and other buildings after the surrender of the Pakistan Army. Medical doctors talked about the forced and secret abortions they performed on daughters and wives of family friends in order to save them from public dishonor. In short, my first exposure to the hidden history of 1971 was sharp and clear, visceral and poignant. The repeated message I received was that in a fleeting moment of violence, dramatic changes took place in women's lives and many live with the consequences, even today. I had entered into the private world of women without previous knowledge, and I had no notion what I could expect next. From Rangpur, Rafi and I went to Saidpur a few miles west and closer to the Indian border.

In Saidpur, as in Rangpur, a variety of people assisted our work. They were professional men and women: journalists, teachers, local activists, social workers, doctors, and representatives of nongovernment organizations. In Saidpur, we met with both Bengali and Bihari women and listened to the unscripted stories of violence that took place in the war. Remembering the moments of violence and what they endured usually produced unsteady emotional states, and often women ended their conversation with tears and sobs. The past would suddenly become a still moment, bloodied in violence, and that is all they could remember in the present. The disruption that the violence caused was unspeakable for most of them; there was no place to retreat and connect to a pristine past. Those who spoke under these conditions, I realized, had rare courage and were expressing immense trust. This realization raised a question about the ethical nature of my research. I was asking women to reveal the secrets of their inner life that might normally come out in situations of great familiarity with people with whom they are intimate. My task, however, was to invite these women to reveal their memories in the public sphere. Was I exploiting women's memories?

The question was given urgency by a woman in Saidpur, Nayatulla Ara. Nayatulla is an elderly Bengali woman. Nayatulla and her husband, a retired accountant, live with their children in a railway colony. Nayatulla recalled that "it was in the twilight hour on a day of rioting between the Bengalis and Biharis when [she] lost [their] seven-year-old daughter, Ayesha."[71] Ayesha was snatched away in a split second as they were trying to flee with their Bihari neighbors to a safe place for refuge. Several days later, Nayatulla heard rumors and gossip that her daughter was seen outside the town, near the military base. In the hope of recovering her daughter, Nayatulla asked her Bengali neighbors to accompany her to the police station to register a case for her "missing" daughter. Her neighbors declined and "refused to bear witness," she said. Her older daughter who was "taken by the military but had returned after several days refused to discuss" with her mother her younger sister's whereabouts. Thirty-four years later, Nayatulla was still waiting to hear from the state about her missing daughter. She asked me: "You've come to listen to our story, of our suffering of violence in the war. I've told you what happened to my family: my eldest daughter was taken by the Pakistanis, but she returned; my two younger children were taken, too, but they never returned. I lost a daughter and a son in the war. Will you bear witness for ordinary people like us who had suffered extraordinary violence that nobody knows about?" Nayatulla thus called upon me to fulfill my responsibility as a historian to pole vault from the abstract descriptions of the war available in history books and engage the process and consequences as experienced by the people. Can we read this call to bear witness by Nayatulla as a larger demand to tell women's memories in the public sphere, to make history an implicated experience, and to make it a continuous engagement?

I raised this issue with each of my interlocutors as I continued to meet and discuss with women about their experiences of the war. Virtually every woman who shared her story did so expecting that I would represent her experiences to others and thus help her and other women to overcome the silence and forgetting that have been imposed on them. They are disillusioned and bitter that even after three decades no one has attempted to redress their condition. Several of them expressed the need to find economic stability in the form of a job or skill training. Others wanted recognition and an end of their outcast status. They suggested that a plaque or memorial dedicated to women who "sacrificed" for the liberation of Bangladesh would help to create public acceptance of women's multiple roles and contributions in the war. Many reminded me that only two women—Taramun Begum (also known as Taramun Bibi) and Dr. Sitara Begum—have been recognized for their sacrifices in the cause of nation making. But there are many more Taramun Begums and Dr. Sitaras that are waiting to be recognized. Will that happen someday? How can my work enable this process? Like the women who told me their experiences as a didactic exercise, I have also assumed that producing the story of the war of 1971 refracted from a single lens of women's experiences will serve a purpose and educate us about the evil of wartime.

Nonetheless, I remained concerned about what kind of an impact a public historical interpretation of their private lives and memories would have on these women. In a village outside Saidpur, I met a schoolteacher who at our very first meeting indicated to me that she wanted to "tell her story." She invited me to her home, but after a meal when we sat down to talk, three other women from the village stopped by to chat and stalled the conversation. Although discouraged, on her insistence I went back to her home the next day hoping to listen to her story. But that day the crowd waiting for me was larger, comprising a mixed group of men and women. The men recounted to me exaggerated stories about their brave feats in 1971. The third day when I went back to her house, a huge crowd of men barred my entry demanding to know why I was repeatedly coming back to speak with the schoolteacher. "What is your interest in her?" they demanded to know. They threatened me, making it clear that they did not want me to return.

Weeks later, I received a letter from the teacher detailing a story of starvation, brutality, and rape by a Bengali neighbor in 1971. She said: "I was only thirteen years old then, and this elderly neighbor whom my family had requested to help me get safe passage out of the camp (where we were kept in custody of the Peace Committee) destroyed me." She forbade me from using her name in my research and "the details recounted in the letter." Her story and her fears were far from unique. There were several instances during my research in Bangladesh when I seriously doubted the effects my work would have.

The larger truth, however, is more encouraging. By and large, the project had a beneficial impact on the women themselves. Almost all the women I interviewed told me that if more people would listen to them, the story of the war would emerge very differently. They also convinced me that the opportunity to talk about their experiences and reflect on their memories and make sense of them was invaluable. At another level, too, my research had an impact. My two field-research assistants, Rafi, a Bengali man, and Taslima, a Bengali woman, both of the post-1971 generation, discovered an aspect of their history unknown to them. The encounters with the women had different impacts on both of them. For Rafi, initially, it was an exciting possibility to travel to different towns and villages of Bangladesh that he had not seen. In the field, he expressed his unhappiness with my inclusion of different groups of women, including the Bihari women, who he considered as "enemies." Hence after a trip to Chittagong, when Rafi quit work without informing me, I assumed he was upset. A week before my departure from Bangladesh, Rafi requested a meeting with me. I learned then that soon after we had returned from Chittagong, Rafi's father suddenly passed away leaving his mother and unmarried sister at a total loss. He concluded by saying, "when I see my mother and sister's face, I understand the helplessness of the women we had met." Rafi's simple but genuinely inclusive use of the word *women* illuminated the impact the research had on him; he was able to see the vulnerable human condition and accept it as a shared reality for everyone, Bengali and Bihari alike.

For Taslima, in turn, the meeting with the women provided her with motivation to take the work a step further and organize dialogues between Bihari and Bengali women in order to overcome the barriers of distrust and hate that have kept them apart. The recognition of similarities between Bengali and Bihari, self and Other, by both Rafi and Taslima have provided me encouragement that new research on the war of 1971 can produce a different narrative that can establish new communities based on understanding. This also taught me the most important lesson: violence can never be total and absolute; it cannot undo the shared human values that make us human.

Following the trip to northern Bangladesh, I traveled to the eastern districts of Maulvi Bazaar, Sri Mongal, and Sylhet, ending our journey near the Meghalaya border of India. There I met with Hindu, Christian, and Muslim Bengali women, as well as women from the ethnic Jayantia community. I made several trips to southeast Bangladesh, particularly Chittagong and the adjoining towns and villages, and there met with Hindu, Muslim, Buddhist, and Christian women who belonged to a variety of ethnic communities. I traveled throughout central Bangladesh as well—including Khulna, Faridpur, Noakhali, Comilla, Jessore, Rajshahi, Mymensingh, Tangail, Narayanganj, and Mirpur where I met with women both individually and collectively to listen to their experiences.

A few obvious questions that may arise for my readers at this point are what was the language of conversation with these women, what was the method of research, and how was contact with survivors initiated.

Since the research involved a variety of women from different groups it required that we deal with different linguistic communities. Bangla is the language of the people of Bangladesh, but there are regional variations. The Bangla language spoken in West Bengal, India, with which I am familiar, was generally our medium of communication, and almost everyone in Bangladesh understood it. In turn, most women spoke in their regional Bangla dialect, and except for the dialect spoken in rural Chittagong, I was able to comprehend all the other dialects without much problem. With the Urdu-speaking Bihari women, I spoke Urdu, which is a commonly spoken language among Indians of North India and with which I am fluent. Some of the Bihari women had a more pronounced regional intonation than others, but, for the most part, the vocabulary was standard.

I sought permission to tape almost all the conversations, and they were recorded with the understanding that they would not be made publicly available beyond my scholarly work. In some instances, women asked me not to record, but they gave me permission to use the general details without directly referring to them. They did not want the "world to know their experiences," but they "felt the urge to share their memories," many said. Additionally, I took extensive notes during the conversations, which I was able to use for corroborating the transcribed materials later on. The conversations were free-flowing discussions, and women talked about issues that they chose—I did not have a list to follow. I saw my role as a listener, and generally the women took the lead in directing the conversations, except for a few broad conceptual issues that I addressed to each woman that enabled me to stay on course with the chronology of personal experiences. Some told life stories; others talked very specifically of an experience or incident. Most of these conversations were in the privacy of a person's home and were one-on-one discussions. The Bihari women did not have the luxury of indulging in private conversation in personal spaces. All of them were public discussions and simultaneous speech during these conversations was common. In many instances, they became interactive and the specific details of an individual's account were left unfinished.

While women's direct experiences of violence in the war remained the focus of my research, I also wanted to hear from women about their work as soldiers, social workers, caregivers, service providers, and other related tasks during the war in order to write a more comprehensive narrative that highlights women's experiences in multiple ways without reducing all of these women's experiences into a poignant story of victimization. Collecting the stories of women who were involved in the struggle for freedom as medical doctors, nurses, social activists, and mukti jouddhas was comparatively easier than the collection of "catastrophic rape stories" (Clandinnen 1999).

All communications, though, were deeply gendered, and for each woman the conversation was a personal and female experience. They rarely talked about detailed facts and war activities, nor did they follow a structured format. Rather what developed in these discussions and dialogues were issues—the chaotic and problematic time of the war that defies strict human understanding was a repeated theme in women's conversation. These rich dialogues established the reality that women experienced the war in many sites, encompassing the public and the private, and to write a history of women's experiences required an intimate and personalized level of engagement, for which oral history is best suited. After a year in Bangladesh, I had on record the memories of more than two hundred women, of which more than fifty recorded testimonies were from survivors of sexual violence.

My meetings with women were facilitated through many channels. As I had mentioned earlier, my initial interview with a survivor of sexual violence was prompted by Beauty. She provided me an introduction to her mother's cohort in the sex camp, and these women, in turn, introduced me to others outside Rangpur. They, in turn, led me to more survivors, and I followed their leads throughout Bangladesh. Sometimes women's revelation of rape was spontaneous. During the course of a general discussion on the war when conversation shifted to sexual violence, sometimes a woman would reveal her horrific memories of rape. These disclosures were underscored with a promise of maintaining secrecy, but the need to vent became the driving force for these women to share their experiences. Perhaps women found it easy to talk to a stranger, for they intuitively knew that their well-guarded secrets wouldn't become known to their neighbors and family. It was in instances like these that the purpose of undertaking oral history became clear as it served as a site for women to make sense of their own experiences and reflect on them verbally without holding back.

Contacts with women who served as social workers, medical professionals, and freedom fighters during the war were facilitated by local interlocutors. There was a general pattern that developed after my first two trips outside Dhaka. My immediate task on arriving in a new town was to find accommodation through the district magistrate's office. Generally, the district administrator also facilitated my research in the area. I also visited the local college or high school to meet with the history teacher. I wanted to establish upfront my research interest and make it a participatory process for the local people. These meetings led to more meetings with local groups, dominated by men, and when they were convinced of my research interest, they deputed a local social worker to assist me in identifying the women I could speak with. Sometimes, help was not forthcoming. In that case, a visit to the local library or women's social welfare office proved very useful. Invariably, a woman in the office would be willing to talk to me. Thus, my contacts grew and expanded, and I was able to invoke their help to undertake research in other areas.

A question that is of concern to oral historians is how much one can depend on people's narratives to construct a reliable picture of an event? Memory, at least what is retrospectively remembered, is a frontier between the verbal word and the historical event. It is not always easy to go there, beyond the limits of what women in Bangladesh had been allowed to remember thus far. Yet the marginalized, suppressed memory was not forgotten altogether; rather it lurks in the background without being integrated into the plethora of war stories that are remembered within a family's or society's narrative. The problem of accuracy of personal memory notwithstanding, it serves an active function to give us a sense of how a woman understands the war through the recollection of memory. If we keep this in mind, we would know not to make factual claims of the past based on the memory of the individual person but accept that this memory is regarded as true by the individual, at least for the time being. Perhaps this narrative will change as new sets of memories become engraved on the present memories and a new narrative will evolve. Thus from the beginning while remaining vigilant with regard to survivors' narratives, I listened to what they had to say and tried to make sense of the larger issues that were embedded within these episodic recollections.

Nearly four decades of silencing have pushed women's memories to the extreme margins of personal memory and have made a coherent narrative of the violent history almost impossible. So when some of the women tried to recall their experiences of violence they could do so only in disjointed fragmentary sentences. On many occasions even this was not possible. A survivor who I will refer to as Rukiya Begum claimed that she could not remember anything, but she told me that she is still in pain. On inquiring about the nature and cause of her pain, she said: "My body is in pain, but I can't tell you what they did to me. I was unconscious throughout my captivity (which lasted eleven days). I was seven months pregnant when they took me to the camp." Her initial captors, it appears, were Bengali men and they handed her over to the Pakistani soldiers. These men brutalized her, but the only way she now remembers the experience is by forgetting the details of the violence. The memories of survivors can be somewhat foggy, and their language is not always sufficient; nevertheless, personal suffering can and should be a social experience (see Das 2000, 2001; Kleinman 1997). Constructing a narrative brings with it the danger of muzzling and not hearing the silence of survivors due to the scholarly obsession with impersonal and rigorous demands for substantiating individual experience with corroborating evidence. Although aware of the shortcomings of personal memory and the multiple gaps filled with silence in women's testimonies, I was keen to engage the spoken and unspoken memories, to approach survivors to transform their horrific memories into some sort of a language to tell in their stead, and to speak the unspeakable to those willing to listen.

It is important to note here, that the word *rape* rarely surfaced in these conversations. Rather, both Bangla and Urdu speakers used euphemistic terms such as abduction, marriage, torture, visit, and the like to convey the forced sexual interaction.[72] Few women talked about their status as birangonas, but almost all of them talked about the pain of neglect they suffer in society today. Rape was a devastating event in their lives, but they endured it in the understanding that during war sacrifices were necessary for the national cause of freedom. The postwar attitude toward them as "deviant women" has recast women's understanding of their loss during the war. Frightened and marginalized, women take recourse to forgetting the event rather than engaging society in a rigorous scrutiny of its proscriptions and expose the violent actions during and after the war. Imposed forgetfulness is not an erasure; the memories haunt and torment women, making their experiences unspeakable.

During our conversations, almost all of the women described the moment of rape as "a state of unconsciousness." There is no language for women to reveal what they suffered at that moment; unconsciousness is the only available vocabulary to resort to when speaking the unspeakable. Partly this is cultural; fear of backlash from the religiously conservative and patriarchal Bangladeshi society is a real threat for women. Women cannot claim knowledge of the rape, but resort to the state of unconsciousness to declare they are "guilt free," otherwise they may be viewed as involved in adultery. As well, it is important to recognize that the horrific impact of rape that is still fresh and unprocessed cannot be accessed with everyday language to fill in for the experience; it is a site of trauma. Hence instead of asking women to "tell me what happened," throughout the research process I remained deeply committed to listening to what they wanted to tell, and a lot was said without words. The subtle nods, the faraway look, the movement from one kind of memory to another, the sudden break in speech accompanied by long silence, shifts in tone and topics of the narrative, a sudden urge to cut short the discussion and prepare tea for me, all of these nonverbalized moments drew me into women's inner experiences. This inner voice of testimony was more powerful than the explicit narrative of the war.

Over and over again, women remembered that the enemy was not the Pakistani soldiers alone. Pakistani men who utilized a variety of state institutions and were endowed with power by the state brutalized women with impunity. If this was the only group of perpetrators, women astutely remarked, there would be social acceptance of their memories in present-day Bangladesh. In fearful and hushed tones women revealed that Bengali and Bihari politicians, strangers, even neighbors, friends, and family members preyed on them during the war and inflicted pain on them that they cannot forget. These men were the ones who led the Pakistani soldiers to their doorsteps. Thus the moment of violence was also simultaneously a moment marked by the loss of faith in community and a breakdown of trust. The enemy, as women revealed, was within, not outside the community of *insān* (human beings). They were ordinary, armed men not some monsters and demons that came from another sphere. This is why many women are forced to forget their memories, but, of course, they do not. Also, women confided that rape was not limited to one group. Rather, women as a whole were targeted. They represented rich and poor, young and old, Bengali, Bihari, Jayantia, Muslim, Hindu, Christian, and Buddhist women of Bangladesh.

The complex ways in which survivors understand violence make the investigation of 1971 from their viewpoint an important and necessary task. But caution is essential here. Revisiting the violence and telling it as a shared experience of Bangladeshi women should not lead to flattening the multifaceted experiences and substituting them with a narrow narrative dominated by speech and retrieval. Survivors behoove us to understand this limitation, while making us aware that official history can never tell the story of 1971 in its entirety, even if it tried. They demonstrate that there is a need and possibility for developing another site to unlearn the habits of believing what is told externally and start a rigorous scrutiny that may lead to dismantling the internal oppressions of institutions and, in turn, make people responsible. Without a discourse of survivors' shared humanity in Bangladesh there is little hope of overcoming the enmity and divisions forced on them by an oppressive history and ethnic nationalism. Women's ability to return to the site of trauma creates a picture of what harmed humans during the war, and we begin to learn what is necessary for human well-being in postcolonial

South Asia. Survivors' picture of humanity is not total or free from the culture that shapes it; it is historical and limited. Nevertheless this picture is a beginning sketch that questions the oppressive discourses that divide and mystify people and aim to destroy the development of shared responsibility.

Survivors' experiences have led them to question the ethical dimension of nationalism and the cost of nation building. They clearly understand now, that in 1971 in East Pakistan there was no distinct and decipherable zone of conflict; violence was used by the powerful as a tool to act out power at the expense of the vulnerable. Some of the survivors compared their sacrifices with that of men and criticized the failure of the government to recognize their courage for fighting the enemy. They believed it was state-sponsored gender discrimination after liberation that enabled men to overlook the contributions of women during the war, particularly the work done by poor women in the war. Some of them demanded women like themselves should be recognized as mukti jouddhas and not reduced to birangonas. They reasoned that it was in the context of the war that they were apprehended and abducted by their enemies. They were raped because they supported the freedom of Bangladesh. These women are bitter that despite the "double violence" they experienced—arrest and torture for fighting for freedom and rape because of their gender—there are no commemorative symbols to remind the nation of women's sacrifices and contributions on behalf of national freedom. The price women paid for nation building was easily forgotten.

In the course of the research, it became evident that women who were identified as birangonas by the state were the most exploited after the war. The majority of these women live in poverty, struggling hard to support themselves and their children. Many of them also told stories of abandonment by their husband or natal families who perceived them as an object of disgrace after the war. Those even less fortunate were sold into the sex trade by their guardians to support their poor economic condition. Mumtaz and Anwara are two women I met in Dhaka whose families had forced them to become sex workers. It appears that Mumtaz's father sold her mother and sister to the Pakistani soldiers during the war to support his drinking habit. After 1971 Mumtaz followed her mother's profession in order to support herself. During the war, Anwara's mother abandoned her, and her grandmother took care of her until she was forced to sell Anwara because she did not have the resources to support her. Both Mumtaz and Anwara are now active in an organization called Ulka Nari Songha (an organization that protects and promotes sex workers' social and human rights) in Dhaka. Not all women who suffered violence during the war, however, have been able to develop their own agency and transform their lives in meaningful ways.

Aparna, whom I met in a village in Chittagong, remorsefully commented on her miserable life after the war, which encapsulates the general condition of marginalization and neglect that most birangonas suffer. She lamented that in the last thirty years nobody has asked her how she is "doing and what does [she] want from [her] life. The government has neglected thousands of women, like [her]," she said. "One of my hands is paralyzed, but I have another hand and I want to work and earn a living. The government has not given me that scope, it does not care whether we live or die. I don't have a normal human life and cannot fulfill my most basic needs. I can't even wear a nice sari." The established gender predispositions in a patriarchal society have played a catalyzing role in transforming birangonas into pariahs. The social mood of neglect has manifested into making survivors of 1971 invisible in society.

Women's narratives unmask the multiple faces of conflict and hidden within are several different layers of memory, history, and violence. In several instances women brought into the conversation memories of the most ordinary things alongside the horrific event of violence. Sometimes they preferred to talk of the everyday work they did rather than about the dramatic events. The iconic memory for many women was not about what they knew but what they did not know or would never know, like the sufferings of their parents (as in the case of Syed Nur Jahan whose narrative in the next chapter highlights this), the betrayal of a family member or the "disappearance" of a loved one. I remember one such narrative of a woman in Sylhet who told me about her "father sacrificing his only son and revealing his hiding place to the Pakistani soldiers because he wanted to live at the cost of his son." To this day, Mrs. Jewel (a pseudonym) cannot forget the scene: her brother trying to cling on to their father's feet who was sitting in a chair, besieging him to save him from the Pakistanis. Her father, she remembered, sat there crying but did not make a move to protect his son. Mrs. Jewel could not understand whether her father was crying in relief for having saved himself or in remorse for her brother who was taken away to his death. She will never know the pain of either her brother or her father, both of them had become absent from her life. There is no speech to tell of this multiple loss that happened in one instant in the inner space of a person's life.

At other times, by clinging to the memory of the everyday and ordinary, women tried to reconvene a different sense of self, which was beyond the violated self reconstructed in their narrative. Once when I asked a survivor called Mumtaza Begum (her real name) what her worst memory of the war was; she thought for a long time and then said, "I did not get rice to eat or oil for my hair during the five months of captivity. I looked so bad that when I was released from the camp in Jessore, people chased me away as if I was a beggar." In another instance, a woman in Chittagong remembered that she had watched a relative being raped, but what bothered her was that when the dead body was found "there was only a petticoat on her." She felt ashamed that strangers "saw her naked." Yet another woman in Noakhali told me in great detail about how her husband was betrayed by his Bengali office colleagues and later inhumanly killed in their own compound by the Pakistanis, leaving her a widow, childless, and penniless, but she finally remarked that she wished she had the typewriter her husband owned. She wanted to show me the instrument in which he wrote his communiqués. Yet another woman in Khulna, after recounting the brutal murders of her daughter and son-in-law in front of her eyes added: "They took away all our belongings. We did not even have a glass to drink water from."

It was during one of my last conversations with a Bihari woman, whom I will refer to as Zaibunisa, that I heard the most poignant account of how women's ordinary lives were made extraordinary and abnormal due to men's violence.[73] Initially, when Zaibunisa started her narrative it appeared to be an ordinary war tale, and since she recalled her memories with little show of emotion I was not prepared to hear the devastating details that soon followed. As she continued to tell the story, I slowly began to grasp the depth of the misery that women like her suffered in wartime East Pakistan. It was the combination of the seemingly ordinary with the abnormal violence that ravaged women's lives, which Zaibunisa's narrative reminds us of and makes the memories tormenting and difficult to deal with nearly four decades later. There was nothing heroic about the war of Bangladesh (or any war for that matter); it etched a path of undying memories of pain for those who experienced it firsthand, as Zaibunisa's account so eloquently and poignantly reveals.

Zaibunisa recalled that in 1971 she lived with her husband and four children in Khulna, in south central East Pakistan. A few days before the war ended, her husband, a security guard in a local paper mill, was summoned by their Bengali neighbors and taken outside the house. Zaibunisa's husband never returned home. Soon after Bangladesh was liberated on December 16, 1971, violence became an indulgence of the victorious Bengalis against the Biharis. Fearing total unrest, the local authorities in Khulna put the Biharis in a local jail for their safety; Zaibunisa with her four daughters, ages twelve, eight, three years, and six months, lived in the jail for several months. Having no resources for supporting her young and dependent family, Zaibunisa and her children often went to bed hungry. She recounted that one morning, "the three-year-old and the six-month-old baby refused to get up from their sleep. They died of hunger in the night."[74]

She began to worry about what to do with the bodies of her children. Burial was not an option that she could afford. Her jailer, who was sympathetic to her condition, agreed to "throw the bodies away." Zaibunisa accepted the offer since she had no other option. Having said this, Zaibunisa abruptly stopped her narrative. Silence became our communication; it was charged with meaning. No more speech was necessary. An ordinary life was not so ordinary after all in its suffering. The war had taken its greatest toll on common people like Zaibunisa and her children. They are so like us, yet their lives seemed so different in the end—bereft, unaccounted, and erased by violence, and no one even took notice. The initial description of her normal world before the war seemed so close to my own; like everyone else's it was in ebb and flow, yet her suffering in the war was totally abnormal, defying any sense of human logic. Her story shocked me and continues to even today.

After a long while she turned to me with tears in her eyes and said in a quiet voice, "they were human too."[75] In that moment, in a simple, emotive statement, Zaibunisa told me more than a story of her children. Her narrative encapsulated what had happened to women and girls, as a whole, in 1971 and provided knowledge about what needs to be remembered today. Females were deemed objects, things, nonhuman Others and were used, abused, and discarded in the war without anyone taking note of it. People forgot that women were human too. Those who experienced the gendered crimes of society and community and lived beyond it were unceremoniously pushed aside, their pain was reduced into disposable memory, and the nation moved forward to celebrate victory and the liberation of Bangladesh. An abstract concept called nation became more important than the human beings who were lost in the violence.

Women's memories enable us to see the inner experience of the war in people's lives. Their stories humanize the narrative, and their speech and silence provides transcendence and gives meaning to an individual's experience to make it a collective encounter. Through women's voices we are urged to see and to encounter the inhuman acts of violence and to remember the sites of humanity. The story of human resilience despite the losses women suffered creates a different human perspective that is recounted in their stories.

WOMEN'S HUMANITY

The feminine that was attacked and marginalized in the war, women remind us, was not a simple biological category, but it was the domain of interiority, the location of emotion, and the place called home that was transgressed. Men, who were co-citizens, neighbors, even friends and family members undermined and violated women. There was no distinction between the zone of conflict and peace; it was all around and inside for women. Women ask us to go behind the text of history produced by the national institutions and consider a different narrative authored by them to interrogate the dominant story. This was eloquently summed up by an elderly Bihari refugee woman living in a camp in Saidpur, whom I interviewed in February of 2001. I will refer to her as Sakeena. After providing a graphic account of different scenes of rape and torture of women that she had witnessed, Sakeena ended her narrative in these words:

> One evening, someone dumped the half-dead body of a child outside the mosque. The child was bleeding profusely. She was in shock and could not speak. . . . I tried to save her, but she died three days later. I can never forget her. You ask me, who could have possibly done this to a child? Don't ask me who killed whom, who raped whom, what was the religion, ethnic, or linguistic background of the people who died in the war. The victims in the war were the women of this country—mothers who lost children, sisters who lost their brothers, wives who lost their husbands, women who lost

everything—their honor and dignity. In the war men victimized women. It was a year of anarchy. *Insāniyat* [humanity] had died. How can I explain this?

Survivors, like Zaibunisa, Sakeena, Beauty, Nur Begum, Mumtaza, Aparna, and many others in Bangladesh demand a rethinking of gendered violence in the war in a totally fresh way that foregrounds women's dehumanization in violence. Women's testimonies thus act as resistance against forgetting, and the remembrance of the memories calls into question the figure of the enemy that they identify as the hypermasculinized state, which used its agents, men who represented a variety of ethnic, linguistic, and religious communities, to execute violence in the name of nationalism by putting power before human values. Individual women who made up part of an integral whole were Otherized and handed over to be brutalized and tormented. By making them anonymous, the impersonal state and society pretended to free itself of a responsible obligation and relationship after its brutal acts. But survivors refuse to forget.

In listening to their memories, we hear the celebration of human exchanges, and we are poignantly reminded of the fragility of being human that was constantly put to the test in the inhumane moments of the war. Women's stories constitute the tenacious site of humanity and create hope beyond the bitter endurance of violence and loss. Ultimately women's stories voice the voiceless humanity, and in listening to them we hear the stories that have not died, even in the face of wanton violence. Listening exorcises memories and loss, granting them new meanings and educating those who remember and listen.

The common concern of women—Bengali, Bihari, Muslim, or Hindu—was that in war and violence the socially accepted status of humanity, a given condition in normal times, was undone. The mechanical calculation of increasing the impact of terror meant violence had to be enacted on the site of the vulnerable, and using the tool of nationalism the state endowed men with the capacity to kill and terrorize. The violence women experienced, they tell us, must be understood for its physical impact and beyond. It was an attack on their personhood, their dignity, their worth as human beings. This is what made the violence so powerful and useful to their perpetrators. Women served the purpose of being objects for men to carry out the will of terror required by the state for establishing its power. The transformation and perversity of the time that made the political quest for nationhood superior to human beings are not lost to survivors. Women refuse to forget that in the sociopolitical world of South Asia they are both inside and outside the nation. The war and violence drove home the point most starkly.

Women in Bangladesh, as elsewhere in South Asia, are fully aware that because of a variety of reasons—biological, religious, cultural, and economic—they are deemed "below men," but as *ma* and *boun* (mother and sister) they also occupy a special position of reverence. The status of a mother, in particular, is a near-sacred status in South Asia. The duality of their existence as mothers, who is the most revered within the inner domains of a family, and the lowly status of a subordinated female person within the external structure of the national community made them vulnerable even after surviving rape. With men abusing women with sexual violence, the sacred image of women as mothers was undone, and the vulnerable woman who became the object of men's sexual violence was exposed to further abuse. Women remind their listeners that their rehumanized but objectified bodies as birangonas were used by men as a nationalistic prop, as the swelling numbers of abused women gave men evidence to demand redress from the "enemies" who violated their so-called sacred mothers and sisters. In making this demand, women astutely remark, men asserted their manly rights to be recognized as the guardians of the community. The women who were made "impure" by men, once more, became the objective site to elevate men to a new prominent role as guardians of the nation. There is thus a profound connection between the person, acting or being acted upon, and the realm of structures created by human power and need that turn against humanity, time and again. And so, women's speech concerning their devaluation as human makes us aware of the norms and values that *should* provide the undergird to civil society in postcolonial South Asia and simultaneously leads us to question how power endowed to institutions could triumph over the humans who created them.

How do women understand their place within the human community? It is of course not an easy question to answer. In Bangladesh, the vast majority of women have not heard about the Universal Declaration of Human Rights adopted by the United Nations in December 1948. They are not exposed to feminist discourses, nor do they identify with the academic politics of gender studies or philosophical discourses on humanity and metaphysics. But they do know that they deserve respect as humans, and that this basic right was denied in wartime East Pakistan.

Their responses and understanding thus must be evaluated within what one may call women's intuitive humanism.

Women try to understand the complex systems at work during the war based on the actions of human individuals and focus on their worth as human beings by referencing the devaluation they suffered in violence. The moral yardstick of humanity had changed. The capacity to choose right from wrong became contingent on the exigencies of the time. Hyper-masculinity and militarized nationalism went hand-in-hand, and men took their anger out on the inner domain of the communities marked as "enemy." By shedding their humanity, these men took pride in violence. Men, women explain, became opportunists, aggressors, bystanders, but ceased to be human. Moral rules that should enable human behavior were dead. Women ask: is humanity a contingent condition? Through their narratives they reveal the vulnerability associated with being human. The awareness of women's dehumanization is absorbed after suffering violence. To know oneself as not only raped but rapable has a distinct affect on women's notion of self (Calhill 2001). The topography of being human is not a question before the event of rape. It is in the experience of violence that the knowledge of the loss of their humanity is generated and becomes a site of suffering and then a site where demand for restoration is born.

Should the transformed voices of the speakers and listeners constitute a site for truth and reconciliation? Is a war crime tribunal an alternative? My immediate response to the latter question is to raise two more questions: Who will try the criminals? And who has the authority to do so? Reconciliation and forgiveness are subjects of enormous ethical possibility, but the will to execute them requires political determination of both governments—Pakistan and Bangladesh—as well as public opinion that favors the process of reopening the wounds of 1971 for a final closure. It is a little hasty to suggest a TRC-like project for Bangladesh and Pakistan under the present circumstances of distrust and the rhetoric of vengeance in the public sphere.[76] Also, I do not think a trial of war criminals with the hope to punish perpetrators would solve women's problems. Individual raped bodies are a testimony of power that is at work on many levels—cultural, social, religious, as well as national. Liberation lies in our ability to see them as the sites of these inscriptions of power. A close scrutiny of these dynamics at work in the South Asian context is essential for creating space for individuals to question and undermine the disciplinary power that shapes women's lives and limits their possibilities. Women must be acknowledged as wholesome human beings and their grievances fully heard for developing policies for redress. Otherwise, women will be raped and continue to be rapable.

The will to remember and listen to women's stories is not yet formed or explicit in the subcontinent. The cultures of religion that dominate people's lives and shape their outlook on the issue of gender violence do not encourage public discussion on rape. Engaging the constructs of culture and society informed by religion is critical for finding a solution. Returning to the religio-cultural site of lived Islam in Pakistan and Bangladesh may actually serve as an emancipatory space where we can move beyond silence and the erasure of women's experiences and reintegrate a vocabulary understood by the people for settling unresolved grievances. I would hasten to add a word of caution here that this is not a suggestion to return to the Islamic religious legal system of Shari'a law. Nor can the legal, moral, and ethical issues linked to the war and violence be conflated and made compatible with the Western concept of human rights. Rather, I would emphasize what one can loosely call "Islamic values" (Dallmayr 2002) that accommodate religious principles with cultural concerns, keeping in mind the dynamic nature of society and culture in the predominantly Indo-Islamic countries of Pakistan and Bangladesh.

There are, of course, no ready-made answers available to reach simple solutions to the complex set of problems posed in the aftermath of gender violence in the war of 1971. Nonetheless, an exploration of certain fundamental principles that resonate within the Muslim communities in Pakistan and Bangladesh may serve as a starting point for new possibilities. Privileging a people's language emerging from within the context of their religion and culture would be the test of our decolonization and offer a creative potential to alter the story of official history on 1971. We may be able to tell the story of 1971 in our own words, writing a people's history in the region. To explore this possibility, the discourse of rights and obligations within Islamic law offer an opening for a genuine dialogue between the aggrieved parties.

Traditionally speaking, in Islam there are two kinds of rights or *haqq*: the rights of God or *huquq Allah* (plural of *haqq*) and the rights of persons or *huquq-al-ibād*. The rights of God are directly related to the Five Pillars of Islam, but what we are concerned with here are the rights of persons that are secular and are due to people, including rights owed to the poor and the weaker and more vulnerable members of society.[77] These rights are fundamental and unconditional and cannot be denied to any person. Huquq-al-ibād is not equivalent to human rights, though; there are some overlaps between them but it is not possible to package them together (see An-Na'im 1990, 2008; Moosa 2000). Rape, which is viewed as a sin or transgression committed by men against women, is a matter of huquq-al-ibād. The obligation to admit and act on the realization of the transgression of a women's haqq to her human dignity is a perpetrator's responsibility, and the reciprocation of forgiveness is the right of the victim. To invoke this right and implement the obligation requires an active engagement by both parties—it cannot be decided unilaterally. No one can absolve the perpetrator of the crime of rape except the victim or in the event of her death by the surviving relatives of the deceased who have the authority of *wali al-dam*.[78]

The concept of wali al-dam is found under the general principles of Islamic law and is mostly related to homicide cases. This concept refers to the guardian of the life of the deceased who has the authority to decide whether to forgive and completely release the perpetrator, accept *diya* (compensation), or insist on *qisas* (an eye-for-an-eye principle) depending on the facts and circumstances of the case.[79] Ultimately, it is the victim or the family of the victim who has the prerogative to forgive and assist the perpetrator in the recovery of their humanity through the process. The act of seeking forgiveness cannot be done from a distance and not by the nation or by the community at large on behalf of the perpetrator. It must be actively sought by the perpetrator who must first acknowledge and recognize the full and holistic humanity of the victim and then appeal for forgiveness. To a large measure the reformed outlook of the perpetrator toward the victim is a necessary beginning step and must accompany the act of submission and humility in relation to the victim, seeking their compassion and forgiveness, which they can refuse to grant. The victim is encouraged to forgive the repentant rather than seek retribution for the well-being of peace and harmony in the community and to help the perpetrator recover their humanity and fulfill their obligation of upholding the principle of huquq-al-ibād.

Forgiveness accordingly is not an affair of the state or nonvictims or those unrelated to the victim. In Pakistan an effort was made by the Women's Action Forum to apologize on behalf of their nation to the women of Bangladesh for the crimes committed by the Pakistan Army in 1971. To my understanding this gesture, although commendable, cannot be a substitute to perpetrators seeking forgiveness from the victims. Perpetrators, who committed violence, whether they are Pakistani, Bengali, Bihari, or others, must be identified by the state and society, and they must be encouraged to seek women's forgiveness. It will not do to absolve them of their crime by others seeking forgiveness on their account. In Pakistan and Bangladesh men even today have not willed themselves to hear the call for justice by women. When one can hear and become ready to engage the body of women as a crucial text, a site of the abuse of men's power, and a source of testimony about the war of 1971, then a movement in the direction of reconciliation and forgiveness or justice is possible.

In order for perpetrators to acknowledge and repent for their crime the active engagement of the governments of Pakistan and Bangladesh is critical. Individual men committed crimes of sexual violence sometimes with the knowledge of their superiors and sometimes without the knowledge of others. During the war, the West Pakistani government had called upon individual men to subjugate the rebels in the east, and, in turn, these men attacked the vulnerable to display power. Violence spawned and the nationalist Bengalis heeding to the call of their leaders turned against their supposed enemy—Pakistanis and Biharis—in their midst. In liberated Bangladesh the mukti jouddhas later formed the government. It is time for the states of Pakistan and Bangladesh, who were involved in creating and facilitating the violence, to execute their national will and take responsibility for their crimes. The admission on the part of the state and government of their actions and inactions during the war will encourage and empower their citizens to recognize their individual actions and the crimes they committed in the name of nationalism. A language of responsibility and justice can emerge in that case to bring closure and open avenues to a new future. In the absence of the governments taking responsibility, individuals cannot implement the principles of justice and forgiveness—even if they have the tools to imagine the possibilities. At this juncture, the narrative testimony of men admitting to their crimes and the states acknowledging their misuse of power against the vulnerable is the first challenge.[80]

The narratives of women provided in this book are graphic recollections of painful experiences. Some of them are explicit in sexual references and tell of the carnal passion of violence. By reinserting these candid and unedited visceral memories of survivors into the text of historical memory of 1971, my purpose is not to regurgitate the absurd or sensationalize history. Like Primo Levi, I see my interlocutors using "a certain dose of rhetoric . . . for the memory to persist" (1986, 20).

History or the narration of the past in people's lives is polyversal and multifocal. It is malleable and flexible and is not the same as written, institutional official history. The boundaries between history and memory in people's narratives are not clarified. People's history is always in the present, and they can relate to it only when they can tell stories about what they know. They tell about high politics that drive events and impact the collective and simultaneously talk of history as an individual, personal experience. When an event is great enough to enable them to make a linkage between the high political story and their personal encounters, they claim it as their story. Understanding the relationship between the two—history that becomes officially recognized and people's history, which is active but not institutional—is a challenging task, but once we can grasp the message, the multidimensional story of history becomes a lively, animated process constantly becoming and unbecoming in sites where it is created, lived, and experienced.

The history of nation-state formation in South Asia is a site of memory that is both celebratory and painful. There are conflicting passions and emotions that are embedded within them because nation matters to people in India, Pakistan, and Bangladesh, like elsewhere. They had won their freedom and created sovereign states after long and bitter struggles initially fought against the British colonial masters, and later they had to settle scores among themselves. They continue to fight over unresolved national issues, even today.[81] The citizens within the nation-states, in turn, look toward their governments with the hope that they will deliver the promise of a good life, security, and protection. For their part, they are willing to kill and die for the nation. The site of nationalism for most people in South Asia is political, but they are also aware that politics divides the networks of shared memories that were constituted in exchanges between the different groups over a long period of time, before the nation-states came into being. Social and collective memories of the past and the ongoing present therefore take both real and imagined shapes, and they span the entire spectrum of pleasant and horrific encounters.

The war of 1971 is one of the worst memories in the region. The event illuminates both a spoken and a silent past and traces a history that frightens us because to look at it may mean seeing the continuous violence that frames the story and in which we are both victims and perpetrators.

The survivors of 1971, however, ask us to engage with the violence. They demand an answer: whose purpose did the violence serve? In writing this book in their words, I do not assume to arrive at a transcendental truth. Writing cannot be a replication of experience. Nonetheless, writing enables us to move closer to the possibility of confronting the amnesiac memory of war and educate ourselves about what was done in those forgotten moments of violence. Many in South Asia may find the bitter effect of suffering in 1971 as grounds for revenge, rather than a site to develop a language of understanding and to claim the story produced by survivors to move beyond the horrific moment. Some may also claim that an acknowledgment of "composite heritage," much in vogue these days in the dialogue between the Indians and Pakistanis seeking to move beyond the horrific partition of 1947, is the next step to follow and make our "common suffering" the ground to reconvene in the subcontinent. The Ernest Renan-like approach advocating for the recognition of suffering or *gham* as the location for thinking beyond violence to form nation and community could be a useful tool.[82] But first there has to be increased determination to listen to what the voiceless survivors of violence are saying. How has their suffering of violence transformed their worlds? In the world of South Asia where this voice of survivors has not emerged and become accepted, we cannot be at ease and claim their suffering as a slogan for national or community interest. Searching for an understanding of the violence of 1971—to know what women suffered in their excruciating details, to come to terms with what it was, and what we are capable of doing to each other—is done with expectations for a different future in the subcontinent. Historical justice is a horizon that extends but cannot be exhausted (see Derrida 1994). To narrow the gap between the horizon and evident, present reality, a conscious effort must be made to develop ethicality as a concrete historical need, capable of developing actions, politics, and organization. Thus, can we dare to write from within the abyss of violence a people's history of the subcontinent, and make it a site for understanding and claiming human dignity that is our due? The survivors of 1971 urge us to answer this question and embark on this task.

PART II  SURVIVORS SPEAK

3

VICTIMS' MEMORIES

NUR BEGUM AND BEAUTY, RANGPUR

I could not even remember my name, who I was,
or what happened to me. —NUR BEGUM

I don't have a human life,
even though I may look human. —BEAUTY

After several months of researching the documents and records in the Liberation War Museum, National Archive, Radio Archive, and the libraries of the Ain-o-Salish Kendra, Bangla Academy, and Dhaka University, I remained puzzled about how I could write a history of 1971. In the materials there was no actual story of the war as it happened, rather the purpose of the documentation was to retrieve and preserve the memories of the war. The archivists and staff in these institutions made frequent references to the ongoing work aimed at collecting and recording everything, such as identification and excavation of the killing fields, preparing the list of *rajakars*, and finding survivors to compile their testimonies in oral, written, and audiovisual formats. This work will be a rich resource for historians in the future, but for my immediate purposes in 2001, there was little I could use to start my investigation of wartime East Pakistan. I decided that whatever understanding I had to develop would have to emerge from survivors, women who could tell me what they experienced and can remember about the dark days of 1971.

From discussions with intellectuals, decorated veterans, social activists, and historians, I realized that the majority of the survivors had been unceremoniously pushed aside and forced to remain silent, leaving no traces to gain access to their experiences nearly thirty years after the war. On the face of this evidence, it seemed daunting to undertake oral history research in Bangladesh. But I also knew that as humans we have a need to talk, to find words even though language may not fully convey experience, and to organize memories into narratives so that we may voice our silent, unspoken thoughts and ideas.

My first trip outside Dhaka to Rangpur in northern Bangladesh, a predominantly Bengali area, confirmed my intuitive conviction that survivors of 1971 would be willing to talk. On the second day of my stay there, I met Beauty. She was bursting with stories and no longer wanted to keep the fact that she was a war baby of 1971 a secret. Following a group meeting with the cultural association that Beauty is a member of, she requested a private meeting that afternoon. During this meeting in the home of an associate, she told me her story. The fluency of her speech interspersed with spontaneous outbursts of emotional ramblings made me think that Beauty has told the story to herself many times, in private, but that she had not told her fears and experiences to another person, a stranger at that, publicly before. Hence her story has both a sense of continuity and discontinuity, as the past is enmeshed with the present, but she does not want to carry it into the future since her personal history has become her worst liability.

For more than two hours, Beauty told me about her hopeless life and marginal social identity because she was a war baby. Many times in her narrative she referred to herself as a cadaver. Her agony is that Bengali society and, more importantly for her, her mother have refused to acknowledge her identity. When she was a child and lived in an orphanage, she did not search for her personal identity because she was surrounded by other orphans, like herself. But as a grown-up, Beauty found that she was suddenly alone, transplanted, and displaced from a familiar world and thrown into a different milieu of people who judged her and reduced her into a pariah. They shunned her. The interior self-narrative that she had created came undone and ruptured. Now Beauty does not know how she can mend and make a new beginning for herself. In despair she has contemplated suicide as a last resort to unshackle and free herself from the inhuman condition of her life. If Beauty acts out on this thought, it will be a great loss; she is a single voice that forces us to recognize the incalculable loss of human capacity to see its own acts of violence but is quick in judging others for their cruelty.

Fortunately for us, Beauty wants to continue her search for her identity in the hope that a new life is possible. Beauty wants to first establish the past, the truth about her birth. Hence she wanted me to speak with her mother and excavate the truth about her pregnancy during the war. The next day, on her request, I met with Beauty and her mother, Nur Begum, in the government circuit house where I was staying. It was a telling moment when Nur Begum came to the government house. Obviously, the staff was very uncomfortable, but they could not bar her entry since she was my guest. They lingered around my room appearing to be cleaning some imaginary dust and cobwebs. After a while, I asked them to leave so that I could have a private conversation with Nur Begum and her daughter, and they obliged grudgingly. During this meeting, my assistant Rafi was present for a while, but as the conversation moved to more explicit sexual descriptions of violence and torture that Nur Begum had suffered, Rafi excused himself. This enabled Nur Begum to talk more openly about the intimate topics of violence and rape, although she never named the experience. Her descriptions of sexual violence are graphic and horrifying, and her speech conveyed the intensity of the pain she suffered.

I started the conversation by encouraging Nur Begum to tell me her memories of wartime East Pakistan, but quickly Beauty took over the conversation and interrogated her mother with pointed questions, demanding that she tell the truth concerning her birth. It was an unusual and rare moment in my oral history research in Bangladesh. For the first and only time throughout my research with survivors, I had the opportunity of listening to a mother and her daughter share their memories in tandem. Creating synchronicity in their memories was not the purpose of the exchange between mother and daughter, rather both sides wanted to tell and find a version of a story that was acceptable and useful. Needless to say, the conversation between mother and daughter was marked by agitated speech, poignant emotions, and painful reminiscences.

Nur Begum maintained one story line: that she was married to Beauty's father before the war had started, and that she was pregnant at the time when she was abducted by the *hanadar*[1] (also referred to as Pakistan) army, who killed her husband during a raid. Beauty refused to accept this story and revealed to her mother that she had done some personal research since she had met several of her mother's companions from the sex camp. Beauty's mother did not change her story, but she was pressed to do so by Beauty, who gathered information that she was born several months after her mother's rehabilitation in a mental hospital in Pabna (in northern Bangladesh) toward the end of 1972, which suggests that

Nur Begum could not have been pregnant before she was abducted. Nur Begum feigned forgetfulness, invoking her loss of memory as the problem. She insisted that Beauty should accept the version of the story that she had told her—that Beauty had a father who died in the war—and make peace with herself and her past.

Beauty was not satisfied with her mother's approach of hiding behind a lie, and she demanded that Nur Begum acknowledge the truth of her rape and admit that Beauty is a child born of rape and not of wedlock. Beauty claimed that her mother's admission of the truth of what happened to her during the war would free her from social ostracization and would give her agency to claim her identity as a war baby. She will no longer have to face the taunts of society that has passed judgment on her mother for being complicit in the crime of her rape and deem her a prostitute. Her interrogation, however, was fruitless. Her mother did not change her story. At the end of over two hours of conversation, without reaching a conclusive decision whose version is the "authentic" memory, we ended our discussion.

Nur Begum's testimony was very complicated both in its narrative style and in what it wanted to convey. At one level she wanted to share her story to release the tormenting memories that she has lived with in her mind since the war. But, at the same time, she did not want to open herself and her memories to scrutiny. There were sudden changes in her tone and train of thought during our conversation. Obviously, there is a private and public space in her testimony, and she occasionally allows her listener to see that disjunction in her narrative. These and other complexities as well as the chronology of the events and the people she invoked from memory to make her testimony "authentic" made the narrative very difficult to follow. The testimony is wavering, moving from one moment to another, at times without connections between them. The narrative obviously is of a person deeply troubled, as the violence of the war resulted in an intense emotional loss and became a site of finding oneself within the context of a community made up by strangers. In the transformed post-liberated Bangladesh, Nur Begum had no familiar human frame of reference, no family to return to after she emerged as a *birangona*.

Nur Begum feels an extreme sense of guilt for her rape. Her guilt silences her, and she has to make up a story that works for her public account. Her rape, unlike some other victims who were raped at home, was a public act. She was repeatedly raped in the camp along with other women, so that all those who were present witnessed the assault on her body. It dehumanized her, and she is terribly ashamed that she hit the rock bottom of her womanhood because she had become an object for penetration. In her testimony she tries to hide that sense of public exposure she suffered by creating a new private story of marriage and pregnancy to legitimize the memory for her daughter, Beauty.

Her silence about what happened to her is a form of testimony to protect her daughter from being condemned to live with and suffer from the memories. By telling and retelling her story framed within marriage and pregnancy before rape, Nur Begum wills Beauty to erase the stories she knows and has found out from the other survivors of the sex camp. In turn, she wants Beauty to believe in her version because Nur Begum believes that her story can be an instrument for Beauty's survival and creation of a normal life. Nur Begum does not want to provide concrete details, which she thinks will burden Beauty's life even more. She does not want Beauty's life to be like hers, although it seems to be very similar. By denying the similarity, Nur Begum thinks she can make Beauty's life better than hers, more wholesome and real, unlike hers. She does not want to understand Beauty's desire to know the truth of her rape. Nur Begum is conscious of the society and culture that will condemn her for this knowledge. But does her denial really protect Beauty? Does refusing to speak the truth help Nur Begum and Beauty? Quite clearly, the discontinuity between the two narratives creates more stress and restlessness in Beauty. Knowing the truth will perhaps help her to understand and accept, but Nur Begum does not acknowledge this. Toward the end of our conversation, Nur Begum requested that I help Beauty find a job somewhere outside Rangpur, "where she can find some peace of mind and make her own life." In parting she told me the most disturbing thing: "Take her with you to America. She will be your servant forever." The bleak future that Nur Begum anticipates for Beauty, to become an exploited and voiceless servant girl serving someone else, once again undermines Beauty's quest for personal liberation and finding her autonomous self.

Despite her despair, Beauty shows incredible fortitude. She refuses to accept the verdict pronounced by others, including her mother and the Bengali world of Rangpur. She is determined to find the truth concerning her mother's pregnancy in 1971, which, she believes, will help her to reconstruct a self. Now, will the social collective in Bangladesh allow her to search so that she can achieve her goal?

NUR BEGUM'S STORY

My name is Nur Begum. My original village was in Dinajpur. I was married in 1971 and was living in my husband's house. It was in Chirirbondor, near the border. The place is called Fulbari, Dinajpur. I was living there, but when the war started my husband, his brother, and father all fled to India. None of the young people could stay there. They all went to India. The women were at home. My husband used to come to visit us at night and return before dawn. In the course of coming and going, my husband was caught. It was some time in the middle period, just before liberation. This girl [pointing to Beauty] was in my womb. I was caught in the middle; it was fifteen or twenty days before independence. They killed my husband. My husband came home to visit me. The rajakars from our village informed the Pakistanis that my husband was at home. The rajakars were all Bengali. When my husband came, they caught him and tortured him. They hung him from a tree. We had been married only one year, and he was very young, maybe twenty, twenty-five years old. A woman came and told me, "They have hanged your husband and have probably already killed him." I asked her who had caught him. She told me, "the rajakars." I rushed to the place. I was five- or six-months pregnant then. They shot my husband in front of me. Before that they had tortured him in many ways, but he did not die. He was reciting verses from the Holy Quran. They gouged his eyes, crushed his body, yet he did not die. Then they shot him. When he died from the bullet wound, his head had leaned to one side. I started screaming and held one rajakar by his arm and shouted at him. Then one *khan*, I mean Pakistani soldier, kicked me with his boot. I tumbled forward and fell down. I lost consciousness, and I can't remember any more.

They had caught all my family members. A month before this incident they killed my parents. My parent's village was near the town, just one mile away. I learned about their death from different people. Those days, people were coming and going from everywhere. Mukti Bahini soldiers were especially moving about, coming from and going to India. Beauty's father had also informed me that my parents had been killed. There was no one in my parent's house. It was a wild and desolate field, he told me. There were only cows, goats, paddy, and rice — nothing else. No human beings were alive. There were some dead bodies lying here and there. The dogs, foxes, and vultures were devouring them. I lost my entire family in the war, my own parents and my husband's family too.

I was marked with violence in 1971. Look at the bite marks on my breasts. When I was first captured, the Pakistani military kept me naked. I was unconscious when it happened. When I gained consciousness, I was wondering where I was. I did not have any clothes on. They had tied me to a chair with my hair, my hair was very long. One after another they tortured me. I could not speak. My lips were swollen, my face was puffed up, and my entire body had bite marks. They cut my arms with blades because I was shouting. How long could I bear it? Here, look at my right hand. I was tortured until independence; they tortured me one after another. I saw two dead girls, they tortured even their dead bodies; they were dead already.

I saw many girls in the bunker. There were fifty or sixty of us. My sister-in-law was there also, but she died. She died in the bunker. She died because of torture; three women died there. I don't know even today how many women died after they were rescued. Some women died in the rehabilitation center in Dhanmondi, in Dhaka, in the hospital.

The Pakistanis came in groups—group after group. You seemed surprised to hear it. They did it in front of everyone. It was wide open in the bunker. Nobody was looking at the others. It was a condition that no one asked or questioned. The majority were young girls; there were no older women there. In my estimation, the girls ranged from fourteen to twenty-two years old. The soldiers cut the girls' hair short so that they could not strangle themselves using their hair. Their arms were smashed, so they could not raise their arms [showing her own left arm], my arm was also smashed. Because my husband was a freedom fighter, I was tortured relentlessly. They used to say "Mukti, Mukti." My arms and legs were smashed. They tortured me terribly.

They tied me down. I could not even move my head in any direction. I saw the girls who were in front of me, but I could not turn and look if there were others. They had stretched my hands and legs wide apart, just like being in a sitting position, so that they could use me. They kept me in that position. On the day of liberation, I was tortured brutally. On that day, in the bunker I could hear the sound, "Bangladesh, Bangladesh, independent Bangladesh." The khans could not come that day to me, from 3 A.M. they could not enter the bunker. The Mukti Bahini soldiers were pouring hot water inside the bunker. They thought that there were khans in the bunker. Then they heard us shouting, "Help us, save us, fathers and sons, please save us!" They turned the bunker upside down and found us without any clothes. The freedom fighters took off their shirts and hid our nudity. They were looking away from us. I was in a daze, I didn't know anything, I didn't have sense, I didn't have the sense where I was being taken, where I was brought, and what they were doing.

The freedom fighters that rescued me also arranged for my treatment. I was in Dhanmondi, in the rehabilitation center for five to seven months, but I don't remember anything, how the days and nights passed. I was not in a normal condition. People used to come to see us. There were many foreigners, some well-known and renowned people of Dhaka, ministers, and so forth, came to visit us. They used to bring us food, and also they took care of us. They arranged for our treatment. From there I was taken to Uttar Bongo [in northern Bangladesh]. They sent me to the mental hospital, I mean Pabna Mental Hospital. They said I was a mental health patient. I went to Pabna Mental Hospital after staying in Dhanmondi. I lived in the hospital for five years, I think. My daughter was born there. I was pregnant, all this time I was pregnant. I was in that hospital for a long time. See the marks on my ankle, I was in chains for a long time, I was there for a long time, the scar is still there. The doctor said I would be all right slowly, if I would be under treatment. They told me they would not give me electric shock or put me through any other kind of "torture." The doctor said, "She should live the way she wants, do whatever she likes, no one should stop her." I was suffering from memory loss.

The doctor in Pabna Hospital advised that I should be integrated with people and given regular work with others. "Work will help her to forget, she will forget her past and will be able to live her present life," he said. The board accepted the recommendation, and I was discharged from the hospital. I was taken to the Nari Punorbashon (Women's Rehabilitation Center) from Pabna Hospital. I was married off from there. My husband used to live in Gaibandha, near here. After marriage he started to torture me, after he got a job because he had married a birangona. The government gave him a job for rehabilitating me, a birangona. After he got his job, though, he threw me out of his house. I went back to my father's house, but no one was there.

I used to roam about here and there. I went to Harun Saheb and other freedom fighters and appealed to them to help me. People used to bother me a lot; I could not go to my village because no one would talk to me. I could not show my face to anybody. I used to roam about with the child. Her grandfather and grandmother didn't give me shelter. I used to cry a lot. Harun Rashid, he was a freedom fighter, was assistant district collector then. Based on the recommendation of the doctor from Pabna Hospital, Harun Rashid and the freedom fighters who had rescued me sent an application to the civil surgeon of Rangpur, and I was given a job. This happened between 1976 and 1977, I don't remember exactly. After I got a job and was somewhat normal, I looked for my daughter. I found her in the Gaibandha orphanage. But I could not bring her from there. I was always at work and I was living in another place, in Rangpur, and Beauty was in another place, in Gaibandha. They sent her to an orphanage when I was in the Pabna Mental Hospital.

Now with this daughter of mine, with Beauty, too, it is the same situation. I brought her back when I was released from the hospital. I brought her back from the orphanage. A man had married her forcibly, but after he found out about her father's identity he abandoned her. I tried with all my might to save her marriage. I screamed and shouted that her father was Mahmud Chowdhury of PG and he died, but he would not believe me. He said, "I have come to know that she is the daughter of khans, she is the daughter of several fathers, there is no trace of her fathers, and the whole of Bangladesh is her father." My daughter doesn't have a family, she has two children, but she still doesn't have a family. I tried to help her. I told her husband, "I will not have any contact with her since I am a bad person, but my daughter is innocent, she was a child. She doesn't know anything. Does she have any fault? She doesn't have any fault, why are you treating her like this? Let her have her children and family back." But they broke the marriage. What do I do with this girl? I got married for the second time, but she can't live with me and my husband nor does she have her own family.

My present husband is a non-Bengali man. He used to live in the Bihari camp before. Since he married me, he moved out of there and bought a piece of land. He built a house for me. I hope that I'll die in his hands. My husband says that what I suffered was for the country. The country had done this. He makes them understand that it was not an intentional thing that girls did. They did not go there willingly. It just happened. I was forced to go there. I should not be blamed for what happened to me.

Regarding Beauty he does not say anything. I'm in great distress because of this girl. She has no happiness in her life, nor is she able to take care of herself. She does not have a job. I have tried my best to get her a job. I knocked on every door and asked everyone I could think of to help her. I went to Dhaka and pursued many ministers. But everyone wants bribes. I have sacrificed my life, my dignity, my entire family was martyred; not a single person from my family is alive. I have high blood pressure and am suffering from heart disease. I may die any moment. Since she is an accomplished artist, she had learned music and dance and is involved in a cultural organization—some of the people in the group help her. She lives on charity. She is a helpless orphan. Allah has given her beauty and an able mind and body. But she is not blessed with family. She suffers because I, her mother, was a birangona. They reject her because her mother was taken by the Pakistani military and tortured? When I tell people that I did not go there intentionally, they refuse to believe me. What can I do?

Nowadays, many people have forged documents and they claim to be freedom fighters with fake certificates. There are many fake birangonas. I am an *original* birangona. My name is not included in any gazette. I don't have any record. All my papers and documents have been destroyed. A fake freedom fighter promised to marry me, to create a family with me. They got us married, and he was given a government job, which he continues to enjoy. He is living happily with his wife and children, but I couldn't enjoy the same benefits or have a family with him. My child has suffered. Tell me what kind of country is this? People laugh at me, they jeer me. Where can I get peace? It would have been better if I had died then. It is fruitless to live in this Bangladesh. Has it produced any result for people like us? I am asking you. Do you think this country will do anything good for us? I am expressing my inner sorrows to people like you. Even as I am talking to you, you can see that my daughter is feeling disgraced. People mock her that she is the daughter of a birangona. But do they understand what a birangona is? Why I became a birangona? To fight for our freedom, to protect our country I became a birangona.

You can see, Beauty keeps asking me why I gave her up to the orphanage. I had no choice. I was in the mental hospital, and she was born there. I had to give her up because I had no family who could take care of her. I could not even remember my name, who I was, or what had happened to me. Why don't you try to understand this, Beauty? Now I can't remember whether you were born in Dinajpur Hospital or Pabna Hospital. Beauty was born before my marriage to my second husband that is all I can remember. I want her to believe me, but she refuses. I don't know what to do, how can I help her? I don't know what will happen to her? Can you help her get a job somewhere where she will find peace? You can take her to America; she will be your servant forever.

BEAUTY'S STORY

I can't live well; I can't make my living. Wherever I go people want to make use of me. They think my mother had a poor character and I was born due to her disgrace, so they want to exploit me now. This, in short, is my life. I have no house, no family; I want to do some work, but I can't find a job. Where do I go at this time? What do I do for a living? What do I do with my life, my time? I can't seem to find an answer. I am struggling with my life and I am facing a lot of challenges. Sometimes I have food for two days, and the next day I starve. I am living my life without direction or a sense of security. My mother does not want to see me or spend time with me, she is afraid. She doesn't want to recognize me as her daughter. I have no identity. I keep on thinking: who is my father, where is he? My mother can't tell me if I have any relatives. I would go to someone who cared for me. But I have no one. My mother told me a few things about her life before I was born. She told me that my father was a good person, he was a soldier. My grandfather was a very pious man, and the people in the village used to respect him a lot. But in the war all of them were killed.

My mother was very young in 1971; she was married to my father at an early age. I have heard that she was very beautiful, everyone used to be amazed at her beauty; she was like an angel. She has grown old now, yet whenever I see her, I smile with happiness. Whenever she wears something nice, she looks pretty. After father's death, she had to struggle a lot. I believe many men wanted to marry her forcibly. Many tortured her.

Circumstances made her marry a Bihari man. What can my mother do? She is an orphan; I am also an orphan. I, too, have no one. My mother has two daughters with her present husband, but I can't visit them. My stepfather doesn't allow it. He doesn't allow it because in the eyes of society I am not acceptable. There are a lot of rumors about my birth; many people have said a lot of nasty and horrible things about my mother. She sent me to an orphanage soon after I was born, I believe. I grew up in the orphanage. My mother was rehabilitated by the government after the war. As a result of it she is known as a birangona, and I am treated like a pariah. Everyone sees me and my mother externally. They think we are bad women, but inside us there is so much pain, humiliation, history. No one ever thinks or writes about these issues, they just say that she had lived her life like a sex worker and that is my origin. Even if my mother shouts a hundred times that she was married and I was her husband's child, no one believes her, and because of this mistrust, my own family broke up. My husband divorced me. He said that he did not want to live with me because I am a daughter of a prostitute. Now I am in this condition, without home or family.

My husband had married me without knowing about my mother's experiences in the war. He knew that I had a stepfather. My stepfather told my husband, "We don't know who Beauty's father is. I married her mother after Beauty's birth." Actually, my present stepfather is my mother's third husband; she was previously married to another man who was selected by the women's group that rehabilitated her. My mother married her second husband after she regained her mental stability after her rehabilitation. At that time, I believe, she did not remember anything. When she returned to a normal state, she didn't even know that I was her child. But she remembered that she was pregnant before she had gone mad. So she inquired about the baby and asked where I was. She learned that she had given birth to me while she was in the Pabna Mental Hospital, and because she was not in a state to take care of me, I was sent to an orphanage in Gaibandha where I grew up.

From the beginning my new stepfather, my mother's third husband, knew all about my mother's experiences in the war. But he accepted her, although her second husband had left her. He is a good man. And if you meet him, you will also realize that. But due to this society, he thinks he cannot accept me. He has accepted my mother although our society does not accept it. But he does not want his daughters' families to interact with me because he is afraid it will cause problems for them and their families may break up because of me. When I visit my mother's house he tells me, "I am happy to see you have come to visit your mother. Please stay and eat with us." But he never encourages me to stay beyond the meal.

Neither my mother nor her husband is bothered where I go, what I eat, whether I have food or not; they don't care about that. When I am with them they talk to me nicely; there is no problem to be nice in words. My mother goes on tolerating everything silently. There is nothing that she can say now. She can't hide from her life story. People look at us as bad women; especially they look at me as deviant. I am "bad," "fallen" in their eyes. I don't have a human life, even though I may look human to you. I have no shelter or shade over my head, there is no one, there is no way I can work and make my living. There is no one to help me, to give me work; I have nowhere to go.

You were asking me about my marriage and husband. My husband burnt me with cigarettes [she points to several wound marks on her arms and neck]. He burnt both my hands. My husband tortured me; he used to beat me and once left me in a sewage drain. He thought I was dead and left me there. A passerby found me and took me to the hospital. This happened six or seven months back. I went to the police station to register the case. But no one is interested to help me get justice.

I was married in 1990. My husband saw me during a cultural performance. I sing Rabindra Sangeet,[2] and I was singing for the orphanage in the show. I was still living in the orphanage because I had nowhere to go. I was sixteen years old or so then. He liked me a lot and proposed marriage to me. I was married off from the orphanage. Initially, he did not know anything about my mother. After ten years he found out about her. He was very upset. I had two sons by then. He decided to abandon me and forbid me from having any relationship with my sons. He took me to Dhaka and sold me there. It was a brothel. He said, "Your mother is a whore, and you are one, too." I escaped from the brothel and came here. But no one wants me. I don't have any place to go. Where will I go now? I wish the government would allow me to stay in the orphanage again. . . .

Where will I stay now, I am just left in the street. I am tortured by the street boys day after day. When I went to the police station to complain about my husband and his abuse, the officer told me, "You can't pay the money we need to take interest in your case, but can you make us happy . . . can you make us happy with *something else?*" I asked, "What is something else?" They said, "You don't understand anything? All right, we will send a man in the evening, you come with him." I thought that some other officer might be willing to listen and that they wanted me to meet him to request his help. Hence they are encouraging me to go and meet this man.

When I arrived there, there were many men, and they started saying indecent things to me. I protested and asked them why they were doing this to me, why they were not interested to help me. They said, "Will you be able to pay the money? If you can't please us with other means leave at once." They called me all kinds of insulting names and forced me out of the office. I went to the superintendent of police and informed him what his men had done to me. Nothing happened to them, and no one punished my husband for abusing me.

In this society, either women like us have to go to the police station with a huge amount of money to file a case, or women like us have no other options but to commit suicide. Those who don't have anyone on earth shouldn't ask for justice, they should rather commit suicide; I think that is the best option. How long can I live alone like this? Here my mother can't take me to her home, and society will not allow me to live peacefully; what other option do I have? Why are children like me born?

FIRDOUSI PRIYABHASANI, DHAKA

It was a nightmare for me. — FIRDOUSI PRIYABHASANI

Firdousi Priyabhasani is a remarkably brave woman who has come out publicly to testify to the rape that she suffered during the war. In a society such as Bangladesh, where rape is deemed a victim's problem and discussion about it is taboo, Firdousi has demonstrated unusual courage in daring to speak out and break the silence. Normative Bengali society deems this act of speaking about rape as a transgression of social practice, but it is intrigued by Firdousi's story and consumes it with the passion of a voyeur. Her testimony of rape is available in many different versions and formats, within and outside Bangladesh, both in English and in Bangla. In Bangladesh, every discussion about sexual violence in 1971 includes a mention of Firdousi's experience. As such, Firdousi has become an emblematic figure; this creates several problems in accessing her as an individual person. Also, the established story about her rape encroaches on our personal understanding of the event and her experiences.

When I arrived in Bangladesh in January 2001, many people recommended that I meet and interview Firdousi. I was very keen to hear her story firsthand. Particularly, I wanted to engage her on the issue of sexual violence as a war strategy. Was rape used to humiliate a community, or was it directed to make women more vulnerable? Did she think that her rapists were acting out nationalism when they raped her? How did her family react when she gave a public statement about her rape during the war? How have her social relationships changed since? In other words, I wanted to explore through her story how the personal sphere

Firdousi Priyabhasani.
(Courtesy of Abu Nasir, University of North Carolina, Central)

of an individual's life was being reshaped and configured by public political acts and speech. I was also interested to hear from her if her story influenced the national production of history in post-liberated Bangladesh. How does she evaluate society and the state of gender politics in Bangladesh now? I was, however, very uncomfortable approaching her with these questions and queries. It seemed intensely personal and prying, and raised several questions for me about research ethics and the outcome of pursuing oral history with living subjects. Thus, even after three months of being in Bangladesh, I did not make the attempt to meet Firdousi.

One afternoon during a casual conversation with Shahriar Kabir in his office, he offered to introduce me to Firdousi, who is a relative of his and an active participant in the Ghatak Dalal Nirmul Committee (GDNC), usually translated as the Committee to Exterminate the Killers and Collaborators, whose mission is to fight for justice on behalf of the Bengali victims of 1971.[3] He indicated that Firdousi would be very keen to meet and talk with me. I accepted Shahriar Kabir's offer; it seemed appropriate since he was deeply concerned about victims' empowerment through voicing their stories. I met Firdousi in her house that evening and followed this initial meeting with several more meetings in her home. Over time, I think I got to know her beyond her story, as a person and as a friend.

I still remember the first time we started talking about 1971 and of her experiences, pain, and suffering. It was a Sunday morning in April 2001. We were sitting outside in the veranda so that Firdousi could keep an eye on and direct the laborer who was building a thatched greenhouse for her plants in preparation of the impending monsoon rains. We were discussing the poetry of Rabindra Nath Tagore, and Firdousi was recit-ing from memory some of his compositions on nature and beauty. She stopped somewhere in mid-sentence and said, "Rabindra's poems are part of our identity; we have maintained it despite so many assaults on it, particularly by the Pakistanis." I cannot recall how we moved from this discussion to her personal story, but Rabindra's poems helped us to break the silence of the unspoken words that were lurking in the back-ground until then. Our conversation about 1971 and her personal experi-ences continued for several days.

Initially, I did not record our conversations. I felt uneasy about re-directing our budding friendship and confining it to a research project; at some level I suppose I did not want my interaction with Firdousi to end. I realized that unless I recorded her words, I would not be able to tell her story in her words. When I addressed this to her, she said, "Of course, you can put everything on tape; I trust you will use it well. I am not ashamed to tell you what I'd suffered. I will tell you my story of 1971 for your book, and you can decide what you want to include or leave out. You and I will be friends beyond this book." Thus I started the process of recording her story. When I transcribed my recordings, though, I found gaps in the narrative, and I decided to return to Bangladesh in the summer of 2006 to meet and talk to Firdousi and some of the other women who had told me their experiences during the war. Firdousi was recuperating at home from major heart surgery, and I decided not to burden her with my questions.

The narrative below is produced verbatim (as are all the others) but is based on several different segments of recordings over a period of many months. Firdousi's story of pain and suffering, as one will find in this telling, does not begin and end in 1971. She tells it as a continuous nar-rative and identifies many different moments of suffering. Her memo-ries of violence during the war are deeply and intimately entwined with previous experiences of misery in her life, and she starts her narrative with a story of her parents' wedding and her mother's unending anguish since then. In Firdousi's story, her mother's suffering is very much a part of Firdousi's own life, and she locates her sexual victimization in 1971 within the larger story of gender violence in Bangladesh, which she experienced through her mother's marital agony.

In the established public representations of Firdousi's rape in 1971, it is described as a "moment," qualifying it as the worst possible experience that she suffered. Her life before and after the rape is unknown to her readers; her entire being is captured and frozen within the moment of rape. Firdousi, according to this representational trope, must be accessed only as a victim because this has become her identity. The victimhood of Firdousi is critically analyzed by scholars and the Bangladeshi public, some even questioning if this is a fictionalized or false portrayal, as Sharmila Bose (2007) has recently argued. Firdousi challenges and undoes this reductive and dehumanizing reading of a false victim in the story she told me. She evaluates her life alongside her mother's as a series of moments of suffering, and she recognizes that this condition is shared by many women in Bangladesh. Rape in 1971 is located within this shared condition of women's sufferings.

Of course, Firdousi cannot forget the repeated sexual violence that she endured during the period of the war. She tries to suppress the memory of the gang rape by the Pakistani officers because it disturbs and unnerves her, but she cannot blot out the experience. As she recalls, it was a moment of total loss, beyond suffering, a moment when life itself was suspended for her. But following this horrific incident, her relationship with a Pakistani captain, who she recalls as Altaf Karim, became a beautiful experience of love for her. One may say that Firdousi is a victim of Stockholm syndrome and her relationship with Altaf Karim must be evaluated through this lens. For Firdousi, though, there is no name she can give to this relationship, but she has a distinct memory of her love for Captain Karim and his for her even three decades later.

Firdousi struggles with the memory of her rape and the pain that followed. What troubles her the most, like most survivors, is the negativity of Bangladeshi society toward them for suffering rape. Firdousi is despised by many in Bangladesh because she publicly told her memories of violence. How dare she tell her story and shame the moral core of Bangladeshi society? Firdousi continues to defy this social sanction and tells her experiences even though she is shunned and ridiculed by those who are closest to her—her natal family.

What do we learn from this brave woman? I have asked myself this question often and have come up with a variety of answers. Most importantly, I have learned from her the power of telling and defying the silence that stifles life. A story cannot encapsulate and tell the entirety of a person's life, but it is the first step toward getting to know the person for recognizing the shared condition of our lives. Women like Firdousi have been able to harness their painful memories to give meaning to their experiences, and the power of their stories makes us grasp that the human self is fragile but resilient, unyielding yet compromising. The secret of being human is to accept this condition without passing judgment on others who are just like us. Firdousi's narrative asks Bangladeshi society to accept victim's suffering as theirs, collectively, and to remember in victim's survival the violence they had to endure.

FIRDOUSI PRIYABHASANI'S STORY

Exploitation happens when there is economic need. If you do not have money, it is your worst crime. I experienced torture due to our poverty right from my childhood. My mother did not come from a poor family; on the contrary, she was from a rather wealthy family. Her father, Abdul Ahmed, was a very successful lawyer in Khulna, later he served as a speaker in the Pakistan Assembly. He was also a well-known philanthropist. My mother's marriage was arranged by some relatives, and my grandfather agreed to the proposal because my father was an educated man. He thought it would be a good match for my mother. My father used to be a college teacher. Even before the wedding, though, there was a lot of tension in my father's family. His father sent a long list of demands to my maternal grandfather. My mother's family was not Syed, like my father's; hence they demanded from my mother's father a huge dowry to get his daughter married to a Syed groom.[4] The list kept growing. My maternal grandfather wrote back, saying that he was not "selling his daughter," and this made my father's family very angry. They refused to attend the wedding. No one came to the wedding. My father showed up at 11 P.M. with only a briefcase in his hand. But my mother's father was a very kind man, and he did not make a scene. He gave his daughter in marriage to my father as promised, and he gave her a lot of gifts and a huge amount of jewelry. But it was not enough for my father's family; they were very greedy. They continued to demand more and more things after the wedding.

Besides his teaching job, my father was involved in cultural activities and used to dance in Afrida Bulbul's troupe. At work, he was considered a progressive person and was a champion of women's education. But at home he was a different person. My father was given a nice house because of his job in the college. We lived in this house when I was growing up. But there was no peace. I remember one day, he dragged me out of school and beat me with his belt all the way home because he had lost his passport. He wanted me to give it to him. He had beaten all my brothers and sisters for that. We did not know what a passport was, so we could not reply. Our neighbors heard us crying. One of them, a writer, Sengupta, intervened and asked my father to stop beating us. My father replied to him that it was a family matter, and the man was too embarrassed and went away.

My mother used to give birth to a child each year, and I had to take care of the baby. I used to be sad because I had to miss school all the time and would do very poorly in the exams. For that my father would beat me mercilessly. Ultimately, my maternal grandfather took me to his house so that I could study there. My father was such a hypocrite. He used to teach girls and tell them that education is very important for women's liberation, but he was against giving me a proper education. I was really interested in my studies, but there was no support from my father, and I couldn't bear to see him torture my mother. For my father, my mother deserved to have no rights.

Even after my mother had six children, he continued to beat and torture her. Sometimes I think given the torture that my mother suffered she should have ended up in a mental asylum. I don't know how she continued to live. You see, Shahriar Kabir's mother is my mother's sister. Seeing my mother's condition, she became extremely afraid to get married. She cried a lot at the time of her marriage; all the girls of my mother's generation were afraid to get married after they saw what had happened to my mother. I want to tell you about a few incidents how my mother was tortured because they are the most painful to me. I think you will understand my life story and experiences in 1971 better if you know what I'd experienced in my childhood.

When my mother was pregnant with her seventh child, our father left us for six or seven months; no one knew where he was. We were staying in my paternal grandparents' home in Faridpur. I was eight years old then. At 6:30 A.M. my mother started having labor pains. She asked me to call the midwife, Nirupama Aunty. My mother suffered from pain until 8 P.M., and my brother was born. But my grandparents did not even come once to see her and didn't give us any food to eat that night. My mother's father used to send plenty of money for my mother's expenses, but my paternal grandparents would never give her the money. We had nothing to sustain us, so my mother wrote a letter to her cousin, who was a police officer in Kustia, and sought his help. He came and took us to his home. He created a really pleasant atmosphere for us so we didn't feel humiliated and embarrassed to stay in a relative's home. In the meantime, my mother contacted her sister-in-law who used to live in Kustia. She asked my mother to come to her house immediately. I protested and begged her not to go, but I couldn't stop my mother. I went to my aunt's house when my mother did not return after a couple of hours. When I reached her house, the servant told me that my father was there too and had beaten my mother mercilessly because she had left her in-laws' home without his permission. This was planned by my aunt, who had invited my mother to get beaten by my father. When I entered the room, I saw my mother was lying in bed, wounded, and my father was sitting and smoking beside her. He asked me to sit with her because she was ill and went away to make some coffee. The baby was with the nanny. I told him she wasn't ill but that he had beaten her and I started crying. My mother told me she had to suffer because she did not listen to me. When she came into the house, her sister-in-law, my aunt, took the baby from her, and my father who was hiding behind the stairs started hitting her when she tried to climb the stairs to fetch the baby. From that day on, I kind of matured and hardened; I stopped talking to my father.

As a result of this incident, our uncle wired my maternal grandfather, who, in turn, sent a person to fetch us. My grandfather was serving in the high court then. He was wealthy and could support us. We were seven brothers and sisters, and he gave us shelter. But we were not loved. Nobody wanted us there except my grandfather. Our uncles were very unhappy that my mother had returned to her father's house and that he was paying for all of us. They kept telling my mother that she had to "find her way" and plan for the future. We were served the smallest portions of food as a gesture that they did not want us in the house. My grandfather encouraged my mother to continue her studies and bought her numerous books. My mother started studying and preparing for her exams. But my father found out and sent a messenger to my mother. The person who came on behalf of my father pleaded with my mother to return to her husband and told her that my father will commit suicide if she did not go back to him. He requested my grandfather to give my father another chance and assured him that since my father was teaching in a college and was a brilliant scholar, he would help my mother with her studies and enable her to take the exams. My mother went back to my father and was, once again, treated very shabbily. Once he threw hot tea on her face in front of his students when they were traveling by boat. Whenever my father called my mother to talk to her, we would be very afraid. I and my younger brother followed her to make sure she was not beaten by him, but my father would chase us away. Soon thereafter, we would hear our mother crying and screaming. This is how we grew up, without love and security.

Our father abandoned us when my mother was pregnant again, with her eighth baby. We did not hear from him for a long time but learned that he had remarried. One day all of a sudden, I met him, and he took me out to a restaurant to talk to me. He asked me to tell my mother to return to him. But I told him she was not going to come back given the way he had treated her. Also, it was obvious that our stepmother did not want us to stay in touch with our father, who agreed to it. We lost touch with our father. It was very painful to me. We were poor and everybody knew it.

In the meantime, I had gotten married and was working in a school. It was run by an Aga Khan Foundation. I used to earn eighty Indian rupees and gave tutorials at home. My husband lived on my income, as well, and I supported my brothers and younger sister and my mother, who occasionally lived with me. My biggest grief is that people took advantage of me because they saw that I was vulnerable and poor.

Let me tell you one very early incident in my life. I was only sixteen years old, but was married with two children. We had a neighbor called Hasan, who used to often call me and tell me how beautiful I was and that he loved me, and so on. Since I was in desperate need of money, I needed ten rupees—can you imagine how poor I was—I decided to ask him for his help. He asked me to visit him in the evening in his office. This man used to work for a shipping office in Dhaka. He invited me to come to his office to take the money and promised to give me fifty rupees. When I reached his office, I found there was no one there; the staff members had left. Mr. Hasan locked the door as soon as I entered. I immediately understood his intentions, but I needed the money to feed my children. When he started touching my blouse, I felt very uncomfortable. I suddenly realized that he wouldn't give me the money. I bolted out of the office and started walking; I didn't know where to go. A rickshaw pulled up behind me, and I hastily got into it. When I told the rickshaw puller that I didn't have money to pay him for the fare, he started abusing and insulting me. I offered him my pen. I felt so guilty, I started to cry.

I met Ahmed around that time. He was such a nice man; hence I cannot say anything ill against him. He was also very handsome. Lots of women desired him, and they hated me because he spent time with me. My reputation was sullied because of this. Ahmed visited me often in my house, and one day he expressed interest to live with me. I started to cry and told him that my husband was very upset about his visits and we fought everyday because of him. As a result everyone in the family was also insulting me. Ahmed promised never to leave me. We got intimate and one-half-hour later, Ahmed told me that he had to leave. I couldn't believe it. Only a few moments ago he had told me that he would stay with me forever! I was not angry with him, though. I told myself that if he is in my fate, he will come back to me. I used to love him a great deal, and I couldn't bear to live without him. I was shocked when I realized that.

In the meantime, I had to find a new job to take care of my family. I was working in the school run by the Aga Khan Foundation and earned a hundred rupees as a salary. But it was not enough to feed an entire family—my two children, husband, and mother-in-law, as well as the domestic help we had at home. They all depended on my income. I used to be always hungry and couldn't teach well. I often fell asleep in the classroom. The children came from rich families and never respected me. They saw me tired, sleepy, and I always wore the same sari. I could not even contribute to the teachers' fund to have tea. I was rejected by them, too.

It was Karamat Ali Shah who had helped me to get the job. I was recently married, and my husband was studying in college. My husband's name was Yunus Islam. He was a very good student, and I thought I should support him to study further. But I did not know how I could help. Incidentally there was a job advertised in the District Commissioner's Office. The district commissioner was Karamat Ali Shah. I applied and was called for an interview. When he saw me, I think he realized that something was wrong. He was very kind to me and asked me if I had eaten anything. Nowadays it is hard to find people who care for others like he did. He told me that since I looked too young I wouldn't have authority in the office and no one will listen to me. But I was very keen to get the job because it paid one hundred and fifty rupees as a salary for a few hours of work. I told him that I was married and had a child who was five days old. He felt very sorry for me and referred me to Junaid Sheikh, who gave me the teaching job. But I couldn't concentrate on the job, as I told you, because I used to be hungry and always worried about money for my husband's school fees, food, and so on.

Added to this was the torture that my mother-in-law meted out to me. Although I was the only earning member in the family, my mother-in-law used to be very cruel toward me, particularly when it came to food. She used to hide the food from me. She would feed herself, her son, and even the maid servant before serving me. She was extremely jealous of my relationship with my husband. Often she put a blanket next to him and would lie down herself and ask me not to come close to him. Once my husband and I went out; I was pregnant with my eldest son. We went for a walk and when we came back home we found she had fainted. My husband tickled her feet, and she jumped up laughing; she was pretending, and my husband understood it. She forbade my husband to drink water if I served him because she accused me of having a bad character. He never protested against her dictates.

I found work in a jute mill as a secretary. Aslam bhai [a cousin] was my entry ticket into the jute mill. It was owned by an Aga Khani and Ismaili businessman. Those days I did not know Ahmed. One day, he came into the office and demanded whether I had sent his phonogram. I told him that I had a lot of work to do and had not sent his phonogram. He rebuked me that I was useless and not efficient like Ms. Banu, to which I responded that I was not Ms. Banu. He asked me to make some telephone calls for him, which I did. I did not like him at all, at first.

My husband was very jealous of me. He asked me to borrow five hundred rupees from my cousin Aslam bhai, and I asked him but he refused me the money. Aslam bhai reminded me that I was in this situation because I had married into a hopeless family. My continuous poverty was the root cause of why men took advantage of me. Another time, I needed a hundred rupees, so I went to a businessman called Kalam. He was the husband of an actress called Nazma Anwar. He used to come to Khulna, where he had his business. I asked him for some money, and he promised to give me the money in the evening. When I went to fetch the money from his office, I found he was quite drunk. As soon as I entered the room, he locked the collapsible gate of the office. He came toward me and held me very hard. I started to cry and asked him to let me go. I was helpless, so I could not misbehave because there was no way to get out of the place. I pretended I was a virgin. He derided me telling me that I am not good looking enough for him to rape me. I had seen life very closely, even before 1971.

My husband did horrible things to me. He spread a lot of rumors about me. He went to my boss in the jute mill and told him that I was eloping with Ahmed and that I wouldn't be available to work in the office anymore. Next day, when I went to work the managing director called me and told me that he had sacked me because my husband did not want me to work there. Although I had worked there for four years, I had no recourse. I never received my provident fund or termination salary. I had taken so much salary advance in the past that there was no money left in my account. Thereafter, I got my divorce. My husband called me many times, but I refused to return to him. I had been married to him for ten years. But he never worked for a single day to earn money to take care of the family. He never bought me anything and depended on me for every expense. There was no point returning to a man like him.

I called an old contact of mine in the office, Jahangir, and asked him if I could have my job back. I had known Jahangir for twelve years, and he used to refer to me as *Baji* [sister]. He advised me to go to the office and talk to the officer there. I was not certain if the office was open then. This was after March 25, 1971, after the initial military action in Dhaka. Many people had fled, and even Khulna was quite deserted. Jahangir's wife had also left with his three children. He told me, "Baji, I will take you to the office since it is not safe for you to go alone." But I told him I preferred to take a rickshaw because I was not comfortable sitting on a motorcycle. He gave me the address of the house where I had to go. I had seen this house many times. In fact, every evening on my way back from the office I used to look at the house. It was a beautiful old house. When I entered the house, I saw there were glasses of whiskey and other kinds of booze lying around. It seemed that the owners were not there. Jahangir was there with a couple of other men. He hit me on my face and nose and boxed my ears. I was taken aback; I couldn't understand what was happening. They told me, "Let us have some fun." I was very angry. I kicked one man and asked him to make room for me so that I could leave. He yelled at me. He was very offended that I insulted him, and it hurt his ego that a woman had kicked him. I told him the irony was that I could not even afford to buy slippers, and he was expecting me to amuse him! I told him not to trouble me as I was not in a mood to have fun!

The gang rape happened later. I was back on the job because I had no other way of supporting myself and my family. They dragged me into a taxi. There were four or five people who raped me all together. It was a nightmare for me. I become unconscious when I think about it. Although I try hard to forget the incident, my mind is free and it does not let me control it. Even today when I go out alone in a rickshaw if there are two or three boys together I ask the rickshaw driver to move faster. It was a nightmare for me. When I was not cooperating with them, they opened both the doors of the car. They started rubbing Vicks on my private parts, which, you know, can be dangerous. They could not find soap, and they started cursing and swearing. These men were officers of the Pakistan Army, mostly captains. The others below the rank of captain were worse.

There was an officer among them who helped me after the gang rape. His name was Altaf Kareem, and he served in Brigade 121. He came only one and a half months before the independence of Bangladesh, at least, that is when I met him. If he had come earlier, it would have been better. I would have been more sincere and married him. I still have feelings for him. I was twenty-two and he was thirty years old. We loved each other very much. He was willing to take responsibility for my children and support them. He was an ethical person. When he left me for the last time, he gave me a salute and told me, "Maybe, I will be killed." I never saw him again.

But first let me tell you more about the gang rape. It was after 3 A.M. or so at night. They had tried to rape me for two days before that night. As I said earlier they applied Vicks on my private parts. They gagged me, and it nearly suffocated me. So I indicated to them that I will cooperate with them if they uncovered my mouth. I begged them to finish their business fast. They were driving and stopping and raping me. They tried in Prem Bagh and Picnic Corner. It was near Jessore, before Bakchor. In the picnic ground a guard was there so they couldn't rape me there. They were really enjoying it, it was obvious to me, but I was nearly dead. Once they stopped the car and dragged me out. They pulled me by my hair. It hurt so much I couldn't think whether it was happening to me or someone else. They kept shouting at me, "You are a Hindu. You are a spy." I used to wear a bindi [dot] in those days. They asked me to surrender and admit that I had committed murder. I refused to do so.

I was not a nationalist or anything like that. I did not even love my country then. I was struggling to stay alive, being raped by five men. At home my condition was no better without a husband and with three children that I had to provide for as well as my mother, brothers, and younger sister. Where was the time for me to think about nation and freedom? Neither was I that intelligent to understand politics. But I refused to say I had murdered someone when I hadn't. I said, "Take me to court." There was one person in the group who helped me. He was very nice and also very clever. After they gang-raped me, they took me to a bunker. They showed me the women who were kept there; their condition was truly terrible. They were living in filth, in a hell, so it appeared to me. They told me, "We will make you like them if you don't cooperate." There the women were raped by rank-and-file soldiers, and the condition of the women was inhuman. But I told my perpetrators that they can do anything to me but I was not going to admit to having committed murder.

The officer who had taken pity on me decided to deal with the situation. He told his fellow officers that he will handle me and get the truth out of me. Actually, he used this ruse to protect me. I was thus spared from gang rape again. I became his lover, and, believe me, it was really love. My younger sister, who lived with me, knew about it, but she was very emotional and wanted to commit suicide when she heard what had happened to me. She started screaming and shouting, but I took a sari and shut her mouth. I had another sister; she was shameless. She went to the Pakistani army officers of her own will. No one raped her forcibly. Now she refuses to talk about it. She thinks it will ruin her elder daughter's life. I told her it may be a blessing because her husband does not respect her. I am telling you all this now because the time has come to reveal the truth. I did not tell all this in the testimonies I had given before. Most of the time my interviewers did not want to hear the whole story. They only wanted me tell them about the rape. They refused to hear beyond that.

Life after my gang rape did not change much. I continued to work in the office but I was not forced to have sex. Everyone teased and insulted me, though, on account of my rape, including my ex-mother-in-law and ex-sister-in-law. The Bihari men in our neighborhood used to follow me to work and tease me all the way to the office. Even the Aga Khani men did not spare me. Some army officers came to my office and asked me to serve them too. When I refused to speak to them, they started calling me all kinds of names. Altaf Kareem protected me, and I was his lover. But I also loved Ahmed. He had left me a few months before this happened. He was frightened, I think. He went to the village, and I was grief stricken. If I were in his shoes, I would have never left him, but he left me. What could I do? I could have run away from Khulna, but I did not want Ahmed to look for me. I wanted him to find me in the place where I always lived and worked. I didn't leave because I hoped he would return. Ahmed never came to meet me during this time; he was married and morally obligated to his wife. He called me a couple of times, and I told him that I didn't need an apology and hung up the telephone. He had nothing else to say.

After 1971, I was considered the "number one" prostitute in Bangladesh, at least, by my family. I was not allowed to attend wedding ceremonies because they considered me inauspicious. The only person who did not tell me anything rude and mean was my mother. She was a broadminded person, and as she was a widow she depended on me. She did not want to create bad feelings between me and her. After her death when I read her diary, I found that she had written about me that I had never hurt her in her life. For me that is my greatest achievement, that I had never hurt my mother.

The first time I came out publicly about my victimization in 1971 was in 1999. It took me twenty years to regain some sense of self-respect and be able to talk about it. People didn't like to hear about it initially. Strangers used to call and insult me, asking me the price for my service. My mother was alive when my first interview came out in a magazine called *Bichitra*. She looked at the article, but she did not say anything. She could not speak because she had a stroke. I was encouraged to talk about my experiences by Hamida Hussain. She called me to her office and told me, "You have worked so well in the Taslima case, please collect a testimony of rape in 1971." Later Shaheen Akhtar, who also worked in the office (Ain-o-Salish Kendra), called me. She told me that they could pay 50,000 rupees for the testimony.[5] I told them that I will try and find out if someone will testify about their rape. I told myself, "[Hamida] Apa does not know that there is darkness below the lamp." I went home and thought about it. You know, I was always in need of money, and 50,000 rupees was a lot of money that they were offering. I convinced myself that I will tell them my story in the third person as if it had happened to someone else whom I knew. Thus, I would protect my identity. I had not yet really come to terms about the rape to publicly talk about it. While recounting the story to Shaheen the next day, however, I started to cry at some point and used my name rather than the other person's. Shaheen immediately noted the slip and encouraged me to tell my story. I told her and Hamida Apa, and they helped me to tell my story to the magazine. I told them then and I will tell you now that what I regret most is what happened to women after 1971. I cry for our lives post-1971. We were physically assaulted in 1971, but after 1971 we were both physically and mentally assaulted. Today, I have no shame to say I am a victim. But I continue to ask why are only the victims identified? Where are their rapists? Why are their pictures not taken and put on the front-page?

Despite the torture I suffered, I still remember one pleasant memory. I had experienced the love of one man during this horrific ordeal. There is no ego or pride in love, and I want to talk about Altaf Kareem's love for me, but in Bangladesh no one wants me to talk about it. I have to tell an incomplete story of 1971 every time I give an interview. This is the first time I am telling my entire experience before and after 1971.

TASLIMA'S MOTHER, DINAJPUR

They came from behind, I became unconscious. — TASLIMA'S MOTHER

I arrived in Dinajpur, in northwest Bangladesh from Saidpur toward the end of February. In Saidpur, where I stayed for several days following my extended stay in Rangpur that had been my first research site, I set up meetings with several different groups of journalists, local activists representing different community and interest groups, as well as school teachers and administrators to enable me to conduct research there. They facilitated my meetings with a number of survivors who represented the Hindus and Muslims from the Bengali and Bihari communities. Women told me a variety of stories concerning 1971; each conversation was heavy with sorrow. The stories of violence that women told were horrific and painful to hear. Sexual violence, women recalled, was rampant during the war. Listening to these women's memories, day after day, I came to the conclusion that almost anyone in Saidpur could tell me a story because the people of that town and the neighboring villages—the Biharis, Marwaris, and Bengalis, Hindus, Muslims, and Adivasis (tribal or indigenous groups)—as a whole had suffered. They are all survivors and witnesses to violence.

The men in Saidpur were victims and perpetrators of violence; some colluded with the Pakistani soldiers to victimize Bengalis, and, in turn, some Bengali men assisted the Mukti Bahini guerillas to attack non-Bengali and Bihari communities. Muslims threatened Hindu Marwaris, who were mostly involved in local businesses and many of whom fled to India, and, in turn, they reported their experiences with a great deal of exaggeration in Kolkata, leading to a deepening rift and increased violence between the Hindus and Muslims in India. The distinction between good and evil, victim and perpetrator, became blurry and murky for me in Saidpur. It was an awful realization that depressed me, and I found it difficult to continue the project of collecting women's memories. But there were many in Saidpur who believed in my project, and they urged me to continue the work and move on to Dinajpur, both for a change of scene and to meet with different groups of women who may have diverse stories to tell.

In Dinajpur I did not have established contacts. In searching for local groups to enable me to start my work, I decided to visit the office of the local district administrator. Also, I had an immediate need to find suitable accommodations for our stay. I suppose being a person of Indian descent did not help my situation there. Dinajpur shares a border with India, and I suspect unpleasant border politics and clashes between border security personnel have penetrated and poisoned neighborly relationships in the region. The local district administrator was almost hostile toward me when I invoked his help for accommodations and was further irritated when he learned about the purpose of my visit to Dinajpur—to meet survivors of sexual violence of 1971. He muttered something about it "being a waste of time." Obstinately, he provided me accommodations in a government guest house that was generally used by lower-level security personnel and trainers. I suppose he deemed I deserved to stay with "ordinary men" because of the "ordinary" nature of my research project.[6] Hence, although I had intended to spend an extended period of time in Dinajpur, I could not do so.

Dinajpur being a border town there is a lot of movement of both people and goods. Both formal and informal sectors of the economy are thriving and generate brisk commerce across the border. A sense of busyness and chaos permeated the town, and anonymity marked most interactions, so it seemed to me. It was difficult to engage people, particularly about the events of 1971.[7] Whoever I spoke with mentioned that they were not residing in Dinajpur town during the war but had fled to their village. It appears that violence during the war was intense, and the town came under siege due to heavy fighting between the Pakistani soldiers and the Mukti Bahini guerillas.

I started my research in the Women's Affairs Office and sought their assistance to meet survivors of 1971 to listen to their memories. The office staff was friendly, although lax and indifferent to my request, and expressed their frank opinion that it was useless to try and locate survivors three decades later, since most of them had moved or passed away. After a great deal of persuasion and repeated requests, the officer gave me Taslima's mother's address. I followed up on the lead and finally located Taslima's mother in western Dinajpur district in a village close to the border.

My research assistant, Rafi, and I rode a local bus and then a rickshaw to reach the village where Taslima's mother lived. It was a long way to her home. Taslima's mother, as one will read in the narrative that follows, was living with her daughter at the time I met her. En route, as we walked through what seemed like a desolate byroad, we met an elderly man who directed us to her house. We soon learned that he was Taslima's husband. He took us to the house and explained to her the purpose of our visit, to listen to her experiences in 1971. Thus we were spared an awkward entry and a long explanation regarding the purpose of our visit.

Taslima's mother is a young woman; she is in her early forties, but her husband is considerably older. Their age difference is evident and striking. Initially, she was reluctant to speak with us, although she welcomed us and encouraged us to sit outside and talk with her. With some more encouragement from her husband, she finally invited me inside to sit and talk with her. She did not ask Rafi to come in. This was quite understandable and acceptable to us.

Although Rafi and I had traveled together throughout Bangladesh, during conversations with women Rafi generally had to excuse himself. The reasons were many. Women were generally reluctant to speak in the presence of a man about their memories of sexual violence. For Rafi, too, it was embarrassing for him to listen to their memories because most of these women represented his mother's generation. These reasons aside, usually when Rafi and I went to a village, our visit would spark a lot of curiosity. The men, in particular, were very anxious to know about the purpose of our visit and about Rafi's relationship with me. He had to pose himself as my brother because in rural Bangladesh it would not be acceptable that a man and a woman who are unrelated to each other travel and spend time together. To them it was not important that I am several years older than Rafi and that his relationship with me was that of an academic colleague. Rafi therefore had the task of talking with the men and presenting a "normal version" (Rafi's words) of my research as a historical project about 1971. Further, he decided to present me as his sister. Often, at the end of the day when Rafi and I compared our notes, he would inform me of the "happenings outside," while I spoke about the "inside." Generally, it appeared that the men's curiosity veered on hostility, but Rafi managed to stave them off by telling about Dhaka, his university experiences, and other stories so that I could continue my conversation with the women.

On entering the compound of her house, I saw that it was made up of several freestanding thatched and mud-baked rooms. Each room served as separate quarters for the families living there. The room belonging to Taslima's parents was separate from hers. On seeing me approach her mother's quarters, Taslima went inside her room. I sat with her mother on the mud plinth of her room, and she asked me several questions about my life, the purpose for undertaking research on 1971, and what I hoped to accomplish. On learning that I was planning to write a book about women's memories, she was very excited. She told me that she had hoped that someday she would be able to write the story of her life, but she was demoralized after she lost her diary in which she had recorded her story "as it had happened at that time." We talked about several other issues for an hour or so, including my travels in Bangladesh, her visits to her relatives' home in India before the war, and her general memories of the place and people before 1971. I did not push her to tell me her story, but both of us were conscious about the purpose of my visit. Although it was late in the afternoon by then, and I was aware that it would be a long trek from the village back to Dinajpur town, I did not want to leave without hearing her memories. She struck me as a person who had a lot to say but was not ready to tell it yet.

"I don't know why, but I want to tell you about my experiences in 1971," she blurted out suddenly. "I want you to call my daughter to listen to what I have to say. She needs to hear it. Her husband is not here now, so she has some free time. She has never understood me and has blamed me for many things. She does not know my suffering." On her request, I walked over to Taslima's quarters and asked her to join us for a cup of tea and some conversation. Taslima hesitated for a moment and then agreed to join us.

Taslima's mother, Taslima, and I sat and talked till late into the evening. Taslima got up once to fetch us some more tea and biscuits. For over two hours her mother told her story; Taslima listened to it but showed no emotion at all. When her mother finished her story, Taslima got up and left without saying goodbye to me. In the meantime, her younger brother who had returned from work came in to greet his mother. Our conversation stopped, and we all sat together and talked for a little while about school, work, and other everyday topics. It was almost dusk when Rafi and I said goodbye to Taslima's parents. We walked to the end of the village and were very fortunate to find a rickshaw to take us to the bus station.

The story that Taslima's mother shared with me is not different from many others that I had heard in rural Bangladesh. The Pakistani soldiers and their local collaborators, rajakars, often went to villages to terrorize the people and find pro-liberation supporters to put an end to the anti-state activities brewing in these rural areas. On many occasions, jealous neighbors called upon the army to "pick them up"—pro-liberation Bengalis or neighbors that they did not like, which provided an opportunity for the Pakistani soldiers to terrorize and humiliate the local people by ransacking their granaries, stealing their chickens, goats, and cows, and, worst of all, sexually abusing any women who caught their fancy. The experiences of Taslima's mother are framed within this scenario. She was attacked by strangers in her own village, but no one defended or protected her from the violence. Rather, all of them, even members of her family, fled from the scene of the crime. The sudden, mindless attack, however, had a long-lasting effect on her life. In fact, in one moment, her life was changed forever, without forewarning.

Women in Bangladesh who suffered the heinous crime of rape during the war have been forced to live with guilt and in silence for the rest of their lives. In telling the story of Taslima's mother, I hope to tell the story of many more women whose voices have not been heard in Bangladesh because they belong to the nondescript masses. They are neither powerful nor confident enough to be able to demand that state and society listen to them and provide justice. But if we take a moment and listen to their silence, we can hear their painful experiences, which to this day haunt and punish them. Their silence forces us to question why victims suffer the punishment for a crime they did not commit.

THE STORY OF TASLIMA'S MOTHER

It is no use talking about it now. I am a destitute woman, and no one has helped me in all these years. I do not even have a house of my own. You have come to meet me in this village, so far away from where I normally live. This is my daughter's house; her name is Taslima. I have lived here for five months. Taslima is not the oldest of my children. I have four children: three girls and a boy. Taslima was my third child. I have two more daughters staying in Dinajpur, in the town. How did you find me here?

No one has ever approached me to hear my story of 1971. They have all forgotten us. Now the country is independent. They got Bangladesh because everyone fought and sacrificed for the nation. The women sacrificed the most, but no one rewarded us for our sacrifices. I went to the Women's Rehabilitation Center and told them my life story. But no one did me justice. I worked in the Mahila Daftar [Office for Women's Affairs] since the fourteenth day of independence. I went to Dinajpur and stayed there for three to four months because I was pregnant. I was only twelve years old then. Now I am more than forty years old. I have suffered all my life. My husband used to work for the Rehabilitation Center, but we earned very little and could not build a house of our own in the town, so we have to live here with our daughter for the time being. This is not even a village, as you can see. There are no people for miles around. When the rains come, we are marooned from the outside world.

My original home was in Paleshbari. My maternal uncle was a business man and used to come to Dinajpur for his work. He asked me to go to the center, which was opened in Dinajpur. The incident happened to me in my village. But I have never spoken about it to anyone, not even my daughters know about it. I did not tell them, and they did not want to hear about it either. I wrote everything down in a diary, and I thought someday I will give it to my children, maybe before I die, but unfortunately the diary got lost. I had kept some money inside my diary. I don't think I should talk about it in front of my children, but I can tell you now because they are not here. My son was keeping very bad company. I think he was doing some kind of bad things like *nisha* [drugs].

He owed the guys money for the nisha but he did not have money to pay them back. I think he told them that I used to hide some money in my diary. So one day, they came to the house when I was not there and stole the diary. I believe they took the money and then threw away the diary. What use would they have of a diary, but for me it was precious, it was my life story.

No one has cared about us. It is no use to tell others what happened to my life, or what have been the problems with my children, and so forth. All kinds of horrible things have happened in my life. The government has never helped people like me. They did not even bother. They could have if they wished. That is the reason I am telling you that there is no point listening to my story now. What kind of benefit will I get in my old age? What good will it do for me even if I get help now? My life was ruined many years ago. But you have come from a distant country and have found me in this unknown place with the purpose to listen to my story. I would feel terrible to send you away without telling you my story. I don't know why, but I feel like telling you all about it. I want to tell you from the beginning. My daughter should also know what I had endured. It is time she listens to me. Will you ask her to join us? She will not listen to me if I ask her. . . .

We went to the Indian border when the war broke out and stayed there for a long time. But I was homesick and wanted to come back to my village. People in the village told us that khans, rajakars, and their helpers were torturing people. I did not know who they were, but the rajakars who came to our village were all Bengali; they came to torture people with the hanadar army. It was seven or ten days after we had returned from the border. It was the month of Asin (late fall, between October and November) in the Bengali calendar, a few months before Bangladesh finally became independent. Villagers were returning to celebrate Eid.

My parents were in the village. They had sent me away because I was the eldest among the children; the others were all younger than me. My father's name was Kazibuddin, and my mother's name was Rubiya. We were all together in the village. Our village was not far from the Indian border.

It was perhaps ten or twelve days after we had returned that rajakars and khans suddenly came to our village. I was sitting by the pond and washing dishes. It was midday, after lunch. I was on the other side of the pond, and they came from behind me. I was facing south, and they came from the north, hence I could not see them. My mother saw them and ran away. She couldn't call me. She had to protect herself. There was no time to think about me. People were running for their own lives. Everyone was only looking out for himself. I shouted and I fainted! I became unconscious.

When I woke up I saw that I was in my house. I came back to my senses after four or five hours. It all happened near the pond. When I regained consciousness, I saw my mother was looking down at me. She kept staring at me, but did not say anything. I was having my monthly cycle at that time, and I became ill for many days, thereafter. I lost a lot of blood and stayed in bed. They told me not to move, and no one talked to me. I got pregnant although it was the fifth day of my menstruation. It was Allah's will. I was twelve or thirteen then and it was for the first time, I knew nothing. My period stopped from the month of July. Initially, my parents did not talk to me at all. Later when my periods stopped and I told my mother, they asked me what had happened. It had happened to me only once.

The rajakars, Punjabi, Pakistani, and khans[8] used to come every seven to ten days, and would remain in the village for two to three hours. They would go around the village and leave after that. Since my father went to work outside the village, he never saw them come and go. He knew nothing about what had happened. My periods stopped from July, and my mother took me to the doctor. My blood and urine were tested, and he told me that I was pregnant. Our country was independent by that time. My mother sent for her brother who used to live in the town. He told us about the Rehabilitation Center. He brought me to the town.

Nobody in our village knew in the beginning that I was pregnant. They came to know of it after I left the village. I became so ill that they had to take me to Rangpur for treatment; it was not possible here in Dinajpur. I was taken there after one month, and the abortion was done twenty-two to twenty-three days after I arrived in Rangpur.[9] It took me one and a half months to recover. My father and uncle both became ill due to my condition. They could not tolerate what had happened to me. They died soon thereafter. I got the news after two and a half months. That is when I decided that I will work here and not return to my village or my home. My brothers and sisters were very young, but people in our village knew about the incident and they passed obscene remarks and gossiped about me. I did not want to go back to the village and be dishonored by them. I also thought there is no chance of getting married because of what had happened to me. I had to find something to do, find a job and earn so that I could take care of myself. But it was Allah's wish, and my husband who was working in the Rehabilitation Center applied and married me. He knew my history.

We started our married life after the abortion and still today we are together. He told me at the time of our marriage that he had rescued several girls from a bunker. After the war, many such girls were found in bunkers. The bunker in which he found the girls was an old depot. This happened soon after the country was liberated. One evening as he was walking by the depot he heard some noises, like screaming and wailing. When he peered inside the building, he saw many girls in a terrible state. They were mostly naked and dirty and were like mad people. He rescued eight girls and brought them to the Rehabilitation Center.

My husband has been very kind to me, *masha' Allah*.[10] After I had my children, I approached the office for work. They gave me cleaning work to do, but the salary was very little. I asked them if they can raise it because it was not enough to support a family on our meager income. It was a growing family. So they gave me training for one month and put me in the production unit. We made small things that were sold in the shop. I worked there for thirteen or fourteen years. I had four children by then, three daughters and one son. The boy is the youngest, and he is fifteen years old now. I worked in the field and also did embroidery and stitching work for the office.

Many people think that birangonas like me were rewarded by the government, that we received monetary compensation. As far as I am concerned, I was not given any money under the birangona program. My office, which is the Women's Rehabilitation Center, did not help me though I asked Apa [the office manager] about my husband's retirement and if she could help us.[11] Maybe, I asked too late. Throughout the time we worked in the office no one offered to help us in any way. We have no savings. The office did not do anything for us, so we had to come here and live with our daughter.

I was not the only woman who went to the Rehabilitation Center. When I was there, many other girls and women were too. Many of them were very young. Every day abortions were performed. A makeshift clinic was set up, and there were many doctors who had come from outside. They did the abortions. There was no privacy or anything. But no one talked about their cases. Girls were strapped to stretchers and taken for abortions. They were like cattle. The abortions were done in tents that were set up for the purpose. After a few months, I think a couple of months or so, the clinic was closed. I know that three girls who came there were married off from the center. Others were taken back by their guardians. No one came to take me. So I never went back home. The first time I returned home was after many years, maybe ten years or so. No one recognized me. My mother was alive then. My sisters were married, and I did not see any one of them. No one was interested to meet me, and I did not want to disturb their family life. Since then I never went back to my village.

Everything that happened to girls like me was recorded. The doctor had the case histories, and Apa kept the files. They should be still available in the *daftar* [office]. You tell me that no one was willing to show you the folders. I believe that. The office staff is very lazy. They don't like to do any work. They used to order people like me to do all the work. "Clean this," "bring this," "do that," they would shout all day. But we were not paid accordingly. No one cares for people like me. Apa died some time back, and the doctor left the place. The doctor who was in the clinic was not able to treat me. So they had sent me to Rangpur to the Sishu Mangal Hospital [Child Welfare Hospital]. There were a lot of girls there; I had seen some of them. Some of them stayed for a short time, maybe seven days or so. Some even stayed for a shorter time than that, but the girls who had no home to go to and were ill stayed there for a long time.

I would have liked to work in that hospital if I was not married. I got married in 1972. The food was free there. Although I got married, I did not get anything from the government. Please note that. My husband actually took pity on me and married me. If he had not married me, my life would have been ruined. No one wanted me. Even my family turned their back on me. How would I have lived? I had very little education. I had studied to grade five. But my life was ruined for no reason.

You are the first person I have spoken to about what I had suffered in 1971 and thereafter. No one has ever asked me my story. As I told you earlier, I wrote all this down in a diary, but it got lost; it was stolen. I wish I could give it to you now. You would have understood everything. There are many other women like me. There is one old woman who lives eleven miles from here in a small village. It will be very hard for you to go there. There is no *pacca* [gravel] road to the village. You will have to walk through paddy fields to reach her. I can give you her address if you want, but I don't recommend you should go to the village. I don't think the people there will receive you well. It is closer to the Indian border. I don't meet her as such, but I get news about her now and then. Women like us have to stay together because no one else cares. When we get together, we talk about those days. But we don't talk about what happened. I don't know why. No one encouraged us; no one talked to us frankly as you are doing. Even my children did not want to hear it. We saw how my daughter behaved when I asked her to sit down and listen to my experience. She was so reluctant. Because you asked her, she obliged. But you noticed how uncomfortable she was. We have kept our silence all this time because others did not want to hear it. What good will come of it if I speak now? Will I be rewarded for anything? You see, no one cares.

I can't change what happened to me. But now I want to live in a good environment and bring up my children in a good place. I want to live with others who are nice and can help us grow and progress. I also want to save some money and earn a nice living. Is that too much to ask?

NURJAHAN BEGUM AND A GROUP OF BIHARI WOMEN, KHULNA

Women are treated like cattle. —NURJAHAN BEGUM

The Bengalis claim 1971 and the trauma of violence as an exclusive experience. Public memory is replete with stories of the suffering of Bengali people, but there is no space to remember the experiences of other groups. The most recent storytelling about 1971 is by Tahmima Anam (2008a) and is based on memories borrowed from her parents and their generation of survivors. It creates an evocative picture of the war and the coping mechanisms of Bengali people during and after the shattering violence. Tahmima asks: Who gave the West Pakistanis the exclusive right to own Pakistan? Wasn't this nation created with loving care by our grandparents' generation? In her story, she weaves the failure of the Pakistan state to deliver its promise of equal treatment to all citizens, thus forcing the Bengalis to fight for their freedom. Obviously, at the center of the narrative is memory, memory that is drenched in the loss of dignity, although the founding of Bangladesh enables some semblance of its recovery. This memory is not a writer's fanciful imagination, it is a story based on lived experiences that are told and retold in Bangladesh. The reassembled memories are now available in a narrative form, which have been standardized in the last three decades since the war.

The internal, private stories of ruptures and the confusion of those who had actually experienced the violence of 1971 have been neatly flattened in the narrative telling, and continuity is created between all Bengali people, then and now; they are all survivors of the same trauma. The events of 1971 belong to them, the Bengalis, who can remember and tell their version of the story and thus make it "their history." Those who are not included within this "memoryscape" are condemned as an enemy; there is no audience to listen to the enemy's tale. Who are the enemies of the Bengalis? Whose story is forbidden in Bangladesh today?

When I arrived in Bangladesh to begin my research, I did not know of these politics and found it hard to understand why my interlocutors were discouraging me from asking questions about the experiences of non-Bengali groups in 1971. Their vague responses of why I should not pursue a larger historical framework that includes the stories of all groups of women in Bangladesh befuddled and confused me. No event is unitary, and even though we may talk of an event in the singular, it is made up of many disparate parts and components that work and interact in multiple ways and are experienced differently by the variety of people involved. As a historian I am trained to look at details, discover the multiple dimensions, and to understand the parts alongside the story that appears as a whole. Even if I set aside the business of being an academic historian, my personal experience in 1999 with Rukhsana, a Bihari woman whom I met in Camp Geneva in Dhaka, continued to haunt me. She had told me in graphic detail about the murder of her parents and the attempted rape that forced her sister and her to escape and find shelter in the camp where they have lived ever since, nearly thirty years. How could I overlook the experiences of this woman, who like the Bengali women, too, had suffered during the war and beyond it?

I could not be persuaded by the Bengalis that the Biharis were enemies of liberation and were pro-Pakistani traitors. Although I respected Bengali sentiment and recognized the Bengali position concerning their suffering in 1971, I also had to stay true to my commitment to find memories of different groups of Bangladeshi women and tell their experiences. Within this term, *Bangladeshi*, as I understood it, is a variety of people — Muslims, Hindus, Christians, and Buddhists, as well as Chakmas, Biharis, Jayantias, and women of indigenous groups. I had to continue the search to find Bangladeshi women's memories, and I was willing to listen to what they had to tell.

Finding Bihari survivors was not easy. The first problem was access to the community. Ostracized as stateless, Biharis continue to live in camps that are ghettoized enclaves. To enter these spaces and generate a conversation one needs insider help. My research assistants both being Bengali had grown up with heavy doses of anti-Bihari rhetoric. They had never crossed the boundaries of their cognitive and emotional worlds to reach out to Biharis and develop casual acquaintances. It was a challenge for Rafi in particular. He had accompanied me on many research trips outside Dhaka. In Saidpur, after we found a local person who was willing to introduce us to Bihari women living in one of the camps, Rafi tried to dissuade me from visiting them. Nevertheless, I persisted and we went to the camp. On our return trip from the camp, Rafi expressed his grievances for "visiting the enemies." I explained to Rafi that my task as a researcher was to excavate and find and not take sides with the witnesses of 1971. It was not a good enough explanation for Rafi, but he conceded to my research agenda.

The second problem was more daunting: how does one speak with women about their intimate memories in public? There is no private space in these camps. The rooms that make up their "homes" are small six feet by eight feet windowless "containers" made of flimsy materials that are separated by thin walls. The condition in Geneva Camp is the worst of all; several generations live together with no privacy or space between them. The squalor and inadequate living conditions in Bihari camps as a whole gave us a bitter taste of the lives of the people living there. The lack of space represented the general paucities in their life. It was a harsh realization, and even Rafi recoiled from this firsthand experience in the Bihari camp.

There are greater difficulties to overcome than dealing with the sheer shock of the physical realities of camp life. When I first entered Camp Geneva in Dhaka, a cacophony of voices demanded I hear them and redress their condition. Yet, when I asked the camp dwellers to tell me their story in details, none of them could create a narrative. Speech is associated with sociability, and narrative with continuity. For the Biharis living in the rootless world made up of camps, having lost most of the members of their families and needing to create new associations with camp companions in extreme conditions, the past was lost. Most of them could not go back to their lives before they came to the camp and the nexus of persons and affections that had made a place called home because it was now obliterated. In its place was a disabling memory of a rupture, and they suffered from the brutality of that internal narrative. That took recourse in dreams and silence.

First a short word on their dreams. During the war of 1971, many of these people, or, at least, people like them, the Urdu-speaking citizens of East Pakistan, took the side of the West Pakistanis. Many of them felt compelled because of their initial impulse to migrate from India to Pakistan, which was conceived and created as a Muslim homeland, to remain true to that homeland, as they admitted to me. How could they abandon the dream of Pakistan in the face of its threat of dismemberment in 1971? These men felt bound by "sacred duty" to *qaum* (nation) to uphold that promise. In consequence they made enemies of their Bengali neighbors, who, in turn, were struggling to free themselves from the shackles of West Pakistani domination. At the end of the struggle, almost everyone in the zone of conflict had witnessed unspeakable horror and crimes in the name of nationalism. The Bihari supporters of Pakistan had lost their place in Bangladesh. They joined the retreating Pakistanis, and both groups became prisoners of war in India. They were repatriated to Pakistan two years later.[12] Many more made their way to (west) Pakistan through clandestine arrangements as well as official routes of repatriation. After April 1974, however, no more Bihari or Urdu-speaking people from Bangladesh were officially allowed into Pakistan.

Those who were stuck in Bangladesh formed the bulk of the camp dwellers, and they linger there in the hope that someday Pakistan will repatriate them. The chances of this actually happening are very dim and many are aware of it, particularly the children who are born and raised in camp life. A young man expressed this with great poignancy: "They [people of my parents' generation] keep on talking about Pakistan. They will go to their graves without ever seeing Pakistan. Who will take them?"

As the days have waned and the memory of 1971 has dimmed in Pakistan, the camp dwellers have been utterly forgotten. In this environment, where no one—neither the Pakistanis or the Bengalis—cares for them, silence has become an expression of the bitter truth that no one cares to listen to them. For many individuals the memory of the violence they suffered or witnessed is raw and they cannot speak of it. There is no story to tell; there is no transcendence in speech. Thus for these camp dwellers, the memory of 1971 lives silently, without speech, in some recess buried under the filth and hopelessness of their lives. The present mocks the past too vividly; they escape its taunts in silence.

We can never be sure what lies behind the silence of Biharis—shame, grief, confusion, hopelessness, remorse, and perhaps even regret. Nevertheless, I continued my search to hear Bihari women's memories. The majority of survivors could not tell me a story. During my initial conversations with camp dwellers in Mirpur and Saidpur, I assumed that it was a problem of the individual; she could not expand on her words and tell her experiences to enable me to comprehend what was done to her and her family. But when this pattern repeated in all subsequent conversations with Bihari women across Bangladesh, I realized Bihari women's experiences defy verbalization. The things that were done to them cannot be spoken of. But occasionally they told stories of what happened to others, of violence they had witnessed.

Violence belonged to the realm of others and was circulated as memory that was not their experience. Initially, I did not understand that this narrative plot is a kind of strategy and believed they were talking of others' sufferings, until one afternoon, after a prolonged conversation with an elderly woman who told me about the atrocities she had "witnessed," her daughter and daughter-in-law confided in me that these were her experiences that she had shared with me as if they had happened to someone else. It had become the narrative of a stranger. Why do Bihari women do this?

Living in the midst of so many people, in camps where privacy is unheard of, the likelihood that others would hear their story of "ruin" was very real. The fear of exposure and loss of honor put these women on guard, and it was not possible to talk about their horrific memories. Women hid behind silence, it was a face-saving mechanism. In rare cases, women whispered the experience of *zulm* (atrocity) in the war. But they never discussed rape. Everyone they knew who was raped had died, they told me.

Thus only the dead knew the full extent of the violence they suffered, and now they were mute. The Bihari women who have survived are not the victims of violence, this they want us to assume. But when I listened to their disjointed, chaotic recollections, I glimpsed the conditions and experiences of their horrific violence; words cannot capture the tumultuous emotions that enveloped the event and left them without words to remember it. Some of them are still trying to make sense of the violence that defies the logic of a human society, which they believe they are a part of.

As I continued to meet Bihari women throughout my travels in Bangladesh—in Dhaka, Mirpur, Saidpur, Chittagong, and Khulna—I began to recognize that they shared a common human condition of suffering, like their counterparts, the Bengali survivors. But did they see this likeness? In Khulna I was astounded by a story I heard that revealed a deeply conscious human understanding of the brutalities that people indulged in during the war, but the story did not stop there and condemn the Other for the violence. Rather, Nurjahan's story that I produce below takes us to another dimension in which the human spirit emerges despite its dehumanization and is capable of expressing empathy for all survivors.

Khulna, where Nurjahan lives, is an important location for documenting the violence that took place between the Bengalis and Biharis. The survivors in Khulna provide us a long durational understanding of the complex and fragile relationship between the different interest groups and the breakdown of these relationships during the war. In fact, ethnic violence did not end there after the war, it carried on much beyond the surrender of the Pakistan Army.

Biharis had a large representation as workers in the jute and paper mills that were owned by West Pakistani and Urdu-speaking Aga Khani businessmen. During the war, the Bengalis were harassed and violated by the Pakistani soldiers and their alleged Bihari supporters because they suspected the Bengalis to be antistate, pro-India, and Hindu-like. Firdousi, whose story we heard before, was a casualty of such suspicion in Khulna. The war became a personal issue as many faced the violence in their own homes, and the ethnic differences between the Bengalis and the Biharis flared up and provided fodder for extreme atrocities. After the surrender of the Pakistan Army to the Indian forces in Dhaka, the Biharis of Khulna suffered massive loss of life and property. Those who survived were evicted from their houses and driven to take refuge in the camp, which is nowadays called the "Bihari colony."

As my readers will note, the stories that Nurjahan and her companions tell are located in the period after the war when Bengali violence against the Biharis escalated. The women's narratives do not maintain an order of narration; there are several simultaneous conversations. Although Nurjahan's retelling of the story of her daughter's life and death frames the main focus of the conversation, the other women speak alongside

Traumatized Bihari women.
(Source withheld)

and in disjointed, scattered sentences they insert their own experiences. There were seven women in the room, and all of them wanted to talk at once. Despite the chaotic cacophony of memories, I learned the sad truth that life during and after the war hasn't changed much for them — it continues to be a saga of violence and loss. It was deeply troubling to hear them talk of the violence in terms of familiarity, of neighbors, identifiable local Bengali people attacking and destroying their families and property. Yet, I was heartened when I heard them problematize and question the very nature of the ethnic conflict between the Biharis and Bengalis and expose its underbelly of constructed hate. Most of all I was touched when I heard them include within the field of survivors Bengali women. These Bihari women recognized the violence that Bengali women had suffered also. This is a unique perspective of empathy for others, even those who consider them enemies. For me, these women are more human than anyone else I met in Bangladesh.

I learned the most crucial lesson from them: it is important to be able to comprehend the nature of life in wartime and be able to distinguish it from peacetime and not blur the boundaries between them. Thus discontinuity is necessary in order to move on. These women have suf-

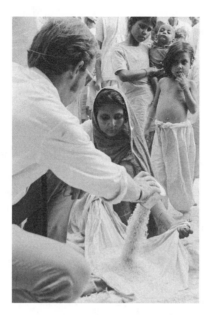

Living on charity in the camp.
(Source withheld)

fered immensely, but they are not stuck in hate. They understand that it was their vulnerability that made them targets of unwonted violence, just like the Bengali women who suffered because they were vulnerable. This understanding enables them to close the yawning gap between the Bengali and Bihari survivors and make peace with them in their hearts. Is it possible to move beyond talk and actualize this sense of peace in Bangladesh today?

THE STORY OF NURJAHAN BEGUM AND
A GROUP OF BIHARI WOMEN

"My name is Nurjahan Begum. I had five sons, brothers, and nephews. They are gone. Here all the women are widows. The men were killed on March 28, 1972. I was able to save only one small son and one daughter. They are with me now. My son is married and has children. I can't tell you who killed my family. Everybody was killing each other then, the killing started before the Mukti Juddho and continued after *swadhinata* [liberation].[13] You can see I am an old woman; I have lost several teeth and have lost almost all my hair. I was young at that time. I don't know my age, but you can write my age as you think, you can see I am old."

"I can't tell you what I saw on that day or even before or after. They are not things to be spoken about, they are not describable. Don't ask me about those days, my blood begins to boil. Don't ask about my daughter. There was a river of blood and slaughtered heads of people were strewn all over. My sons and brothers were killed in front of me; I saw them with my own eyes. I don't want to talk about these things. I feel ashamed [Nurjahan breaks into tears and makes a whimpering noise]."

Another woman starts to speak. She says, "We are alive with our children. That is all we have now. Those we managed to save are with us, those who were killed, Allah knows what happened to them. Some of them we could not even bury. They were slaughtered like chickens. Today, we have no roof over our heads and nothing to depend on. Allah knows when we will be delivered from this hell. Life has no meaning when you live like this, like unwanted outcasts."

Another woman started to speak randomly. "My name is Khairum, and I came from Kolkata. I came here after my marriage." Others also piped in, all of them were speaking simultaneously and they were unstoppable. "I came here after partition," one said. Another woman said, "I came here after the riots." Yet another said, "I came here after the 1947 riot. I used to stay in Lucknow [India]. My parents are still in Lucknow. I came here after fifteen years. I was sixteen years old then. My children were born in Bangladesh. We came from Kolkata in a goods train. We came and made our home here. But they destroyed it, and now they tell us we don't belong here. Where will we go? We have no home? The Bengalis wanted us to leave, but where could we go. Wherever we tried to take shelter people have asked us to leave. Nobody would even give us rice or water. They abused us calling us names 'Shala Biharis.'[14] We are like outsiders here; we have no home or country, neither in Bangladesh nor in Pakistan."

Nurjahan resumed her story: "I came to this country with my husband. Nobody asked me if I wanted to come here. I came here from India. It was after 1947, many years after that. It was in the 1950s, I think. No one asked me. Women are like cattle. They pack us off with the men as if we belong to a herd to be sent off for slaughter. My husband thought that our lives will be better in Pakistan. Hence we left our homeland and came here. My husband worked in the jute mill in Khulna. He was a cashier in the office. One day, he went to the office and never returned.

It was before swadhinata. I had grown-up children then. For their safety, I moved to a Bihari *mohallah* [compound]. Everyone was Urdu speaking there. But we were not safe even there."

"When a war takes place, people write only about the external story, nobody wants to know and hear about the internal, intimate stories. Even today no one has written about it. It was not only Bengali women who were tortured. Everyone was looted and tortured during that time. Both Bengali and Bihari women were dehumanized. You should write about that."

"I saw with my own eyes several incidents. There were some bags of sand and behind it I saw a few men were hiding. When I asked them why they were hiding they said, 'We do not have any grudges against the Biharis. We wouldn't do any harm to them. Our revolt is against the government.' When my husband came out he saw them setting fire to the haystacks. Many women were raped by them. They even killed most of them. There was looting and plundering everywhere. The girls they had raped although they looked alive were almost dead. I saw them pile dead bodies in trucks of both men and women in Khulna. They took them somewhere, I don't know. Many of us saw those truckloads."

Other women in the group affirmed this with many noisy agreements of "yes."

Nurjahan continued, "Once, I even hid with my children in a truck with dead bodies. We were trying to get out of our neighborhood and reach some people we knew. We didn't know how to get there without being identified. So we pretended we were dead and lay down on the dead bodies. It was terrible, but we had no other way to save ourselves. All this happened after the country was independent. Bengalis did the greatest violence then. They were kicking on every door and breaking the doors. I told them not to bother us. 'Please leave us alone,' I begged them. They said, 'No, we will not leave you.' We were given two hours time to leave our homes. They laughed at us and said, 'You can't escape too far. The Indians are killing Biharis. Hindus will kill Muslims, and you are Muslims.' People were being killed all over for nothing. I saw this with my own eyes."

Suddenly, one of the women in the group started to cry loudly.

"What happened to me or my children, or to the women here, who will tell their stories?" Nurjahan demanded. "I don't want to talk. Tell me, can you help us? We want to live a human life, we are human beings, is it possible for us to have a human life? What is the point in telling all this now? We will go to the *kaberstan* [grave] but no one will deliver us from here.

"My daughter was killed in front of my eyes. They came to the mohallah with sticks and *daos* (knifes and sickles). They dragged my son-in-law out of the room. My daughter's *mehendi* was still fresh in her hands.[15] She had gotten married just eight months before. They killed her husband with a dao. Then they went into the room and pulled out Fatima [Nurjahan's daughter]. She was pregnant at that time. They molested her, tore her clothes, and slaughtered her like a chicken. I fainted when I saw it. They tore open her stomach and pulled out the unborn child and killed him, too. They were beasts, like animals. What had my daughter done to them? She was innocent, like all other women in this country. Women are treated like cattle. What was her crime, except that she spoke Urdu? That made her an enemy? She was born in an Urdu-speaking family. What other language could she have spoken? They did not care. My daughter had not harmed anyone, but they killed her because she spoke Urdu. No one has fought for justice for us."

The women in the group started to howl and scream and cry for justice.

Nurjahan said, "Who will speak on our behalf? Allah will do justice someday. That is all we have to hope. What's the use in telling all this now? The truth is no one has asked us before this. This is our first chance to talk. Until this day, no one has even come here to find out what we had suffered. Please tell the world what we suffered. Perhaps some people will understand. Mothers will understand the pain of losing a daughter."

The women were crying and making a lot of noise, "It was *qayamat* [doomsday]," one said. "Our children were killed and destroyed. They tortured us so much. They took away all our belongings."

"We did not even have a glass to drink water from," Nurjahan said, and she was totally silent thereafter.

The other women explained, "We did not do anything to the Bengalis. What could we do? We are women? The Hindustani [Indian] Army protected us. It was the Pakistan Army that burned our people. The Pakistanis tortured the Biharis as well as the Bengalis. People think that the Biharis were protected by the Pakistan Army; not in our village and locality, they did not protect us. They took so many of our men away. We hid our boys in rice sacks and under our beds. In India, Bengalis and Biharis live together, sometimes they even share rooms. They

sit together; even marry each other's daughters. I have seen it myself.
I grew up in India. Here in Bangladesh it can be like that, but it hasn't
been. We are treated like pariahs. If they throw us out of here someday,
we have nothing but Allah's mercy. It is important for women to form a
common organization to fight for women's issues. We are not enemies
of Bengali women. We need to work for our children's future together.
Will you help?"

4

WOMEN'S SERVICES

SUHASINI DEVI, SYLHET

I am a witness to history. —SUHASINI DEVI

After working in the field and collecting women's stories for several months, a clearer picture of the violence and victims started to emerge. Also, I realized that the history of 1971 cannot be told as a simple story of one group fighting another group. Survivors' memories established that violence was both an internal and external phenomenon. Armies and militias trained to kill and terrorize the public had functioned under different guises and banners—the Pakistan Army, Indian Army, and Mukti Bahini. Women's memories confirmed that violence was committed by men, and security that noncombatants expected in the familiar world peopled by family, neighbors, and friends was no longer a guarantee in wartime East Pakistan; they were surrounded by danger within and outside their home. So, how did women respond to the disruptive and encompassing violence?

To seek an answer to this question, in addition to speaking with survivors of sexual violence, I decided to investigate the work of community supporters in these abnormal times. Did women assist other women in times of trouble? If so, what kind of social and community work did women do to provide succor to the aggrieved victims? Who did they help? My initial inquiries concerning social and medical work during wartime produced many eager respondents willing to tell me about their bold acts of service. The vast majority, not unexpectedly, were men. I met several of these local heroes, and, although all of them, I am certain, sincerely believe that they are worthy of the respect and admiration of society, their stories exceeded my expectations of the capacity of human response in moments of crisis. These interlocutors provided me with important clues to map the outbreak of violence in different localities that reconfirmed women's descriptions of the preponderant nature of the enemy, but they did not help me understand how the community coped with the ordeal of war and terror that I was more interested in probing.

Occasionally, when I met women who were introduced to me as important social workers, they could not tell me about their work; it was difficult for them to talk about it. They did not see their activities during the war as particularly meaningful or their postwar contributions as part of the healing process of the nation. Sometimes, they described difficult situations that they encountered and the immediate and intuitive work of assistance that they provided. For them these were not heroic acts but were small gestures owed to family and friends. They talked about them as routine work—to care for others—and they did not claim special status as heroes because they responded to the need of another person. Precisely because women did not talk of the work as conscious acts of bravado but presented them as duty, the work that individual women did during and after the war has gone largely unnoticed in the national register of war memory. I became interested in searching for women's memories of their work and recording their special contributions to the nation-building process. With this aim in mind, I traveled from Moulvi Bazaar to Sylhet in northwest Bangladesh.

Sylhet's location within Bangladesh is complex. It is within and, yet, outside the Bengali culture. Extending almost to the Indian border of Assam and Meghalaya, Sylhet has a long history of association with both nations. In 1947, during the partition of India and Pakistan, a demand was made by the Muslim League group that the entire region of Assam (including Meghalaya, which was a part of erstwhile Assam until the early 1970s) and Sylhet should be united and constituted into a province of East Pakistan, becoming a shared geographical entity and culture with a large Muslim population of more than 30 percent. In the end, the politics of the Indian National Congress (a national political party) demarcated Assam with a Hindu majority to India, and Sylhet, having a Muslim majority, was given to East Pakistan. The division during partition, however, did not drastically alter the interaction between the people of Assam and the Meghalaya area with Sylhet, and a variety of educational, business, social, and personal exchanges, including marriage arrangements between the Sylhetis and Assamese, have continued.

Even today the people of Sylhet refer to themselves as Asamiya in culture and Bangladeshi by nationality. A borderland as such, Sylhet is porous and impacted on by a variety of outside and internal transformations. Its history is portable and fluctuating.

Hence, when I started my work in Sylhet town as an Assamese, I was quite confident that I would find a good response there. Contrary to my expectation and despite the enthusiasm of the administration to assist me in my research, the local Muslim representatives who had assured me introductions to survivors never came through. These interlocutors of the Muslim community in Sylhet disappeared after our initial discussion. As well, the representatives of the ethnic Jayantia community advised me not to visit survivors in their homes to avoid the social ostracization that would follow. These setbacks aside, I was richly rewarded by archival research in Sylhet. I found a variety of very important documents of 1971 in many small offices and libraries connected to the Women's Welfare Department. These documents are invaluable sources that provide an understanding of the nature and extent of sexual violence in Sylhet town during the war. Since my interest was to understand women's responses to victims of violence and the resulting social rehabilitation work they undertook, I searched for names of local social workers who could tell of their activities and work during and after the war.

Immediately, I was directed to speak with Suhasini Devi, who was actively involved in the rehabilitation of women. She was revered by everyone in Sylhet, and I was impressed by the respect she commanded. I wanted to know from her what motivated women, like her, to serve the vulnerable when everyone else had failed them. What were the small acts of duty she performed and who benefited?

My meeting with Suhasini Devi was facilitated by a respected Hindu businessman, an active Awami League (AL) supporter in Sylhet. Suhasini Devi is well known for her social work during the anticolonial struggle under the direct guidance of Mahatma Gandhi. She was intimately connected with the rehabilitation of survivors after the devastating communal riots that broke out in Noakhali before partition in 1946. Since then Suhasini Devi has been an ardent social activist taking many risks in her personal life for the cause of social well-being.

I went to meet Suhasini Devi in her house. She was dressed in a simple white cotton sari without any adornments to disrupt her self-representation as a Hindu widow. She had been widowed almost her entire life; her husband died within a year of their marriage when she was barely in her twenties. Soon after, she became involved in community and social work. The contrast between her vulnerable, unprotected status as a fragile, old woman and the public work that she is involved in cannot fail to catch anyone's immediate attention. For Suhasini Devi one identity does not submerge the other, but rather they complement and free her to work without any selfish motivations. Our conversation about 1971 started in the early afternoon and continued until late evening.

Suhasini Devi was gracious, kind, and forthcoming. I did not feel any hesitation about asking her the most difficult questions, even those concerning her family, and she responded to my queries with honesty and sincerity. She made me see that it was possible, despite the abnormal time of war, to not become enveloped in the madness of hate and violence but to live with a normal expectation of rational justice and an ethical code to respond to others' calls for help. Suhasini Devi continued to work as a social worker in the midst of the war and beyond it because in her moral world too much emotion, either detachment or anger against the perpetrators, was counterproductive, creating a sense of helplessness, which she never indulged in. Her indomitable spirit and social responsibility elicited positive responses from those whose lives she touched with her assistance, and they, in turn, created a life beyond the war as best as they could, not by forgetting, but by living the outcome of the sexual violence with dignity and forbearance.

In Suhasini Devi's account, we find she casts only a sideways glance at the perpetrators and names their violence. She is more concerned with the moral conduct that human beings owe to one another and is shocked that there were some who transgressed that responsibility. Instead of dwelling on them, Suhasini Devi reminds us of the collective work done by women who rose to the occasion and extended their homes and hearts and fulfilled the promise that humanity is capable of selfless gestures in moments of crisis. Suhasini Devi's narrative allows us to see another side of the war and shifts our focus from the deprivation and suffering of victims to a realm of service and hope, which only humans are capable of. I was, however, somewhat disappointed that her compassion did not extend beyond her ethnic boundaries. Suhasini Devi did not know or find out what happened to women who were from the non-Bengali community during the war. Did they also suffer? Who provided them with assistance? While I greatly respect Suhasini Devi for the work she did during and after the war, I continue to remain puzzled as to why her noble gesture was confined to helping only Bengali women. Were the Others less human and thus not deserving of her compassion? I never found out the answer because Suhasini Devi passed away before my next trip to Bangladesh.

SUHASINI DEVI'S STORY

The Mukti Juddho [War of Liberation] was a terrible period for everyone here in Sylhet. There was no certainty about anything anymore. There was no honor left in people's relationships. The situation was very bad; there were no enemies or friends. In fact, the chairman of the Peace Committee in our *para* [neighborhood] was himself disgraced by the military.[1] They tied him to a chair and raped his wife in front of him. These people were supporters of Pakistan. They were not for the liberation of Bangladesh, but they were not spared either by the Pakistan Army.

Rape happened in my own family. It happened to a close relative of mine in this house. She tried to hide in the toilet when she saw the army was approaching our house, but she could not save herself. I haven't told these things to others. No one in the family knows what happened to her. It would be a disgrace, and no one will accept her within the family if they found out. We can't let that happen. It did not happen because she was at fault. How can a woman protect herself when she is under attack like that? Many more things happened right here in Dalia Para. I have seen a lot, I have worked with many women after the war was over. I helped women who were pregnant. I delivered many babies right here, where you are sitting. I brought these babies into the world with my bare hands. Sometimes, I had a midwife to help me. We had to do this in absolute secrecy. I used to keep the girls with me, as if they were my companions. They were very safe here. No one bothered us. People in this neighborhood knew me as a social worker for a long time. So they did not ask me questions about the women who stayed in my house. But it is better not to talk about them. It will open up too many disturbing wounds and cause problems for the families.

A relative of mine was raped. She was married afterwards, but she did not disclose anything about what had happened to her in 1971. Hence, I can't arrange a meeting for you with her personally. It will ruin her life. No one will understand how and what she suffered. [Suhasini Devi did not talk for a while and let silence speak. It appeared that she was thinking, reflecting on what had happened, and revisiting the moment in her mind. Suddenly, she resumed the conversation].

This was not the only incident. My cook was raped, but not in front of me. I had given her a separate house because she was a Brahmin widow. They came to the house at night. She was by herself. They did not spare her. What could a Brahmin widow do after that? She lived like a dead person. She had a son; he was with her then. He was very young, so he did not remember anything. Later, I gave her son another house and money to start a business. Her son is married now. He did not know what happened to his mother and has shown no interest to find out either. Only my cook and I knew about the rape, no one else in the family ever heard about it. Not even my daughter knew about it.

I had another girl here; she was raped by robbers who came to loot our house. She became pregnant because of it and later had a child right here. We named the child Kartik, as he was born in the month of Kartik.[2] I treated her like my own daughter when she lived with me. Later, I sent her to Kolkata after the delivery. We did not want people to gossip about her. I wanted her to learn some skill so that she could support herself. Initially, she could not adjust in Kolkata; also it was hard for her to find work, her baby was too small. Sucheta Kripalini took her to the Rehabilitation Center in Behrampur and admitted her to a craft school.[3] She learned sewing and was later able to find work there. For many years, she kept in touch with me through letters. Sucheta Kripalini tried to convince the girl, and I tried too, that she should leave her son in the care of others and get married again. But she refused. She said that she wanted to live her life like a Hindu widow with her son. Her son to this day does not know about his mother's experiences. He will never find out, I think. He thinks his father had died before he was born. My friends in India, like Sucheta Kripalini, kept me informed of the girls I'd sent there for rehabilitation. Sucheta Kripalini and I worked together since the freedom movement, since the time Gandhiji came to Noakhali.

There were many incidents that happened during the time of the Mukti Juddho. People sacrificed a lot then, but we are not really enjoying independence now. Particularly not the women who were victims of the war for freedom; they got nothing. It is an irony: today our country is ruled by a woman, and she doesn't treat her children equally.[4] I have told this in a public meeting. When I was a student, I got a gold medal for excellence in studies, but now I know it is not important to get a gold medal, it is more important to work for people. In our schoolbooks, we read that the sun never sets on the British Empire, and we praised Queen Victoria [Suhasini Devi breaks into laughter]. We were not told of the violence they committed to acquire the colonies.

I came to Sylhet as a wife at the age of twenty. My original home was in Sunamganj [on the border between present-day Bangladesh and India]. After several years in Sylhet, I joined Gandhiji's freedom movement at the age of twenty-three. Now I am eighty-five years old. I have seen and experienced a lot in this lifetime. I have lived through many regimes of rulers: the British, the Pakistani government, and after liberation several Bangladesh governments. Now I am reaching the end of my life, and I can say from experience that unless the rulers serve people, there cannot be real change. One can change the administration, but that is not enough for real change to take place. We have to work for people, only then we will uplift society and see positive results.

For sixty-two years I worked on my mission. I was widowed soon after my marriage; my daughter was only one month old then. She is now married and lives in the United States. She did her masters and works as a lecturer. Her daughter, my granddaughter, is a doctor. I had saved thirty *bhori*[5] of gold for my daughter and gave it to her at the time of her marriage. I, on the other hand, have worn this *tulsi mala*[6] throughout my life. I never touched gold since I joined Gandhiji's movement [long silence again].

On December 16 we became independent, and I returned to my home in Sylhet on the 17. My house looked so desolate, the plants and shrubs were overgrown; it looked more like a jungle than a person's house. People who met me on the streets told me to go and see my place, where we had previously lived. Now it is the airport area. Dead bodies were lying around; some of them were even visible because they were not properly buried. It looked like they had dug shallow graves and had thrown the bodies into it. There was a foul smell everywhere. I could not look anymore and went away from the place.

On the day of the revolt, I saw a young man shot on the road.[7] The family used to stay in a house near ours, and I saw his mother running out of the house to protect her son. Blood was gushing out from him, and the mother was holding her son and trying to stop the blood from flowing out. The son died soon afterwards. It was so painful to see the mother's condition, she was crying inconsolably. I tried to offer her solace, but what good would words do at times like this. The grief of losing a child cannot ever be overcome.

I heard about another incident around the same time. This happened in Burunda in Dhanbari, some thirty kilometers from here. A joint meeting of Hindus and Muslims was called in a school building. When the people arrived they divided them into two groups. They sent the Muslims to one room and the Hindus to another room. Soon after that the Pakistan Army men entered the room where the Hindus were waiting and tied them with ropes. One man escaped by jumping out of the window, but they shot him. He was hurt in one of his legs, but he managed to escape. The others who were in the room were held prisoner. They were asked to line up and then shot and killed. Many of them were crying "Ma, ma!" Thirty or forty of them were killed. One person survived from this group, although he was shot at too. I met both of these survivors, the one who escaped through the window and the one who escaped the shooting.[8]

Here is another incident. Purendu Babu was alone in his house. His full name is Purendur Kishore Sengupta, and he lived in a lovely old house by himself. He was like a saint. A young girl used to work for him. She used to stay in the house and do all the housework as well as cook for Purendu Babu. One day, the military came to his house. They knew that he was a Hindu man and were suspicious of him, although Purendu Babu was not involved in political activities. He was involved in welfare work for his neighborhood and community. When the Pakistani military men came to his house, they saw the young girl working there. They went away that day, but they returned the next evening for her. They tried to abduct her, but she started shouting and screaming, calling for Purendu Babu. Then she fainted. Purendu Babu, who was praying at the time, stopped his prayers and came out to meet the army men. He told them in English that they were like animals and that all they were concerned about was physical enjoyment, forcing and torturing women to get their physical satisfaction. He also told them that he was certainly not dead although he had not slept with a woman his entire life. The men who had come to rape his maid were surprised. They stood there and listened to him and then told him that it couldn't be true that he had lived a celibate life. They said that it is not humanly possible, but they felt ashamed and left the girl there. They even returned the marble table they were dragging out of the house and other valuables they had packed to take with them. Purendu Babu was eighty years old at that time. You see, I saw all these things happening in front of my eyes.

I am a witness to history. But I am old now and will not live for much longer. I am glad you have come to my house and have asked these things. Otherwise, the things that we experienced, our memories, and our stories will die with us. Your book will help to keep some of this alive. You are very brave to be doing this. I think all women are brave. They need to have exposure to show their worth and stand up for the truth.

You are curious how I got involved in social welfare work. When I had come to Sylhet as a newly married bride, I used to see women who were involved in the Indian National Congress activities walk by our house. They also noticed me. I had very long hair that I used to leave untied and open after a bath sometimes. I would stand by the gate and watch the women walk by. They came to me one day and asked me if I would like to join the Congress Party and do some work. My husband had passed away. I had a small child and that was all I had to do. I asked my brother-in-law, and he gave me permission to join the Congress. I registered my name as an ordinary member and paid twenty-five paisa. My sister-in-law also became a member. Initially, I did not attend the meetings.

There was a conference in Sawda Hall, and my neighbor Madhuri asked me if I would like to go to the conference with her. I used to stay in the house and take care of the housework. That was my world; I never even wore shoes because I never went out. I was living the life of a widow. I liked it that way. But that day what happened in Sawda Hall changed my life. I heard Ashalata Sen speak, and her fervent voice, her impassioned speech, and her personality impressed me very much; I wanted to do social work and be part of the Congress. Ashalata Sen was a leader of the Women's Congress. When I heard her, I realized I had been wasting my time.

Although I was involved in the bookshop that we owned and used to read books and also sing Rabindra Sangeet, I realized it was not enough. I started going to the Mahila Organization [Women's Organization]. There I learned how to weave and also do *katha*.[9] I also started to teach. I used to teach from 1 P.M. to 5 P.M. I became an active member of the Congress Party, and for that I was jailed for nine months. During the time I was in prison, my sister-in-law took care of my daughter. After coming out of jail, I continued to work for women's causes. I was mostly involved in women's social welfare.

I went to see Gandhiji with Sarala di and other girls in Noakhali. We went by train. In Noakhali we joined Gandhiji in a prayer meeting. I decided to work with him there and stayed in the ashram. We worked in the villages with him. I did spinning work and helped the villagers rebuild their houses that were burned down. In 1946, too, women were abducted and taken away from their homes. Many of them had taken shelter in Muslim homes. These Muslim people in Noakhali area were very suspicious of us and did not let us enter their homes. But we stayed there and worked toward organizing relief and provided support whenever and however we could. We stayed in many different villages. Basically, we followed Gandhiji. Wherever he went or sent us, we went there. I think we were in Alunia village when I fell ill. I was suffering from chicken pox. Gandhiji came to see me with Ava and Khanu.[10] I was surprised that Gandhiji has come to see me. He joined his hands to greet me in *namaskar*[11] and told me that I would get well soon. I tried to greet him with a namaskar too, but I simply stared at him. My companions later told me, "Suhasini didi [sister], you forgot to say namaskar to Gandhiji." I told them that I was so thrilled since he came to see me personally, I forgot everything; I was overwhelmed.

It was a long time ago. We got independence from the British and became free. It was such a jubilant moment, but then the violence during partition led many people to migrate. I tried to convince many of them not to leave their homeland. People were concerned about their safety and about their family. We stopped a lot of people from leaving. But after Gandhiji was assassinated, I felt lost. I did not stop my social work, but it was different after that. In 1965, we had some horrible communal riots here. There was a lot of bloodshed. Many Hindu families left for India then. We tried to stop them from leaving even then. But people were scared. There was no peace anywhere. I did not go, why should I? This is my own home. I was born in Sunamganj, and I came as a bride to Sylhet. I will die here. Till death comes I must continue to work. I hope I did my part in helping women in 1971, I hope they are well and have peaceful lives.

DR. SYED AHMED NURJAHAN, CHITTAGONG

I did my duty and performed many abortions. —DR. SYED AHMED NURJAHAN

The terror of sexual violence transformed real women into objects— female bodies became a site of fear. This psychology of fear produced extreme anxiety in families. Women's bodies that were deemed enemy bodies were hidden, dispersed, and exiled from their homes. Parents warned their daughters to stay out of the sight of men and forced them to move from house to house, flee their homes and villages, and seek shelter in strange places. The preemptive fear of rape struck everyone. Even married women were forced to leave their homes and hide in paddy fields, bamboo groves, ditches, even in morgues and graveyards. Although some claimed that these precautionary measures had saved them from the enemy, others remembered the ordeal as unpleasant and cruel. This latter group of women raised an intriguing question: who was protected and who benefited through these subterfuges, women or the men who controlled their lives?

In postwar Bangladesh, the discourse of victims as women without honor, called *birangonas*, resulted in the introduction of harsh measures that, once again, transformed women into mere bodies for developing new scripts of patriarchal power. The government's dramatic claim that two hundred thousand women were raped allowed for drastic action by state and society. Abortion was introduced as a quick and certain measure to cleanse the odious Pakistani presence from the midst of Bangladeshi society. Despite the legitimization of this process by the government as a face-saving device for women's benefit, supposedly enabling them to regain their lost honor, the truth is much harsher. At the very moment of the birth of the nation, both the Bangladeshi state and Bangladeshi society failed their women by taking away women's agency, transgressing their humanity and transforming them into bodies that were manipulated so that men would not have to deal with the unhappy reminders of the past. An interrogation of this process through women's personal experiences seemed important to understanding how this scheme was implemented and what women thought about its outcome.

I was able to probe the issue of abortion and women's medical work in Chittagong, a port city in eastern Bangladesh that is second in importance only to Dhaka, the capital city. I had identified Chittagong as one of my principal research sites and had spent a considerable amount of time there visiting both the Bengali and Bihari communities living in the urban and rural areas. Chittagong's history of 1971 is a bloody and gruesome story of ethnic and armed violence in which no groups were spared. In Chittagong I visited the railway colony and several government buildings, rest houses, colleges, and schools where the Biharis and the Pakistan Army victimized, raped, and killed Bengalis in large numbers to establish their might. I also went to a number of sites where ordinary Biharis were massacred by the Bengalis and left to die in open pits, sewers, and drains. In rural areas and in the town, I listened to women tell me their heartrending stories of sexual violence committed by neighbors and strangers alike. I listened to women who were forced to marry their rapists for fear of social sanction against them. Some of them were Bihari women who had to forget their family and friends and adopt a Bengali persona to survive in postwar Bangladesh. I also listened to men tell me the stories of atrocities that they committed. In short, Chittagong fulfilled the stereotype of a city and people gone awry during the war, thus, research on the outcome there was urgent and compelling.

I decided to start my research on the government's abortion program in the Chittagong Hospital where I met Dr. Nurjahan, a well-known doctor and OB-GYN. After the war, she was appointed by the government to perform emergency abortions on pregnant women. The staggering number of abortions that she did is a test of her courage and professional ability. I met Dr. Nurjahan in her chambers in the Chittagong Hospital and had an extended conversation with her for several hours. She presented her narrative in two registers of emotions: she told with intense feelings her personal story of the loss of family during the war, but talked of her professional work in a matter-of-fact manner. For her, the abortions were *duty*, and she did it without questioning the consequences of her actions. She approached her role in the government program as a responsibility that she undertook in service of her fellow Bengali women. Her narrative makes it clear that women in post-liberated Bangladesh did not have the privilege to exercise choice; the driving force was to purge the past and become "honorable" for social acceptance. Nurjahan is confident that she enabled some women to regain their honor and arrest further humiliation in society, while performing the work the state expected from her and creating an exclusive Bangladesh populated by Bangladeshi people only.

Identity matters to Nurjahan, and she started her narrative by locating herself and her family within the larger Bangladeshi society. She grew up in Sylhet, where her father served as an officer in the government of Pakistan. Her father's important position and Nurjahan's drive to receive higher education made it possible for her to get a state-sponsored fellowship to study abroad in the United Kingdom. On the completion of her studies and her return to East Pakistan, Nurjahan accepted a lucrative academic position in the medical school and became a Pakistan government employee. The war had already started by then.

Although a Bengali, Nurjahan initially did not feel compelled to relinquish her position and to resist the state's violent activities. She remained a loyal employee until the personal loss of both parents—her father was presumably killed by the Pakistan Army, and her mother was abducted and disappeared for a long time—changed Nurjahan's attitude toward the state. She began to silently oppose the state for which both she and her husband were punished. Nurjahan, however, refuses to discuss what her husband and she did to bring about the wrath of the Pakistanis. We can only guess that they were covertly involved in the freedom struggle.

It is in postwar Bangladesh that Nurjahan became publicly active when she provided her services to her Bengali community with her specialized knowledge as an OB-GYN. Nurjahan spoke about the difficult and complicated abortions that she performed with cool detachment and disengagement. Clearly she embarked on her duty with a determination to overcome the humiliation that women suffered and saw the task of abortion as essential to creating a new Bangladesh. But was Nurjahan also exorcising her own past?

Nurjahan does not give us the luxury of delving too deeply into her life story and her losses, but she willingly talks about the new techniques of medical interventions that she introduced and adopted to terminate even late-term pregnancy, which she believes saved many lives. Without boasting about her work, she makes us see the work that doctors, like her, did to assist and rehabilitate victims. To her, it was and remains a call of duty, which she fulfilled without reservation.

I wanted to hear about women's work aimed at helping others. In Nurjahan's narrative there were some troubling dimensions of the state's exercise of power. Taking control of women's bodies was one of its most obvious scripts for implementing unquestionable authority. I found myself asking: Did Nurjahan ever think of her work as transgressing women's rights of choice? Did she see the state working through her and forcing women to agree to live by the rules of a rigid patriarchal order? Perhaps she has considered this, and hence she does not brag of the work she did. She presents abortion as routine medical practice without further consideration of its long-term and deeper implications on government-sponsored family planning that is nowadays hailed as a big success. Its cold rationalization was implemented in 1971 in the government abortion program. Nurjahan does not remark on it, making it appear as though the war had diminished the extent to which compassion and self-reflection worked in post-liberated Bangladesh.

Nurjahan's iconic memory is not about what she knows—the humiliation she suffered in the hands of the Pakistani authorities before Bangladesh's independence or the work of abortion she performed after independence. Her iconic memory is about what she does *not* know, about the experiences of her mother during the war and her trauma. Nurjahan's testimony lingers on what she cannot speak and struggles to make sense of the incomprehensible, the contact between the victim and perpetrator through her mother's experience in the war.

Her mother ended up in the hands of the perpetrator community. The close proximity of the contact and the momentary recognition by one of her perpetrators that she was different from their other abductees changed her status. She was transformed from an object, not to an equal human, but to another subject position. The temporary softening of the Pakistani military's glance spared her further abuse, at least sexually, and she was relegated to the level of an imprisoned servant. Her mother's enslavement is a new narrative but an uneasy one. It cannot be located within the known register of abuse in 1971 of sexual destruction and abortion that followed as a result, which Nurjahan had become familiar with in dealing with victims. For Nurjahan, her mother's suffering as a servant in the home of her perpetrator is an unfamiliar position, and she cannot access what this suffering entailed.

Her mother's refusal to speak about her condition in her perpetrator's home does not enlighten Nurjahan about the face of the perpetrator, thus she cannot box him or them into a narrative to follow. Added to this, her mother's endurance leading to her forgiveness of her perpetrators makes her mother's experiences and conclusions irresolvable for Nurjahan. But there is no way to know and no way to speak about it. Her mother died soon after, before Nurjahan had mustered the courage to really ask. Thus she now tells her mother's story as a matter of duty, paralleling her own work, without filling in the gaps. Nurjahan's trauma is without memory and therefore profoundly troubling to her as well as to her listeners.

In Nurjahan's narrative we encounter the possibilities and limits of women's memories. Women, like her, can tell the story of the work they did to save many from disgrace and dishonor by making exigent decisions to mitigate the past. But they cannot tell their own story because there is no structure to locate their memories. Their memories hover unbalanced, as there is insufficient information about what happened. The price that women like Nurjahan have paid for not knowing the memories of those who were intimately connected to them, while providing service to heal strangers and others, is a paradoxical situation. She helped strangers and facilitated their recovery, but her own wounds remain open and festering. Can this bafflement be resolved?

DR. SYED AHMED NURJAHAN'S STORY

My name is Syed Ahmed Nurjahan, and I am a doctor. I graduated from Dhaka Medical College. Soon after, I left for England to pursue higher education there. In England, I did my [medical] membership and fellowship. I returned to East Pakistan where I joined the PG hospital.[12] Very soon after, I was promoted to assistant professor and later became a professor. I hope to become the vice chancellor in the university that will open in Putiyar. I have a lot of experience in my work and have traveled extensively.

You must keep in mind the rather dismal picture of education in our country before 1971. In East Pakistan, the majority was Muslim, no doubt, but the Hindu minority was better educated than we were. When I was growing up, I saw that the Muslims were not involved in education and a large number of Hindus were coming here as teachers. I don't know where they came from, whether they were migrating from the villages to the cities or had come from across the border from India. But the truth is that education was the purview of the Hindus, and Muslims seemed uninterested in this area.

I was quite young in 1971. In the war, I lost my father, a brother, and later, after liberation, my mother died too. I had an older brother, but he is several years senior to me and used to live in Dhaka. It appears that in 1971, my mother was traveling to Chittagong to visit me. I had returned from England after six years, and the Mukti Juddho was already raging then. I did not know where my parents were, if they were still living in the house in Sylhet or not. I did not want to go there by myself because I did not know anything about their whereabouts. I thought no one would be there. Also, I had my job in Chittagong. I could not go home to visit my parents, hence my mother decided to come over for a visit, but she got lost on the way. She was first seen in Putiyar and later in Noakhali. My mother came back to us five months after the war was over. She came back to my brother's house in Dhaka.

The incident happened to my mother on May 17, 1971. This is what I later learned had happened to my mother: The train that she had taken was one of the last services to Chittagong from Sylhet. The station master in Sylhet, on my father's request, asked a family traveling to Chittagong to let my mother travel with them. It was meant for her safety and protection. The family provided her company. The train left on time, but they moved very slowly. Somewhere, en route, the train was hijacked, and they were attacked. The family my mother was traveling with became very afraid and refused to help her. My mother was abducted by some men who took her to Noakhali. She lived for some time in a place but she could not tell us where it was or any details about it [Nurjahan fell into long silence and did not talk].

A few weeks later, I think, after the situation had improved somewhat, the military district officer came to the place for an inspection. When he saw my mother, he told his men, "This woman does not belong here. She should not be kept here and treated so shabbily." My mother was transferred to a family with whom she lived throughout the period of the war. After the war was over, my brother put out a massive search for her. He was a very high-ranking officer. After several months of searching for her, he found her in Noakhali. He sent a letter to the family with whom she was living, and soon after that he sent someone to fetch her. She returned to Dhaka to my brother's house. My mother kept in touch with the family in Noakhali. During the first Eid after her return, she asked us to write to them and send them gifts. I was not very happy to do this; they had not treated her well while she lived with them. She was like a maid servant in their house, but my mother said, "They provided me shelter and protection, and I am very grateful for that." While my mother was in captivity, which I did not know at that time, a colleague of mine, a doctor, told me that my father had run away to India. I could not believe it and told him he was lying. But he insisted that it was in the record book. I refused to accept it because I knew my father wouldn't run away, no matter what happened. After the war was over, my father did not return home. My mother died in grief soon after, about six months after she returned from Noakhali. Something very interesting had happened before that, which helped me to understand what had happened to my father.

I received a small letter from him written in the back of a Capstan cigarette packet. It was dated sometime in November. He had scribbled there, "They are taking me away. Your mother is lost. Take care of yourself. Love, Baba." I later found out that my father, who was a highly placed officer, was arrested by the Pakistan Army. They took him to the railway station, and, I think, they shot him there. The only personal item that they found later that was identified as belonging to my father was his reading glasses. They found his glasses on the railway tracks. I don't know why my father was killed. He was not at all political and was a very decent and respectable man.

I was not involved in political activities. I am only a doctor, and I continued my work during the freedom struggle. My contribution is little. I did my duty and performed many abortions. There were a lot of pregnant women who came to the hospital. On a given day, we terminated more than two hundred such cases of unwanted pregnancies. Wherever I looked, I saw pregnant women. I could not get so many catheters, so I had to remove it by using antibiotics and other medicines. Pregnancy termination is not easy as these women were more than six weeks pregnant or even more advanced. Sometimes, there was risk to the girl's life. But we had good results, and we saved many girls.

Thirty years ago there was no disposable syringe. The majority of the women who came for pregnancy termination were between the age group of eighteen and twenty-five years old. They were mostly young and unmarried, although there were a few married women too. An entire unit was established to deal with pregnancy termination. I think most of the pregnancies happened a few weeks before and after December 16. Most of these women came from refugee camps, a good number of them were orphans. They were all Bengali. I did not ask them who had raped them, nor was I interested in hearing their life stories. But sometimes they told these stories on their own. In the case of married women, the general pattern in their story was that their home was raided, their husband was killed, and they were raped. In the case of unmarried girls, generally we heard stories that their parents were killed, and they were raped thereafter.

My own brother was killed during the war. His name was Abul Kalam Azad. It appears that some men, Pakistanis, I think, entered his house and demanded to know if he was protecting Hindus. My brother escaped when he saw them approaching and hid in the backyard pond. His entire body was submerged in the water, but the tips of his fingers were visible. The men who were searching for him saw this and pulled him out of the pond and killed him. They had also beaten my husband in front of me. But they did not do anything to me. They did not abuse or yell at me. I can't tell you why, but the Pakistanis did not do anything insulting to me [once again, a long silence].

I want to tell you more about the pregnant women and their families. Most of these women were brought by their mothers, and sometimes another family member, generally a male person, accompanied them. I did not ask anyone about their case history because I was not in a mood to engage them. It was their private matter. I had my own set of worries; I was preoccupied with the disappearance of my parents, the death of my brother. I don't think you will find records about the survivors now, after thirty years. There were no computers then. Also, the government never wanted us to keep records. They simply picked the doctors and gave them the task of performing abortions. In this hospital, Dr. Murshid Aman was the head, and his assistant was Jahan Ara.

The government even today continues to say no to the termination of pregnancy. In 1971, lots of girls died. Families were destroyed, mothers lost their children, but no one took responsibility. A lot of people suffered from psychological problems. What can doctors like us do? Our work is limited, and we had to do as we were told—terminate pregnancies without personal involvement. I did just that. Did anyone benefit because of our work? I hope so. I did what I could, that is all I can say.

I've heard that there were a lot of pregnant non-Bengali women in the refugee camps that were set up by the International Red Cross. But I did not work with them. Their men were very secretive. I did not get information about who had tortured whom. My job was to admit pregnant women and terminate their pregnancies. The women kept their secrets to themselves. The Biharis were arrogant; they did not come here, but they did not know where to go either. Some Red Cross doctors worked with them, I had heard. The Indian soldiers also behaved very badly with the Bengali girls in Chittagong. I believe the local authorities and social workers had to arrange meetings to discuss this and sort out the problem with the Indian Army officers. The torture of women by Indians, however, was much less than what the Pakistanis did. The Indians looted a lot of things from Bangladesh, though. All disposable goods like crockery, cutlery, household things, even cars and machinery, were taken by Indian soldiers.

You know, talking to you after thirty years brings back a lot of old, painful memories that I had suppressed. My husband and I never talk about 1971. He had seen and experienced it; there was no need to discuss it. After we returned from England for the first time, my father promised us that after Bakr Eid [Eid al-Adha] he would throw a party for us. The party never took place. I had gotten married in England. My husband feels sad about 1971; nothing is left now. My parents sold two houses for my brother's and my education. Now we have so many houses and so much money, but my father is not here to see and enjoy it. I have a son, and my brother has four children. Two of them are already doctors, and the third one is also studying to become a doctor. All that happened is the will of Allah; we have to accept that. It is very painful, but that is reality.

JHARNA CHOWDHURY, NOAKHALI, GANDHI ASHRAM

I had responsibility for many children. I had to . . .
make sure that they were protected. —JHARNA CHOWDHURY

The narratives of the Liberation War suffer a curious absence. There are no stories of children told by children. Yet, one can imagine that in wartime East Pakistan the most vulnerable group were children who depended on the protection of adults. It was a reasonable and natural expectation. Did adults provide children the security and comfort that they expected? Many women told me with anguish of the failure of adults to live up to this basic responsibility. Mothers talked about the pain of the loss of young daughters; many are bewildered about where their children disappeared to; some are still waiting for their children to return; yet others vividly remembered their inability to protect children who were destroyed by sexual violence. Outside Bangladesh in Geneva, Switzerland, André Yves Jolliet, who was commissioned by the Red Cross International to create a visual documentation of the war and its effects, told me that he continues to think about the sufferings of children in Bangladesh. He is haunted by the images of children who were blown up in land mine accidents; some had died and others were left disfigured and maimed for life.[13]

The barbaric world of violence engineered and executed by adults must have enormously frightened and confused the children. To me the trauma that children suffered in the war is the worst crime and the saddest outcome of the situation. The unexplored issue of children's experiences in 1971 reveals a hopeless gap that makes all accounts of its history incomplete. Unfortunately, to find children's stories is almost impossible more than thirty-seven years later. The children who had witnessed suffering and had suffered in the war are now adults, and their memories have been reworked and reformed over time. When called upon to tell their memories, they recount an adult person's version of reconstituted childhood memories. Nonetheless, it is worth listening to the adults who can tell about children's experiences and extend our knowledge of the multiple experiences of noncombatants during the war.

One of the advantages of doing oral history is the unpredictability of where one can find evidence. I had traveled to Noakhali, in southeast Bangladesh, due to historical curiosity and, if possible, to trace the path of the journey of Dr. Nurjahan's mother after her abduction and imprisonment. Noakhali is infamous in the subcontinent's history for the bloody religious riots that took place in 1946, which was one of the darkest episodes of India's freedom struggle and that Suhasini Devi alluded to in her narrative. Mahatma Gandhi was forced to put a halt to his political activities in preparation for India's freedom and go to Noakhali to resolve the religious discord. Present-day Noakhali is a Bengali Muslim-dominated area and is a very conservative place. Doing research there was a risk and a challenge that I decided to take.

In Noakhali I found many survivors who were willing to speak with me in private about their memories of 1971, and they asked me to maintain their secrets. But in Noakhali, I found something more. I was directed to meet Jharna Chowdhury in the Gandhi Ashram who provided me a narrative that makes one think about the terror and the cruelty of the war that children suffered through. I was impressed with the immediacy with which she handled several critical situations that demonstrated the possibility of human sensibility and resoluteness in the face of crisis.

In her narrative she traces many historic moments and actors, particularly the role of the Indian agents and leaders who supported and created conditions for the success of the Bengalis in the war, but her focus is on the children, orphans who lived in her care. In the unstable war environment, Jharna had to improvise survival strategies, adopt different identities, and even cheat to find safe places to protect her children. Her narrative style is prosaic and pedestrian. It lacks in sharpness and the images are not vivid. But she makes us clearly aware of the dangers that accompanied every move she and the children made, and we begin to appreciate the children's capacity to adapt and survive in these difficult times. The children don't speak to us in their words, but they structure Jharna's narrative plot that she recounts for our benefit. Often, she asserts it was the element of luck that was crucial for her success in protecting the children.

One thing that her narrative does very clearly is to show the fears that engulfed the minorities in East Pakistan in 1971. No one cared for the vulnerable; and children were viewed as disposable liabilities. Jharna had to move them from place to place because there was no safe home for them. As she tells the story of her experiences, one cannot predict how the situation will end for the children: will they be saved or will they die due to starvation, be killed by animals, or be taken away by the enemy? Fortunately, the surrender of the Pakistan Army to the Indian forces ended this unendurable condition of unpredictability and uncertainty.

After the war ended, Jharna returned to her work of managing the Gandhi Ashram where she provided a safe home to "her" children. Jharna's narrative enables us to cast a glance in the direction of the shadowy and undocumented world of children's lives in wartime. It is a rare and unique opportunity to hear what children endured and what their fears might have been. Jharna's capacity not to buckle under the pressure of these harsh conditions or fail in her commitment to the children makes her a hero. Were the Bihari children in East Pakistan fortunate enough to find a hero like Jharna to save them too?

JHARNA CHOWDHURY'S STORY

I was in Dhaka in 1971. I was in a training camp in a welfare society. We worked for social welfare. I left Dhaka on March 23 and went to Chittagong via Comilla. I was in Chittagong Medical College on March 25. On March 24 the Bangladesh flag was already hoisted there. I saw some of the representatives of the East Pakistan Rifles. They tried to present themselves as if they were from the media. Some of them were wearing *lungi* [sarong], some were wearing pants. There were not many, only seven or eight of them. I heard them tell the crowd that had gathered to listen to them that they [the soldiers] must fight, and they used the roof of a building to hide and fire from there. They wanted to counterattack the cantonment [military compound]. They started firing.[14] There was so much noise. Several hundred people took shelter there. The electricity was shut down; the entire place was in darkness. I saw this with my own eyes.

I was born in 1938, so I have seen the British period, and I saw the communal riots of 1962 and 1963. In 1969, I saw the Bhasha Andolan [Language Movement].[15] There was a great deal of disturbance inside the country then, as well as in 1971. I am sure as a historian you understand this. We went to the board of directors and asked them how they could allow people to fight from inside a women's hostel. The director said, "If Ram kills us we will die; as well, if Rahim kills us we will die. It is better to die in the hands of Ram."[16] There was scarcity of food everywhere. They had to bring food from outside. It was a terrible time; men, women, young children, and old people were dying everywhere.

I was not in charge of the group in Chittagong. There were other staff members from the ashram [Gandhi Ashram in Noakhali] who were in charge. After this incident on March 25, I'd say that the war started. The person in charge of the Medical College at that time was Mr. Talukdar. He sent the old people, children, and sick patients to the village. He sent us to take care of them. I was a teacher and a welfare officer too.

Since I was not married, I was more mobile. In fact, all the people from the Ashram were like a single family, and they were ready to go wherever they were sent. We were all dedicated to the ashram. We made a camp outside Chittagong and started staying there. Many people joined our camp. We took care of them. They killed our Dhirendra Lal Chowdhury along with five other people.[17] We became leaderless. There were about four hundred people staying there.

We were all Hindus in this camp. It was not easy to get food, particularly the staples, rice and dal [lentils], were very hard to find. Since all of us in the camp were Hindu and our diet was the same, we were able to make arrangements and shared our food. My secretary and I arranged for rice, tomato, dal, and drumsticks. We made the dal with drumsticks and served them with rice. Camp life was not at all easy as there was hardly any food to feed the people. We had only one set of clothes with us. We had to stay there with very little because we did not know when we had to move again. This camp that I am talking about was about thirty kilometers from Chittagong. The chairman of the village gave us some rice. We somehow managed to stay alive by collecting food from different sources. During this time of crisis we became one single group, there was no division among the people who stayed in the camp.

We had many old people, women, and children with us. The women had duties. I used to wake them up at 4 A.M. They went to different villages to look and beg for food. Whatever we could gather, rice, dal, pumpkin, and so on, we collected and combined together. Sometimes we had very little, and by evening our stomachs would be empty. We had so little that one meal was all we could manage on most days. The food that we cooked was distributed equally. Everybody got to eat something whenever we had food, but there was not much.

On May 20 the members of the ashram were all taken away.[18] There were five people from the ashram: four of them died, and one was carried away by a fox. Later, I heard that one of them had died of starvation, and that the army killed the rest of them. No one was willing to break this news to me at first. My older brother gave me the news. I couldn't believe it. The time was around 3 P.M., and the children and I were very hungry. I was thinking what should I do? Should I eat or complete the last rituals for the dead? The children were very hungry so I arranged for some food. A person from Chittagong helped us. He had also heard the news of what had happened in the ashram and came to visit us in the camp. I told him that I did not have any money, so I could not feed the children. He gave me fifty rupees. In those days, fifty rupees was a huge amount of money. I bought some *laddos*[19] and divided it among the children. Then I arranged for an earthen pot. I put some rice, dal, and salt in the pot and boiled them together for the evening meal. I gave a small portion of it to the eighteen children who were with me. I also had some older boys who were studying for their school final exams. I gave them a little extra food. Then I sent the boys to bury the dead bodies. I could not allow them to burn the bodies because it would be obvious that it was a Hindu funerary ceremony and that would have attracted a lot of attention. The army would kill us. So we had to bury the bodies like Muslims do, although the dead were Hindus.

We moved to a forest. That was the only place for us. Who would give so many people shelter? In the forest while we were hiding, an old man approached us. He had a lantern in his hand and a stick in the other. We were feeling scared that he will take some of the girls with him. We were afraid that anything can happen and we wouldn't know what to do. There was no escape for us. He came to us and asked us why we were sitting there. "Will you not go?" he inquired. I asked him where we could go. There was no place for us to go as all our people had been killed. He was curious if this meant that we were planning to stay in the forest. He asked us to follow him. So we all followed him. He took us to a house. He asked the girls to go to the first floor and the boys to stay downstairs. There were women upstairs. They left all the rooms for us to use. The next day, in the morning, we went out and dug some trenches in the garden. Once again, the women went out in search of rice and food. That evening we had boiled rice and dal.

We came to this house on May 20, and on May 31 I went back to Chittagong. I took my secretary with me and left the children behind in the house. Neither of us had a set of clean clothes to wear. We had no soap either. We were dressed like sweepers, and we went to Chittagong like that. An acquaintance of mine arranged for two burqas for us. We wore that and boarded a rickshaw. Then we went to visit some people in Chittagong. We needed to get their help to transport the women and children who were in our care. When they met us, our friends cried a lot. These were Christian missionaries. They arranged for us to be dressed like nuns.

We were now dressed in nuns' clothes as if we were Christian missionaries. Underneath we were wearing polyester saris, shoes, and glasses. Those days polyester was a popular material for saris. We got in touch with the Catholic mission. With the help of the church authorities, we slowly started bringing the children from the place where they were hiding. We brought them in groups of two and three. We used to dress them up differently every time so that the army did not suspect us to be of the same group. We also changed the children's names and their last names so that the Pakistani soldiers could not guess that these children were Hindu. We also went all over Chittagong to look for other homeless children and brought them to the mission. I and Nila di used to fill out the forms for Hindu and Muslim children.

In Chittagong we initially stayed in a house of the Mondals. We were very scared. They [the Pakistanis] had killed all our relatives; our own people were all dead. So we used to cry a lot. Dora Mondal, our host, was not very welcoming though. She would tell us, "Don't cry so much, my bed will get wet." The owner of the house was Albert Sukumar Mondal. He told us that he would eat with us, as Hindus do, and I used to cook for all of them. I like cooking so it was not a chore.

One day, when we all sat down to pray, someone knocked on the door. Mr. Mondal was very frightened and asked us to leave his house immediately. So we had to leave with the children; we had only the rickshaw fare with us. It was 9 P.M. then. We asked the rickshaw puller to take us to a nearby church, but when we reached the place we found that the gates were closed. We went to the next house seeking help, but the owners asked us to leave. We returned to the church and found that the small gate on the side was open, and two of us managed to get through. We helped the others; we had eight people inside the church. At that very moment just as we all got inside, two army trucks passed by. They missed us by a couple of seconds. If they had seen us, they would have killed us. I went to the priest and told him that we were Dora and Mary (the names of Mrs. Mondal's nieces). So he opened the door, and we cried a lot then. The next morning we tried to make arrangements for the eight people to provide them shelter elsewhere. I did not know where we could take them. Mr. Mondal had thrown us out of his house. While I contemplated what to do, I received a call from him. He was concerned if we were alive and how we were doing.

I faced the Pakistan Army once in the Chittagong police station. I told them that we were Christians. Thus we were saved. Another time, I had to face them in Mr. Mondal's house. Mrs. Mondal was very friendly toward them. She used to joke with them and invite them to her house. She introduced us as her relatives. When the Pakistanis came to the house they asked for drinks, and she served them Coke or Fanta. She also introduced us as her nieces, Dora and Mary. Mrs. Mondal was very brave. She was very comfortable with them. I never came out to visit with them. I stayed in the kitchen and cooked.

A minister from India helped me to leave Chittagong and cross the border. Two students accompanied me on the trip. My old mother and my family also went with me. By family, I mean my brother and his daughter. When I met the minister, I told him that I did not have ID cards for anyone in the group. I asked him what I should do. He believed me and issued me a special card. I had to have a proper name because I had to meet different people like Charuji.[20] I was allowed to meet him alone, and I asked him for assistance for the work I was doing. I realized that this meeting will have some consequences, and I will become visible to too many people and they will become aware of my work. I was still wearing the clothes of a nun, and it was a spectacle to see a nun go to meet Charuji. I met many important people in India then. Generally people know me as Jharna, but my official name then was Mani Bala Rai Chowdhury. I saw that lots of young Bengali girls from East Pakistan were working and helping in different capacities in Tripura. Maleka Begum was there; also Sultana Kamal and her sister were there. Sultana was staying in the women's hostel, and I had lunch with her one day.

I received a lot of help from the Shadinota Camp and sent the stuff I collected to Chandan Nagar [near Kolkata]. Then I went to Kalka and got in touch with more people there. Indira Gandhi sent her messenger to meet me. She asked me to write down everything that I had seen and experienced. Whenever I tried to write I felt sick, as if I had been stabbed in my chest. I was very emotional. I had lost one girl in the group. I think she was taken away by some animal. My girls and children were suffering so much, I could not write all this down as if they were in the past. I knew that they were still suffering. I wrote what I could, but I was not allowed to tell anyone who I was. I could not even tell them that I was a teacher.

Many people would ask me if I was sad for leaving behind my husband and child in Bangladesh. I would say yes, but I was afraid that if they asked more, I would not know what to say. I was not even married, but I had to pretend that I was so that no one would suspect what work I did and my involvement in the ashram. In the meantime, one of the two students staying with me had dysentery. She was also running a high temperature. I was very worried for her. I gave her an injection. I was afraid that something horrible might happen to her at night. I did not know what I would do then.

I saw lots of small children, mostly Bengali Muslim children, playing with gold ornaments. They had so many watches, boxes of things, and trunks full of goods. I was staying in a Muslim person's house at that time. His name was Hasan. He was a political person, but I did not tell him anything. Later, when our own people came from the camp to fetch me, I left with them. I saw a lot of people had benefited during the war; they were all Muslims.

I had also seen women being raped, kidnapped, killed, and mutilated. I had myself buried five bodies. The people around me told me that I was not supposed to use that ground. I had to remove those bodies and rebury them elsewhere. I treated many sick people in the villages. I knew a little about medicine, and I used whatever knowledge I had to help people who needed my help. I had responsibility for many children. I had to arrange their food, as well as make sure that they were protected. Around this time, my brother's wife was expecting her baby. I had to take care of her too.

I returned to Bangladesh after some time. I wrote the report that Indira Gandhi wanted me to. I told her all that I knew. Many international visitors also met with me then. There were many young men who were working in the intelligence service, and they met with me to discuss what was happening inside East Pakistan. I went to Kolkata from there, and I got in touch with everyone I could there. I returned to Bangladesh after we got independence. It was on January 1 or 3 that I went back to Jessore. I could not find anyone there. I stayed there for two nights or so. I was hosted by the owner of a local cinema there. He was a Muslim person. I was very scared to stay in his house. They were scared, too. But they helped me. From Jessore, I went to Khulna. From there I went to Dhaka Ram Krishna Mission. I asked them to help me bring back the orphans from India. Slowly, they started coming back to Dhaka.

During 1971 the whole place was in chaos. I was, as you have heard, involved in the social welfare of destitute women and children. It was a horrible time; everyone was torturing, killing, looting, and destroying everyone else. They were grabbing each other's things, entering their homes, destroying their women; it was like hell. Some of my acquaintances, women of my age group, were also raped. Some were even killed. So many women lost their husbands, fathers, and brothers. Most of them were very troubled, lonely, desperate, and I was worried what they would do. Now, however, life has changed for them. If you meet them now, they look happy; they have settled down. So much time has passed. People have healed their wounds. I have also stopped thinking about 1971. It makes me feel badly when I think about those days, but generally I never think about it. I am talking about it after nearly thirty years.

Bihari children living like prisoners. (*Source withheld*)

Dying slowly from hunger. (*Source withheld*)

5

WOMEN'S WAR

LAILA AHMED, RAJSHAHI AND DHAKA

There was a revolt, you can say,
by women, and it had a great impact.

—LAILA AHMED

The story of the Liberation War would have become a kind of religious artifact in Bangladesh, pure and inaccessible, a deified object of worship if we did not have Bangladeshi women to report on it. In a variety of voices, these women raise our awareness of the multiple experiences of the war from many different locations as victims, collaborators, supporters, caregivers, soldiers, bystanders, and survivors. Their memories make us realize the war's terrifying power of violence that wreaked havoc among the communities of women, and, simultaneously, we learn to appreciate those individual women who resisted the dehumanization of their gender against all odds.

The desire to fight and become agents of the state and nation provided motivation to many women to join in the war efforts. The dream to be freedom fighters was for the majority of women in the realm of imagination, they could not find an entry point in the male-dominated war. A few did and got the taste of fighting some battles firsthand, which was an important turning point in their lives.[1] Generally women were pushed out of the battlefield to secondary and invisible places like infirmaries and clinics as first-aid workers and nurses to take care of wounded soldiers. Women were thus, once again, reduced into the service of men, and their hope to be equal partners in founding a new nation was severely restricted.

To understand the power of the attraction of war for women and their ambition to become soldiers on behalf of the nation, we have to hear from the women who were enthralled by the rhetoric of nationalism and promise of an independent nation, which inspired them to overcome the patriarchal order of Bengali society and make individual decisions to risk their lives in the hope of service to their country. What were these women's experiences in war? How should we judge women who decided to fight and kill for nation? The hands-on and deliberate killing that men did in war with the aim to destroy their real and imagined enemies makes it easier to pass judgment on men as perpetrators. It seems many women also desired to do the same work as men did, but they could not execute these actions because of the barriers that gender posed. If we simply go by the rhetoric of ethnic nationalism to free Bangladesh from the clutches of the Pakistani rulers that some women recite in remembering their war memories, it would not be difficult to call them potential perpetrators. The problem of understanding and explaining the hopes of Bengali women and comparing them with their actions and activities during and after the war, however, produces a far more complex and nuanced narrative of women's experiences, which clearly establishes the different experiences of Bengali women versus men. Women's reality as secondary citizens limited the exercise of their agency even before independent Bangladesh was born.

In Laila Ahmed's narrative, we hear a firsthand report of the lived experiences of discrimination that women had to combat within the fluctuating situation of the war. Women's roles were not outlined or developed within the war plans, and their inclusion was on an ad hoc basis. It is in episodes like Laila's that women's fractured inclusion in the nation-making process becomes evident, and we clearly see the discrimination at work that has plagued Bangladesh's history right from the beginning and continues even now. How did a woman like Laila change an adverse situation into an opportunity to create awareness of women's work and a site of hope for others? How do we judge her struggle that has continued beyond the battleground? Has liberation delivered the promise of freedom and equality to women in Bangladesh? Tracing the experiences of Laila gives us an understanding and some answers to these questions.

Laila Ahmed lives and works in Dhaka, where I met her a few times. She is a single woman and is well known socially and professionally in her field of work. Our discussions were generally conducted in the private space of her home, which provided opportunities to have long and frank conversations on many topics. She was generally forthcoming and willing to engage, but was not comfortable in talking about witnessing or enabling violence. Hence, after a few attempts, I decided not to interrogate her on that delicate subject. She was more interested in talking about the process of her involvement (or lack of it) in the war, and I focused our conversations on that topic.

The war had a dramatic impact on Laila, as we find in the narrative below. From living a protected and sheltered life at home as a student in the medical college, she was transformed into a homeless revolutionary; a self-image she liked to present and talk about at great length during our discussions.

Laila's testimony is a narrative road to personal forgetting of family and friends who constituted her world. In its place she created a new world based on purpose and service to nation, which she actualized after the war. But first she had to make sense of emotions and experiences that arrived at the doorstep of her home when the war broke out and changed the familiar into the strange. She realized that her father's death and the utter lack of respect for her female body by kin made her into a liability. The world in which she was protected and respected was gone. The harsh lesson the war taught her was that her body made her vulnerable, and others would survive by disclaiming association with her because of this. She had to pay the price of the dissolution of her family. Rather than relinquishing and accepting her fate, she struggled to come to terms with the end of her old self, but she created a new purpose through discipline and a forward-looking will, becoming a participant and not remaining a bystander in the war. The troubling realities of the unscripted acts of violence that she encountered in this new mission opened a space for another level of interrogation. She continued to find a pattern behind the planned and unplanned assaults on her. She found that gender discrimination was a designed social system to destroy the private and political being of women.

Strangers became kin in her flight to find a purpose, and in the alien land of India she found a location to carry on her struggle. Laila had to undertake a personal journey as a woman, and she emerged as a free agent after a long and hard struggle. In Kolkata she trained to fight in battle. Unfortunately for her, the war ended before she received notice of deployment. She did not have the opportunity to carry arms and fight on behalf of her nation, and this has remained her greatest regret.

Laila's testimony makes us question what women were capable of doing during the war. We suddenly find we do not know the Bangladeshi women. Our lens was focused on a single vision thus far. We saw Bangladeshi women as victims of sexual violence and caregivers. We did not encounter Bangladeshi women as aggressive agents, desiring to kill and be killed on behalf of territory and nation. We believe we knew them as pacific voices against violence. We have a conventional image, and we want to hold on to it. We are biased. Laila's testimony tells another story. A woman like Laila was motivated by the cold rationalization of political issues to support the war effort. Laila believed that wartime participation was a necessary price for full citizenship in the future. Her youthful infatuation with the romance of war and longing to become a frontline participant by committing violence to make nation and find a place as a full member in the newly created nation were not fulfilled.[2]

The harsh conditions of living and training in an alien and male-dominated environment were difficult for Laila, but she endured it in the hope that she, too, would be a war hero. The ideological training in the classes that she received was important for her. She felt worthy. But it was not enough. She needed to see the war upfront and find a place for herself within the rank of soldiers. She never achieved that purpose despite several trips to the border camps. In the face of failure, which she experienced time and again, being denied the opportunity to fight for Bangladesh, Laila now clings to every detail of the listless days past — the schedules they maintained in the women's training division, the daily work they did, and the sacrifices they made. Her detailed memory of the places and the people she had encountered during the process of preparing to become a soldier is marvelous, but it makes one ask why does she remember so much. Why is this memory so important to her more than three decades later?

The period of the war was a turbulent time for Laila. It was ruthless on her body and mind. She has committed to memory every person she met along the way in her recovery and becoming an agent for change, each episode in the process, every gesture of friendship, because she needs to make sense of the disruption that the war entailed and the changes she made. The war is plotted as the point of transition in her life. For Laila to remember everything that happened in the process is crucial. Laila is convinced that women would have been "delivered" from their restricted female form and become truly free from the clutches of a male-dominated society if the war hadn't ended so soon. An extended war would have demanded women's participation in the front and, in that case, Laila and many others like her would have found a place among the respectable war heroes. War was a hope for another possible future for women like Laila, but it never delivered that promise. It is an unusual viewpoint coming from a person who desired a peaceful Bangladesh.

In the face of the failure to become a war hero and no home to return to, Laila became bold and defiant. She refused to marry and settle down. On completing her medical courses, she decided to take a leadership role in providing healthcare to the rural poor. She has since dedicated herself to the primary healthcare program for disempowered rural women with the hope of making them masters of their lives and bodies, which women of her generation could not achieve. Laila understands that women have limited privileges within the nation-state even after liberation; she had suffered many levels of discrimination. She is determined to facilitate others to overcome the restrictions of gender that are imposed on them. Were women like Laila really deemed partners in a war that men fought? She waits and longs to find that place, and every bit of the past—the war and violence that promised fulfillment—she gathers and preserves in the hope that she will be able to make sense of her life someday. For now the question lingers: can women be accepted as architects of the nation-building process in post-liberated Bangladesh?

LAILA AHMED'S STORY

My father was an intelligence officer and was posted in the Central Intelligence Division. I had five brothers. I am the only daughter. Our ancestral village is in Kustia, near the India and Bangladesh border. We lived in Rajshahi town, and our house was directly on the riverbank. On one side of the river is India; on the other side is Bangladesh. I had a cousin who served in the Air Force as an officer during the war. After March 25, Rajshahi was under the control of the *mukti jouddhas* [freedom fighters], but not for long. They kept the Pakistani officers captive there. A new regiment of the Pakistan Army was sent from Dhaka. In the town, though, all the units—like the BDR [Bangladesh Rifles], East Bengal Regiment, and Intelligence Department—were supporting the freedom fighters.

On April 13, the Pakistan Army captured the Police Training Institute near Rajshahi. They entered the university and caused a massacre. Rajshahi town fell that night after fierce fighting. We took shelter in an old building with the families of other intelligence officers. We were afraid to stay in our own house because it was like a bungalow and the roof was made of straw and tin that would catch fire if the Pakistan Army shot at it. The freedom fighters did not alert people when they left; people were not aware that the Pakistan Army had taken Rajshahi town. If they had done that, rung the alarm bells all over town, so many people wouldn't have died.

The Pak Army came into our town with their tanks and ammunition. This was on Wednesday, April 14, 1971, and in Bangla it is Chaitra 31. They were well equipped and well informed. They came into town at 10 P.M. and captured Saheb Bazaar without any opposition from the Bengalis. The whole day, they went from place to place arresting ordinary people who they thought were anti-Pakistan. They broke open the gate leading to the house where we were all taking shelter. They entered the house and looted it. My mother and two small brothers were in the house. Two other brothers had fled to my elder brother's house. Many local people were fleeing to India by the river way, and one of my brothers went away with one such group, about which we did not know until later.

I was a student of Rajshahi Medical College at that time, and our college was closed since March 23. I was a day-scholar; that is, I lived at home and attended college from there. College was not far from our house. There were fifteen to sixteen girls in our house when the Pak Army entered our house. We were asked to stay behind and not come out in front of them. We saw them from a distance. They asked all the men to line up—my father was also in the line-up—and they marched them out of the house. They took them some distance away from the gate, out of sight of the people, and then brush fired them. This I learned later on. Everybody could hear the sound of gunfire, but we were not certain what had happened.

At around 4 P.M. that afternoon, we went up to the terrace to see what was happening in town. The entire place looked desolate. We heard the sound of firing; it was continuous, and soon we saw there was a fire in our neighborhood. We thought, "Our house will be burned in this fire." The fire was so intense and fierce that people from the Indian side of the border and across from the river Padma saw it too. People were suddenly very scared. They did not know what to do since the Pakistani soldiers had surrounded the town and the people.

My family told me to hide. I hid in a place with the other girls for the night. No one came to see us that night. If they'd come to check on us, the Pakistanis would have come to know that there were girls hiding there. Across from where we were hiding was a wall. Dead bodies were on the other side. We heard people walking there; they were making sounds and breaking twigs and things like that. We were praying that the fire would go out and whoever was on the other side of our hideout wouldn't find us. We were very afraid. It rained that night. In the campus where we stayed, there were other women too. Mothers were trying to protect their young girls because everyone knew that when the Pakistani soldiers came they raped young girls. We were all afraid of that. They had taken away girls from the university hall in Dhaka. The small towns came under their control after Dhaka. Our main motto was to save our lives and the honor of girls. Girls suffer the risk of torture, rape, and death. Boys, on the other hand, fear that they will be captured, tortured, and put to death. Now when I think back on it, I wonder if the people in the villages were also concerned about these problems. For certain, those who were somewhat educated and were aware of the nature of the Pakistan Army men were well aware of the dangers that we had to deal with.

Ninety people had taken shelter in the place I was hiding that night. They included men, women, and children. In the morning, people left the place. It was still raining. The dead bodies were wet, and some were rotten and lying in the muck and water. We, the young girls, requested that the bodies be brought inside, to a decent place. But everyone, particularly the men, refused us. They told us that the army might come again, and if they don't see the dead bodies they will know that the local people were involved and will find us. On the other hand, if they see the dead bodies lying outside, they will think there is no one alive in the neighborhood. Hence, they wanted to use the dead bodies for their own safety. I really felt badly about it; I told them we can run away instead of using the dead bodies for our protection. But no one listened to me.

People were going on with their daily business as if nothing had happened. They were cooking, taking care of children, and generally talking. When I asked my mother what had happened, she told me that the night before when we were in hiding my father was taken away by the army. She had waited for me to return so that she could move us to another building where there were many people hiding, more than a hundred people or so. When I heard this from my mother, I wondered if my father's body was also lying outside in the mud on the road.

I had to find out if my father was lying in the cold out there. So I peeked out of the building we were hiding in. From the crack in the door, I saw my father's face, and his body was swollen and he was making some sounds. I could not go out because the road was visible from the main door, and the people who were staying inside the building had posted a watchman on the door to prevent people from going out and coming in. I was feeling very sad. My father was lying outside, almost dead, and others were taking advantage of it. I was the oldest child in my family. I was watching him helplessly and unable to do anything. I was very close to my father. My mother did not say a thing to the people in the building. She kept quiet. She wanted to live, I think, and did not want to risk her life for her husband. I had two younger brothers too; they were not with us then. One was eleven and the other two-and-a-half years old. Also, my younger sister was missing. We did not have information about them. My mother sat there the whole day and did not even move. She refused to ask the men to help her bring her husband inside. I went about trying to get my mind off the problem and started giving first aid to those who were inside and needed some help. Being a woman, my body was considered to be dangerous to myself and others, but I could not do anything because everyone was afraid. So we waited and hid inside the abandoned building all day. Inside the building, they had divided the place into two sectors. There was a section for women and children and another for the men.

In the evening, a truck came. It was full of dead bodies. The men who were collecting dead bodies were in civilian clothes, but I think they were army men. They inspected the ground, and then brought out the dead bodies from the truck. They dug a shallow grave and piled these bodies with the ones lying on the ground together and put some earth over them. The bodies were not well buried at all. They left them like that and went away. We heard the sound of windows being broken, but nothing happened that night. On Friday, we heard an announcement that the army had left our town. I came out of the building and saw that my father's body was barely covered with earth. The body parts were visible and rotting away, but no one cared that he did not get a decent burial. I requested that the men help me to bury my father properly. In the meantime, my brother who was missing came looking for us, and he helped me to put some earth on the exposed dead bodies. But he did not understand or know who had died and who we were burying. We decided to leave that building. It was not a safe place to stay. The house had a five-foot wall and a thatched roof with tin over it, and it could be burned down at any time by the army. So we returned to our house, which was not too far from the place where we had taken shelter.

We heard that the army was going to open all the offices the day after Jumma [Friday] and force people to return to work. My mother decided to retrieve the property documents from the strong room in my father's office where he had kept them. My mother was a strong person. She was a teacher in Calcutta in the British era, and she was practical and aware of the situation. We did not have information about my elder brother, and some people told us that he left on April 13 with others. We later got news of my elder brother and his family, that they were alive. He had one daughter and two sons. One of them was in the air force. They were all captured and taken as prisoners. We were dumbfounded when we got the news.

My father's two brothers came to our house. We used to live on the border of Kustia. My uncles were much younger than my father. One was studying in the university. It was not easy for them to come to our house. They had to cross the border to the Indian side and come to us through Behrampur, Murshidabad. We were on the bank of Padma in Rajshahi town, but the people who lived across from us were not citizens of East Pakistan but India. My uncles were living on the island in Padma. While they were hiding there, they heard that the entire town of Rajshahi was under the control of the Pakistan Army. The Pakistani soldiers used to fire on the island whenever they saw any movement there. People staying on the island were given an hour's break from the curfew-like conditions to go to the market in Rajshahi. My uncles dressed up like people of the island and came to our house along with the people from that island when they came for the daily shopping. My uncles wanted to take us with them, but my mother refused to leave her house. She told them that it would be difficult to raise six children on the island without a proper place to stay and without assets to support her. She requested my uncles to take me with them. She was very concerned about me. My eleven-year-old brother also came with us, but my elder brother wanted to stay with my mother and also my youngest brother stayed with her.

My uncles came to fetch us on May 11, and we moved on May 12. I dressed up like a girl from the island and walked with other women past the army. We went to Behrampur, Jalangi, and Nadia and reached my grandfather's house in Kustia. It took us a whole day and night to walk through the island to reach the place. We reached Kustia and found that it was a free land. The whole border was free at that time; but later after occupying the towns, the Pakistan Army started closing the borders. For four or five days, there was no trouble. Men and women from Faridpur were crossing the border [to India] from this side. They were refugees.

My grandfather's house was huge. It was located in the village of Dharmoda in Shikarpur. The house was on eight *bighas*[3] of land, and he had a lovely garden with a tube well and everything. When I lived there, my normal day consisted of providing first aid to the people who came from across the border. I used to give them water, food like puffed rice, and anything else I found and they could manage to find. I also gave them information of the army postings, and this was of great help at that time. We also had a small house in the compound that we used as a rest house for the refugees.

However, later when the army came to the village, the whole situation changed. I saw them rape many girls. Once I saw them rape a girl from a good middle-class home, and they left her bleeding. She was no more than eighteen years of age. But no one could do anything for her. Rape was not the only torture they did to the women here. To be forced to leave one's house is another kind of torture, and so many women had to leave their homes because of fear of the army. They had to move to unknown places without their family, at times, without their children or food, and they had to stay in that condition for days, weeks. Sometimes they never met their families again.

Soon the army started coming regularly to our village and asked the people to vacate it. They stopped coming at night because the mukti jouddhas, who used to have a camp on the other side of the bank, used to come to the village at night. The Pakistan Army was not able to identify them, so they wanted the people to vacate the village.

The army came twice and told the people to leave. Their camp was two miles away, and they used to take two hours to walk through the bank. We could see them as they approached us. The young women used to cross the narrow rivers on banana rafts and go to the other side and hide there. We would come out at night when the Pakistani soldiers had left. Some potters went to the other side of the river, to the Indian side, and lived there. We did not move there.

The Indian Army started firing towards this border, where we were, from the other side of the border during the daytime. This side of the border was higher than the other side, so it was quite visible. The freedom fighters had joined them, too. Our families told us to go into the interior of the village, more than a mile inside, and stay there. We used to return only in the evening. Ten or twelve of us were doing this daily; my aunt was with us. The rest were all young women. On May 24 the army came to empty the village. My aunt and the others wanted to go to the other side of the river. My uncle asked me if I would like to go with them. My aunt's family was from the village and used to live in the interior, about three miles inland. My aunt wanted me to go with her there, but I refused because there was no certainty about the army's behavior. They could easily go there too, and then we would be in trouble.

There was a massive battle there for a day. The entire day there was firing from both sides. I stayed in the house of a potter. I was alone there with my uncle and brother. That night a Christian boy called Dipu came to take me to a temporary shelter, but my uncle didn't want to let me go since he had promised my mother to take care of me. I did not want him to decide about my life; I wanted to take my own responsibility. He wanted me to give this in writing to him so that my mother would not hold him responsible.

My maternal grandmother used to stay in Nadia. We did not have any connection with her, but I had her address. I decided to go to her house. I got shelter in a *zamindar*'s [landowner's] house that night. His daughter, I found out, was a student in Kolkata and was educated. When she found out that I was a medical student, she was very upset that I was in this condition moving from place to place like a homeless person. Next day, I went to my grandmother's house. She was very old at that time. She had lost two of her sons within six months in two car accidents. Her youngest son who lived in Kolkata took care of her. Now, when I arrived at her house, I gave her the news of her son-in-law's—my father's—death. I had reached her house after three days journey, although in normal conditions it takes no more than three hours to get there. On the way to my grandmother's, I stayed in Dipu Kabiraj's house. His mother and other family members were there.

The death of my father was the turning point in my life. After that, many incidents, big and small, took place, but they did not affect me as much. When I was growing up my father never allowed me to go anywhere alone, although I was a medical student. He was very conservative. I had never been to a students' picnic. I had a fixed rickshaw, and the rickshaw puller used to drop me and pick me up from college. My father never allowed us to go to any party or join politics. Being in the intelligence branch, he knew everything that was happening in politics and the government. I grew up in a protected and sheltered home.

Today people say that they were with the freedom fighters from the beginning. It was not easy, although many people claim that they went to war. It is true that many people in East Pakistan supported the mass uprising. Many Bengali officers [who defected from the Pakistan Army] also supported the freedom struggle. I don't know if my father was involved, but he was killed during the time of the takeover. It was not that easy to become a freedom fighter when the Pakistan Army was watching everything that the Bengali officers were doing. It was May 24 and the process of forming a government-in-exile in India had already started a few weeks before. The structure of the government was not clear at that time. Freedom fighters who were from the ex-East Bengal Regiment [EBR] and East Pakistan Rifle [EPR], who knew how to handle guns, were setting up camps of freedom fighters and training men. I had some relatives who were in the Bengal Regiment, and I contacted them. I made these contacts very early on when I was staying in the potter's home. I forgot to tell you that when I was staying in my grandfather's house, the villagers there had asked him to leave his house and take shelter elsewhere. But he refused. He reasoned that the army would not bother an old man like him. He was mistaken. When the Pakistani soldiers came to the village, they forcibly occupied his house and hung him with his own *lungi* [sarong]. They wanted his house, which was on higher ground and from where they could see the enemy's movements. Also, the house was surrounded by a wall and was beside the river, which made it easier for them to catch the people who were using the river to escape.

Dipu Kabiraj told me to go to Kolkata since the government-in-exile had formed, and the important members were available there. I wanted to join the medical wing of the Mukti Bahini, since I was a medical student. I went to Kolkata and contacted the ministry. One of my father's friends was the minister of the Health Department in the new government. He advised me to meet someone in Theater Road,[4] and that person asked me to join the office and work there for a while. They offered me a salary of one hundred and fifty rupees per month. I refused to take this job. Since I refused, they asked me to go and meet General Osmani in Kaylani, where he was staying. They told me that he can appoint me to the medical wing, and in that case I could go and help the freedom fighters. I did not know where Kaylani was, so I asked Dipu Kabiraj if he would accompany me. I trusted him as an Indian more than I would a Bangladeshi man. There were nine refugee camps in Kaylani, and General Osmani's office was also there. I could not meet General Osmani because we were late. The tram in which we were traveling had an electric failure, so we were delayed. We went back to Kolkata without meeting the general. My younger brother was also with me then. Since I decided to join the freedom fighters, I sent my brother back home. It was very hard for me to make that decision since I knew our house, being in Shikarpur on the border, was a vulnerable target. My grandmother was not aware of anything that we were planning. She wouldn't have allowed me if she knew.

There was an elderly doctor who used to practice in Krishna Nagar in Nadia. His office was near the train station. I decided to go to Kaylani again. Some local people there told me that they could take me to Kaylani. But I refused their help. I had a sixth sense that they were not good people. I was very cautious and used to take shelter in safe places like the doctor's chambers. I never went anywhere with a strange person. The doctor sent me to Theater Road in Kolkata in one of his patient's taxi. I tried contacting people there so many times. I was tired. I was twenty years old and had to sell everything I owned, like my gold chain, to generate money to pay for my expenses. I tried not to take taxis and public transport in order to save my money. So I walked as much as I could. My legs were swollen, and I had apses and a kidney infection. Kidney infection was a common disease at that time. Sodhukha Choudhury was there at that time. He was a minister and was helping educated women to get training before sending them to the field. This was toward the end of June. He selected me to get trained.

We stayed in Gobra Camp; it was a garden house of a rich man in the middle of the biggest burial ground in Kolkata. In that compound there was also a factory, but it was closed due to the Naxalite problem. This compound was now given to the Bangladesh government-in-exile for its use. It was outside the main city of Kolkata. Naxalites used to make bombs there and also used it as their shelter. Regular people did not visit this place. There were some people who did not want us to be there. They used to throw stones at us.

There were very few women in the camp in the beginning. Many joined afterwards. St. John's Ambulance Association of India started giving us first-aid training. They also trained us for espionage, short arms training, and nursing. All these tasks women could do easily. Also, we had to attend a variety of classes on different subjects. These classes were taught by women from different colleges and universities. There was Mira Di from Lady Braborne College, another from Jadavpur University, and one more teacher. They were preparing the girls mentally to go to the battlefield and fight. They used to tell us the history of war and fighting on the borders, and about Fidel Castro and Che Guevara. Mira Di also gave us physical training, and her brother, who was serving in the Indian Air Force, used to teach us about arms and ammunition. This training was arranged by the Indian government, but they did not give us arms. After our regular classes were over, I used to teach in the medical camp about first aid.

Most of the girls who were in this camp were actively involved in politics during their student days, before 1971. They had come on their own to the camp, like I did. They came from various places in Bangladesh, like Dhaka, Chittagong, and some of them came from the refugee camps because they wanted to do something for the country. There was one girl from a rather rich family in Bangladesh. Her father was killed, and her mother was abducted on the way when they were trying to cross the border to India. She was well trained in horse riding. She came to this camp to train with us. Now she lives in Kolkata and is married.

There were strict rules in the camp. We used to get thirty-five rupees in Indian currency for personal expenses. Everything else was free. Our food was free; we were also given two white saris each, our bedclothes, and mattress. All of us in the camp had taken an oath not to use a pillow as long as our country was not free. We cooked for ourselves, and when we were not in class or training, we spent our time singing war songs. I had to bring medicine from the medical unit in Theater Road. Generally I got tetanus injections, vitamins, ointments, and creams for injuries and pain, medicine for infection, and so on. We used to join protest rallies against international and national policies that were not in favor of Bangladesh. We also used to give public speeches on what was happening in East Pakistan and about the suffering of our people. We were also helping the Ramkrishna Mission and others who were working on behalf of the refugees.

Generally, we were not given permission to go out of the camp on our own or alone. I had to get permission to go out of the camp to fetch medicines from Theater Road. Likewise, if anyone wanted to come to the camp from outside, they had to first get permission to visit. There was strict enforcement of security after 5 P.M. For practical training, we were sent in batches of fifteen girls to B. R. Singh Railway Hospital. There were two batches for training. I went with both the batches.

After receiving practical training, the girls were sent for fieldwork. The first batch was sent to the Field Hospital of Ganashasta in Agartala, Tripura, from Kolkata. They were sent by train. Geeta, Mira, and many others were in that batch. They are still alive; you may want to talk to them. There were freedom fighters too, in the first batch. I can give you the names of the first batch, because I have all their names written down. Three sisters went together: Geeta, Ira, and Mukti. Their father and uncle had been killed.

The second batch was ready to go, but the country become free before the batch had an opportunity to serve. There were also other batches that were being prepared, but they were not required anymore. Gobra Camp became known as the Women's Freedom Fighter's Training Camp and was recognized by the Bangladesh government. The camp was closed on December 25. We were the last to leave the camp. Many of the girls went to their relatives. I was out of touch with my family for many days. When I was in the camp, I used to occasionally go to the Shikarpur border and meet with Dipu Kabiraj and the freedom fighters there. During these visits I got news about what was happening in the village.

After liberation it became known that many young women students from the university were victims of the war and were pregnant. I had returned to Bangladesh and had rejoined the medical college as a student. We heard that a medical team had come from India, from Mumbia, to carry out the work of abortion. This was not done openly in the hospital, but they set up some special units for this work. Since we are a conservative Muslim society, nobody wanted that the women should be identified. They were all concerned about the future of these girls. Hence, although people knew that rape had taken place during the war, no one talked about it or discussed about the abortions.

When I returned from Gobra Camp, nobody in Bangladesh was eager to know about our experiences. I joined the Medical College again. I met many of my old classmates, and they did not bother me, neither honoring nor dishonoring me. Honestly, I don't have memories aboutthat time. Our family was struggling for survival, and we had no economic stability. My mother was not like a typical Bengali woman. She used to read a lot of books, even as a child I remember discussing books with her. She had to manage a small pharmacy that we owned. My brother used to help her while he also attended college. That was our only source of income. My mother had to really struggle, as did the rest of the extended family. My cousin who had been in the Air Force returned to Bangladesh after 1973, and this helped the family a little. But none of our lives were settled for a long time.

My mother asked me to get married after I graduated from medical college. But I was now my own woman and could not be forced. It wouldn't have been possible if my father was alive. I couldn't have even dreamed of joining the freedom struggle, going to the other side, to India, on my own, let alone cross the river. After the war, I had really grown up. I knew what I wanted, and no one could force me to accept their ways.

For two years I worked as a lecturer in the Department of Anatomy in Rajshahi University. I did my higher degree from Dhaka P. G. Hospital in anatomy. I changed my mind about continuing in this field. I discussed this with the registrar and expressed interest to work with him to develop a program on rural women's health. It was the Ganashasta program. I was very keen to develop something that would benefit the country after the war. Although the program was not exclusively for women, but was a rural upliftment program, women, being the most backward and isolated group, were given more attention within this program. I asked my mother if I should pursue this career, and she told me to make my own decision. I was young and educated and there were lots of marriage proposals for me, but I refused them. I joined the program in 1976 and devoted myself to development work. In most places, I lived in very limited accommodations, in tin sheds and tents.

In the field, I found that the rural people had no knowledge about how to prevent the spread of disease. Women were suffering from complicated deliveries. We started a vaccination program. The village elders were discouraging women from coming to our centers. They really found it difficult to accept that the women field workers were moving around the villages on bicycles. These were women from their villages that we had employed to help us with the work. The village men and even the army guys used to pass bad remarks about these women. Even truck drivers used to threaten these women on cycles and hit them. We did not stop our work, though, and tried to overcome these obstacles by making the rural people, both men and women, aware of their health problems and the remedies that they could use for preventing the spread of disease. You will find it hard to imagine the obstacles we fought then. It was a very different world. But we persisted, and the women who came to work with us were breaking many rules and taking risks to assist us. There was a revolt, you can say, by women, and it had a great impact. You cannot understand it now. The Liberation War had made this possible.

The sad part is that the contribution of women in the freedom movement is very little known. It has not been recorded, at that time no one thought about it. Now they are trying to get information about women's activities at that time. If they had done it before, many more facts would have become evident; most of us have forgotten the details, and many have died. What you find even now is about the women who were in Dhaka and their work in politics, but there were many more women who contributed actively to the freedom struggle in Sylhet, Jessore, Kustia, Khulna, and other places. I was from Rajshahi, as you know. In 1997, for the first time they asked me about my experiences. It took them more than twenty-five years to find people like me.

I think women are more sincere and dedicated—as a mother, wife, widow, at home and in her workplace, even in politics. Bangladesh would have been more beautiful and prosperous if we were less selfish and really loved our country. In the field of politics, many have taken undue advantage of their involvement during the freedom struggle. But there are many more people who have really sacrificed for this country, but they have not benefited from the politics after liberation.

MUMTAZ BEGUM, JESSORE

I was discriminated against because of my gender.—MUMTAZ BEGUM

The work of the war was considered to be physically tough, mentally strenuous, and emotionally shocking. Men assumed that they alone were capable of handling these demands; war was not a game for women to play. Reluctantly few women were selected and admitted to the ranks, not as leaders and commanders but as agents and spies to help the movement of men who fought the war directly. Men needed to keep women safe and protected, they claimed. Hence, the women were not allowed to bear arms equally with the men. Women who continued to resist this exclusionary practice and demanded inclusion often encountered neglect and harsh treatment from their male counterparts. They were

seen as "misguided" and distracting to men's work and were advised to
return home to domesticity and caregiving. How did women respond to
the discrimination? What stories do women who were at the war front
tell? Curiously, these women's narratives stand in sharp contrast to the
official story that has produced a fantastic image of women as full and
armed participants in the war.[5] Women's narratives from the war front
question the veracity of this official tale.

Mumtaz's narrative is an intriguing and challenging story that chron-
icles in detail her initial love affair with violent nationalism and experiences of marginality within the nation-making structures, which led her
to a gradual understanding that a woman's place was not at the center
stage, although women deserved and were capable of assuming leadership roles and responsibility. She establishes in her narrative that the
nation-building project, of which the war was an integral part, was a male
space. This understanding has not left her bitter but somewhat wiser
and resilient to future manipulations by external agendas. Mumtaz now
lives a quiet life in Jessore and is involved in community work on her
own terms.

It was not easy to reach the point of clarity and maturity that Mumtaz now has. She had to leave the safety of her home and community in
Jessore, in central Bangladesh, in the thick of the war. She jumped into
politics hoping to land on the battlefront, but she found a harsh and un-
welcoming world. Despite her training and knowledge to bear arms and
fight, she was amazed that she was not selected to be a soldier. Her male
students, on the other hand, in Mumtaz's words, were rewarded with a
rifle and encouraged to fight. Discouraged, but undeterred, Mumtaz left
her base in Jessore and moved toward the Bengal border, in India, in the
hope that she would find a place in the freedom fighters' camp and join
the fight with them. On arriving at the camp, she found no one wanted
her there. She was snubbed.

Mumtaz charted her own course of action by forming a girls' camp.
Occasionally, she found someone who was willing to help and include
her girls' group in the war efforts, but this would be immediately coun-
teracted by another male act of discrimination. In the end, it seems
Mumtaz found it easy to take charge and fight on her own. Interestingly, in the narrative she does not give us details of her female team
performing active duty or fighting in battles.

A few things that Mumtaz learned very well in the male space of war
were the intricacies of the politics of the big actors and the fears of the

state. She reports in detail about the fear the Indian state felt about the revolutionary Naxalite movement and the continuous precautions they took lest the disgruntled Bengali fighters like her moved into their orbit.[6] She was not surprised when the Indians suspected her of being a Naxalite. Mumtaz also draws a very clear picture of the unstable politics within Bangladesh in the postwar period. Immediately after the war ended, there was a raging power struggle between different factions who were supporting different leaders: the Sheikh Mujib group versus the supporters of Tajuddin Ahmed. Tajuddin had headed the government-in-exile in India when Sheikh Mujib was held prisoner in Pakistan.

Mumtaz's group did not belong to either camp but had a different agenda. They wanted to inaugurate the direct participation and exercise of power in politics by people, but their platform became unpopular in the face of the powerful actors in the central government. Pushed to the margin and under suspicion of promoting socialist politics, Mumtaz was declared an antistate agent and sentenced to five years of imprisonment. In prison, she reeducated herself and freed herself of her own delusions of violent nationalism. She ends her narrative asking—not in regret, but in hope—if women have won the basic right of liberty and equality after the liberation struggle. Throughout Bangladesh in my fifteen months of research, I had heard this question raised by many women, and women are still waiting for an answer.

MUMTAZ BEGUM'S STORY

In 1971 I was a young woman, about twenty years old. I was a member of the Students League [SL] while I was a college student. I was the secretary of the Jessore Students League. My brothers and sisters were also members of the league. Our father was a police inspector. He was a supporter of Awami League [AL], but being a government servant he could not show his support openly. At home, he used to discuss with us various matters of politics; he wanted Bangladesh to be independent. Hence, he encouraged us to be active in student politics. In fact, he gave me my first rifle training in 1961. Before the war had started, our school arranged for training the students, and my father gave me permission to get combat training. He always encouraged me. One of my younger sisters accompanied me to the training. My other sisters were very young at that time.

My mother, too, contributed immensely during the freedom movement. She was always with us and supported us. She stayed up with us
for the entire night the day before independence and helped us stitch
a flag of Bangladesh. My mother was very brave. She used to hide our
weapons that we had brought from India. These weapons were with us
when we hoisted the flag of Bangladesh on March 23. When the police
raided our house, they couldn't find the weapons, but they did not give
up. They continued to raid our house several times. During the combing
operation, which was ordered by Brigadier Huda, they searched everything in our house, even the pots and pans, the containers of rice, pulses,
and everything else that we had in the house. They got the weapons outside, buried in the compound, and they arrested my father. Since I was
a young girl, they did not suspect that I was involved in politics. My
mother managed the situation very well. They had no idea what we were
doing for freedom.

Since you are interested to hear my story and involvement in politics,
I have to start from the beginning. It was 1966, but I was not yet a member of the SL then. A nucleus formed within the SL that used to say that
we should be independent. The details about this are written in many
history books, and you can read it there. These students started using
the platform of the AL and wanted to form an armed force. They motivated the people from this area to join their struggle. That is how I
learned about and joined the movement.

The desire for freedom was not implanted by India, as far as I know.
People of Bangladesh wanted independence. If there was the involvement of India, it was on a higher level. We did not know about it, but
we got a whiff that something was happening at the higher level of
politics.

Soon after my father was arrested and it became unsafe to stay in
our house, we decided to leave the place. We went into hiding. I never
thought of fleeing to India. I wanted to return to Jessore. When we were
going back to town, we saw no one was there. Jessore town was on fire.
People were running away, and several people were running toward me.
Among them were a student in the league, a doctor, and another was a
neighbor of ours. They told me that we cannot go to Jessore. "Where
shall we go?" I wondered. I am a practical person, not emotional and
sentimental about things. That helped me make a decision on the spot.
Also, we had suffered a lot during our childhood when we were under

Pakistan's rule. We used to carry a knife to protect ourselves. Our father used to tell us how the West Pakistanis discriminated against the Bengalis. The disparity had led to the demand for freedom. In 1965, the Indians had dropped bombs on Jessore. You don't know about it. Pakistan did not protect us. They had their administration in West Pakistan, all the bigwigs lived there; they had power and money, while we in East Pakistan had to suffer. Indians would come and go, act however they liked with us, but no one from the central government in Pakistan bothered about us. They lived like kings in West Pakistan. I used to think about all these things and had taken an oath by touching fire that we will fight to free our country. I thought about it in this critical moment when we were on the road and decided to join a fighting group.

The place was under curfew; as I told you there was no one in Jessore then. I was wearing long pants and a *kameez*,[7] and the Pakistan Army took me to be a Pakistani. I am also quite tall, as you can see. So they did not think I was a Bengali. They did not fire at me, although at one point one of them pointed his gun at me. I thought that they would shoot at my leg with their Chinese gun, as they had done to some of our SL members. So I checked if they had shot at my leg. Luckily, they hadn't. I crossed the town on my own, alone. A rickshaw puller, who was a party member, gave me a ride out of town.

In the meantime, one group had gone to fetch weapons from India. Our group divided into smaller groups and decided to go to Bonga. I and my partner from the SL walked to Bonga. We had to take a long route to avoid being detected. In Bonga, almost all the volunteers who were there were from the SL. This was in April 1971. We engaged in an armed combat in Bonga. This was not the first time I had fought in a combat operation. I had fought another time in March, when we started the armed struggle. In Bonga, we had a training camp.

From Bonga, we crossed over to the Indian border. We went to the Bangladesh office in Theater Road. Then, we went to Prinsep Street.[8] After that I got in touch with a cabinet minister.[9] There was no system for anything then. I did not know what to do. Because I was a girl, they were simply not bothered. I told myself that I would do the training. There must be girls like me who are also interested. I thought, "I have to find them." In the office they told me, "You have to wait. It will happen, but we can't tell you when and how." They did not help me find accommodations in Kolkata. So I stayed in my *nanabari* [grandparent's home]. In the meantime, I got in touch with the Forward Block of Netaji Subash Bose. I got my training from them. There was a camp called Gobra Camp, but I was not there. Gobra Camp was set up by the government [in-exile] toward the end of the war. The cabinet minister had given me an option to take charge of it. But I was not interested in being an instructor. The general training in Gobra was nursing. I told them that I have come here to learn how to fight, not to do bloody stitching. I had left my parents and come here to fight for my country. I returned to Bonga and found my own way. But I did not stay there and depend on them [the government-in-exile] to find me a group to join. I returned to Bangladesh after receiving my training.

The district collector of Bogura [in western Bangladesh] helped me.[10] He found me a place to stay, and the relief officer arranged for our food. I set up a camp there. We had nine girls in the camp. The bravest among them was Sandhya. She is still alive. You may want to talk to her. I found Mumtaz [another girl] living with a family. They were poor people. I asked her mother for permission to take her, and I brought her with me. We asked the Bangladeshis to give us arms, but they did not give us any. They wanted us to get our training from the Indian Army. We said, "No. We don't want any training. We want arms." At that time, the Bangladesh government-in-exile was being set up, and camps also were being developed in the border area.

I went to the Border Security Forces (BSF) camp and took some girls with me. This camp was called Baghda or Chakda. I can't remember its exact name. I went there because I had heard that every night they fight from that camp. They were trying to clear the way for entering Bangladesh. They were trying to enter the border areas of Bangladesh. I took my first chance in Itimda Camp. No one paid me any attention. I was discriminated against because of my gender. I even argued with some of the leaders there. I told them that they were discriminating against me because I am a girl. What gave them the exclusive right to fight for the liberation of our country and deny women the same right and privilege? They told me that I could go to the press meeting with them, and that was all they would offer me. They told me that they were under the control of the Indian Army rules, which only allowed boys in the camp. "How can you go there?" they admonished me. I did not waste any more time with them.

I went to the BSF guys directly and asked them to give me training in wireless and message interception. There I learned that many girls were being arrested by the Indian Army because they suspected them to be

Naxalites. The Indian government was very sensitive about the Naxalites at this time. Indira Gandhi was the prime minister, and she was determined to finish the Naxalites. I got into trouble because someone suspected that I was a Naxalite. They would have arrested me, but I was saved by a Congress leader. He was from the sl. This report was sent to the Research and Analytical Wing (RAW).[11]

An officer came to question me. The leader in the camp warned me about it and told me to be careful as the officer was coming especially to interrogate me. For three days he interrogated me. He was an elderly man. He even asked me if I wanted to go with him to see a movie. I told him that I did not watch movies. Throughout the interrogation he showed me a lot of respect. By the third day, he understood that I was not a Naxalite. He told me that it was not safe for me to stay in the area and started to address me as *tumi*.[12] He asked me to go with him to Bonga. He was not alone. There was another interrogator, Mr. Mookherjee, and both of them had to submit reports to RAW about their findings. He asked me to travel with him in the BSF jeep. I understood that he had indirectly arrested me. I realized that I must not resist it. In Bonga, I stayed in a camp. The camp that I am talking about was a one-room set-up, like this room. We used to call it a camp. But we did not have any weapons there. I sent a message and went to Salsha. Since I was tall, I was easily spotted in a crowd. Also, I was easy to notice because there were very few smart, young girls in the area. From Salsha, I tried to return with a family.

The family let me stay with them in their house in Hamidpur. We arranged to leave from there by boat. I was about to leave when I received a message from the commander not to go. Everyone who went on that operation was killed. We had less people and even less weapons to fight with. I was saved because of that commander. The four others who were on the boat died. Our leader had retreated, but he had not warned us. I am not saying that he should not have retreated. But he did not warn us of his decision and movement. All the other commanders said that I should not stay there any longer. They feared the boys would get spoiled. There were two other women there from the ashram.[13] The area I am referring to here was called Bahadur. It was a nice place.

Even after this incident the commanders were not letting me enter Bangladesh through the border. They were afraid that in my attempt to enter the border, I may be picked up by the Pakistani soldiers and that would jeopardize the chances for the men to enter Bangladesh through that area. We had many verbal arguments. It was toward the end of November that the Indian Army entered Bangladesh through that belt. The chief minister said that now the war would be over very soon. How did the minister know, I have often wondered. This thought still worries me. A liberation war can continue for ages, no one can foretell when it will end. How could an Indian minister guess that the war will end soon? In less than a month, our country was free. I soon found that I could not return home that easily. I had no arms with me, so I could not start my own camp. Then I started to collect money for the camp; we needed help. While I was doing this work, I also tried to enter the country. I could not get through despite several attempts. I met Jamal Beg and S. P. Mohammad,[14] but they did not pay heed to my request. I tried to find a way to get in. I had heard some rumor that the ministers who had taken training in the camps would be entering Bangladesh. I wanted to go with them.

When I finally came to Jessore on January 6, our country was free. When I entered the area, I saw there were some Indian army men still there. I did not find my family members. I was concerned whether the assistant cabinet minister would recognize us and how he would deal with us. Whether he would give us anything or not? We were pro-Mujib at that time. We were not certain about his approach toward our political views. Tajuddin Ahmed was not giving us recognition because he was not following Mujib.[15]

We had one assignment after we returned. We had to activate our group. We were all concerned that if Mujib did not recognize us what we would do. Till today, we have not been recognized for the work we did during the liberation struggle. We had to prepare for this eventuality. We feared that in case Mujib refused to meet with us, we would be crushed by the other opposition groups. I can't explain to you what the situation was like in those days in our country. It was free, but very tense. There was so much uncertainty at that time. There were so many groups that were involved; no one knew who was playing politics with whom. We did not know how the political leaders would behave toward us now that the war was over. We did not even know whether Sheikh Mujib would be freed. These were our prime concerns. Neither did we know how he would behave toward us if he returned to Bangladesh. We did not know what his mentality was since he was in prison.[16] Whether he would crush us or not? Whether the Shorashtra Mantri [Home Minister] would give us anything or not? We were doing socialist work, but we were keeping it secret. Our condition was like "na ghar ka aur na ghat ka."[17]

I asked myself, "Now what will I do? Under which political shade will I stand?" Our group jointly decided that we would surrender our weapons. This was the problem not only in Jessore but all across Bangladesh. There was a great deal of uncertainty. Even before we had started the freedom movement, those of us who were in the AL were aware that we had to fight for freedom. But there were many who were opposed to joining the freedom movement. After the liberation movement, those groups became opposed to us once again. We were able to understand that if we did not remain united and powerful they would destroy us and cause us great harm. In Jessore our group was powerful. We still had our weapons with us. If we had given up our weapons, the others who opposed us would have killed us. It was during this period of uncertainty that Mujib returned.

When he returned, he did not give us recognition. He set up a Rakhi Bahini.[18] We had asked him not to. We were at that time fully organized. We were spread throughout Bangladesh. The SL invited Mujib as their chief guest. The SL was divided into two groups by that time. Both called for a conference on the same day: one was in Saroj, and the other was in Paltan. We were in the Paltan group and did not know about the Saroj meeting. We were going to raise our manifesto there: Banganik Samaj Tontro [Republic of the Bengali People]. We had our flag. But the country was divided. We came back to Jessore.

From a woman's point of view, I will say that the Liberation War did help us to achieve our dream. The men suffered a lot. Many young students were arrested and put in jail. There was an arrest warrant for me, but they were not able to arrest me. I was able to escape. Afterwards, a vacuum was created as the students got scattered, mostly due to the fear of arrest and punishment. Later, however, I got arrested when one among us, who was from Dhaka, betrayed me. I was in jail for five years thereafter. I was in the first division in the jail so I did not suffer as much. I had decent food; I got two daily newspapers. In jail we continued to fight for improvement of the conditions for everyone and were successful on two or three demands. Since I was not married then, I used the period of incarceration to get higher education.

I completed my bachelor's degree while in jail. I was able to sit for two exams, but could not take the other two. Hence, my overall marks in the exam were lower. They gave me a special degree for my graduation. In fact, the best thing that happened to me in the jail was that I met my husband. He was the jailer.

I was not the only member of my family who was involved in the freedom struggle. My younger sister and brother had also joined the movement. My father was arrested during the liberation struggle. They had arrested him in order to punish him so that he would reveal some information to the Pakistan Army. But when he was lined up, one person in the group recognized him, as he had fought in the 1947 Indo-Pak War. This man brought him to Khulna, where he was later united with my mother. My mother had also suffered. She was separated from us and was in a different place from the rest of the family. She had to leave the house because the Pakistan Army was searching for me, and they came to the house everyday to harass her. I was in India by then. That was the reason my mother had to leave the house. She was finally taken by her family to Khulna, but there she had to go to the local police station every morning to report. She was what we call *nazar bandi*.[19] My father found her and brought her back after the war.

While in India, I met a writer who asked me to tell him my story. He wrote my story and broadcasted it on All Indian Radio. Those days everyone used to listen to the radio, and my parents also heard the story on radio. They immediately recognized that it was about me. That is how they learned that I was still alive. It was very interesting how they found me, so to say.

I regret one thing though. On March 26, no March 28, 1971, our command went under the control of some young male students. We were there when weapons were given out to the students to fight. Everyone was given a rifle, but they gave me a gun with two bullets. I was very angry because they had discriminated against me because of my gender. I had arranged for their training, but I was not given a rifle! How could they do this? We were nine girls who had dedicated ourselves to fight the Liberation War, but we were not recognized by any politician. They never asked us about our well-being, if we had money to buy food, if we had any food at all. In India they were very strict about checking for ticketless passengers traveling in the train. We had no money to buy train tickets. So we used to travel before the collectors started their duty and leave after their shift was over. We did not have money to eat. From where were we going to spare money to buy train tickets? In my camp, I had nine girls, but no one was recognized for the work they did during the liberation struggle. In my batch were Diya, Firoza, and

Sayeeda. From Jessore, there were thirty girls who had directly joined the freedom struggle. Even Dhaka did not have so many women volunteers. Charu Bala's case became well known. She was in the news because she was shot from the TNT building, while she was sitting outside on her veranda. She was not fighting. There was a *basti* [settlement] near the TNT tower. The Biharis lived there. During 1971, the Biharis did not have it easy either. Their girls were tortured, and their belongings were looted from them. Many of these Biharis went to the Pakistanis hoping for protection, and they [the Biharis] randomly killed Bengalis, in turn. Charu Bala died in one such incident.

The Indian Army came much later to Bangladesh. They were not there when the freedom movement started. The Indians thought they would fight with the [East] Pakistanis and divide the country and take away Bangladesh. Our mother has seen how the Indians attacked them [the Bengalis who demanded the India Army to leave after the surrender]. She wrote a poem about it. Our mother says that for them our country was only good to exploit and use. The Indians did not care about us; they were fighting the [West] Pakistanis in Bangladesh. It is not important to me what the Indians and Pakistanis did; but it is very important to me that we got Bangladesh. Despite freedom, we have not attained equality though.

PART III  A NEW BEGINNING

Postscript

 ❧

LESSONS OF VIOLENCE

Toward the end of November 2001 after eleven months of being in Bangladesh and having collected over fifty survivors' accounts, over one hundred testimonies of women who had suffered losses in the war, and having researched countless documents, many of which were damaged, dusty, dispersed, and scattered—being the unarchived materials of the history of the war—I believed my work was done. I envisaged that the research I had completed would enable me to write a book on women and war in Bangladesh. But something unpredictable happened. I met a person whom I will refer to as Kajol who pushed the limits of my knowledge of gender violence in the war and my capacity to endure difficult stories.

Kajol told me his troubled story, about his vicious attempt to rape a neighbor's daughter, who until then he considered to be like a sister. In wartime East Pakistan, she was reduced to a label—a Bihari and pro-Pakistani supporter—and symbolized the enemy that Kajol had to destroy. Thirty years later, Kajol found his release by speaking to me. He had revealed his guilty secret to me, a stranger, and freed himself from a burden that was too heavy to carry any longer. In turn, he made me responsible for searching out another hidden story of the war, men's memories of their acts of gender violence. My multi-sited research methodology was put to a true test. Should I explore the question and follow the new direction that appeared before me and continue the research? I was at the end of my research grant and leave. I had to put the question on hold and return to my teaching duties.

A few years later, in 2004, I received another research grant. I decided to utilize it to explore men's memories of the war of 1971. What were men's experiences of the war? Did violence transform them? How do perpetrators recall their memories, and how have these memories impacted their lives? Because of Kajol and his confessional testimony, I felt compelled to search for the perpetrators' memories.

Since the Pakistanis are identified by the Bangladeshis as the obvious perpetrators within the story of 1971, I decided to start my research on perpetrators' memories there. I was particularly interested to trace what the attraction of war for men is and the process of how ordinary men transformed into soldiers and then became perpetrators in consequence. I assumed that it was a slow linear regression and Pakistani armed men were enthralled by the magic of power they had over others in killing and terrorizing them. It was definitely a naive and jaundiced approach that I realized afterward was conditioned and developed by reading too much history of 1971 produced by the states of India and Bangladesh that cast the Others—mainly Pakistanis—as obsessed with hate for the Bengalis and waiting for the war to live out their inherited tendencies. I did not question the narrative that pathologized the "enemy" army. But once I entered the field a complicated picture started to take shape, and it led me to search and analyze the process of the devolution of soldiers into perpetrators. Within that distorted location, much to my surprise, emerged the language of a human being after the war. Drawing upon a popular local expression of *insāniyat*, many Pakistani soldiers told the story of the war as a breakdown of the human condition, reminding me of the fragility and responsibility entailed in being human, which, unfortunately, they failed to live up to, they regretfully said. In the process of committing violence, some of these men encountered and recognized the human desires of their victims—the emotions of love and hate, deep anxiety, as well as attachment to life and fear of death. In becoming aware of their victims' human emotions perpetrators recognized that what is within them is also within their enemies. Their lives became interconnected even though the external markers of identity such as nation, ethnicity, religion, and gender separated and distinguished them and motivated them to fight and destroy each other. The blurring of differences, at least temporarily, enabled perpetrators to see their victims as human and understand the limited power of violence that cannot undo humanity. An understanding of the shared insāniyat between the self and others emerged and produced a new and thoughtful narrative that perpetrators reported on. Some of the perpetrators of 1971 that I spoke with used the term *insāniyat* in the context of the loss of their human self during the war. To them this meaning had relevance because it shifted and expanded the discourse of the war, enabling them to tell a different story beyond the violence and based on humanistic memories. It is this narrative of the loss and recovery of *insān* and insāniyat that they now report on that offers a new take on the understanding of postcolonial nation-state formation, enriching us with the lived experiences of people and helping us to see the common human condition even in violence.

A word of caution here is necessary. In highlighting the transformation of soldiers into perpetrators and turning the narrative back to recognize their humanity, I do not mean to posit a banal idea that perpetrators and victims deserve similar understanding. Nor am I suggesting that focusing on perpetrators' regained sense of human responsibility exonerates them of the crime of rape; this is not my prerogative. Victims alone have the right to forgive the repentant, and they can do so if they want. Nonetheless, listening to perpetrators' stories is an important engagement for us, the audience of history, to understand the complexities that are at stake in the field of violence. I have throughout the book privileged the religio-cultural site of insāniyat to understand what women suffered and want to recover, and this site can be used to probe perpetrators' obligations learned from lived experience. The reconvened language of humanity can aid in reforming the ruptured national, collective, and personal selves in South Asia. The struggles of the perpetrators to regain their humanity alongside others should not be romanticized, but the enormous personal work that each individual had to undertake to reach this refined awareness cannot be underestimated either.

When perpetrators come full circle and seek this refined awareness, their acknowledgment of their own fragile human identity along with that of their enemy's humanizes them. Perpetrators' narratives show the dynamic potential of being human characterized by the rich cultural background of South Asia that offers multiple resources for continuously generating a language of understanding as people confront new situations in their multiplex world. Thus by returning to the lessons of humanization taught by Rumi and Lalon, I read perpetrators' insāniyat as both ethical politics and an emotional impulse to connect with others like them, while simultaneously empowering humanity in South Asia to reform and become better.

In exploring soldiers' narratives, I began to gradually understand that killing and violence are not natural impulses but they were learned, taught, and cultivated as duty within the institution of the army (see Grossman 1995). The Pakistani soldiers performed their duty, that is, they killed on behalf of the nation to establish power and force enemies into submission. The armed violence against unarmed noncombatants produced different consequences of loss and failure for Pakistan and became a site for personal transformation for some soldiers who had experienced the war firsthand. An ethics of humanity emerged, motivating them to question the call of duty. In short, one can say, some perpetrators were humanized in war. The ethical dimension of this memory cannot be predated to the period before the war, but it is in war and the experiences of violence that we begin to see the emergence of an ethics itself. It was this story of insāniyat that I became interested in investigating further in my research in Pakistan in order to find and voice the emotions, experiences, and knowledge of insān that transcend the boundaries of divided nation-states. What is the architecture of the memory of the war of 1971 in present day Pakistan? How do individuals negotiate between state and personal memories? Can retrospective memories now tell us what happened then? Why should we listen to killers and perpetrators, and what lessons do we learn from their experiences?

I lived for a year in Pakistan (2004–2005) and met with a variety of Pakistan Army men—high-ranking officers and ordinary soldiers, civil staff and media people who were in East Pakistan in 1971. I was surprised that despite the delicate nature of my research topic no one put up obstacles, and I was allowed to investigate the story and the historical sources without any problems.[1] Over a period of a year's research, I collected a wide range of testimonies, including testimony from perpetrators who had terrorized the vulnerable Bengalis with mass killings and wanton violence to attempt to force them to give up their struggle for freedom. Many talked of their memories of the war as duty and boasted about their valor. They regretted the loss of East Pakistan, but reminded me that they fought bravely to the end. A few ventured to show a little more trust in me and expressed their remorse of what had happened in the war. They seemed aware that the violence they committed led to the loss of their humanity, which I had not expected to hear. Although a marginal group, these men disrupted the pattern and wrinkled the smooth surface of national history.

The curious juxtaposition of my location as a researcher and being treated as a guest by almost everyone I encountered in Pakistan enabled me to interact with the representatives of the Pakistan Army at a very close and personal level. In the course of my interviews, I repeatedly encountered a pattern of extreme hospitality, but my hosts were uncomfortable about discussing critical issues about the war and talked down to me as a woman.[2] Their outlook toward the people of Bangladesh was, likewise, fractured. The rhetoric of Bangladeshis as brothers occupied the same space as the representation of them as "betrayers" and "Indian-like," that is, the Other or "Hindu-like." Despite this, I was able to persist and probe the experiences of the Pakistani military in 1971, often making many of the representatives very uncomfortable with my insistence.

I interviewed 123 Pakistani military personnel who represented different ranks. The vast majority of retired officers live in Lahore and Rawalpindi. I was often welcomed to their homes and got to know their families quite well. To conduct interviews with rank-and-file soldiers, I lived in villages. This provided me with the opportunity to discuss with young and old people their memories of the war. Particularly, with women I was able to discuss intimate topics about their conjugal life and marital problems after their husbands returned from the war. On many occasions women told me that their lives have not been the same since their men left for Bengal. This hinted at a change in their relationship, but I was not able to explore this subject in greater detail without upsetting my hosts, so I decided against it. In the villages I was dependent on the men to take me from one house to another and even walk me from one village to the next to conduct my interviews.[3] Ironically, the men who had been presented to me as perpetrators became my protectors while conducting the research.

Putting aside two interviews with two very high-ranking military officers, who I will refer to as Amin and Alam, almost all the others had some recognizable characteristic patterns that I had come to expect from reading books on 1971 and conducting oral history.[4] The Pakistan Army officers and soldiers generally confirmed those patterns, highlighting issues of duty, love for nation, economic compulsions, and peer pressure as reasons for their actions and activities in the war. They talked of others committing violence but rarely owned up to their own crimes, if they had committed them. The narrative of strangers as aggressors allowed them to hide and proclaim themselves as "good." Of course, when this became a pattern I realized it was a narrative style and not necessarily an account of witnessing. I had to pay attention to what they refused to answer, which were questions such as: Did you rape a woman in East Pakistan? Do you remember how many people you killed there? Have you thought of the people and place of Bangladesh since? Paying attention to their explanations that they performed "duty as commanded," or "I fought for my unit," or "I was not in a position to question the orders of my superior officer," and so on, provided a different and new scenario I had to grasp. With explanations like these, we can come to some sort of an understanding of the individual lack of choice within the institution of the army, and we can begin to understand how people are persuaded to join in the horrific activities, and why they later contrive and distance themselves from what they had done. Amin and Alam, however, cannot be framed within this category of soldiers. They refused to accept that what they did in East Pakistan was wrong, and even worse, still pretend that violence never happened there. Their indifference and total denial of their actions speaks volumes about their actions.

Although on the surface Amin and Alam appear to be different and their personas have nothing in common, both of them have some common features of a perpetrator, which I recognized when we discussed the violence they committed or ordered. They made violence in the war look like it was a normal thing. In meeting them I saw the face of what Hannah Arendt calls "the banality of evil" (Arendt 1965, 252). Both Amin and Alam talked about violence in a normal, matter-of-fact tone to explain that they performed *duty* that was required of them as military administrators. I want to present these interviews with Amin and Alam in brief to explicate the banal approach to violence and their role as perpetrators, which they refused to see.

The first thing that struck me when I met Amin was his obsession with gardening. He invited me to tour his meticulously groomed garden, and as we walked along he gave me a report on each plant. He told me about the quality of the seeds that he imports from London, the slow process of germinating the seeds while he designs the layout of the flowerbeds, the careful transplanting, growing, watering, and his enjoyment in seeing the flowers in full bloom. The careful planning process, grooming of each plant, arrangement of color, and the selection of the mix and variety that he maintains would make one think this fussy gardener is only concerned with his plants surviving and blooming. But this is not what Amin is all about, and neither do his colleagues think he can fool them with his passion for gardening. They had insisted that I should "ask about the violence he committed" in East Pakistan.

I was not prepared, though, to meet a man like Amin who celebrates violence as masculine valor and denounces human morality as weakness. The stories of killing he told me became increasingly gory as he became more comfortable talking to me, and for two-and-a-half hours I listened to one horrific story after another.[5] I can still recall his cold, careful voice chronicling the various events of killing, *duty* is his term for it, which he engineered and executed so that he could "clean Pakistan of the betrayers, the Bengalis."

Amin started the story of his career in East Pakistan in 1971 by recounting the first order he gave that entailed the mass killing of Bengalis in Santahar, a railway town in northern East Pakistan, because, in his opinion, they, the Bengalis, had killed "over 17,000 Biharis." The vast pile of bodies that were stacked in the railway building was clear evidence of the 17,000 missing Biharis, he concluded, and so he ordered the mass killing of Bengalis in revenge. Amin did not bother to make an investigation about the reliability of this number. He took pride in claiming that men like him "saw the problem on the ground. The Bengalis were deceiving the Pakistanis, and they had to be taught a lesson."

This was followed by the killing of intellectuals in Rajshahi University and an attack on Dhaka University to teach the Bengali students a lesson to be good citizens—thus, he "justified" his actions. Particularly in the Dhaka University incident, it is well known that rape of many women students also took place. When I raised the question of the violence against women in Dhaka University he said, "no one raped anyone. Those who complain about it were looking for trouble." In response to the violence against civilians that he ordered in Joydevpur, he responded, they were "armed rebels who were ready for combat against the army. No innocent people were killed in that instance." The violence that he indulged in East Pakistan exceeded the tolerance of the establishment, so it seemed. He was removed from East Pakistan, and the army court-martialed him. But an injury in operation beforehand provided a lucky break, and he could appeal for leave on medical grounds. After several months, Amin was reinstated and was posted to the western sector.

Much to his dismay, he found that the war ended there as quickly as it started, within twelve days (December 3–16), and he could not execute his plans "to kill as many Indians [Hindus] as possible."

It would be unfair to say that Amin hated the Bengalis and Hindus only. For him killing is an activity that he does with passion without consideration for ethnicity, religion, or gender, but he masks his violence as acts of love for nation. His morbid passion became evident when I asked about the guns on display in his living room; there were over a dozen with several rings on each of them. The question provided him an opportunity to chronicle the story of each gun and the ruthless killing his ancestors did, the rings indicated the number of people killed. These guns were his inheritance, and he displayed them like trophies to announce the "manliness that distinguishes his family from many others in Pakistan."

Alam, on the other hand, is a soft-spoken, quiet man. I had to strain my ears to hear him. Unlike Amin, Alam did not flaunt his bravado in war, nor he did he speak carelessly about the Bengalis. He never once hinted about his participation in violent activities in East Pakistan that would incriminate him as a perpetrator. He denied knowledge of violence in his administrative area of Comilla (southeast East Pakistan), despite written evidence of his activities there (see Mascarenhas 1972). He claimed he only obeyed orders and tried to maintain law and order. Although crude soldiering was not his style, Alam is known in the circle of veterans for his plots that involved arresting Bengali civilian officers, some of them were his "friends," and later they "disappeared" without a trace.[6] Of course Alam did not answer these questions when I raised them. He told me that he rose to the top of the military administration because of his abilities and merit. No one could have risen to such a powerful office in Pakistan, as Alam did, by obeying orders. The cultivated presentation of Alam as a quiet, sophisticated man and his actions in war, which speak more than he is willing to claim, contradict sharply, yet, we know from eyewitness accounts that Alam is not what he says he is. Like many other perpetrators representing the Pakistani and the Indian military, Alam buries the violence he committed in his soft, calculated speech, and his faux-ignorance about horrible things happening in the war. The recognition of the contradiction in his speech and the reality of his life and position disturbed me immensely.

Not all veterans of 1971 can be categorized as Amin- or Alam-like. Violence was not a tested experience for a vast number of officers and rank-and-file soldiers in the Pakistan Army, although many of them had fought in the 1965 war against India. That was a strategic war fought on the border. Both the armies, it is clear, were not prepared in 1971 to deal with human issues that emerged in consequence of the violence.[7] This became especially evident when the Pakistani soldiers were exposed to the realities of a people's unrest, which they initially thought was no more than a rebellion. Gradually when it grew intense and the East Pakistani Bengalis responded with their own violence, the West Pakistanis reeled under its impact and were broken. Aggravated violence became their language to negotiate power that slipped out of their control.

In interpreting Pakistani soldiers' actions, many reminded me it is crucial to remember that most of them were relocated from West to East Pakistan to "bring back law and order in the region, even at the cost of violence." Pulled out of their familiar environment and sent to a strange land where they could not understand the language and customs, the soldiers reacted with fear and fulfilled the mission they were brainwashed into believing, that they were going there to kill Hindus. The majority of soldiers came from hopelessly backward villages and had little or no education. These men generally believed whatever they were told; they had no other resources to enable them to think otherwise.[8]

For most of these men the army provided an outlet to see and interact with the larger world outside their village and community. The encounter with the outside world was, as expected, not easy for them, and, more often than not, it produced many wild fears and deep anxieties. When they arrived in East Pakistan many confessed that they found the swampy terrain frightfully unfamiliar and were terrified because they could not swim. Many soldiers drowned in the small rivers and streams. The unfamiliarity of the language was another site of discomfort. Many of them told me that when they came across small groups of Bengalis, they immediately reacted because they could not understand their speech and suspected the Bengalis were conspiring against them. Often they resorted to violence like beating to disperse the crowd because they were afraid for their own safety. In the unfamiliar terrain of war, ethnic and religious differences mixed with personal fears of life and death, creating conditions for men to forget that the people they were killing and brutalizing were fellow countrymen. The majority of the Bengalis were Muslims and not "Hindu-like," as they were told. The Pakistanis had to legitimize themselves for fighting a war against their own citizens, who were predominantly Muslim. Their leaders told them that they represented the national ethos, while Bengalis were transformed into "enemies," "traitors," and "anti-Pakistani." Violent nationalism limited the ability of these armed men to see others as similar to them, as citizens and, above all, as fellow human beings.

Over and over again during my interviews, I probed soldiers' memories of the experience of killing and sexual violence. It was always at this point of recounting their experiences that silence entered the narrative. Abruptly, many soldiers stopped telling their stories or changed the subject of our discussion. The traumatic memory of the destructive force of their violence is at the heart of perpetrators' silence. One can say silence marks the moment as a crisis of remembering and reveals the complex intersection of an unforgettable memory and a need to forget a violent history. Silence is not devoid of language, but the inability to put the memory into a perspective that can allow a new text of the war to emerge is what these men are struggling with and have to work through to make sense of their experiences.

Culturally uneducated about Bengali society, Pakistani soldiers could not understand Bengali body language either, and interpreted Bengali curiosity as an assault. Added to this was the cultivation of manliness and bravado, which is part of all armies. Men were afraid of shaming themselves in front of their fellow soldiers for being weak, and the high value on physical toughness had to be shown periodically, even invented. For instance, an officer told me, "there is a famous picture of a Pakistani officer holding a limb of a dead man and almost eating it over Bhairab Bazaar Bridge. This picture was circulated among the officers to boost their egos. . . . This was a posed picture. The man at heart was a coward, but he became celebrated as a hero."[9]

The myth of power over the Bengalis was displayed by rank-and-file soldiers too, leading them to believe they could easily win the war. Humiliation was one of the tactics they used to show power. Often at check points, young Bengali men traveling with their elderly and female relatives were asked to remove their *lungis* for the Pakistani soldier to inspect whether they were circumcised, to prove that they were indeed Muslim. The insult had a very deep impact leading many to join the Mukti Bahini to fight against the Pakistanis and throw them out of their country.[10] The Pakistani establishment and soldiers wanted to force the Bengalis to acknowledge their superior power, but it resulted in antagonizing the local populace, turning many into avowed enemies.

Not everyone in the establishment agreed with the logic of project-
ing supposed military prowess. Sahabzada Yakub Khan, who was the
Pakistani commander in the east, was one of them. When rumors of an
impending war started to circulate after the National Assembly was disbanded on March 3, Sahabzada Yakub Khan sent desperate telegrams
to Islamabad asking for a halt to the military solution. Failing to convince President Yahya Khan, Sahabzada Yakub Khan resigned from his
position on the grounds that a military solution was not acceptable.[11]
Strange though it may seem, the chief commander of the Pakistan Army
in the eastern wing became a conscientious objector, for which he was
punished. In recalling the violence in the war, he said, "We did not hear
the many *azāns* rising from the pulpits of East Pakistan." The Pakistani
administration, he interpreted, had failed to hear the different voices
of their co-citizens in the east—the Bengalis—who were calling upon
them to bear witness to the injustices of the regime. In turn, the Pakistanis used violence to submerge their voices. Perhaps there were many
more men like Sahabzada Yakub Khan who did not want to execute a
military solution, but no one listened to them.

Today, those who supported the decision to go to war and fought on
behalf of Pakistan are afraid to examine and address their experiences.
They use the common rhetoric of nationalism in order to justify their
violent actions in East Pakistan. The general explanation I received was,
"The Bengali people were initially not against us. Many of them continued to be pro-Pakistani to the end. But the Indians had infiltrated and
manipulated the Bengalis, and with the help of Hindu intellectuals, they
engineered the civil war. . . . We were simultaneously fighting a variety of
enemies there." Some of them tried to sanitize the events by explaining
that "not too many people were killed in East Pakistan, perhaps fifty or
sixty thousand." The one million that India and Bangladesh claim were
killed, they said, "is an exaggeration." Frequently, they talked about violence being "part of human nature" to dilute their own actions in East
Pakistan and sometimes defended their violence as "necessary," but
rarely did they address the issue of rape. Occasionally, they admitted
to having "relationships," "affairs," and "girlfriends" in East Pakistan.
Even if I accepted the rhetoric of "relationship," which was not rape
according to them, the reporting of these interactions by Pakistani men
without taking into account the hierarchies of power at work was truly
disturbing. How could a Pakistan Army officer, a representative of the
master class, not be aware of the compulsions that led women to these

"relationships," and the limited options women had to reject their over-tures? Was it really mutual? Also the explanation for killing co-citizens in a normalized tone and representing violence as part of human nature, alongside the interpretation of the Bengali demand for justice as a de-rivative politics engineered by the Indian "masterminds," undermine the enormity of the issues that led to the disintegration of Pakistan.

Clearly, many in Pakistan view the violence as not of their making but a situation that they were dragged into, and the traumatic loss of half of their country haunts them but remains unanalyzed at almost all levels—scholarly, administratively, and politically. Had it not been for the hu-miliating consequence of the war for the Pakistan Army that became POWs in India, the events of 1971 would have been written out of the texts of the Pakistani nation. In the absence of a collective public mem-ory the experience of loss was not conceptualized and the traumatic memory remained confined to the private domain of perpetrators' lives. Public forgetfulness and private pain framed the story of 1971 in Paki-stan.[12] The whitewashing of bloody murders as duty for the nation and distancing the reality of the use of force on women by calling it an affair are external explanations of individual actions, but this does not address why ordinary Pakistani officers killed and raped East Pakistani civilians in war time. In my interviews I pushed this issue further and many of-ficers responded to my query. Together we investigated the distinctive elements of the war of 1971 and the emotional narratives of loss that emerged at an individual level because of the violence they either wit-nessed, committed, or both.

A question that arose for me then, and one that I continue to ask, is why should we believe perpetrators' confessions that are told now, more than three decades after the event? If they were not remorseful then, why are they repentant now? I was afraid that by probing their memo-ries I would provide them with an opportunity to rationalize their ac-tions, minimize their responsibility, blame others for the violence, and contribute to renewed tension between the Bangladeshis and Pakistanis (see Payne 2008).[13] I was also concerned that my research would expose the vulnerable subaltern soldier while the top generals of the Pakistani military who ordered the violence would never be held accountable for their actions. Even when I avoided asking difficult questions concern-ing personal memories, almost every soldier I spoke to brought the memories of East Pakistan to the center of his story. Many among them spoke with deep remorse and wanted to undo what had happened in

Bengal. I had to listen to these stories because these men wanted to tell them. The more I listened to the men I realized it was the most important memory for them, and it provided an entry point to hear another narrative, not constituted by state history or driven by political ends, nor with the hope for truth and reconciliation. They were simply memories unrehearsed and hidden in the public sphere, but in the private sphere of a person's life they survived and generated troubled thoughts and secrets. In the unhappy space of silent memories a human self emerged and conveyed a powerful lesson that violence can never be total or complete. Violence destroys but cannot obliterate the human capacity, these men reminded me. Recovering their destroyed self is a task that persists beyond the violence, but not everyone involved in the war has excavated the buried remains. I started listening to the narratives of men who have done the hard work of reconvening themselves and the victims in their minds at least.

The voice of Colonel Nadir Ali was one of the first ones that I heard when I started work in Lahore. Friends asked me to meet him because he is remembered by many as "the colonel who lost his mind during the war." They presented him to me as a man who was deeply troubled by the violence that the Pakistan Army men experienced in the East. But when I met Colonel Ali he provided a narrative that was both poignant and assertive. He did not take sides, nor did he ask for forgiveness on behalf of the Pakistanis. Rather he told me as truthfully as he could that the Punjabi Pakistanis had never accounted for the culturally plural society that made up Pakistan and failed to unite it despite their claim to controlling state power. The western half of the country had failed to understand itself and thus could not even try to understand the eastern half, he reminded me. His concern was that the lack of self-doubt has produced a society that has no concern for moral turpitude, and it is a collective and not an individual problem. During our very first conversation on August 11, 2004, he told me this:

> When you are part of the machinery called state, nation, you see it face to face. You see how comical and farcical it is. I had served in East Pakistan from 1962–1966 and went back again in April 1971. Before the war, the Pakistanis used to treat the area as if it was their colony or a holiday resort, where everything was permissible to them. We brought with us the same arrogance when we went to fight the Bengalis. In the officers' mess, we were shown pictures of the atrocities that the Bengalis were committing,

particularly in Chittagong and Santahar. This was our side of the story of the Bengalis killing Biharis and Pakistanis. In another instance, a little Pakistani girl, a daughter of a major, who was the sole survivor of a family that was brutally murdered, was taken from house to house to show how the Bengalis had orphaned her. This girl could not even speak. She was in shock and the army told her story on her behalf. There was so much fear, everyone was afraid of the other. Exaggerated stories were made up on both sides without verification and evidence. For instance, in Joydevpur an officer was killed by his own men. There were no Bengalis involved in it. Later, however, the story was told differently.

Colonel Ali and I met several times over my yearlong stay in Pakistan, and he continued to talk to me about his multiple experiences and provided different readings for each, from the Pakistani and Bengali point of view. He continued to remind me there is no single story of 1971. Admittedly, the variety of incidents, groups, and institutions involved in the war left him totally confused and he quickly lost sight of the purpose of the war. He started imagining that the entire war was a devious plot masterminded by some "outside" enemy and he felt hopeless and helpless because he had no control and no leaders to follow. He recalled his feelings in these words:

> In the subcontinent, we live in a false consciousness of the enemy. Often there is no foundation in the real, but we take recourse to it. When an opportunity arises we act it out violently, maybe it makes us feel heroic, masculine, autonomous. Most people in the war had no idea what they were fighting against, there was no plan. It became empty with each passing day without any leadership. We were all worried about ourselves, we were fighting ourselves. Nobody could see; we were all blind. . . . I carried out a guerilla operation on July 15, 1971. It was the infamous train incident in which many people were killed. It was one of our first successful ventures across the Indian border. In the evening, when I returned to Dhaka and listened to the BBC report, I learned that fifty-six people were killed. I felt justified that we killed some Indians, as they were killing us. I felt very proud then. The general called me and gave me a pat on the back. Later that evening, in the Dhaka Club everyone celebrated the news. A few weeks later, I gradually slipped into madness. . . . War is madness, how can a thinking person be heroic in that? I was recommended for a gallantry award. You have to be a son of a bitch to get an award for killing people. No one was willing to see me as a person, weak and haunted by my own life. The Pakistanis claim I

had seen too much violence of the Bengalis and that drove me nuts. I hear the Bengalis claim me as conscience of the Pakistani violence. I was given credit for the breakdown. But in reality it was a lot different. It took me thirty years to figure it out. . . . I am just human. When I was inside the machine called the army, I was a part of it. I have spent a lot of time thinking about it. Now I know much better. But I don't talk about it. The biggest problem to deal with is the emptiness. How can one write stories after killing civilians or fellow soldiers and ask people to celebrate?

In Colonel Ali's admission he did not fight against the violence; rather he contributed to the war machine until his psychological breakdown. The experience of mindless violence, the impersonal state machinery, and his own dehumanization in the process forced Colonel Ali to grapple with his fragile human condition. His state of madness freed him, and he stopped playing the role of a soldier. Later, after regaining his equilibrium, he was able to recognize his and his "enemies'" humanity and fill the empty space wrecked by violence to develop speech and tell the story of the war in his own language, Punjabi, which he considers will enable him to convey his deepest feelings and emotions.[14]

Of all the interviews that I did in Pakistan, only a small fraction, no doubt, touch on these human matters. As many explained to me, they did not see what was happening to them and those around them when they were inside it. Now they think differently. Brigadier Aga (in 1971 he was a colonel and martial law administrator in southwest East Pakistan) confessed: "I have now reached an age when I have to be honest about what I know and experienced. . . . In the past, when my wife told stories to our children, about the Bengalis killing and brutalizing the Pakistani families in East Pakistan, I did not contradict her. But now when I hear her tell the same stories to our grandchildren, I tell her 'there is no point in hiding the truth. The Bengalis did kill and brutalize many Pakistani men and women. They orphaned a lot of Pakistani children. But you and I know that the Pakistan Army retaliated against them with greater violence, which far exceeds what the Bengalis did to us. . . . There was no good or bad party in 1971. We all committed violence. Don't take sides and distort the truth.'"

The retrospective significance that these men are giving to their experiences and their willingness to take responsibility of their actions reveal their struggle, and the disturbing remains of the past continue to challenge their humanity. Their disjointed and unclear testimonies may not allow historians to create a "thick description" of the war that is authenticated by cross-reference and evidence for corroborating the soldiers' stories. Nonetheless, the individual voices of the soldiers that emerge from inside the vortex of the war machine decenter the master narrative of national history and illuminate us, however obliquely, with a powerful truth that focuses on the loss of insāniyat, which rests on a thin line between doing duty and killing. It is in the condition of war that they suddenly encounter and realize the difference between the two. Malik is one such interlocutor who learned this lesson and, in turn, he now teaches us the difference between violence and human duty.

Malik came from a very poor family in the area of the Salt Range in the Punjab, which at one time boasted of the highest recruitment of soldiers in the Pakistan Army. His widowed mother made a bare-bones living by selling sugar cane and *channa* (fried peas) in front of a local school. In 1968, when Malik was sixteen years old, he found employment in the army. After a couple of months training, he was posted to East Pakistan. For three years he lived there and did his normal duties. In 1971 when the war broke out, his unit was not well prepared; the collection of rations was a recurring problem. Malik along with a few others was given the responsibility of acquiring food for the mess hall. Since the Bengali merchants and shopkeepers refused to sell them food, he had to go out to the villages and acquire rations for the soldiers. He said, "I looted some shops and beat Bengalis in the process. Some of them probably died. But I did not see it as violence. I was told to provide rations by my superior officer, and I carried out his orders. In the army we are not allowed to question orders. We obey the commands and do as we are told." When I asked if in the process of acquiring rations for his unit, he committed violence against women, he said, "I did not beat or assault woman. But I did not do anything to save a woman. My peers [common soldiers] did rape many women in East Pakistan. Some even brought them to the camp, married, and lived with them. No one stopped them. Since you ask, and I must tell you the truth, I will admit that there were occasions when my senior officers raped women. At times I had to stand outside the house and guard it. I knew why they had gone inside the house; they went there to rape the women. But I could not stop them. I was a sepoy. It was not my place to disobey the commands of my officers. My duty was to stand guard and that is what I did."[15]

Malik's explanation of obeying commands, performing duty without asking questions, his complete subordination to the orders of his superiors perplexed me. Yet, he seemed to draw a line of his limit to obey. When I asked him why he did not rape enemy women to create terror or force the Bengali villagers to submit to the will of the occupying Pakistani soldiers, he took a while to answer my question. Slowly, he said, "my *zameer* (conscience) would not let me commit such a crime." I was perplexed by this remark. How can a man who was surrounded by violence on all sides and had the official sanction to indulge in it refuse to go the whole way? What motivated him to punctuate his actions with a philosophical understanding of his responsibility as a human being and choose between good and evil action? How could he distinguish and demarcate between duty and ethics? Some actions connected to the army in his estimation were valid, they are part of his duty, but other actions were not. What is his source of knowledge for his insāniyat?

To understand the source of his moral vision he invited me to meet his mother. Even before I met her, Malik expressed to me that he was inflicted by remorse and a sense of justice on behalf of the victims "whom [he] and the Pakistan Army had wronged." He described himself, "as a troubled soul." But he did not have the language to talk about what he did, saw, and experienced, or what needs to be done now to redress the victims' suffering. Malik lives in a state of limbo stuck in the ruptured moment of 1971. The continuous replay of the violence in his mind creates a sense of moral relationship to the victims, and his experience of suffering does not diminish, even after three decades. To understand his suffering, he asked me to talk to his mother with whom he had shared some of his pain. His mother is an old, invalid woman.[16] When I met her in Malik's home, she blessed me for my endeavor and told me,

> My son used to write letters to me from East Pakistan and later from the POW camp. I could not read his letters because I am illiterate. I took the letters to the local schoolmaster and all the women gathered to hear what Malik wrote. We used to be very proud to hear about the battles he participated in. But the violence troubled everyone. The women blamed the East Pakistanis for the violence. But I'd sit in a corner and think about the violence that my son was witnessing and my heart cried out, "tauba, tauba" [forgive us]. I was very sorry that my son was part of such violence. But I knew he would not do bad things to women because he was raised by me, his mother. So I prayed to Allah to save him from committing violence and to save the women and children of East Pakistan because no women should suffer the loss of a child or be dishonored in war. I know my son still thinks

about East Pakistan and what he witnessed there. The memory cannot be erased. He has taken refuge in religion to seek Allah's forgiveness. That is all we can do.

The mother and son's narratives do not illuminate some secret knowledge about the war and violence, but their anguished, untutored speech clearly move beyond the national slogan and raise fundamental questions on individual responsibility and ethics. The recognition by mother and son that ordinary people like them were actors in crime has great consequences. The state had called upon men like Malik to execute the duty of killing, and the propaganda of hate against the Bengalis, the manipulation of minds using the rhetoric of saving Islam, and the political greed of the warring parties contesting for state power transformed these ordinary people into killers and murderers of other ordinary people in East Pakistan. Nonetheless, it is the person, the perpetrator, who has to bear the consequences of his actions. No longer can he hide behind the veil of having performed duty, but he must acknowledge his individual failure to be an insān during the war, that is, the loss of the capacity to choose good over evil deeds. The loss of this capacity is Malik's brooding concern, and his confession of crimes told in an awkward manner to me, a stranger, is the best he can muster because there is no escape in his mind.

The engagement with tumultuous inner thoughts and secret evil actions that are not recorded in the history books of Pakistan is not an easy process for Malik and many like him. Malik's mother believes repentance is the beginning of the healing process. This is a very heavy demand because to repent involves acknowledging the crime not simply in the juridical or collective sense but at a personal and individual level, which Malik knows must accompany the acceptance of punishment from a higher external authority other than the state. Coming to terms with the religious obligation of *huquq-al-ibād* or the rights of humans that he transgressed during the war obliges Malik to accept the consequences that would follow beyond this lifetime. It causes fear and remorse, and everyday life has become abnormal in Malik's mind and heart. There is no space in Pakistan for men like Malik to discuss their experiences and the renewed understanding of the losses in destroying others like themselves during the violence of the war. Not unlike their victims, a perpetrator like Malik, too, lives his life in silence and shame, being repulsed and tormented by brutal memories.

Mohammad came to my apartment in Lahore on his own initiative because "he needed to talk about the war." Mohammad started his account in these words:

> I am from Attock. My father was in the army, and I joined the forces because that was the only source of employment for us. I had to support a widowed mother and several brothers. In April 1971, I arrived in East Pakistan. Soon after, our unit was sent to a border town in northern Bangladesh. We were told that a large number of Biharis were slaughtered by the Bengalis. We had to teach the Bengalis a lesson. Eleven of us were sent to carry out the mission. After a day of fighting, we took many Bengalis captive. We sent them to the unit headquarters; I don't know what they did to those men and women. At the end of the day, when I looked around, I saw the whole place was strewn with body parts. There were decapitated bodies, heads without bodies, dismembered arms and legs littered all over the place. Dogs were roaming about, dogs without any hair on them. They were feeding on human beings. Scores of vultures were descending too, and the dogs and vultures were fighting over human body parts. I thought, "He was a human being like me. Is this what a human being does to another human being?" I thought and felt sick knowing that I was a part of it. Humanity had died (Insāniyat khatam ho geya).[17]

Once he started this story, the floodgates of brutal memories were unleashed, and he talked for several hours about the violence they committed. His graphic description of the destruction of the human person clearly indicated the trauma that haunts him. He cannot forget the unknown Bengalis and strangers that he and his peers attacked, killed, and dismembered, but now he reconvenes them piece by piece, acknowledging them as wholesome human beings once again. Mohammad recognizes that his victims must always have a place in his mind because that is the only way he can dignify them beyond their destruction.

He continued to recount in detail other campaigns, the initial successes and the gradual loss of control on the part of the Pakistan Army leading to their surrender to the Indian forces on December 16, 1971. In explanation he said, "Our officers were very corrupt. But the Bengalis were loyal to their land. Even when we took their families hostage and shot them, some of them died crying, 'Joi Bangla!' How can anyone conquer a people who love their land so much? No force can succeed against them. I knew this early on, but like the other soldiers, I fought for my country. We were disciplined. We did what we were told to do."

Later reflecting on his experiences in the POW camp in India, he said, "There I became human" (waha insān bana). Mohammad's acknowledgment that in the enemy territory of India and in a nondescript status as POW he found his human identity was indeed a dramatic statement. He recalled this process in a disjointed narrative. In his cell there were thirty-six men, and for several months they hid from each other what they did in East Pakistan, he recounted. Once they started talking, slowly and gradually the men started to unburden the memory of the war that was haunting them. Only three of the thirty-six, Mohammad reported, could honestly admit that they did not commit unnecessary violence in East Pakistan. Discussions with his cellmates made him realize that during the war they had became tools in the war machine. Fear and anxiety and a desire to live at the cost of others drove them to cloak themselves in the garb of nationalism and commit violence in the name of doing duty on behalf of the nation. But, in the victims' violent death, perpetrators like them saw their own emotional and psychological fragility and vulnerability. The mirroring effect of the victim enabled them to see how the rhetoric of West Pakistani nationalism, casting the Bengalis as enemies, transformed them, ordinary men, to become murderers of other ordinary men and women in East Pakistan. But in talking about it and acknowledging their crimes, these men were able to dismantle the received narratives and rewrite their own script centering a human story.

The acknowledgment of the shared human condition with their victim was a profound turning point in Mohammad's life. It carried him beyond the befuddled ambiguities of learned nationalism to another place where he understood the subordination of the constructed reality of political power. He was able to strip the power of the men he held in reverence to a basic position in which they no longer mattered in the larger scheme of things. This realization did not come easy, and in its place a deep and troubling fear of punishment for failing fellow humans became dominant. Deed and action, he realized, are intricately connected with reward and punishment, and the inevitability of punishment compelled the need to repent, as it is the only way to mitigate and take responsibility of the crime and possibly a means of regaining one's lost humanity. This meant vigorous religious and spiritual work. Mohammad turned to learning the Quran and for two years he "prayed for forgiveness" because he "was able to recognize his action as *gunah* [sin], and committing gunah," he said, "can never be hidden behind the rhetoric of performing duty." He said, "when we acknowledged our gunah, and did *tauba* [penance] from our heart, we became free.[18] Even the barbed wire of the camp, daily inspection and parading by the Indians, trundling empty days of listlessness did not bother us. We became insān, free, and unencumbered, no longer fearful and following the orders of men above us. We had found our freedom." When I reminded him that it is not enough to do tauba, an act of repentance to God, but he must seek forgiveness from his victims, he responded, "it is important that Pakistan and Bangladesh governments must talk. I am ready to testify to my victims in Bangladesh and seek their understanding and forgiveness."

As a beginning step in the direction of showing true repentance, after two years of suffering imprisonment in India, Mohammad returned to Pakistan and although jobless and poor, he resigned from the army because he said, "I had found my insāniyat." In this single delicately told sentence Mohammad addressed the entire reality of his being and that of the world, the world of human beings that was lost in war. The careful education of violence as manly duty and ideological instruction by the institution of the army against the enemy had to be unlearned, and the gradual recognition that violence is crime transmitted an understanding of a humanistic ethos—it was a painful personal journey. Mohammad makes us realize the triumph of the human capacity to acknowledge, suffer, and seek redemption in repentance in order to become human, once again, alongside their victims. It is an arduous and incomplete journey, but a movement to a better, more human place as he found out in the process. Mohammad's story is not unique in Pakistan. Several perpetrators I met during my stay continue to struggle in their incomplete human journey.

A simple truth of humanity was totally forgotten in the violence during the war and no one even took notice. Even if they did, they marched on, ruining everything in their way, and, in the end, a nonhuman order was put in place and people accepted the logic of inhumanity and called it love for the nation.[19] State, nation, and territory took precedence over human beings, and man became anonymous, his actions irresponsible. However, it is not productive to loathe the perpetrator and take sides with the victim when looking for an understanding of a historical event and engaging with the dynamism of human capacity. A different sensibility is required to hear what men like Mohammad, Colonel Ali, Malik, Brigadier Aga, Sahabzada Yakub Khan, and many others I met

Civilians seeking release from POW camps in India.

Red Cross officers and volunteers at work in POW camps. (*Source withheld*)

and spoke with in Pakistan, who were agents of a violent history, had to say and are asking of us. Their humanity is, like that of others, complex as well as fragile, fluctuating, delicate, yet, resilient. The intersubjective connection between man and man was forgotten in the period of the war, but by remembering the loss, some of these men have reconstituted their human selves and those they thought they had destroyed.

Listening to the variety of soldiers' memories in Pakistan I became aware that there is no final analysis or neat conceptualization that can encapsulate their experiences. Being haunted by the memory of the Other and telling their crimes, these men deliver a justice to their victim that no tribunal, state, or court of law can deliver, and in that same gesture they make us aware that their existence as a human rests on the Other. The perpetrator realizes that he owes his life as a human to another, his victim, whom he tried to destroy. This is the story that history cannot speak, the truth lies with the survivors—perpetrators and victims—who let us enter a murky world of memories and show us the possibility of moving beyond it toward closure. Can the governments of Pakistan and Bangladesh show similar courage and move forward to resolve the wounds of 1971? It is a question to which I did not receive a clear answer from important state actors in Pakistan. No one wants to initiate the process and seek forgiveness from the Bangladeshi public, although many of them showed interest in starting a peace initiative with their other and more arduous enemy, India.

Engaging the perpetrators of 1971 from Pakistan led me to extend my research even further and reach out to probe the experiences of men from India and Bangladesh, who had joined and contributed to the war efforts with violence. Thus my research expanded to cover the work of the Indian armed forces and civilian agents, which I undertook in the summer and winter of 2005. The following year, in the summer of 2006, I returned to Dhaka to document the memories of men who fought in the War of Liberation.

A common problem that I encountered in talking to men both in India and Bangladesh was their inability to articulate their memories in personal terms. They refused to admit that they committed violence although many of them talked of their brave acts of killing Biharis and Pakistanis. The unwillingness of these men to come to terms with their actions beyond the vocabulary of duty is a mask they wear well. Today, many of them have pushed the personal memories aside, as the talk about trying war criminals in Bangladesh is getting louder and louder.[20]

The self-representations of their own actions were veiled and clothed with terms like soldiers and freedom fighters. But, I also met a few men like Kajol in Bangladesh, who had taken the time to reflect on the work of nationalism they had done and the lessons they had learned in 1971. They talked about the violence and regretted the terrible acts committed against others. In particular I remember the admission of violence by Bir Pratik Major Faroukh and Bangladesh's most highly decorated freedom fighter, Bongo Bir Abdul Kader Siddique.

Kader Siddique, it seemed to me, was waiting for an opportunity to tell his memories during the war. My questions provided him with such an opportunity to reveal some of them (the burden of memories seemed to weigh heavy on him). Kader Siddique, a civilian, was the only sector commander of a unit of the Mukti Bahini, generally known as Kader Bahini, who fought within East Pakistan throughout the war. As such, he was most closely and intimately involved in planning, strategizing, and carrying out violence against the Pakistanis in East Pakistan.

The first time I met Kader Siddique at his home he spoke to me quite candidly. That day he seemed most interested to talk about the dehumanization of the Biharis, which the Bengalis enjoyed under his watch and leadership and which he regretted, as it was unnecessary. He talked about his public killing of Bihari men in a stadium full of people. He admitted that at that time he thought he was punishing them for their deeds; they had opposed the liberation of Bangladesh. He felt empowered when he "shot them down in full public view. It appeased the Bengali crowd," he recalled. People applauded his cold-blooded act on behalf of the nation. Now when he thinks about that incident he feels sad, almost repelled by the memory. In his rational approach today's Bangladesh is far more corrupt, its leaders far more dangerous to the people and body politic than the Biharis ever were. Only retrospectively he realizes that his judgment and violence against the Biharis for supporting Pakistan was much harsher than they deserved. Their humanity is now clearer to him as he struggles to understand what happened to Bangladesh, the liberated nation after the war.

An interesting side note that clarifies his ongoing struggle is evident in another action, a more recent one, which Kader Siddique shared with me. This concerns his infant daughter, who he confessed is an adopted child. He and his wife brought her from a hospital where she was left by a rickshaw puller who had rescued the abandoned baby from wild dogs and crows that were attacking her. The predators had already picked on her cheeks and deformed her face when the rickshaw puller found and saved her. Responding to a newspaper story, Kader Siddique and his wife visited the hospital as part of their civic duty and like many others showed their concern with gifts of baby formula and clothes. The helpless face of the little infant girl was unforgettable to them. Returning home they discussed the story of the child with their two teenage children and with their permission, Kader Siddique and his wife decided to adopt the baby. He does not know who she is—a Bihari or Bengali, Muslim or Hindu baby. For Kader Siddique it is immaterial because, as he admitted, this human gesture has made him wholesome again, the ghosts of the war that had haunted him are now at rest. The perpetrator has made a full circle. Recognizing and celebrating the humanity of a stranger, the baby, he finds himself a human capable of responding to his human needs and that of another, and he finds peace.

We had many meetings after that initial discussion, and Kader Siddique talked at length of his war memories, his leadership abilities, and his unit's discipline, the brave deeds his men performed, the ideal of freedom that motivated their passionate actions, the supporting role of the Indian government and armed forces in the war, and about the violence that was a part of it. To me Kader Siddique's ability to see with refined clarity his actions during and after the war epitomized the Bengali passion for freedom and their deeds toward achieving this goal for which there is no easy and simplistic documentation.

Major Faroukh (in 1971 he was a captain) talked at length about the war and his role in it. He started by giving a detailed account of how he had escaped death at the hands of his Pakistani colleagues who locked the Bengali officers in a room and shot at them with the intent of killing them. This incident happened in Chittagong on March 25, 1971. Despite being wounded he escaped through a window and saved himself. During the war, Captain Faroukh was in charge of a unit that operated from the western border of Tripura in India. In recalling some of the activities and battles his Mukti Bahini men fought against the "enemy," which he qualified as the Pakistan Army, he recalled one painful incident that exposed the brutality of "his people" toward a dead Pakistani soldier. He had hunted and killed the man like one would an animal, he admitted. His triumph over his enemy was put up for display by his juniors, and for the entire day the village people gathered to see the dead Pakistani. Many hurled epithets at the dead man calling him a "monster," "demon," and used crude "unutterable names." They were happy to have the power to humiliate the dead body, he recalled. To prove that they despised the Pakistan Army as a whole, many of the onlookers, including women, kicked and spat on the dead man.

Major Faroukh recalled that until then he was not perturbed, but when he saw everyone attacking the dead man and kicking his body something inside him recoiled. He could not take the "crude violence" any longer and with his own hands dug a shallow grave to bury the dead man. But he forgot to mark the grave. He has often wondered if the family members of the Pakistanis who died in the war had found the graves of their loved ones. It troubles him that although he fought bravely, he did not quite understand the violence that accompanied it, and he struggles to remember his own actions and crimes. He remains haunted by "a soldier," although an enemy, that deserved more respect and by his inability to ensure it by marking the grave for posterity to recognize the fallen in war.

The ability to acknowledge the violence and admit to the crime is a powerful testimonial. It is not an unchallengeable testimony, though. Difficult as they are to comprehend and sometimes even believe, we know that these men were there in the battlefront in 1971. We were not there. The words of these men come to us through a formidable act of remembrance, and they are brave enough to do so, even though they may be emotional testimonies. Based on their experiences as they understand it these men can now appeal to us to reconsider the contingent nature of the outward forms of subjective national identities and focus on the unmarked ground of humanity in the subcontinent. On this ground multiple identities crafted by nations and states exist, but there is also enough space for a new understanding of a shared humanity that is at the center of subcontinental memory, although occasionally forgotten in times of violence. These men, who take on that responsibility, allow us access to their thoughts and let us interrogate them. They show the possibility of becoming human in the truest sense, weak but resilient, confounded but not destroyed. In telling us their memories they are doing more than registering some sort of guilt, pain, fear, grief, or anger. Rather, in continuously searching for the meaning of their actions, at least in their minds, they have allowed themselves to be disturbed, upset, and even overwhelmed by the memory of the others. In listening to their stories we become keenly aware that like them, we too have become disturbed by others (for which memory and not history is

Still hiding behind walls. (*Source withheld*)

The work of healing:
Firdousi Priyabhasani with another survivor.
(*Courtesy of Shahriar Kabir/Forum for Secular Bangladesh
and Trial of War Criminals of 1971*)

a possible place), and we can see a clearer image of humanity destroyed in a violent war.

This book, I hope, will contribute in providing a possible direction for rethinking historical documentation of the war and its history that impact the entire region of the subcontinent. The Bangladesh war of 1971 is only one such horrific incident in the twentieth century, which raises some fundamental questions regarding our historical consciousness. The reasons for war and the use of violence against the vulnerable, especially women, children, and the elderly, is a pattern repeated in all wars and in all parts of the world. Shining a spotlight on the 1971 war and incorporating its documentation from the lived experiences of people may move us closer to creating a broader template of war memories, and writing an inclusive story of the remembered and the forgotten to begin the process of knowing the shared condition of humanity, within and outside Bangladesh. Specifically, I hope by listening and engaging the narratives of survivors a new and believable people's history of 1971 will emerge for promoting decolonized narratives and fostering better understanding among people in the subcontinent. Without a discourse about our shared humanity, we, the divided citizens of the multiple nation-states in South Asia are without guidance how to choose between competing discourses that differentiate and instill fear and hate inhibiting our human functioning. We need clarity about what we are trying to liberate ourselves from—our colonial past and the learned fear of the Other or our present disempowerment within our respective nation-states—and relearn the lesson of humanity that we are capable of.

NOTES

1. I am borrowing "polyversal" from Zillah Eiesenstein (2004), who uses it in the context of the plural worlds and the diverse spaces of our lives and realities that produce multiple ways of knowing self and others.

2. Only two women thus far have been recognized as *mukti jouddhas* — Taramun Bibi and Dr. Sitara Begum. The countless other women who fought, supported, and actively facilitated the war are unsung heroes whose silence and inability to claim their place in the annals of Bangladesh's history is a telling reminder of the marginalization of women during and after the liberation of Bangladesh.

1. TOLD AND UNTOLD STORIES OF 1971

1. The term *Bihari* is not meant to identify the people of Bihar. Instead, a variety of Urdu-speaking people who had migrated from India to East Pakistan after partition were commonly referred to as Bihari in order to distinguish them from the local Bengalis.

2. The term *colonialism* was first used in 1969 in Justice Shabuddin's report to describe the feelings of the East Pakistani Bengalis toward the state of Pakistan (Choudhury 1974).

3. Lieutenant General Niazi's (1998) book *The Betrayal of East Pakistan* sums up this concept. In Pakistan, by and large, the discourse on 1971 vacillates between two representations: One is of a family gone awry, of brothers

fighting against brothers, and the second representation is starkly opposite and Otherizes the people of East Pakistan as "Hindu-like." Their affinity with India, a Hindu country in Pakistan's imagination, was obvious. In short, the blame is laid on the Bengali people for dismembering Pakistan, and the state's role in instigating the event is not critically evaluated.

4. I am using "multi-sited" in a conceptual sense, as used by George Marcus (1998). Each segment and location of the research generated new questions and texts pointing me in new directions to explore and interpret. The research became like a detective plot continuously unfolding at each stage.

5. For example, see Mascarenhas 1971; Siddiq 1977; Choudhury 1975; Cohen 1984; and Sisson and Rose 1990.

6. For an excellent example of the clash between the different ways of knowing self and Other, identity and history, colonial history and local narratives, see Chatterjee (2002).

7. Very rich scholarship on the impact of Sufism in South Asia is available. For example, see Eaton 1994 and Nizami 2004.

8. Insāniyat is both a word and a concept and can be loosely translated as humanity or the moral and ethical obligations of a person to self and others. An extended discussion of the etymology and application of insāniyat is provided in chapter 2.

9. Once when I asked a survivor if the sacrifices she had made in the war—suffering rape, loss of home and husband, and expulsion from her village—were worth it, without hesitating she said, "Freedom was worth it." Similar admissions occurred in conversations with other women, although women also problematized the issue by asking why they have not been allowed to enjoy the benefits of liberation.

10. Emmanuel Levinas's discussion on the subject of ethical humanism engages the issue of *responsibility to the Other*. The ethical obligation to Other is not directed to make common platforms for creating an instrumentalist agenda to overcome differences (see Levinas 1972, 1981).

11. Recently, there has been a considerable amount of scholarly interest toward understanding Muslim views on ethics, rights, and morality that constitute the basis of humanism. See, for example, Goodman 2003; An-Na'im 1991, 2008; Joansen 1997; Oh 2007; and Davies 2008. As pointed out by Muhammad Iqbal (1986), the words *bashar* or *insān* reserve for man in his capacity of God's vice-regent on earth.

12. James Booth in *Communities of Memory* (2007) provocatively argues that no commemorative action can serve the cause of developing an ethical memory more than "bearing witness." The witness is more than an eyewitness

and can broadly include the statements and actions of those in the present who have received firsthand accounts from others. My report of women's testimonies is an act of bearing witness to the state's action that elected to terrorize, kill, and undermine women and their families.

13. Several early Islamic humanists have emphasized that the principal part of humanism is eloquent discourse. Abdullah Ibn al-Muqaffa (eighth century), Ibn Rushd (twelfth century), and Jalaluddin Rumi (thirteenth century), to name a few, are proponents of the humanist turn in Islam, both in religion and philosophy.

14. The relation between the humanist speaker and listener is reciprocal, for the purpose of hearing is not only to learn but to turn that learning into a vivid medium of speech or writing for creating new narratives for renewed understanding. In Assam, where I am from, the reciprocal relationship between speaker and listener is defined as the principal location for understanding. All exchanges are plotted within a form of a dialogue between the speaker and listener and are encapsulated within two words—*hunisane* (are you listening) and *hunisu* (I am listening). All verbal exchanges are framed within these two words. A speaker has to ask his or her audience at crucial points of the speech or discussion if she, he, or they are listening *to* understand, and the listener is obliged to reply if listening is leading to understanding. This humanist approach resonates in the 1971 survivors' speech.

15. Africanists were at the forefront of developing oral history for methodological and epistemological inquiry nearly fifty years ago. In Latin American history, testimonial narratives have produced counterstatist accounts that challenge the production of history from the archive and documents of the state to show the extraordinary range of contexts in which history and narratives are produced. India has an oral tradition that goes back to the foundational narratives of Hindu culture expressed in memorizing and telling the Vedas, the Mahabharata, and Ramayana. Unfortunately, the oral tradition of India as a source for writing communitarian texts was undermined with the development of history produced by the colonial state, which became dominant. The colonial scholars and administrators coerced oral narratives from the "natives" to outline an ancient history of India and then discarded it by calling it nonhistory. The subjected public in India has since interacted with a state history as "real" and oral tradition as "myth."

16. See essays in Patai and Gluck (1991). Also for ethnography of the interaction and impact of fieldwork on research method and outcome, see Behar (1993) and Abu-Lughod (1993).

17. An excellent research bibliography on partition has been compiled and

made available by Vinay Lal at http://www.sscnet.ucla.edu/southasia/index
.html.

18. The recent backlash against Jaswant Singh for his book *Jinnah: India, Partition, Independence* (2009), in which he identifies the main actors of partition as Jawaharlal Nehru and Vallabhai Patel, shifts the blame from Mohammad Ali Jinnah and the Muslim League. This position is unacceptable to the Indians and the Indian press and media, including some scholars who have vociferously argued against it. Indian public opinion refuses to see the agency of Indian actors in partitioning British India.

19. The representation of 1947 as the determinant moment of history has led to some myopic assessments of the violence. Seen as an Indian trauma (since Pakistan was forcibly created from within the body politic and territory of India), the stories and experiences of people who came to India from across the border of Pakistan or left India for West Pakistan are better known and researched. The experience of the people of East Pakistan is often represented as not violent and a process of slow migration that spanned several years. The stories of displacement and refugeeism of the East Pakistani Bengalis are recorded only after their arrival in India. The partition narrative thus works on two registers of people leaving from West and East Pakistan, and the general tendency is to overlook the experiences of the rest of the people in the subcontinent. Did partition affect their lives in any way? What did the moment 1947 mean to them?

Also, the approach to 1947 as a unique event is a temporal hubris because it reduces the moment into a static date. From 1947 to 1971 the people of East Pakistan underwent massive changes in their relationship with the state of Pakistan, and their sense of identity and the glue of religion binding them together came apart; linguistic and ethnic issues became more prominent. It is important to study the history of 1947 as a process interspersed with many events, occurring before, during, and after 1947. Included in these events is the war of 1971.

20. Within the story of 1971 there are multiple narratives of disruption and violence, and a variety of histories can be written on the episodes within 1971. I have focused on the experiences of violence against women, but another episode that needs our urgent attention is the experience of the people of Tripura in 1971. Thus far, their story is completely overlooked. Tripuris were pushed out from the capital city of Agartala to the hills and were transformed into a minority group in their own homeland due to the settlement of large groups of Bangladeshi Hindu refugees during and after the war. Their language—Kok Borok was overrun by Bangla, which was

declared the state language. After several decades of marginalization, the local Tripuris have demanded a reinsertion of their language into the public space and recognition of their status. These efforts are viewed with a great deal of suspicion by the government in New Delhi. In response the government has stationed several battalions of the Border Security Force (BSF) and Indian army in Tripura to control and stifle the voices of dissent. Local groups have reacted to this by forming militant organizations to carry out ambushes and guerilla attacks against the Indian forces. This has led to a spiraling of the problem with little or no gains for the ordinary citizens of Tripura. Who will tell Tripura's story and the imposed silence? The plight of the people of Tripura who are still suffering the repercussions of an international conflict is disturbingly familiar.

21. I have consulted the 1978 publication of Faiz Ahmed Faiz'a poems reproduced in *Sham-i-shahr-i-yaran*. The translation is mine.

22. Fred Dallmayr (2002) has argued for the process of "humanization" in developing a more inclusive human rights agenda in our times.

23. This was particularly evident for Muslims who had to leave Delhi for Pakistan and lost their connection with Nizamuddin Auliya's shrine. For the Sikhs of Pakistan partition also wrenched them away from the shrines of some of their most important gurus. For many the loss of association with the shrine of Baba Farid, a friend of Guru Nanak, and one of the most revered Chisti Sufi saints of the subcontinent, was a devastating blow. See Bigelow (2009) for a further discussion on the subject of the lived realities of people and the interaction of Sufis and shrines at Malerkotla, who refused to take sides in the partition saga with either India or Pakistan.

24. There are various translations of Rumi's *The Masnavi*, and I have consulted Book One, translated by Mojaddedi (2004).

25. See Chand (1954) and Hussian (2007).

26. Some interesting work has been recently published on Sufi shrines, music, and ritual practice in developing a local culture of shared tolerance. See Wolf (2006) and van der Veer (1992).

27. In Assam, singer, song writer, and poet Bhupen Hazarika has repeatedly invoked the concept and term *manabata* to urge his audience to take responsibility for actions toward fellow human beings.

28. In *Divan-i-Ghalib*, the famous poet Mirza Ghalib writes, "Bas ke dushwar hain, Har kam kain asna hona, Admi ko bhi muyashar nahi Insān hona"—A difficult task does not become easy by simply saying so, alas, it seems impossible for man to be human! (Khan 2000; translation mine). This sentiment echoes over and over again in remembering 1947, and Sadaat Hasan

Manto's writings (1987, 1999) drives home this point most eloquently. The critique that man has failed to be human is gaining voice in the state of insecurity and terror in the region.

29. Although 1971 is barely addressed in Pakistani Urdu literature there have been some probing stories and commentaries on the war that highlight the basic instincts of humans and the capacity of violence that is latent within, which, in turn, results in loss of insāniyat. During the 1971 Bangladesh crisis, Shaikh Ayaz, a much-celebrated Sindhi poet, wrote a poem on war and dedicated it to his exiled friend and poet Narayan Shyam, who had left during the partition. In the poem Ayaz lamented how could he fire a gun at this friend standing before him. Ayaz was imprisoned in Sukkur prison for almost eight months for writing this poem. Intizar Hussain (1973) is perhaps the only Pakistani Urdu novelist who seems to have given some serious thought to the national disintegration and the perceptions toward the event at personal and collective levels. He has written several short stories on this subject. I consulted two well-known short stories, *Shahr-e-afsos* and *Voh jo khoe-gae*.

30. Foucault in the *Archeology of Knowledge* (1969) analyzed "epistemic violence" in the nexus between power and production of knowledge. Edward Said's *Orientalism* (1979) grounded Foucault's theoretical discourse in the study of the colonial apparatus and the construction of the Other in the Orient that negated and suppressed the realities of subject communities and made them static portals of received history that enclosed them within rigid boundaries of identities.

31. See the critical essays on the subject of Pakistani history writing by Ali (2002) and Jalal (1995).

32. This discourse has been popularized by politicians and *kar sevaks* (rank and file workers) of the Bharatiya Janata Party (BJP). They are not the first to do so, though. In the early period of the Indian National Congress, leaders like Bal Gangadhar Tilak developed a very narrow definition of Indian as "Hindu" and devised a variety of public festivals and rituals to develop collective consciousness of the Hindus. Peter van der Veer (1992, 1994, 2001); David Ludden (2005); Romila Thapar (2004); Thomas Blom Hansen (1999, 2001); Sumit Sarkar (2002); Christopher Jeffrelot (1995); and Tapan Basu (1993), among others, have explored the project of *Hindutva* history that seeks to make all of Indian history into "Hindu history." Their research has enriched our understanding of the process and outcome of the *Hindutva* rewriting of Indian history within a narrow and exclusionary frame that

privileges religion as the prism for understanding the past, which makes the Indian present and future belong to one community of people, that is, the Hindus.

33. The nineteenth-century Bengali poet Bankim Chandra in his poem "Vande Mataram" (Hail to the motherland) (1876) sowed the seeds of a poisonous knowledge of Muslims as occupiers and endorsed violence against them to cleanse India and regain her original pristine character. In contrast to this view, contemporary historians like Asim Roy, M. R. Tarafdar, and Richard Eaton argue that the process of Muslim conversion and settlement in many parts of India, including Bengal, was peaceful and was generated through expansion of Sufism (or through the work of the Sufis). Eaton (1994), in particular, maps the impact of Sufi teachings and the expansion of agricultural practices that enabled conversion and settlement of new Muslim groups in Bengal.

34. Declassified Files Pertaining to the Ministry of Education, file no. 18/CF/49–183, microfilm no. 1948, National Documentation Center, Islamabad, Pakistan.

35. The objectives of the Islamic Research Institute were defined as follows: "(i) To define Islam by bringing out its fundamentals in a rational and liberal manner and to emphasize among others, the basic ideals of universal brotherhood tolerance and social justice. (ii) To interpret the teachings of Islam in such a way as to bring out its dynamic character in the context of world and intellectual and scientific progress. (iii) To carry out research in Islam's contributions in this world of thought, science and culture with a view to enabling the Muslims once again to recapture the position of preeminence in these fields. (iv) To take appropriate measures in encouraging research in Islamic History, Philosophy, Law and Jurisprudence" (Declassified Files Pertaining to the Ministry of Education, 324/CF/59/1956–16, microfilm no. 2274, National Documentation Center, Islamabad, Pakistan).

36. Declassified Files Pertaining to the Ministry of Education, file no. 30/CF/65–19, microfilm no. 2478, National Documentation Center, Islamabad, Pakistan.

37. Declassified Files Pertaining to the Cabinet Secretariat, file no. 341/CF/66, microfilm no. 2544, National Documentation Centers, Islamabad, Pakistan.

38. Declassified Files Pertaining to the Cabinet, file no. 348/CF/66–5, microfilm no. 2544, National Documentation Center, Islamabad, Pakistan.

39. Willem Van Schendel (2009) tries to provide some corrective to this "colonization" trope of Bangladeshi history. He, too, however, focuses on the

economic and political marginalization of East Pakistan without comparing this regional story with other marginalized regions in West Pakistan, such as Baluchistan, North West Frontier, and Sind, before 1971.

40. In another context Ashis Nandy (1983) has argued that the intimacy and fear of the Indian colonial subject in relation to the British colonial masters had created a peculiar problem of forgetting self, and the way to regain it is by engaging the violence of colonialism.

41. "We are, it seems then, hopelessly caught in a bind. For, to define ourselves, we have to now define our neighbors. Our [Indian] liberal present has to produce a not so liberal neighbor [Bangladesh], our secularism has to find a fundamentalism there . . . our economic progress is counter-posed to her poverty. And this we do, not only to define our triumphant self, we do it to resolve the quarrel and tensions in our many voices. . . . The first produces history out of half-truth, the second counterposes possibility to history in order to drag history into the region of mythography" (Samadar 2001, 863).

42. In my previous research on the history of the Tai-Ahom in Assam, I encountered this phenomenon continuously. People in Assam have almost forgotten the Tai-Ahom legacy, including the language, culture, and religion. Yet, when I asked my Tai-Ahom informants what made them different from the Assamese Hindus they quoted to me the story of history about Tai-Ahom that Edward Gait, the commissioner of colonial Assam, wrote in 1906. The history inscribed by the colonial administrative masters about Assam and her people informed the Assamese collective memory and circulates as the "local" version of Assam's history. The colonial and local memory of Tai-Ahom have blurred and become one and the same. The inner domain of how people remember was totally transformed during colonialism and it persists in survival.

2. CREATING THE HISTORY OF 1971

1. In 2005, I taught a seminar titled "Communalism and Nationalism in South Asia." One of the assignments for the students was to do a riot report. Students' research showed that in each instance of riot in India, barring the great Calcutta riot of 1946, all other riots were triggered and initiated by members of the majority groups, that is, Hindus. If these findings represent a pattern of riots in India, we can conclude that majoritarian politics and violence are intimately connected.

2. This speech should not be read as a sudden and new turn in Jinnah's vision after the formation of Pakistan. In fact, a close reading of the Muslim League papers from 1937 to 1947 shows that they clearly indicate Jinnah's strong appeal for a separation between church and state and for the rights of citizenship to be accorded equally to all groups irrespective of religion. (See Declassified Papers, MH Series 3.1, "Muslim League," microfilm no. 1500, NDC, Islamabad.)

3. The question of the state's identity as an Islamic republic came to the forefront in the early 1950s when an evaluation had to be made about the Ahmadi question and their Muslim identity. The Munir Report that was produced as a result of it did not conclusively answer the question of Muslim identity. The question of whether the Ahmadis constituted a Muslim group remained moot because the ulema could not decide if the definition of Muslim could be clearly established (see Ahmad 2010).

4. The Urdu-speaking people of Pakistan constituted 3.5 percent but controlled 21 percent of the jobs in the Pakistani civil service, and this made the group immensely influential in the central administration. For assessing the policy of discrimination see Pandey and Samad 2007.

5. Ibid., 93.

6. Although the political parties in West Pakistan were not expecting this result, the president of the National Awami Party, Wali Khan, and Mian Mumtaz Daulatana, the president of the Muslim League, both agreed to attend the National Assembly in Dhaka and resolve the issue of transfer of power to a civilian government in order to "maintain the country's integrity at all costs" (Radio Pakistan, morning newscast, March 10, 1971). Similar requests to start a dialogue for preserving Pakistan were made by multiple members of the Jama'at-e-Islami party, but Zulfikar Ali Bhutto refused to relinquish power to a Bengali leader and even threatened West Pakistani political representatives that he'd "break their legs" if they attended the National Assembly in Dhaka (Radio Pakistan, morning newscast, March 11, 1971).

7. I interviewed Yahya Khan's son, Ali Yahya, about his father's actions in East Pakistan. Ali Yahya confessed that his father did not believe in the use of force in East Pakistan, but he was compelled by the manipulation of Zulfikar Ali Bhutto to do so. If this is true, it was Pakistan's political and military elite that actually broke up Pakistan rather than the Bengalis.

8. Multiple references to India's involvement in East Pakistan are available in military documents in India, and the public records of Radio Pakistan and

Radio Pakistan Monitoring Reports. These archival documents are available in both New Delhi and Islamabad.

9. Radio Pakistan News, March 26, 1971, National Archives of Pakistan, Islamabad.

10. Verbal message to a reporter on Bhutto's return to Pakistan after March 25. See Khalid Hasan, "Excerpts: Did Bhutto Break Up Pakistan?," Sixhour.com (http://www.sixhour.com/did_bhutt_%20break_up_pakistan .htm). This message was reproduced in newspapers and broadcast on Radio Pakistan on March 26, 1971.

11. Photographic evidence to this effect is available in the UN Center for Documentation and Research housed within the Military Archive in New Delhi. These photographs cannot be reproduced without permission from the external affairs ministry, which is not forthcoming since the Indian government has not yet declassified the 1971 papers. I was privileged to see the albums of these pictures. As well, I interviewed General Jacobs of the Indian Army who was second in command to General Arora, who was in charge of the Indian Army operations in East Pakistan, and Sapan Chakravorty and R. Badrinath, who were involved in the refugee rehabilitation program at the West Bengal border. Both of these sources confirmed that regular announcements were made over megaphone to encourage people to leave their homes at the border and move to the peaceful zone, to the Indian camps. As well, announcements were made by the Indian Army to the Pakistan Army to lay down their arms and surrender because they would be destroyed if they engaged India in battle.

12. The Bihari issue is a vexed problem. While no definition of Bihari can be provided except that they were the Urdu-speaking communities of East Pakistan, their role in the war of 1971 remains crucial but generally unexplored by Bengali scholars in Bangladesh. The Biharis are deemed enemies on two counts: anti-Bangla and pro-Pakistan, thus they are also viewed as the group that constituted the *rajakars* or supporters of the Pakistan Army in the war.

13. At the end of the war, Pakistan, having purged the Hindu from its body politic, emerged more firmly as a Muslim state, claiming connection with the Muslim countries of Central and West Asia. India, on the other hand, continued its rhetoric of secularism but became increasingly and publicly Hindu. The wedding of religion and politics in the subcontinent was thus established. It is in the light of the consequences that followed that we have to reevaluate the construction of Hindu and Muslim in the period of the war.

14. These stories are detailed in the Urdu- and English-language newspapers in Pakistan. I have consulted the daily reports of the *Imroz* and the *Dawn* from March to December 1971. Administrator and writer Masood Mufti also provides detailed sketches of the ethnic violence of the Bengalis against the non-Bengalis in his quasi-historical narratives such as *Lemhe* (1995), *Chehre* (1996a), and *Raize* (1996b).

15. In a recent conversation with a retired chief engineer of Crescent Jute Mill, a Bangladeshi, I learned that on March 25, 1971, more than six hundred Biharis, including women and children, were slaughtered in Khulna. He knew of this violence, and although he did not order it he encouraged the Bengalis to throw the dead into the river because there was no time to bury them. The elderly engineer who was and continues to be a supporter of the Muslim League candidly admitted that the violence was not one-sided, Bengalis and Biharis killed and brutalized one another, but the worst violence was committed by the Pakistan Army against innocent people.

16. An extensive report on the violence against the Biharis and their isolation in camps after the war is found in Withaker, Guest, and Ennals (1975). Also, Aziz (1974) provides a useful firsthand account of the violence that the Biharis suffered during and immediately after the war. Selective repatriation was granted to the Biharis to go to Pakistan after the war. Bihari women suffered the most as a result of this selective policy. Unmarried women were not considered for official immigration. Sometimes married women had to sacrifice their "allotment" for immigration and let their husbands avail the opportunity in the hope that they will soon send for them after making some money in Pakistan. Often, these men abandoned their families. After 1975 the official process of repatriation ended. Those Biharis who are left behind in Bangladesh live in enclosed campsites and are labeled "stranded Pakistanis." Two leaders of the camp dwellers are Nasim Khan and Ejaz Siddiqui. They have divided the camp dwellers into factional groups. The rhetoric that they will repatriate their followers to Pakistan enables them to exercise and hold on to power.

17. Recently, in June 2008 the children of Biharis who were born after 1971 were given right of citizenship in Bangladesh. This, indeed, is a positive and important gesture toward resolving the condition of the post-liberated Bangladeshi Biharis. But what about the parents of the Bihari children who were young and uninvolved in the war of 1971? If the parents are not integrated into the nation-state of Bangladesh the fissures of distrust and separation will continue to breed in the Bihari camps, and it will undermine the efforts of integrating the different communities in Bangladesh.

18. On several occasions during fieldwork in Bangladesh, I met survivors of "brush firing." Their experiences of seeing death and then escaping it temporarily had a variety of impacts on their lives. In one case, I met a person who, having survived an incident of brush firing, decided to convert and become a Muslim. He was previously a Hindu from the Marwari community. He was not willing to discuss what drove him to take the religion of his enemy and perpetrators.

19. Parliamentary Debates, vol. VIII, nos. 6–10, Nov, 22–26, 1971; vol. XI, March 17, 1972; vol. 24, March 15, 1973, Nehru Memorial and Museum Library, New Delhi.

20. A similar process followed in the Assamese identity movement. During the initial period, the All Assam Students Union (AASU) leaders demanded the removal of all Bangladeshis from Assam. Over time, it was accepted that the Hindu Bangladeshis did not have to return to Bangladesh; being part of the majority Hindu community of India they should be accommodated within the country. Consequently, the only Bangladeshis they wanted to expel from Assam were the Muslims. This shift in the politics of AASU was not well received by many in Assam because it made the identity struggle into a communitarian issue based on religion rather than language or socioeconomic concerns, which were the driving force for mass support of the movement. The emergence of the militant organization called the United Liberation Front of Assam (ULFA) in the late 1980s reoriented the politics of identity. The ULFA staged their battle against New Delhi and demanded autonomy for Assam. In turn, their recognition of the "new Assamese" enabled a variety of Bengali groups, both Hindus and Muslims, who had adopted the Assamese language and culture, to become part of the Assamese social milieu, and they were protected from violence.

    The most recent attacks against so-called Bangladeshi Muslim immigrants were in Maharashtra. Indiscriminately, Bangla speakers in the capital city of Mumbai were attacked as "Bangladeshis" and threatened with eviction by the political party called Shiv Sena (see news reports in Indian national newspapers, such as the *Hindu* and the *Times of India*, from March 8, 2008).

21. There are also several references to these policies of displacement and changing the internal demography of East Pakistan in the Pakistan Parliamentary Debates, 1966–1970, National Archives of Pakistan, Islamabad.

22. Indira Gandhi's speech at Columbia University, New York on November 6, 1971, enunciated the policy of war that was soon to follow. She persuaded her listeners to accept it as the best strategy (see Prasad 1992, 819–20).

23. In the United Services Library and the UN Center for Documentation and Research in New Delhi, the research officer showed me a photo album of Indian soldiers who were used as infiltrators by the Indian government for purposes of intelligence gathering and espionage in 1971. These photographs document the involvement of Indian agents in East Pakistan before the actual outbreak of the international war on November 26, 1971. In fact, the visual evidence establishes the presence of the Indian soldiers from January 1971 inside East Pakistan.

24. There are no reliable figures to account for the victims of the war. Bangladesh and India claim that ten million persons became refugees, nearly a million died, and two hundred thousand women were raped. Both countries are silent on the so-called Bihari problem. Pakistan rejects these numbers and claims they are exaggerated. I do not think the problem is a question of numbers or the claims for recognizing the "real" victims. The more serious problem is that combatants belonging to armies and militias attacked and killed noncombatants. This crucial issue needs to be explored and investigated for a better understanding of the impact of war on ordinary people, who are neither the architects of war, nor do they have any power to stop the violence. The rise of combatant violence against noncombatants has been increasing since World War II, and data shows that it rose disproportionately during Operation Desert Storm, the first war against Iraq in 1991, and has since increased exponentially (see Waller and Rycenga 2000). Because the war of 1971 has not been critically analyzed, it is not possible to conclude whether it was the turning point for the dramatic increase in the ratio of noncombatant to combatant deaths.

25. On March 3, 1971, in Mymensingh, located in northern Bangladesh, ethnic violence broke out between the Biharis and Bengalis. The Biharis were attacked in their homes, and many were brutally butchered. It appears there was a bloodbath because a few days later when a team of women from Dhaka representing the Anjuman-e-Khawatin-e-Islam arrived they found more than thirty orphans, ranging from the age of six months to fourteen years old, huddled together in a makeshift Red Cross shelter. Among the orphans was a six-month-old baby draped in bandages. Her throat was slit open during the attack. She and her eight-year-old brother were rescued from a drain by the Red Cross volunteers. Their parents were killed in their homes. The Mymensingh incident was the first spark in the long series of hostile exchanges between the Bengalis and Biharis that continued to mar their relationship throughout the period of the war and beyond. I had met these survivors and the women who had rescued them in Dhaka. There

is visual evidence of the killings of the Biharis by the Bengalis, but they have been suppressed and never shown in public spaces because they undo the conventional Bangladeshi position as the victim community (see Anam 2008b).

26. In February 27, 2008, the conference "Genocide in 1971" was held in Dhaka. As the title suggests the problem of naming is an ongoing concern. Although it is widely agreed that there is an urgent need to address and search for more information concerning the violence that happened in the war, it is not possible to establish that the Bangladesh case was genocide. The term *genocide* was coined by Raphael Lemkin in 1944. According to the UN Convention on the Prevention and Punishment of the Crime of Genocide, genocide is "acts committed with intent to destroy, in whole or part, a national, ethnical, racial, or religious group." For comparative studies on genocide, see Totten and Jacobs (2002) and Stone (2008).

27. Dafur is the first ongoing crisis that the United States publicly and conclusively labeled as genocide.

28. Scholars who have studied the Holocaust draw a sharp distinction between the world in which the Nazis lived compared to that of the Jewish people. The Nazis who masterminded the Holocaust continued to live their "normal" lives, such as enjoying operas, picnics, music, and family, while their victims were boarded up like animals in cattle cars and sent to labor and concentration camps, from where they went to their deaths in gas chambers. This is a dramatically different scenario from what happened in East Pakistan, which was a war torn, violent space in 1971. Everyone there lived in fear and anxiety. Looting, rape, and killing were activities that anyone with power indulged in against the less powerful. It was a dog-eat-dog world. In this world of destructive, rampant violence there were many victims and perpetrators. No single group can be identified as the only victim or perpetrator community.

29. Personal testimony of General Abul Lais, a Bengali man who now lives in Rawalpindi, Pakistan. I met General Lais in 2004 in Islamabad, and he revealed to me an untold story of the violence of the Mukti Bahini during the war. His father was "inhumanly" tortured and killed by the Mukti Bahini because he did not support their efforts to break away from Pakistan. He reasoned that his father had once fought for the creation of Pakistan. How could he, in a matter of a few years, turn away from that commitment and make another cause his political platform? This was not a political position that the Mukti Bahini accepted, and they tortured the old man for his politics. Furthermore, his unwillingness to divulge information about

his son, who was then serving as a major in the Pakistan Army, provided further cause for punishment leading to his death. Likewise, a journalist from Dhaka told me that on numerous occasions, Mukti Bahini soldiers committed wanton violence in his village against the Bengali people who did not support their cause.

30. I have done extensive interviews with soldiers and officers of the Pakistan Army who served in the war of 1971. Over and over again, I heard that fear drove them to violence. Killing was used as a tactic to force the Bengalis to give up their claim for liberation and make Pakistan safe from the Indian enemy. But the Pakistanis failed miserably, and East Pakistan broke away and became Bangladesh, an independent country.

31. In 1971 Tariq Rahman, presently distinguished professor of Pakistan studies at Quaid-i-Azam University, Islamabad, was a cadet in the Pakistan Army. He was training to be a soldier when the war broke out. He remembered that the violence in East Pakistan was reported back to the western sector as a state of rebellion that needed to be put down. By presenting the Bengalis as recalcitrant, unruly subjects, West Pakistanis justified their violence. Tariq Rahman resigned from his position in the army during this period of upheaval (personal conversations, September 2004 and March 2009, Islamabad).

32. Mumtaza Begum and her two co-prisoners, Rukiya and Fatima, who were held in a sex camp in Jessore told about their dehumanization in vivid details. Their experiences were brutal and tragic, but what was even sadder was their helplessness and abject obedience to do as they were commanded because they did not even have the will or the strength to resist.

33. Additionally, in a recent conversation with Bongo Bir Kader Siddique he revealed to me an incident of violence committed by one of his Mukti Bahini soldiers. One of his men stole an expensive shawl from the home of a Bengali family during one of their routine visits to the village to collect arms. When Kader Siddique found out about it, he shot the young soldier to teach the others a lesson to not plunder the villagers during their visits for arms collection. He believed that the punishment of death was a lesson for fighting an honest war. Kader Siddique also discussed with me the event when he had shot and killed several Biharis after the war in the Dhaka Stadium. He said that at the time of the incident he did not think of his act as a crime against humanity, being swayed by the Bengali public sentiment for revenge. Today he knows that both the acts—killing a young soldier for a petty theft and killing the Biharis for being different from the Bengalis— were public acts of violence disguised under the label of national morale to

establish the power of the Bengalis and claim victory, but they were violent acts, nonetheless, and he is pained by his past.

34. A recent publication by Jahan (2004) reproduces the same understanding evident in the term *genocide*.

35. For a previous discussion on this subject see Barbara Harff, T. R. Gurr, and A. Unger, "Preconditions of Genocide and Politicide: 1955–1998," a paper presented at the conference "Differing Approaches to Assessing Potential Genocide, Politicides, and Mass Killings," Vienna, Virginia, 1999. The paper is quoted in Staub (2000). For the distinction between gendercide and genocide, see Jones (2000).

36. Derived from a Persian word, the term *rajakars* means "volunteers." Manned by non-Bengali (often Urdu-speaking Bihari) and Bengali men, this loosely constituted group assisted the Pakistan Army during the war. They were pro-Jama'at-e-Islami in their political affiliation and were Pakistan supporters. Most rajakars operated at a local level and provided information and assistance to the Pakistan Army in apprehending, arresting, and committing violence against the Bengalis. In almost all my interviews, women mentioned the active role of rajakars and identified them as both Bengali and non-Bengali men. Under the guise of being a rajakar, men sexually violated and exploited "enemy" women, although the majority of these women were not involved in politics. In my estimation, the rajakars were opportunists who took advantage of the terrible situation of war and used violence to commit crimes.

37. The nation is consciously or unconsciously imagined as masculine, even by the acclaimed author Benedict Anderson (1991, 172).

38. "Bastard Pakistanis" is a term used by Jahangir Haider, who was in charge of the Women's Rehab program as health minister and worked with Rahman Sobhan, the chair of the Rehab Commission, after the war. He explained that Sheikh Mujibur Rahman was particularly concerned about the problem and wanted to erase the evidence (personal conversations, September 2001, Dhaka, Bangladesh).

39. In one of my conversations with a Bihari woman in Mirpur, she told me that she had "seen with [her] own eyes men throwing away bags which contained parts of women's bodies into the river." The Bihari families, like the Bengali families, could not create a space to accommodate the dishonored women in their homes. A Bengali woman, who is now married to a Bihari man, told me that her family disowned her when they found she had survived rape during the war. Although she was married twice to Bengali men of her choice, they abandoned her when they found out about her past.

40. I am using "iconic" as a personal memory that supersedes all other memories. The visual picture of the memory is in the head of the one who remembers. Image and story are merged and a new reality is shaped that becomes the story that is replayed in one's mind, but it is not incorporated into the plethora of "acceptable" memory. Iconic becomes unforgettable and yet fleeting because it is inchoate.

41. Iris Chang, the author of *The Rape of Nanking*, in a public presentation at Carleton College in March 1998 mentioned that the rape of women in the war of 1971 was probably the worst case of gender violence in twentieth-century conflict, but it has not been studied, unlike the cases of mass rape of German women during World War II, Bosnian and Croatian women in the Balkan Wars in the 1990s, and Hutu and Tutsi women in Rwanda in 1994. In two recent articles, Sharmila Bose (2005 and 2007) has argued that rape was not a common violence in the war of 1971. Bose's argument troubles me because it suggests that the grievances of women in Bangladesh concerning rape are made up. The official version of the published supplement of the Hamoodur Rahman Commission Report on 1971 prepared in Pakistan establishes that rape was a common occurrence in the war. The silencing of gender violence in the sites of academia does terrible harm and undermines the victims' experiences, rendering women's direct experience in the war invisible and unspeakable. A slow but steady appearance of essays on the subject of gender violence in the war is now available, but it circulates mostly within the Western academy (for example, see Mookherjee 2006; D'Costa 2005; Sharlach 2000; and Saikia 2004a and 2006).

42. Contrasting this silence, in the case of America we have several testimonies of rape of black women in the Memphis riots of 1866, even at a time when discussion of rape outside the sites of judicial practice was not common (see Rosen 1999).

43. This was reported in newspapers in 2001, during the thirtieth anniversary of the war.

44. While conducting research in Bangladesh many told me the story of Khaleda Zia's captivity during the war and that she was confined in the military camp in Dhaka by the Pakistan Army. I naively asked why she has not spoken up on behalf of birangonas and if she had ever divulged her own story of captivity and unequal interaction with the Pakistani military. Perhaps, if Begum Zia would have had the courage to speak about her own experiences during the war the outlook of society toward birangonas would change somewhat in Bangladesh. Today, when one refers to birangonas the figure of a marginal, poor, and helpless woman comes to mind. Such a

figure is easier to pity rather than engaging them as architects of a history of Bangladesh that is mostly unknown due to suppression and deliberate forgetting.

45. Foucault's notion that history is never about what people really experience, but is made in archives and spaces of power that determine what can be said, by whom, and when, is useful in the context of Bangladesh. The imposed forgetting of women's experiences suits the production of history as part of a nation-building process after the war and creates a collective memory of triumphant Bengali nationhood.

46. Bina D'Costa (2005) has done some interesting preliminary work on the problem of war babies who were products of rape. Her work is focused on the role of missionaries and doctors who were involved in the state abortion program in Bangladesh after the war. The babies that survived despite the state abortion program were generally put up for adoption abroad through various international organizations, including the Sisters of Charity headed by Mother Teresa. Most of these children were adopted by families in Canada and the Netherlands. Bangladesh was desperate to remove all traces of the Pakistani presence in their midst. A small number of war babies remained in Bangladesh, though, and Beauty is one of them. In the course of my research in Bangladesh, I met two other war babies who are aware of their status and discussed it with me. They, however, did not want to make their stories public.

47. A nun who was present throughout the war and continues to live in Dhaka told me some adoption stories during a flight from Jessore to Dhaka in April 2001. I did not ask her name, nor did she offer it to me. Mustafa Chowdhury, a Canadian-Bangladeshi and social worker, is currently working on the outcome of the first contingent of fifteen war babies who were adopted in Canada through an initiative of the Montreal-based Families for Children.

48. Dina Siddiqui corrected my use of the term *other* for Bihari women in a conference presentation entitled "Bengali, Bihari, and the War of Liberation of 1971: Speaking Silence and Displacement," Asian Studies Conference, March 28, 2003, New York. She admitted that the Biharis are not even considered human by the Bengalis because of their betrayal in 1971, and there is no place available to them, even today, in the memories of 1971 to be spoken about as the Other.

49. Gayatri Spivak (1988) has questioned whether there can be a moment when the marginalized can speak. In her consideration, the silencing of the marginal constitutes the lack of agency. The fundamental issue that power is

located in specific sites and is exercised by the architects of power is an important consideration to bear in mind. The construction of the voicelessness of subalterns, like women, needs to be critically evaluated in the Bangladesh case because it is not simply a matter of agency of the one who does not and cannot speak. It is also a matter of listening: do we hear what they cannot say?

50. Shelly Feldman has been studying the history and politics of the Mukti Juddho Jadughar. She delivered a paper at the Center for South Asian Studies, North Carolina, titled "Claiming a Past, Making a Future: The Liberation War Museum (Dhaka) as a Site of Struggle."

51. "Background Documents 1996," *Bangladesh Observer*, March 26, 1995.

52. Many Pakistani scholars were surprised that I was searching for a history of 1971. Some told me that it was not an important topic, and others cautioned me that the "military rulers will be unhappy about such research." Curiously, the students I met were very keen to know about Bangladesh. Many did not even know that Bangladesh was born out of Pakistani violence in the war. For me their enthusiasm to learn and ignorance about their history was both encouraging and distressing. During my stay in Pakistan, I hired a young woman from the Punjab University to be my research assistant, and her dedication to find obscure literary materials and search the history going back to 1947 made the research an enriching experience. These and other interactions with students in Pakistan made me realize that the younger generation is more open to knowing the past for what it is. The experience was similar in Bangladesh.

53. The East Bengal Regiment (EBR) revolted on March 25, 1971. The story has an element of drama. It appears that during dinner, the Bengali officers stood up and fired on their fellow West Pakistani officers and killed many of them. Soon after this revolt, Ziaur Rahman, who later became president of Bangladesh, declared the independence of Bangladesh in a radio broadcast from Chittagong on March 26, 1971.

54. Many officers of the Pakistan Army expressed this sentiment concerning the EBR. For Ikram Seghal, whose father, Chand Seghal, had commanded the 2 East Bengal Regiment of the Pakistan Army, the import of this statement is heartfelt. Ikram Seghal as he himself states (he has written many columns on this issue) is a Punjabi and a Bengali, and he refuses to embrace one label over the other. His mother was a Bengali from Bogra in East Pakistan (in present-day Bangladesh), and his father was from Sialkot in West Punjab (in present-day Pakistan). Ikram Seghal started his career as a second lieutenant in the 2 East Bengal. After the EBR revolted, Ikram's identity

became a matter of suspicion for everyone. The Bengalis saw him as an enemy because of his Punjabi connections, and the Punjabis suspected him due to his Bengali roots. In the end Ikram was court-martialed and released from active duty. Today, when Ikram remembers the war of 1971 he continues to refuse to take sides with either group because it would mean a betrayal of his parents, his Bengali mother and his Punjabi father. For Ikram, it was a war between family members, and he resists their divisions, at least, emotionally. He told me during one of our conversations, "I was really devastated in 1971. I always thought Pakistan was the finest experiment in nationhood, two distinct parts bonding together" (personal conversations February–March 2005).

55. Ashok Mitra, who was closely involved in the reconstruction of Bangladesh's economy, and General Lakshman Singh Lehl, who was deputed to help in the rebuilding of the infrastructure, talked candidly about the Indian attitude of looting Bangladesh after the war.

56. In probing the issue of the sexual violence of Indian soldiers against local Bengali women after the war, General Lehl acknowledged that there were many instances when town hall meetings were called in which Bengalis complained about the Indians soldiers' behavior and claimed they were "not different from the Pakistani soldiers." General Lehl admitted this was an eye-opener because men in these circumstances whether Pakistani or Indian behaved in a similar manner.

57. There is vast documentation on Prime Minister Indira Gandhi's role in the war. To substantiate the official records, I met with many officers who were actively involved in the planning and rehabilitation of refugees. In personal interviews with Ashok Mitra, Sapan Chakraborty, Hirak Ghosh, and R. Badrinath, all of them confirmed Mrs. Gandhi's active role in the refugee rehabilitation program.

58. This was a very popular slogan for creating fear in Assam. The rhetoric of uncontrolled population growth of Bangladeshis served its purpose to motivate the entire population of Assam to back the AASU-led identity struggle. It was through negative identification vis-à-vis the Bangladeshis that the Assamese communities suddenly found motivation to publicly claim an identity of their own. What and who is an Assamese is an unanswered question.

59. The massacre of thousands of so-called Bangladeshi people in the village of Nellie in the Nowgong district of Assam in 1983 has not been investigated even twenty-five years later. The Assamese people pretend the work of killing innocent people was done by "outsiders," and thus they are not

accountable for the crime. Most importantly, the AASU leaders seem to forget that the Assamese identity movement that they organized and led was premised on the demand of driving out the Bangladeshis from Assam, and it was this political demand that provided the impetus to a variety of people to act, leading to the violence in Nellie. Thus both the AASU and the people of Assam were complicit, if not culpable, of committing the crime.

60. A special meat and rice dish that is a specialty of old Dhaka; it is generally prepared during festive occasions like Eid ul-Fitr to celebrate the end of Ramadan.

61. As mentioned earlier, the term *Bihari* as it is used in Bangladesh does not necessarily refer to the people of Bihar, India. *Bihari* is a pejorative term used to identify the non-Bengali, Urdu speakers, who are considered enemies of Bangladesh's liberation. The reference to Bihari as a singular category of people undermines the complexities and varieties of Urdu-speaking people who had migrated to East Pakistan in 1947. In 1971 this label was attached to the hated Other. For a historical analysis of the process of migration, displacement, and reduction of so-called Biharis into an enemy category during and after partition, see Papiya Ghosh (1998 and 2007).

62. The case of the Biharis in the South Asian context provides an empirical location to engage the conceptual category of Giorgio Agamben's "homo sacer" (1998). The Bihari communities live outside the juridical framework of Bangladesh, in a state of exception, and by controlling their lives and deaths the state of Bangladesh has transformed them into bodies for killing and destruction.

63. Ashis Nandy (1995) argues that the limited, Western academic method of writing history is a totalizing discourse disenfranchising and oppressing people who do not organize the memory of the past in those terms. He has called for South Asian historians to unshackle themselves from this derived discourse and search for alternative ways of telling people's experiences on their terms.

64. I find the narratives of survivors of 1971 to be very different from the narratives of survivors of the Holocaust. Hannah Arendt's (1945, 1953a, 1953b, 1958, and 1965) and Primo Levi's (1961 and 1986) accounts were the exceptions to this rule. Their narratives put the Holocaust under complex scrutiny to reveal both the trivial and complex processes that worked simultaneously and effectively to produce devastating outcomes. In their writings we are able to find the personal stories of Holocaust alongside a critical examination of the institutional structures and people who engineered and made

violence possible. In short, a horrific episode of history became eloquent in Levi's and Arendt's narrative styles, revealing the limited and elastic nature of human behavior.

65. The issue of rajakars has, once again, surfaced in Bangladesh after the general elections in 2008. The Freedom Fighters Forum has made a demand that Bengali rajakars who have not been punished, unlike their Bihari counterparts who have been exiled into camps, should be identified and tried as war criminals because they opposed the freedom of Bangladesh. They claim that the leaders and principal actors of the Muslim League Party are the Bengali rajakars (see BBC News report on March 20, 2008, Al-Jazeera, "East Bangladeshis Seeking Justice against Genocide in Bangladesh," April 17, 2008).

66. This is not unique to Bangladesh. In the case of Bosnia and Croatia similar arguments have been made (see Waller and Rycenga 2000).

67. A well-known slogan of Sheikh Mujibur Rahman was "the people of Bangladesh—the Hindus, Muslims, Christians, and Buddhists—we are all Bengali." A reproduction of the poster is in Willem van Schendel's *History of Bangladesh* (Cambridge University Press, 2009).

68. I originally interviewed this veteran of the war of 1971 in November 2001. In the summer of 2006, I went back to Bangladesh to do some interviews with the war heroes for writing another book. During this visit, I had the opportunity to re-interview this decorated veteran, and this time he admitted he was wrong in writing off the issue of violence against women. He encouraged me not to give up the quest but to make people aware of the terror suffered by women during wartime. In inquiring about the reason for the change in his perception and articulation, I learned that his daughter has retrained him to think differently. He now understands her fears and vulnerability and can empathize with women's condition. He wants to see Bangladesh become a safer space for women.

69. Nayanika Mookherjee (2006) suggests that talk about rape can be read as "scorn" in local Bengali society that deems rape as sex, and therefore it is shameful and dishonorable. This is true if we approach the discussion of rape from the viewpoint of South Asian patriarchy, but for survivors the memory is too powerful and cannot be conveniently put aside as "dishonor."

70. Sharmila Bose (2007) argues against the possibility of multiple tellings and questions the veracity of memories, particularly those belonging to victims. She suggests that the horror of sexual violence in the war is exaggerated in the Bangladeshi narratives, and they need to be reevaluated for questioning

their truth. In turn, she creates another narrative by tracking a few individual actors in Pakistan and Bangladesh, and by using their stories disproves the earlier versions. While it is an important and relevant exercise to continue the search for what happened in 1971 and the memories that have been generated, the reduction of the complex story of people's losses and sufferings into a banal scoring of numbers and statistics undermines several crucial questions: Was the violence necessary? Why did combatants commit violence against noncombatants? How was religion and ethnicity used to manipulate people to commit violence?

71. The names of the women used in the narratives of part II are their real names, except Nur Begum. Otherwise, throughout the text only pseudonyms have been used to refer to the women, whose stories I quote in short excerpts.

72. Women used terms like *oitochar, zulm, shaadi, koshto, gaib*, and so on to describe the violence. None of these terms translate into the English as *rape*.

73. Zaibunisa was repatriated to Karachi, from Bangladesh in 1974.

74. Zaibunisa does not reveal how they died. Did starvation lead to their death or did she kill them in her helplessness because she could not feed them? We will never know because there is no simple narrative for Zaibunisa to tell.

75. Her exact words were "woe bhi insān tha."

76. Several women in Pakistan representing the Women's Action Forum have told me that their organization had sent a letter of apology to the women of Bangladesh for the crimes committed against them in 1971. Can women of Pakistan ask for forgiveness to Bangladeshi women when they have not committed the crime? Should women of Pakistan align and claim themselves as national actors when they were not included in the national discussion process of wartime activities? Who can forgive who has been a question of much debate in recent times. An enlightening book on this question in context to the Holocaust is Simon Wiesenthal's *The Sunflower* (1998).

77. The Five Pillars constitute belief in one god, praying five times a day, paying charity, observing the annual fasting during Ramadan, and performing the pilgrimage called *Haj*. In qualifying what constitutes *huquq-al-ibād* some schools of Islamic thought also include murder, although in the modern legal system the crime of murder cannot be mutually resolved by two aggrieved parties.

78. I am grateful to Abdullahi An-Na'im for drawing my attention to this principle that allows us to move forward in addressing the crime of rape in 1971

and seeking a solution. As well, I am deeply thankful for the conversations with Khalid Masud, Bruce Lawrence, and Carl Ernst on Islam and the lived practices of the religion—they added to my understanding of religion, culture, and justice.

79. To claim retribution, oaths of *qasama* have to be taken by fifty blood relatives of the victim from the paternal line. In the Hanafi law the root of qasama was an oath of innocence taken by fifty men that they were not involved in the killing of a man found in their midst. Faced with this oath, the blood relatives of the deceased could not demand blood retaliation but blood price was paid as compensation. In the Maliki law qasama was a collective oath (also sworn by fifty relatives) through which they formally accused and demanded vengeance of the alleged perpetrator of the crime of murder. The oath of qasama was retained in Islam from pre-Islamic practice (see Humphreys 1990).

80. On March 27, 2009, I gave a talk in Islamabad on the invitation of the Council of Social Science. At the end of my presentation a person from the audience virulently attacked me for speaking about victims' experiences of rape and the perpetrators' retrospective sense of guilt, which I suggested is a beginning point to start working through the common trauma in order to move beyond it. He told me that research on the violence of 1971 can be written off in one paragraph and since all of mankind is capable of violence it is pointless to probe this specific event, rather we should investigate the psychology of mankind that makes them violent. In other words, he was absolving Pakistan of the crimes that the men committed in East Pakistan by his assertion that violence inherent in man is the problem and not the episode itself. The willful neglect of history and inability to engage the crimes of community is an alarming issue because by hiding under human nature people try to justify or distance their actions and not hold themselves responsible or accountable. I would like to add that this is not a specific Pakistani problem. In the subcontinent the will to hear and acknowledge crimes that are being committed and those that have been committed is a major obstacle for research.

81. Pakistan and India have fought three wars over Kashmir (1948, 1965, and 1999). After 1971 the hostilities between India and Bangladesh began to surface over issues of illegal migration, water politics, economic strangulation, and other issues.

82. In his lecture of 1882, "Qu'est-ce qu'une nation?," Ernest Renan raised the question of what makes a nation. He responds that although nations can-

not be based on race, language, interests, religious affinity, geography, and military necessity, a nation can be made in another site: "To have suffered together is of greater value than identity of custom houses and frontiers . . . for indeed common suffering unites more strongly than rejoicing. Among national memories, sorrows have greater value than victories, for they impose duties and demand common effort." In this passage Renan makes us aware of the potency of suffering that elevates the victim to a moral position to claim and give agency to self and others who share and empathize with the survivors (the lecture is reproduced in Dahbour and Ishay 1999).

3. VICTIMS' MEMORIES

1. The term *hanadar*, it appears, was introduced in the late 1970s and early 1980s, after the assassination of Sheikh Mujib and the establishment of martial rule under Ziaur Rahman and General Ershad. Since the memory of 1971 is a highly politicized and factionalized topic within Bangladesh and people are very sensitive about it there has been a raging debate regarding its use. The Awami League (AL) and Bangladesh National Party (BNP) have battled over the term and its representation. The supporters of the AL claim that the use of the term *hanadar* dilutes and makes the enemy into a faceless entity. They want the perpetrators to be identified as Pakistanis and *rajakars*. The supporters of the BNP, on the other hand, prefer to use the term *hanadar* to refer to the armed forces that perpetrated violence against the people of Bangladesh. The dividing issue is not whether the Pakistan Army did violence in the war of 1971. The battle is between the two political groups in Bangladesh, with each of them claiming the exclusive right to write and represent, on their own terms, the history of 1971 based on their political leanings.

2. They are songs composed by the Nobel poet laureate Rabindra Nath Tagore. Rabindra Sangeet or Tagore songs, as they are referred to in English, are very popular in both West Bengal and Bangladesh.

3. Under the leadership of Jahanara Iman, a founding leader of the Ghatak Dalal Nirmul Committee (GDNC), the main aim of the GDNC was to organize trials of people who committed crimes against the Bengalis in the 1971 war in collaboration with the Pakistani forces. In a highly symbolic act, the GDNC set up mock trials in Dhaka in March 1992 known as Gonoadalot (People's Court) and sentenced war criminals as well as created public testimonies of rape of women.

4. Syed is an honorific title given to the male descendants of the family of Prophet Muhammad. Both Shias and Sunnis claim this title. In the sub-continent, the class constituted of Syed, Sheikh, Mughal, and Pathan were referred to as Ashraf and they differentiated themselves from the Ajlaf or lower-class caste groups. The Ashrafs claimed a foreign ancestry in the distant past. This peculiar hierarchical development within Indian Islam was borrowed from Hindu social practices and communal divisions that vertically divided society into groups of empowered and disempowered people.

5. In 1999, 50,000 Indian rupees were equivalent to 1,000 US dollars.

6. "Ordinary men," in this context, refer to men who are not backed by social class and economic position that distinguish them. Ordinary men, who are not constrained by the limitations of their position, suffer the disrepute of not following normative practices. My research project appeared to the officer to be lacking in honor. He expressed his opinion in the lack of respect that he showed to me.

7. In 1947 Dinajpur was randomly partitioned between India and Pakistan, but the memory of the place and people could not be divided so easily. Even today, the people of Dinajpur seem to have brisk interaction and exchanges with people across the border in India. I was curious and interested in visiting Dinajpur because of the stories that I had heard from my father about Parbatipur, the grand railway junction in undivided Dinajpur district. In the 1940s, anyone traveling from Assam to Calcutta or Dhaka by train had to travel through Parbatipur. My father had journeyed through Parbatipur many times to and from Assam to Calcutta and Dhaka. I wanted to visit this place to retrace my father's footprints. Unfortunately, I did not have the opportunity to visit Parbatipur due to my short stay in Dinajpur.

8. The distinction between Punjabi, Pakistani, and khan that Taslima's mother refers to is interesting, but she does not establish who constitutes the different groups. At times, she refers to them within the category called hanadar, like Nur Begum did.

9. If we go by Taslima's mother's calculation, she was more than seven months pregnant at the time of her abortion. Late-term termination of pregnancy was done by the order of the government. It was mandatory for women who came to the state healthcare center to go through abortion before they received any kind of assistance. The government's effort to get rid of the "bastard Pakistani" meant renewed violence on women's bodies. Women had no option but to bear the pain of violence all over again.

10. This is an acknowledgment of Allah's grace and bounty that accentuates

the belief that fate is determined by Allah. It is a commonly used expression by South Asian Muslims.

11. Here she is using a familial term of sister to refer to her boss, the head of the office. This is common practice in South Asia where honorifics such as *Mr.* and *Ms.* are easily replaced with familial terms of *brother* or *sister* to show respect and create an "imagined" family within which the boss is seen as the patron of his or her workers.

12. Of the 92,000 prisoners of war, more than 50,000 were civilians.

13. Mukti Juddho is a Bangla term to refer to the war of Bangladesh in 1971 and translates into English as "The Liberation War," not to be confused with *mukti jouddha* referring to the freedom fighters. It is curious that Nurjahan, a Bihari immigrant, considered an enemy of Bengalis, uses the Bangla term, unaware of the politics of semantics and the history associated with the word.

14. A dismissive term to abuse the Urdu-speaking people.

15. The *mehendi* ceremony is a marriage ritual among Muslims in the subcontinent. It is performed in the bride's home before the actual wedding or *nikaah*, and the bride's hands and feet are decorated with henna. Here Nurjahan alludes to the fact that her daughter was newly married and the patterns of henna were still fresh on her hands. In other words, she had not yet started doing the regular chores of running the household. She was still in the initial stages of her marriage, in the honeymoon period, so to speak.

4. WOMEN'S SERVICES

1. During the war, the active supporters of the Muslim League Party, the political party that founded Pakistan, continued to resist the independence of East Pakistan. They founded peace committees, and, as the name suggests, the effort was to create normalcy within East Pakistan with the assistance of local supporters and the Pakistani administration.

2. Kartik is the eighth lunar month according to the Hindu calendar and coincides with October and November in the Gregorian solar calendar.

3. She was a well-known freedom fighter and worked closely with Mahatma Gandhi. In 1963 she became the chief minister of Uttar Pradesh, the first woman to hold the position in an Indian state.

4. Suhasini Devi is referring to the tenure of Sheikh Hasina as prime minister.

5. A measurement of gold used in Bengal. One *bhori* is equivalent to ten grams.

6. *Mala* is a string of beads used for prayer. *Tulsi* or basil plant is considered sacred by Hindus. Widows generally wear a *tulsi mala* to signify their status and disassociate with worldly things.

7. After the General Assembly was disbanded on March 3, common people in East Pakistan took to the streets demanding justice from the Pakistani government. The riots that followed were bloody and chaotic, and armed groups of Bengalis went on a rampage against the non-Bengalis to target them with violence as a reaction to the Pakistani government's failure to accept Sheikh Mujibur as the prime minister. The incident that Suhasini Devi is referring to here is related to this period of the struggle.

8. I have heard similar stories from several people in Bangladesh. Two of them were imprinted in my memory because both of them are somewhat unusual in their outcome. The first incident is from Saidpur and happened on March 23, 1971. It appears that a number of men, young and old, who were suspected of being involved in antistate activities, were arrested and taken outside the town and shot there. Almost all of them were killed, except two who survived. One of them was a Marwari Hindu man. He introduced himself to me as Kamal Ahmed. Later he admitted that he was previously Hindu, and his name was Kamla Prasad. He said, "Saidpur was under curfew then. I came out of my house to shave and saw the army outside. My brother, Narayan Prasad [who later fled to India] was being beaten. I wanted to take the back road and disappear. But they saw me and arrested both of us. My mother pleaded with the army to let one of us go. I was taken to the cantonment where I saw lots of important people—doctors, members of the Parliament, and so on. We were beaten for an hour every evening and were interrogated. We had nothing to tell, though. We were kept like that until sometime in April when they decided to move us because of the lack of space. We were taken to Uper Saher [uptown]. Two rows of men before us were shot at; then they fired on us. The bullet went through my leg and I fell. I was half-buried. Soon after that it rained and everyone left. After several hours, someone came and helped me out of the pit. They took me to a hospital and registered me under a Muslim name— Ahmed Hussain. They warned me never to reveal my old identity.... My family did not accept my conversion. My brother asked me to reconvert and promised he would help me financially, but I refused. I have lived as a Muslim since." He revealed that he has shared his story with his daughter.

Major Faroukh is another survivor. In 1971, he was serving as a captain in the East Bengal Regiment (EBR). After the EBR revolted on March 25, 1971, he and some of his Bengali colleagues were rounded up by the Pakistanis.

They were locked in a room and shot at. This happened in Chittagong. Captain Faroukh broke open a window and escaped through it although he had suffered gunshot wounds. He walked several miles in the dark before he received assistance. Afterward, he joined the Mukti Bahini and fought against the Pakistan Army as a major. He led many guerilla attacks into the border from Tripua. After Bangladesh was liberated, Major Faroukh was awarded the title of Bir Pratik for his service in the war. After 1975, Major Faroukh resigned from the army because he was deemed a suspect in the Sheikh Mujibur assassination conspiracy, was punished on the suspicion of being an antistate agent, and was put under surveillance. He said, "I had survived the Pakistan Army's attempt to kill me, but I was hunted by my own people. It made no sense anymore."

9. *Katha* is a kind of embroidery work practiced in Bengal. Kathas were originally used for babies and were made of leftover fabric and used clothes. To decorate and stitch together the patchwork, embroidery was done. Later, it became a style. Today, many women are involved in this trade, and their handiworks are sold in boutiques and women's cooperatives all over Bangladesh.

10. Ava and Khanu are Gandhi's nieces.

11. Namaskar is an Indian form of greeting.

12. Institute of Postgraduate Medicine and Research was established in December 1965, before the independence of Bangladesh, by the government of Pakistan. The hospital is commonly referred to as PG. It was renamed Bangabandhu Sheikh Mujib Medical University in 1998.

13. Personal interview with André Yves Jolliet in June 2006, Geneva, Switzerland.

14. During my research in Pakistan, I corroborated this event from Brigadier Karar Ali Aga, who gave me a detailed account of the incident. The Bengalis besieged and held the Pakistanis hostage within the cantonment for a few hours, but the Pakistanis retaliated and there was a bloodbath on both sides. This story was also verified by Brigadier Shafi, who was in command of the forces in Chittagong in 1971. Brigadier Shafi took a personal interest in my work being an old boy of Aligarh Muslim University, and he was totally honest in sharing even the most painful memories of 1971 with me. I spent several days in his house, and both he and his wife, Shahnaz Shafi, were gracious hosts and honest witnesses of 1971. Shahnaz Shafi has an unusual story. She was previously married to a Bengali civil servant who was posted in Eastern Europe at the time of the war. He resigned his position during the war and became a persona non grata within the Pakistani

administration as a result of it. A few years after the liberation of Bangladesh, her husband passed away and Shahnaz returned to Pakistan. She remarried Brigadier Shafi several years later, but the two of them never discussed their personal memories of 1971. Shahnaz Shafi was writing a book of her personal memories of 1947 and 1971 when I met her in Rawalpindi, Pakistan during 2004 and 2005.

15. In 1948, the Government of Pakistan declared Urdu as the national language of Pakistan, which was immediately opposed by the Bengalis of East Pakistan. In turn, they started a language movement demanding the recognition of Bangla as a national language. In 1952, protest marches led to clashes between students and police and many were killed. In 1956, the government accepted Bangla as an official language of Pakistan. Nevertheless, Bengali resentment against the ruling group in West Pakistan continued to fester and was expressed in various demands, culminating in the Six Points demand made by Mujibur Rahman, the leader of the Awami League, in 1970. Jharna Chowdhury's mention of the riots in 1969 must be contextualized within this environment of agitation and struggle that started with the language question and developed into the liberation struggle in 1971.

16. Is this a reference to the Indian agents in Bangladesh? The mention of Ram hints that Indian and Hindu agents were helping the Bengalis against the Pakistan Army. Rahim, on the other hand, is one of the ninety-nine names of Allah and is used here to refer to the representatives of the Muslim community in the form of the Pakistan Army. From the point of historical evidence, I am curious if these men who had taken over the Medical College were the same men who are documented in the photo album available in the United Forces Library and the UN Center for Documentation and Research in New Delhi. If so, we have both oral and visual evidence to corroborate the incident in Chittagong.

17. It is not clear who killed Dhirendra Lal Chowdhury and where this incident happened. From her narrative it appears that the incident took place in the camp and not in the ashram. In a later statement, Jharna Chowdhury mentions that several people were killed in the ashram. In Jharna Chowdhury's narrative one encounters several confusing situations because she does not explain the context and details. As listeners we have to make some connections between the events that she mentions in different sections of her narratives to grasp the fear of the Hindu minorities during the war that she highlights.

18. Jharna Chowdhury does not clearly establish who had taken the people from the ashram. We have to assume from the narrative that it was the

Pakistan Army men who were the perpetrators against the Hindu community living in the ashram and the camp.

19. *Laddos* refers to a common Indian sweet.

20. Jharna does not spell out for us who Charuji is. Obviously, it is a nickname and not a given name. Most likely she was referring to Swaran Singh, who was one of the ministers in Indira Gandhi's cabinet and was actively involved in the war efforts. It is obvious from her narrative that the Indian Congress ministry actively supported Jharna Chowdhury.

5. WOMEN'S WAR

1. The number of women who took up arms and fought in battle is very few. Taramun Begum and Dr. Sitara Begum are two recognized heroes of the war. There are many more women who fought on behalf of Bangladesh but were not recognized. The women who are officially recognized as *mukti jouddhas* served mostly as first-aid workers and nurses in the different camps that were located in India.

2. Laila's testimony reminds me of Virginia Woolf's complaint in her book *Three Guineas* (1938). She writes, "Our country . . . throughout the greater part of history has treated me as a slave; it has denied me education or any share of its possessions . . . in fact, as a woman, I have no country. As a woman I want no country. As a woman my country is the whole world" (107–9).

3. *Bigha* is a traditional unit of land area in South Asia. The size of a bigha varies from one region to another. In Bengal (both in Bangladesh and in West Bengal, India), the bigha was standardized under British colonial rule at 1,600 square yards and is often interpreted as being one-third of an acre.

4. Theater Road, renamed Shakespeare Sarani, is in central Kolkata. It was developed during the British colonial period. As such it was and continues to be an active and vibrant public space. In 1971 the government-in-exile of Bangladesh was housed on this street.

5. A few pictures of college-going women from Dhaka undergoing physical exercise training are available in the Liberation War Museum. Compared to the pictures of the training of male mukti jouddhas, who are in different outfits, representing a variety of class and regional groups, and are in different settings, the pictures of women's training are too controlled; they look posed. In a recently held exhibition in Rivington Place in London during April 2008, some of these pictures were put on display to remember the 1971 War. What the eye sees can be deceptive when compared to what

women who joined the armed struggle have to say. Whose version can we believe?

6. The Naxalite movement was started by Charu Majumdar and Kanu Sanyal in West Bengal in 1967. It was a violent revolutionary movement that followed the path of Maoism. The response of the government headed by Indira Gandhi was to brutally suppress the movement with draconian countermeasures. In 1972, after Majumdar was captured and died in prison, the movement lost its impact. Thereafter, Indira Gandhi was able to make a comeback in West Bengal politics after winning the war against Pakistan on behalf of Bangladesh.

7. A long shirt worn by women over their pants or *salwar*, ethnically a Punjabi dress, but nowadays it is worn by women all over South Asia.

8. The street was named after James Prinsep who was a keen meteorological expert and scholar of Indian antiquity. He deciphered the Asokan inscriptions in Brahmi script. In Kolkata there are many public spaces named after James Prinsep, such as the Prinsep Ghat, Prinsep Park, besides a street that is named after him in central Kolkata.

9. The reference is not clear. Did she meet a cabinet minister of the Indian government or the Bangladesh government-in-exile that was formed in West Bengal, India, and functioned from there? The government-in-exile was formed in April 1971, and the incident that Mumtaz reports on could have happened during this early stage of the government.

10. There was much movement from West Bengal, India, to Bogura during the nine months of war. Many different groups used this path to enter and leave East Pakistan, now Bangladesh.

11. The Research and Analytical Wing (RAW) is India's intelligence agency. It was formed in 1968, after the 1962 Sino-India and the 1965 Indo-Pak wars. Its primary function is intelligence gathering and covert operations.

12. In Bangla the reference to *tumi* establishes a kind of familiarity or talking down to a person. When it is used in the context of a conversation between people representing different age groups, the reference to the younger person as tumi establishes primacy of the senior speaker.

13. This may be a reference to Jharna Chowdhury from the Gandhi Ashram, who was also in the border area. Since Mumtaz does not tell us clearly which ashram she is referring to, it is difficult to establish this with certainty. My meeting with Jharna Chowdhury preceded this conversation with Mumtaz.

14. It is not clear who these men were and what their role was in the war.

15. Immediately after the war ended and the Pakistan Army surrendered, there was a power vacuum in Bangladesh. Tajuddin Ahmed, the prime minister of the Bangladesh government-in-exile, returned from India on December 22, 1971, and took charge. This was before the return of Sheikh Mujibur Rahman, who was widely viewed as the father of the Bangladesh nation and the leader of the people. The early months of 1972 were a period of turmoil and uncertainty in Bangladesh and impacted future politics. In 1975, soon after the assassination of Sheikh Mujibur Rahman, Tajuddin Ahmed, too, was arrested, and he died in prison in an incident of "jail killings" along with two other members of the disbanded government.

16. As soon as civil unrest broke out in East Pakistan, the Pakistan Army arrested Sheikh Mujibur Rahman and deported him to West Pakistan where he was imprisoned throughout the period of the war. After the war, he was released and returned to Bangladesh to become the first president and later the elected prime minister of the country.

17. A Hindustani phrase meaning they suddenly found themselves on the wrong side of the political fence. It is interesting that she uses a Hindustani phrase to explain their unstable predicament after they returned to post-liberated Bangladesh.

18. The Rakhi Bahini was the private army that Sheikh Mujibur Rahman set up for his protection and to disarm the previously armed students and militia groups. This measure became extremely unpopular in Bangladesh, and Mujib immediately lost many of his erstwhile Student League supporters who formed another underground organization called the Jatiya Samajtantrik Dal.

19. *Nazar bandi* is a form of house arrest. In turn, it required the suspect to make a personal appearance everyday at the police station to verify their presence in the area.

POSTSCRIPT: LESSONS OF VIOLENCE

1. The materials that one can access on the events of 1971 in Pakistan are many. Many public and private institutions and libraries in Lahore and Islamabad, including the private library of Ahmed Salim, the Pakistan National Archives, the National Documentation Center, and the Defense University Library in Islamabad maintained by the Armed Forces, have sizeable collections of public papers, documents, journals, newspapers, transcripts of speeches, Radio Pakistan transcripts, parliamentary debates, memoirs,

and secondary books in Urdu and English. The Hamoodur Rahman Commission Report, which is, by far, the most important official document on 1971 is, however, not available for scholarly use, neither are the records at the General Head Quarters (GHQ). In addition to undertaking archival research, I benefited a great deal from discussions with the officers at the Fauji Foundation University and Defense University Library in Islamabad. In particular Brigadier Talat Saeed Khan of the Fauji Foundation University provided me invaluable support and introduction to the top level of the military administration, including veterans and serving officers in the Pakistan Army. I am indebted to him for his support of my research.

2. Many of them advised me on my research methodology, gave me long lectures on the history of the subcontinent and the military history of Muslim conquerors, and told me stories about violence to flaunt their bravado.

3. The villages that I visited in the Kushab valley and the Salt Range region are remote and generally inaccessible by car. Donkeys and mules are the main source of transport, and they are used for carrying firewood and fodder for the cattle. Most of these villages do not have electricity or running water. Women spend a lot of time fetching water, fodder, firewood, and the essentials for cooking. The men I interviewed live a retired life, which led many women to comment, "They are good for nothing except for smoking hookah and talking."

4. Except for Colonel Nadir Ali and Brigadier Aga, who requested that I use their names, all other names of the Pakistani soldiers and officers mentioned here are pseudonyms to protect their identity.

5. This interview was conducted in the General's house in Karachi on March 2, 2005. He refused to be put on tape. He told me that in all these years he has refused to talk to outsiders about his experiences in East Pakistan. Presumably, I am the first person he allowed an interview.

6. I had interviewed a wife of a "disappeared" doctor in Chittagong in 2001. Her husband was well known to Alam. When he was arrested for the first time by the Pakistani intelligence, Alam helped to secure his release. But a second arrest led to his disappearance. The wife of the doctor, however, continued to believe that Alam was not capable of brutal actions. "He was such a soft-spoken, quiet man," she told me. But having said this, she wondered, "Alam would have known what happened, he was the head of the administration those days."

7. A case in point for the Indian Army is in the northeast region of India where it operates through coercion and terror and has created a huge rift between the people and government. In Pakistan, the record of the army is

very poor in Baluchistan and Northern Waziristan, in particular. There the army rules rather than governs.

8. One soldier told me, "In the Pakistan Army whatever you feed the soldiers they will believe and follow. Nobody spoke up. We were told 'vahan pe sab hindu humko musalman banana hai. Indian ne pura Dhaka kabza kar liya, aapko ja ke bachana hai'" (there, you have to convert the Hindus to Islam and make them Muslims. The Indians have besieged Dhaka. You have to free it and provide protection).

9. Information based on a personal conversation with an officer in Lahore.

10. Similar incidents were reported by many during my conversations with some of the prominent *mukti jouddhas* in Bangladesh.

11. Sahabzada Yakub Khan resigned as Commander of the eastern wing when he failed to convince President Yahya Khan and his advisors to follow a political solution. He was recalled to Pakistan, demoted from his position, and court-martialed. Later, when the war was over and Sahibzada's advice was proven right, he was appointed as the foreign minister of Pakistan during the prime ministership of Zulfikar Ali Bhutto.

12. Curiously, at the level of ordinary people discussions on 1971 seemed more animated and candid whenever I engaged them to recount their memories. They all agreed that both military and politicians, particularly Bhutto, were at the heart of the breakup of Pakistan, and many referred to it as the "Partition of Pakistan."

13. Leigh Payne (2008) argues that perpetrators' confessions can be contentious and not genuine. Rather than leading to reconciliation, confessions of perpetrators can generate more anguish and bitterness among different groups, particularly the aggrieved.

14. Colonel Ali is writing a novel on 1971.

15. Personal interview with Malik on July 31, 2004, in Pakistan.

16. Malik's mother passed away in July 2006.

17. Personal interview with Mohammad on December 2004, in Pakistan.

18. To understand the concept of *tauba* that Mohammad and previously Malik and his mother draw our attention to, one needs to engage with the issue of personal responsibility for action and thought or *niyat*, which is a salient concept in Islam, the religious worldview that informs Pakistani society. For Muslim men to admit that their niyat was misguided and that they committed crimes in the war is an unsettling realization and has important consequences for the possibility of facing divine wrath. This acknowledgment does not happen easily for most men in a country such as Pakistan where patriarchy dominates and rarely holds men accountable for their

deeds and crimes. But the fear of divine punishment in this and the other world cannot be ignored by these Muslim men, and therefore they have to personally arrive at the moment of their crime and do tauba or appeal for forgiveness. Since the crime of violence in the war was against other human beings, perpetrators' tauba is not complete unless the victim forgives them. For Pakistani soldiers there is no returning to their victim in Bangladesh without governmental arrangement, and the lack of closure haunts and creates extreme disturbance in their present lives.

19. One of the soldiers told me that they were ordered to burn, kill, and destroy everything that came in their way to create fear and panic among the Bengalis. He reported that as they marched along they killed men, women, children, and cattle and ransacked the villages. The long march from Dhaka to Halwaghat in Mymensingh took several days, and at the end of it they had devastated the countryside. The violence was unbearable to this soldier, and he had a psychological breakdown.

20. Sheikh Hasina, the newly elected prime minister of Bangladesh, has promised to try the war criminals to seek justice on behalf of the aggrieved in Bangladesh today. Of course, this public statement made by the head of the state has caused some concern and led to the outbreak of violence. Some have suggested that the mutiny of the Bangladesh Rifles in February 25, 2009, is part of this sudden anxiety that 1971 will be unearthed and people will be made to pay for their crimes, within and outside Bangladesh.

REFERENCES

ARCHIVAL MATERIALS

Declassified files pertaining to the Cabinet, National Documentation Center, Islamabad.

Declassified files pertaining to Education, National Documentation Center, Islamabad.

Parliamentary Debates, vol. 8, nos. 6–10, Nov 22–26, 1971; vol. 11, March 17, 1972; vol. 24, March 15, 1973, Nehru Memorial and Museum Library, New Delhi.

Parliamentary Debates, 1966–1970, National Archives of Pakistan, Islamabad.

Radio Journals and Letters on 1971, Bangladesh Radio Archive, Dhaka, 2001.

Radio Pakistan Monitoring Report, National Archives of Pakistan, 1972.

Radio Pakistan News, National Archives of Pakistan, 1971–1973.

Radio Speeches of Yahya Khan, personal recordings provided by Ali Yahya, Yahya Khan's son, Rawalpindi, Pakistan, 2006.

NEWSPAPERS

Bangladesh Observer, Dhaka, Jan.–June 1972.

Bhorer Kagaj, daily newspaper, 1996, 1999.

Daily Star, daily newspaper, Dhaka, 1996, 2001.

Dainik Bangla, daily newspaper, Jan.–June 1972.

Imroz, daily newspaper, Pakistan, 1971–1972.

Jang, daily newspaper, Pakistan, 1971–1972.

Jugantor, daily newspaper, Dhaka, 1972–1975.

Pratham Alo, daily newspaper, Dhaka, 2001.

BOOKS AND ARTICLES

Abu-Lughod, Lila. 1993. *Writing Women's World: Bedouin Stories*. Berkeley: University of California Press.

Adam, Jones. 2000. "Gendercide and Genocide." *Journal of Genocide Research* 2, no. 2 (June): 185–211.

Agamben, Giorgio. 1991. *Language and Death: The Place of Negativity*. Minneapolis: University of Minnesota Press.

———. 1998. *Homo Sacer: Sovereign Power and Bare Life*. Translated by D. Heller-Roazen. Stanford: Stanford University Press.

———. 1999. *Remnants of Auschwitz: The Witness and the Archive*. Translated by D. Heller-Roazen. New York: Zone Books.

Ahmed, Asad. 2010. "The Paradoxes of the Ahmadiyya Identity: Legal Appropriation of Muslimness and the Construction of Ahmadiyya Difference." In *Beyond Crisis: Re-evaluating Pakistan*, edited by Naveeda Khan, 273–314. New Delhi: Routledge.

Ahmed, Kamruddin. 1975. *A Socio Political History of Bengal and the Birth of Bangladesh*. Dhaka: Inside Library.

Ahmed, Rafiuddin. 1988. *The Bengali Muslims: A Quest for Identity, 1871–1906*. Delhi: Oxford University Press.

Ahsan, Aitzaz. 1996. *The Indus Saga and the Making of Pakistan*. Karachi: Oxford University Press.

Akhtar, S. S. Begum, H. Hussain, S. Kamal, and M. Guha Thakurata. 2001. *Narir Ekatur O Judho Poroborti Katho Kahini* [Women's 1971 and thereafter]. Dhaka: Ain-O-Salish Kendra.

Alam, Habibul. 2006. *Brave of Heart*. Dhaka: Academic Press.

Ali, Mubarak. 2002. "History, Ideology and Curriculum." *Economic and Political Weekly* (Nov. 2–15): 4530–31.

Ali, Rao Farman. 1992. *How Pakistan Got Divided*. Lahore: Jang Publishers.

Allen, Beverly. 1996. *Rape Warfare: The Hidden Genocide in Bosnia-Herzegovina and Croatia*. Minneapolis: University of Minnesota Press.

Amin, Shahid. 1996. *Event, Metaphor, and Memory: Chauri Chaura, 1922–1992*. Delhi: Oxford University Press.

———. 2005. "Un Saint Guerer: Sur le Conquete de l'inde du Nord par les

Turcs aux XI siècle." *Annales, Histoire, Sciences Sociale* 60 (March–April): 265–92.

——. 2005. "Representing Musalman: Then and Now, Now and Then." In *Subaltern Studies*, vol. 12, *Muslims, Dalits, and the Fabrications of History*, edited by Shail Mayaram, M. S. S. Pandian, and Ajay Skaria, 1–35. Delhi: Permanent Black and Ravi Dayal Publisher.

Amy, Lori. 1999. "Contemporary Travel Narratives and Old Style Politics: American Women Reporting After the Gulf War." *Women's Studies International Forum* 22, no. 5: 525–41.

Anam, Tahmima. 2008a. *A Golden Age: A Novel*. New York: Harper.

——. 2008b. "The War that Time Forgot." *Guardian*, April 10.

Anand, Som. 1998. *Lahore: Portrait of a Lost City*. Lahore: Vanguard Books.

Ancsel, Eva. 1988. *The Silence of History*. Budapest: Akademia Kiado.

Anderson, Benedict. 1991. *Imagined Communities: Reflections on the Origins and Spread of Nationalism*. New York: Verso.

An-Na'im, Abdullahi Ahmed. 1990. *Toward an Islamic Reformation*. Syracuse: University of Syracuse Press.

——. 1991. "A Kinder, Gentler Islam." *Transition*, no. 52: 4–16.

——. 2008. *Future of Shari'a: Negotiating Islam in the Context of a Secular State*. Cambridge: Harvard University Press.

Appadurai, Arjun. 1993. "South Asia: Responses to the Ajodhya Crisis." Special issue, *Asian Survey* 33:645–737.

——. 1995. "Ethnographic States of Emergency." In *Fieldwork Under Fire: Contemporary Studies of Violence and Survival*, edited by Carolyn Nordstrom and Antonius C. Robben, 224–52. Berkeley: University of California Press.

Arendt, H. 1945. "Approaches to the 'German Problem.'" *Partisan Review*: 93–106.

Arendt, Hannah. 1953a. "Understanding and Politics." *Partisan Review* 20, no. 4: 377–92.

——. 1953b. "On the Nature of Totalitarianism: An Essay in Understanding." In *Essays in Understanding*, edited by Jerome Kohn, 328–60. New York: Harcourt Brace, 1994.

——. 1958. *The Human Condition*. Chicago: University of Chicago Press.

——. 1994. *Eichmann in Jerusalem: A Report on the Banality of Evil*. Revised and enlarged edition. New York: Penguin.

Arif, M. A. 2001. *Khaki Shadows: Pakistan 1947–1997*. Karachi: Oxford University Press.

Aziz, Qutubuddin. 1974. *Blood and Tears*. Karachi: United Press of Pakistan.

Bagchi, Jasodhara, and Subhoranjan Dasgupta. 2003. *The Trauma and the Triumph: Gender and Partition in Eastern India*. Kolkata: Stree, distributed by Popular Prakashan.

Bandyapadhyay, Sekhar. 2004. *From Plassey to Partition: A History of Modern India*. New Delhi: Orient Longman, 2006.

Bar On, Bat-Ami. 2002. *The Subject of Violence: Arendtean Exercises in Understanding*. New York: Rowman and Littlefield Publishers.

Barstow, Anne Llewellyn, ed. 2000. *War's Dirty Secret: Rape, Prostitution, and Other Crimes Against Women*. Cleveland: Pilgrim Press.

Bartky, Sandra Lee. 2002. *"Sympathy and Solidarity" and Other Essays*. Lanham: Rowman and Littlefield.

Basu, Tapan, ed. 1993. *Khakhi Shorts and Saffron Flags: A Critique of the Hindu Right*. Hyderabad: Orient Longman.

Begum, Forqan. 1998. *Swadhinata Shangram and Muktijuddya Name* [Women in the Independence Movement and the Liberation War]. Narayanganj: N. K.

Begum, Malika. 2001. *Ekatorer Nari* [Women of 1971]. Dhaka: Mukti Judha Banga Bandhu and Bangladesh Research Institute, National University.

Begum, Mumtaz. 1989. *Ila Mitra*. Dhaka: Gyan Praskahan.

Behar, Ruth. 1993. *Translated Women: Crossing the Border with Esperanza's Story*. Boston: Beacon Press.

Berenbaum, Michael. 1995. "When Memory Triumphs." *Oral History Review* 22, no. 2: 91–95.

Berger, James. 1997. "Trauma and Literary Theory." *Contemporary Literature* 38, no. 3: 569–82.

Bhalla, Alok. 1994. *Stories about the Partition of India*. 3 vols. New Delhi: Harper Collins.

Bhasin, Kamla, and Ritu Menon. 1998. *Borders and Boundaries: Women in India's Partition*. New Brunswick, N.J.: Rutgers University Press.

Bhattacharya, Deben. 1999. *The Mirrors of the Sky: Songs of the Bauls of Bengal*. Arizona: Hohm Press.

Bhuianh, S. A. 1972. *Mukti Judhar Na-mash* [The nine months of the Liberation War]. Dhaka: Ahmed Publishing House.

Bhutto, Zulfikar Ali. 1972. *Marching Towards Democracy: Nineteen Seventy to Nineteen Seventy One*. Edited by H. Jalal and K. Hasan. Karachi: Pakistan Publications.

Bigelow, Anna. 2009. "Saved by the Saint: Refusing and Reversing Partition in Muslim North India." *Journal of Asian Studies* 68, no. 2: 435–64.

Blanchot, Maurice. 1986. *The Writing of the Disaster*. Translated by Ann Smock. Lincoln: University of Nebraska.

Boose, Lynda. 2002. "Crossing the River Drina: Bosnian Rape Camps, Turkish Impalement and Serb Cultural Memory." *Signs* 28, no. 1, Gender and Cultural Memory (autumn): 71–96.

Booth, James, W. 2006. *Communities of Memory: On Witness, Identity, and Justice.* Ithaca: Cornell University Press.

Bordo, Susan. 1991. "Docile Bodies, Rebellious Bodies: Foucauldian Perspectives on Female Psychopathology." In *Writing the Politics of Difference,* edited by Hugh J. Silverman, 203–16. Albany: State University of New York Press.

Bose, Sharmila. 2005. "Anatomy of Violence: Analysis of Civil War in East Pakistan in 1971." Special Articles, *Economic and Political Weekly* (October 8): 4463–70.

———. 2007. "Losing the Victims: Problems of Using Women as Weapons in Recounting the Bangladesh War." *Economic and Political Weekly* (September 22): 3864–71.

Bourdieu, Pierre. 1980. *Le Sens pratique.* Paris: Minuit.

Braidotti, Rosi. 1994. *Nomadic Subjects: Embodiment and Sexual Difference in Contemporary Feminist Theory.* New York: Columbia University Press.

Brass, Paul. 1985. *Ethnic Groups and the State.* London: Crown Helm.

Brison, Susan. 2002. *Aftermath: Violence and the Remaking of Self.* Princeton: Princeton University Press.

Browning, Christopher. 1992. *Ordinary Men: Reserve Police Battalion 101 and the Final Solution in Poland.* New York: Harper Collins.

Brownmiller, Susan. 1975. *Against Our Will: Men, Women, and Rape.* New York: Penguin Books.

Bundy, Colin. 2000. "The Beast of the Past: History and TRC." In *After the TRC: Reflections on the Truth and Reconciliation in South Africa,* edited by James Wilmot and Linda van de Vijver, 1–13. Cape Town: David Phillips Publishers.

Burton, Antoinette, ed. 2005. *Archive Stories: Facts, Fictions, and the Writing of History.* Durham: Duke University Press.

Butalia, Urvashi, ed. 1998. *The Other Side of Silence: Voices from the Partition of India.* New Delhi: Penguin; Durham: Duke University Press.

Butler, Judith. 1993. *Bodies That Matter: On the Discursive Limits of "Sex."* New York: Routledge.

Calhill, Ann. 2001. *Rethinking Rape.* Ithaca: Cornell University Press.

Caruth, Cathy. 1996. *Unclaimed Experiences: Trauma, Narrative, and History.* Baltimore: Johns Hopkins University Press.

Chakrabarty, Dipesh. 1992a. "Postcoloniality and the Artifice of History: Who Speaks for 'Indian' Pasts?" *Representations,* no. 37 (winter): 1–26.

————. 1992b. "The Death of History." *Public Culture* 4, no. 2: 47–65.

Chand, Tara. 1954. *Influence of Islam in Indian Culture*. Allahabad: India Press.

Charlton, Thomas, Lois Myers, and Rebecca Sharpless, eds. 2007. *History of Oral History*. Lanham and New York: Alta Mira Press.

Chatterjee, Joya. 1998. "The Bengali Muslim: A Contradiction in Terms? An overview of the Debate of the Bengali Muslim Identity." In *Islam, Communities, and the Nation: Muslim Identities in South Asia and Beyond*, edited by Mushirul Hasan, 265–82. New Delhi: Manohar.

Chatterjee, Partha. 1992. "History and the Nationalization of Hinduism." *Social Research* 59, no. 1: 111–49.

————. 1993. *Nationalist Thought and the Colonial World: A Derivative Discourse*. Minnesota: University of Minnesota Press.

————. 1995. *Nation and Its Fragments*. Princeton: Princeton University Press.

————. 1997. "Claims on the Past: The Genealogy of Modern Historiography in Bengal." In *Subaltern Studies, Volume VIII, Essays in Honor of Ranajit Guha*, edited by David Arnold and David Hardiman, 1–49. New Delhi: Oxford University Press India.

————. 2002. *A Princely Imposter? A Strange and Universal History of the Kumar of Bhawal*. Princeton: Princeton University Press.

Choudhury, G. W. 1974. *The Last Days of United Pakistan*. London: C. Hurst and Company.

Chowdhury, Najma, Hamida Begum, Mahmuda Islam, and Nazmunnessa Mahtab. 1994. *Women and Politics*. Dhaka: Women for Women.

Clandinnen, Inga. 1999. *Reading the Holocaust*. Cambridge: Cambridge University Press.

Cohen, Bernard. 1987. *An Anthropologist among the Historians and Other Essays*. New York and Delhi: Oxford University Press.

Cohen, Stephen. 1984. *The Pakistan Army*. Berkeley: University of California Press.

D'Costa, Bina. 2005. "Coming to Terms with the Past in Bangladesh: Forming Feminist Alliance across Borders." In *Women, Power, and Justice: Global Feminist Perspectives, Volume I, Politics and Activism: Ensuring the Protection of Women's Fundamental Human Rights*, edited by Luciana Ricciutelli, Angela Miles, and Margaret McFadden, 227–47. London: Zed Publishers.

————. 2006. "Marginalized Identity: New Frontiers of Research for IR?" In *Feminist Methodologies for International Relations*, edited by Brooke A. Ackerly, Maria Stern, and Jacqui True, 129–52. New York: Cambridge University Press.

Cowasjee, S., and Duggal, K. S., eds. 1995. *Orphans of the Storm: Stories on the Partition of India*. New Delhi: UBS Publishers.

Dahbour, Omar, and Micheline Ishay, eds. 1999. *The Nationalism Reader*. New York: Humanity Books.

Dale, Stephen. 1990. "Trade, Conversion and the Growth of the Islamic Community in Kerala, South India." *Studia Islamica* 71:155–75.

Dallmayr, Fred. 2002. "'Asian Values' and Global Human Rights." *Philosophy East and West* 52, no. 2 (April): 173–89.

Daniel, Valentine. 1996. *Charred Lullabies*. Princeton: Princeton University Press.

Das, Veena. 1995. *Critical Events: An Anthropological Perspective on Contemporary India*. Delhi: Oxford University Press.

―――. 2000. "The Act of Witnessing: Violence, Poisonous Knowledge and Subjectivity." In *Violence and Subjectivities*, edited by Veena Das, Arthur Kleinman, Mamphela Ramphale, and Pamela Reynolds, 205–25. Berkeley: University of California Press.

―――. 2001. "Crisis and Representation: Rumor and the Circulation of Hate." In *Disturbing Remains: Memory, History, and Crisis in the Twentieth Century*, edited by M. Roth and C. Salas, 37–62. Los Angeles: The Getty Research Institute.

―――. 2003. "Forms, Life and Killable Bodies." Keynote Speech at *Women and the Contested State: Religion, Violence and Agency in South Asia*, April 11, John B. Kroc Institute, Notre Dame University.

Dasgupta, S. 1978. *Midnight Massacre in Dacca*. Delhi: Vikas Publishing House.

Datta, Pradip Kumar. 1999. *Carving Blocs: Communal Ideology in Early Twentieth Century Bengal*. New York: Oxford University Press.

Davies, Tony. 2008. *Humanism: The New Critical Idiom*. 2nd ed. London: Routledge.

Derrida, Jacques. 1994. *Specters of Marx: The State of the Debt, the Work of Modernity, and the New International*. New York: Routledge.

Dixit, Jitendra Nath. 1999. *Liberation and Beyond*. New Delhi: Konark Publishers.

Donals, Michael Bernard. 2001. "Beyond the Question of Authenticity: Witness and Testimony in the Fragments Controversy." *PMLA* 116, no. 5: 1302–15.

Eaton, Richard. 1994. *The Rise of Islam and the Bengal Frontier*. Berkeley: University of California Press.

Eisenstein, Zillah. 2004. *Against Empire*. London: ZED Press.

Enloe, Cynthia. 1990. *Bananas, Beaches, and Bases: Making Feminist Sense of International Politics*. Berkeley: University of California Press.

Faiz, Ahmed Faiz. 1978. *Sham-I shar-i-yaran* [Urdu]. Lahore: Maktabah-yi Karvan.

Felman, Shoshana. 1995. "Education and Crisis; or, the Vicissitudes of Teaching." In *Trauma*, edited by Cathy Caruth, 13–60. Baltimore: Johns Hopkins University Press.

Felman, Shoshana, and Dori Laub. 1992. *Testimony: Crises of Witnessing in Literature, Psychoanalysis, and History*. New York: Routledge.

Fentress, James, and Chris Wickham. 1992. *Social Memory*. Oxford: Blackwell.

Firdousi, Ishrat. 1996. *The Year That Was*. Dhaka: Bastu Prakashan.

Foucault, Michel. 1969. *The Archaeology of Knowledge*. Translated by A. M. Sheridan Smith. New York: Routledge.

———. 1977. *Discipline and Punish*. Harmondsworth: Penguin Books.

———. 1979. *The History of Sexuality, Vol. 1: An Introduction*. Trans. R. Hurley. London: Allen Lane.

Frederick, Sharon, and AWARE. 2001. *Rape: Weapon of Terror*. New Jersey: Global Publishing Company.

French, Stanley, Wanda Teays, and Laura Purdy. 1988. *Violence Against Women: Philosophical Perspectives*. Ithaca: Cornell University Press.

Fujitani, T., Geoffrey M. White, and Lisa Yoneyama, eds. 2001. *Perilous Memories: The Asia-Pacific War(s)*. Durham: Duke University Press.

Gaborieau, Marc. 1985. "From Al-Beruni to Jinnah: Idiom, Ritual, and Ideology of the Hindu-Muslim Confrontation in South Asia." *Anthropology Today* 1, no. 3: 7–14.

Geertz, Clifford. 1973. "Thick Description: Towards an Interpretive Theory of Culture." In *The Interpretation of Cultures: Selected Essays*, Clifford Geertz. New York: Basic Books.

Ghosh, Papiya. 1998. "Partition's Biharis." In *Islam, Communities, and the Nation: Muslim Identities in South Asia and Beyond*, edited by Mushirul Hasan, 229–64. New Delhi: Manohar.

———. 2007. *Partition and the South Asian Diaspora: Extending the Subcontinent*. New Delhi, Routledge.

Giddens, Anthony. 1987. *The Nation-State and Violence*. Berkeley: University of California Press.

Goodman, Lenn. 2003. *Islamic Humanism*. New York: Oxford University Press.

Gopal, Sarvepalli. 1993. *The Anatomy of a Confrontation: The Babri Masjid—Ramjanmabhumi Issue*. 2nd ed. London: ZED Books.

Government of Pakistan. 2001. *The Report of the Hamoodur Rehman Commission of Inquiry into the 1971 War*. Lahore, Karachi, Islamabad: Vanguard.

Grossman, Dave. 1995. *On Killing: The Psychological Cost of Learning to Kill in War and Society*. Boston: Little and Brown.

Guha, Ramachandra. 1995. "Subaltern and Bhadrolok Studies." Review of *Subaltern Studies, Vol. VIII, Essays in Honor of Ranajit Guha*, edited by David Arnold and David Hardiman. *Economic and Political Weekly* (August 19): 2056–58.

Guhathakurta, Meghna. 1996. "Violence and Victimization: Responses of the Women's Movement." Paper presented at the International Conference on Bangladesh 1971, London.

Hansen, Thomas Blom. 1999. *The Saffron Wave: Democracy and Hindu Nationalism in Modern India*. Princeton: Princeton University Press.

————. 2001. *Wages of Violence: Naming and Identity in Postcolonial Bombay*. Princeton: Princeton University Press.

Haqqani, Husain. 2005. *Pakistan: Between Mosque and Military*. Washington: Carnegie Endowment for International Peace.

Harff, Barbara. 2003. "No Lessons Learned from the Holocaust: Assessing the Risk of Genocide and Political Mass Murder since 1955." *American Political Science Review* 97, no. 1 (February): 57–73.

Hasan, Moidul. 1986. *Muldhara* [Bengali]. Dhaka: University Press Limited.

Hasan, Mushirul, ed. 1995. *India Partitioned: The Other Face of Freedom*. 2 vols. New Delhi: Roli Books.

————. 1998. *Islam Communities and the Nation: Muslim Identities in South Asia and Beyond*. Delhi: Manohar.

Headley, John. 2008. *The Europeanization of the World: On the Origins of Human Rights and Democracy*. Princeton: Princeton University Press.

Hein, Laura. 1999. "Savage Irony: The Imaginative Power of the 'Military Comfort Women' in the 1990s." *Gender and History* 11, no. 2: 336–72.

Held, Virginia. 1993. *Feminist Morality: Transforming Culture, Society, and Politics*. Chicago: University of Chicago Press.

Herzfeld, Jean. 2005. *Machete Season: The Killers of Rwanda Speak*. New York: Farrar, Straus and Giroux.

Hesford, Wendy. 1999. "Reading Rape Stories: Material Rhetoric and the Trauma of Representations." *College English* 62, no. 2 (Nov.): 192–221.

Hester, Marianne, Liz Kelly, and Jill Radford, eds. 1996. *Women, Violence, and Male Power*. Buckingham: Open University Press.

Hodgson, Marshall. 1974. *The Venture of Islam*. Chicago: University of Chicago Press.

Horowitz, Sara. 1992. "Rethinking Holocaust Testimony: The Making and Unmaking of the Witness." *Cardozo Studies in Law and Literature* 4, no. 1 (spring–summer): 45–62.

Humphreys, Stephen, trans. 1990. *The History of Al-Tabari, Vol. XV, The Crisis of the Early Caliphate*. Albany: State University of New York Press.

Hunt, Swanee. 2004. *This Was Not Our War: Bosnian Women Reclaiming the Peace*. Durham: Duke University Press.

Hussain, Abu Mohammad Delwar. 2007. *Muktijudder Ancholik Itihas* [Bengali]. 3 vols. Dhaka: Sahitya Press.

Hussain, Hamid. 2007. *Sufism and Bhakti: Eternal Relevance*, New Delhi: Manak Publications.

Hussain, Intizār. 1973. *Shahr-e-afsos* [The city of sorrow] [Urdu]. Lahore: Maktaba-e-Kārvān.

———. 1973. *Voh jo khoe-gae* [Those who got lost] [Urdu]. Lahore: Maktaba-e-Kārvān.

Ibrahim, Nilima. 1998. *Ami Birangona Bolchi* [Birangonas speak] [Bengali]. Dhaka: Jagrati Prakashan.

Imam, Jahanara. 1986. *Ekatturer Dinguli* [The days and nights of 1971] [Bengali]. Dhaka: Sandhani Publishers.

———. 1991. *Of Blood and Fire: The Untold Story of Bangladesh's War of Independence*. 2nd ed. Translated by Mustafizur Rahman. Dhaka: Academic Publishers.

Iqbal, Muhammad. 1986. *The Reconstruction of Religious Thought in Islam*. Edited and annotated by M. Saeed Sheikh. Lahore: Institute of Islamic Culture.

Iqbal, Muhammad Jafar. 1991. *Bish Bachhor Par* [Twenty years later] [Bengali]. Published by Dr. Nurun Nabi and Sajjad Choudhury.

Islam, Rafiqul. 1981. *A Tale of Millions: The War of Liberation, 1971*. Dhaka: Ananya.

———. 1991. *Narhatya O Nari Nirjantanar Kansa 1971* [The tales of the murder and atrocities against women, 1971] [Bengali]. Dhaka: Ananya.

Jacob, Jack Fredrick Ralph. 1997. *Surrender at Dacca: Birth of a Nation*. New Delhi: Manohar Publishers.

Jacobs, Susie, Ruth Jacobson, and Jen Marchbank, eds. 2000. *States of Conflict: Gender, Violence, and Resistance*. London: ZED Books.

Jahan, Rounaq. 1972. *Pakistan: The Failure of National Integration*. New York: Columbia University Press.

———. 1975. "Women in Bangladesh." In *Women Cross Culturally: Change and Challenge*, edited by Ruby Rohrlich-Leavitt, 5–30. The Hague: Mouton Publishers.

———. 2004. *Genocide in Bangladesh*. New York: Routledge.

Jalal, Ayesha. 1995. "Conjuring Pakistan: History as Official Imagining." *International Journal of Middle East Studies* 8, no. 4: 73–89.

Jeffrelot, Christophe. 1995. *The Hindu Nationalist Movement, 1925–1992: Social and Political Strategies*. New Delhi: Penguin.

Joansen, Robert C. 1997. "Radical Islam and Nonviolence: A Case Study of Religious Empowerment and Constraint among Pakhtuns." *Journal of Peace Research* 34, no. 1: 53–71.

Jones, Adam. 2000 "Gendercide and Genocide." *Journal of Genocide Research* 2, no. 2: 185–211.

Joyce, James. 1922. *Ulysses*. Oxford: Oxford University Press.

Kabir, Shahriar. 1999. *Tormenting Seventy One: An Account of the Pakistani Army Atrocities*. Dhaka: Liberation War Museum.

Kakar, Sudhir. 1994. "Some Unconscious Aspects of Ethnic Violence in India." In *Mirrors of Violence: Communities, Riots, and Survivors*, edited by Veena Das, 135–45. Delhi: Oxford University Press.

Kamra, Sukeshi. 2002. *Bearing Witness: Partition, Independence, and the End of the Raj*. Canada: University of Calgary Press.

Kaul, Suvir, ed. 2002. *The Partitions of Memory: The After Life of the Division of India*. Bloomington: Indiana University Press.

Kay, Judith W. 1994. "Politics without Human Nature? Reconstructing a Common Humanity." *Hypatia* 9, no. 1 (winter): 21–52.

Khan, F. A. 1998. *Spring 1971: A Center Stage Account of Bangladesh War of Liberation*. Dhaka: The University Press Limited.

Khan, Mirza Asadullah. 2000. *Divan-i-Ghalib: nuskhah- yi Khyajah ta'aruf, tauzihat aur izafat Sayyid Muinurrhman* [Urdu]. Lahore: al-Vaqir Pablikeshanz.

Kleinman, Arthur. 1997. "Everything That Really Matters: Social Suffering, Subjectivity, and the Remaking of Human Experience in a Disordering World." *Harvard Theological Review* 90, no. 3: 315–35.

Kleinman, Arthur, Veena Das, and Margaret Lock, eds. 1997. *Social Suffering*. Berkeley: University of California Press.

Kumar, Sukrita Paul. 2004. *Narrating Partition: Texts, Interpretations, Ideas*. New Delhi: Indialog Publications Pvt. Ltd.

Kumar, Sunil. 2001. "Qutb and Modern Memory." In *Partitions of Memory: The Afterlife in the Division of India*, edited by Suvir Kaul, 140–82. New Delhi: Permanent Black.

LaCapra, Dominick. 1994. *Representing the Holocaust: History, Theory, Trauma*. Ithaca: Cornell University Press.

————. 1999. "Trauma, Absence, Loss." *Critical Inquiry* 25, no. 4: 696–727.

Lahiri, Anjali. 1999. *Smriti O Katha* [Memories speak] [Bengali]. Dhaka: Ain-o-Salish Kendra.

Langer, Lawrence. 1991. *Holocaust Testimonies: The Ruins of Memory.* New Haven: Yale University Press.

Latina Feminist Group. 2001. *Telling to Live: Latina Feminist Testimonies.* Durham: Duke University Press.

Le Goff, Jacques. 1992. *History and Memory.* Translated by Steven Rendall and Elizabeth Claman. New York: Columbia University Press.

Levi, Primo. 1961. *Survival in Auschwitz: The Nazi Assault on Humanity.* Translated by Stuart Woolf. New York: Collier.

————. 1986. *The Drowned and the Saved.* Translated by Raymond Rosenthal. New York: Summit Books.

Levinas, Emmanuel. 1972. *Humanism of the Other.* Translated by Nidra Poller. Urbana: University of Illinois Press.

————. 1981. *Otherwise than Being; or, Beyond Essence.* Translated by Alphonso Lingis. The Hague: Martinus Nihhoff Publishers.

————. 1986. *Collected Philosophical Papers of Emmanuel Levinas.* Translated by Alphonso Lingis. The Hague: Martinus Nihhoff Publishers.

Liberation War Museum. 1987. *Genocide '71: An Account of the Killers and Collaborators.* Dhaka: Liberation War Museum.

————. 1994. *Documents on Crimes against Humanity Committed by the Pakistan Army and Their Agents in Bangladesh during 1971.* Dhaka: Liberation War Museum.

Lifschultz, Lawrence. 1979. *Bangladesh: The Unfinished Revolution.* London: ZED Books.

Lifton, Robert Jay. 1979. *The Broken Connection: On Death and the Continuity of Life.* New York: Simon and Schuster.

Loshak, David. 1971. *Pakistan Crisis.* New York: William Heinemann.

Ludden, David. 2005. *Making India Hindu: Religion, Community, and the Politics of Democracy in India.* New Delhi: Oxford University Press.

Majnu, Shekhawat Hussain. 1994. *Ekatorer Mukti Judhe Shahar Chattagrame Nirjatan Kendra O Badyabhumi* [The sites of atrocities and killing fields in the city of Chittagong, 1971] [Bengali]. Chittagong: Bangladeshar Mukti Sangram O Mukti Judho Gabashana Kendra.

Malik, Amita. 1972. *The Year of the Vulture.* New Delhi: Orient Longman Limited.

Mamdani, Mahmood. 2001. *When Victims Become Killers: Colonialism, Nativism and Genocide in Rwanda.* Princeton: Princeton University Press.

————. 2002. "Amnesty or Impunity? A Preliminary Critique of the Report of the Truth and Reconciliation Commission of South Africa (TRC)." *Diacritics* 32, nos. 3–4: 33–59.

Mamoon, Muntasir. 2000. *The Vanquished Generals and the Liberation War of Bangladesh*. Translated by Kushal Ibrahim. Dhaka: Somoy Prokashon.

Manto, Sadaat Hasan. 1987. *Kingdom's End and Other Stories*. London: Verso.

————. 1999. *Thanda Gosht* [Cold meat] [Urdu]. Dili: Saqi Buk Dipo.

Marcus, George. 1998. *Ethnography through Thick and Thin*. Princeton: Princeton University Press.

Mascarenhas, Anthony. 1972. *The Rape of Bangladesh*. New Delhi: Vikas Publications.

Matinuddin, Kamal. 1993. *Tragedy of Errors: East Pakistan Crisis, 1968–1971*. Lahore: Services Book Club.

Mayaram, Shail. 2003. *Against History, Against State: Counterperspectives from the Margin*. New York: Columbia University Press.

McEwan, Cheryl. 2003. "Building a Postcolonial Archive: Gender, Collective Memory and Citizenship in Post-Apartheid South Africa." *Journal of Southern African Studies* 29, no. 3: 739–57.

Memon, Muhamad Umar. 1983. "Pakistani Urdu Creative Writing on National Disintegration: The Case of Bangladesh." *Journal of Asian Studies* 43, no. 1 (Nov.): 105–27.

————. 1998. *An Epic Unwritten: The Penguin Book of Partition Stories*. New Delhi: Penguin.

Menon, Ritu, and Kamla Bhasin. 1998. *Borders and Boundaries: Women in India's Partition*. New Brunswick: Rutgers University Press.

Mojaddedi, Jawid, trans. 2004. *The Masnavi: Book One*. New York: Oxford University Press.

Mookherjee, Nayanika. 2003. "Gendered Embodiments: Mapping the Body Politic of the Raped Woman and the Nation in Bangladesh." In *South Asian Women in the Diaspora*, edited by Nirmal Puwar and Parvati Raghuram, 157–77. New York: Berg.

————. 2004. "'My Man (Honour) Is Lost but I Still Have My Iman (Principle)': Sexual Violence and Articulations of Masculinity." In *South Asian Masculinities*, edited by R. Chopra, C. Osella, and F. Osella, 131–59. New Delhi: Kali for Women.

————. 2006. "'Remembering to Forget': Public Secrecy and Memory of Sexual Violence in the Bangladesh War of 1971." *Journal of the Royal Anthropological Institute*, n.s., 12: 433–50.

Moore, J. P. 2006. *Muslim Identity, Print Culture and the Dravidian Factor*. Delhi: Oxford University Press.

Moosa, Ebrahim. 2000. "The Dilemma of Islamic Rights Scheme." *Journal of Law and Religion* 15, nos. 1 and 2: 185–215.

Mufti, Masood. 1995. *Lemhe* [Urdu]. Islamabad: Dost Publications.

————. 1996a. *Chehre* [Urdu]. Islamabad: Dost Publication.

————. 1996b. *Raize* [Urdu]. Islamabad: Dost Publication.

Mumtaz, Soofia, Jean-Luc Racine, and Imran Anwar Ali. 2002. *Pakistan: The Contours of State and Society*. Karachi: Oxford University Press.

Nandy, Ashis. 1983. *The Intimate Enemy: Loss and Recovery of Self under Colonialism*. New York: Oxford University Press.

————. 1995. "History's Forgotten Doubles." In "World Historians and their Critics." Special issue, *History and Theory* 34, no. 2 (May): 44–56.

————. 2002. "Telling the Story of Communal Conflicts in South Asia: Interim Report on a Personal Search for Defying Myths." *Ethnic and Racial Studies* 25, no. 1: 1–19.

————. 2006. "Democratic Culture and Images of the State: India's Unending Ambivalence." In *The State in India: Past and Present*, edited by Masaaki Kimura and Akiro Tanabe, 282–301. New Delhi: Oxford University Press.

————. 2008. "Gujarat: Blame the Middle Class." *Times of India*, January 14.

Nandy, Ashis, Shikha Trivedy, Shail Mayaram, and A. Yagnik. 1995. *Creating a Nationality: The Ramjanmabhumi and Fear of the Self*. Delhi: Oxford University Press.

Needham, Anuradha, and Rajeshwari Sundar Raajan, eds. 2006. *The Crisis of Secularism in India*. Durham: Duke University Press.

Newbury, David. 1998. "Understanding Genocide." *African Studies Review* 41 (April): 73–97.

Niazi, A. A. K. 1998. *The Betrayal of East Pakistan*. New Delhi: Manohar Publishers.

Nizami, Khaliq Ahmed. 2004. *Sheikh Nizamuddin Auliya*. New Delhi: National Book Trust.

Nora, Pierre. 1989. "Between Memory and History." Translated by Marc Roudebush. *Representations* 26:7–25.

Nussbaum, Martha. 2007. *The Clash Within: Democracy, Religious Violence, and India's Future*. Cambridge: Harvard University Press.

Ofer, Dalia, and Lenore Weitzman, eds. 1998. *Women in the Holocaust*. New Haven: Yale University Press.

Oh, Irene. 2007. *The Rights of God: Islam, Human Rights, and Comparative Ethics*. Washington: Georgetown University Press.

Palit, D. K. 1972. *The Lightning Campaign: The Indo Pak War of 1971*. New Delhi: Compton Press Ltd.

Pandey, Gyanendra. 1990. *The Construction of Communalism is Colonial North India*. New Delhi: Oxford University Press.

———. 1992. "In Defence of the Fragment: Writing About Hindu-Muslim Riots in India Today." *Representations* 37 (Winter): 27–55.

———. 1994. "The Prose of Otherness." In *Subaltern Studies, Vol. VIII, Essays in Honour of Ranajit Guha*, edited by David Arnold and David Hardiman, 188–221. Delhi: Oxford University Press.

———. 2001. *Remembering Partition: Violence, Nationalism, and History in India*. Cambridge: Cambridge University Press.

———. 2006. *Routine Violence: Nations, Fragments, Histories*. Stanford: Stanford University Press.

Pandey, Gyanendra, and Yunas Samad. 2007. *Fault Lines of Nationhood*. New Delhi: Roli Books.

Panikar, K. N. 1995. *Culture, Ideology, and Hegemony: Intellectuals and Social Consciousness in Colonial India*. New Delhi: Tulika.

Patai, Daphne, and Sherna Gluck. 1991. *Women's Words*. New York and London: Routledge.

Payne, Leigh A. 2008. *Unsettling Accounts: Neither Truth nor Reconciliation in Confession of State Violence*. Durham: Duke University Press.

Perks, R., and Alistair Thomson. 1998. *The Oral History Reader*. New York: Routledge.

Phillips, Anne. 1991. "Citizenship and Feminist Politics." In *Citizenship*, edited by Goeff Andrews, 76–88. London: Lawrence and Wishart.

Prasad, S. N., ed. 1992. *History of Indo-Pak War, 1971*. 5 vols. Unpublished material. New Delhi: Ministry of Defence, Govt. of India.

Qureshi, H. A. 2003. *The 1971 Indo-Pak War: A Soldiers Narrative*. Lahore: Oxford University Press.

Rahman, Hasan Hafizur, ed. 1982–1985. *Bangladesera svadhinata yuddha: Dalilapatra* [History of the Bangladesh war of independence: documents]. 15 vols. Dhaka: Ministry of Information, Government of the People's Republic of Bangladesh.

Redlich, Simon. 2002. *Together and Apart in Brzenzany: Poles, Jews, and Ukrainians, 1919–1945*. Bloomington: Indiana University Press.

Reilly, N., ed. 1996. *Without Reservation: The Beijing Tribunal on Accountability for Women's Human Rights*. New Brunswick: Rutgers University Press.

Richards, John F. 1994. "Islamic Frontier in the East: Expansionism into South Asia." *South Asia* 4:91–109

Rizvi, Hasan-Askari. 2000. *Military, State, and Society in Pakistan*. London: Palgrave Macmillan.

Robinson, Francis. 2000. *Islam and Muslim History in South Asia*. New Delhi: Oxford University Press.

Rosen, Hannah. 1999. "'Not That Sort of Women': Race, Gender, and Sexual Violence During the Memphis Riot of 1866." In *Sex, Love, Race: Crossing Boundaries in North American History*, edited by Martha Hodes, 267–94. New York: New York University Press.

Safdar, Mahmood. 1993. *Pakistan Divided: Study of the Factors and Forces Leading to the Break Up of Pakistan in 1971*. N. K.: Kazi Pubn.

Sahni, Bhisham. 1988. *Tamas* [English trans.]. New Delhi: Penguin.

Said, Edward. 1979. *Orientalism*. New York: Vintage.

Saikia, Yasmin. 2004a. "Beyond the Archive of Silence: Narratives of Violence of the 1971 Liberation War of Bangladesh." *History Workshop Journal* 58:275–87.

———. 2004b. *Fragmented Memories: Struggling to be Tai-Ahom in India*. Durham: Duke University Press and New Delhi: Permanent Black.

———. 2006. "Overcoming the Silent Archive in Bangladesh: Women Bearing Witness to Violence in the 1971 'Liberation War.'" In *Women and the Contested State: Religion, Violence, and Agency in South and Southeast Asia*, edited by Monique Skidmore and Patricia Lawrence, 64–82. Notre Dame: University of Notre Dame Press.

Salomon, Carol. 1991. "The Cosmic Riddles of Lalan Fakir." In *Gender, Genre, and Power in South Asian Expressive Traditions*, edited by Arjun Appadurai, Frank J. Korom, and Margaret A. Mills, 267–304. Philadelphia: University of Pennsylvania Press.

Samadar, Ranabir. 1997. "On Problems of Writing a Comprehensive History of the Bangladesh Liberation War." Azad Institute Paper 6. Maulana Abul Kalam Azad Institute of Asian Studies, Calcutta.

———. 2001. "Friends, Foes, and Understanding." *Economic and Political Weekly* (March 10–16): 861–70.

Sander, Helke, and Stuart Liebman. 1995. "Remembering/Forgetting." In "Berlin in 1945: War and Rape, 'Liberators Take Liberties.'" Special issue, *October* 72:15–26.

Santner, Eric L. 1992. "History Beyond the Pleasure Principle: Some Thoughts on the Representation of Trauma." In *Probing the Limits of Representation: Nazism and the "Final Solution,"* edited by Saul Friedlander, 142–54. Cambridge: Harvard University Press.

Sarkar, Sumit. 2002. *Beyond Nationalist Frames: Relocating Postmodernism, Hindutva, and History*. New Delhi: Permanent Black.

Sarkar, Tanika. 2001. *Hindu Wife, Hindu Nation: Community, Religion, and Cultural Nationalism*. London: Hurst.

Savarkar, Domadar. 1969. *Hindutva: What Is Hindu?* Bombay: Veer Savarkar Publication.

Scarry, Elaine. 1985. *The Body in Pain: The Making and Unmaking of the World*. New York: Oxford University Press.

Schendel, Willem Van. 2001. "Modern Times in Bangladesh." In *Time Matters: Global and Local Time in Asian Societies*, 35–55. Amsterdam: VU University Press.

———. 2009. *A History of Bangladesh*, Cambridge: Cambridge University Press.

Scott, J. 1988. *Gender and the Politics of History*. New York: Columbia University Press.

Sereny, Gita. 1983. *Into That Darkness: An Examination of Conscience*. New York: Vintage Books.

Shafiullah, K. M. 1995. *Bangladesh at War*. 2nd ed. Dhaka: Academic Publishers.

Sharlach, Lisa. 2000. "Rape as Genocide: Bangladesh, the Former Yugoslavia, and Rwanda." *New Political Science* 22, no. 1: 89–102.

Siddiq, Salik. 1977. *Witness to Surrender*. Karachi: Oxford University Press.

Siddiqui, Kader. 1985. *Shaadhinata '71* [Freedom, 1971]. 2 vols. Calcutta: Dey's Publishing.

Siddiqui, Kalim. 1972. *Conflict, Crisis, and War in Pakistan*. New York: Praeger.

Singer, Wendy. 1997. *Creating Histories: Oral Narrative and the Politics of History Making in 1930s India*. Delhi: Oxford University Press.

Singh, Jaswant. 2009. *Jinnah: India, Partition, Independence*. New Delhi, Rupa and Company.

Singh, Khushwant. 1956. *Train to Pakistan*. London: Chatto and Windus.

Singh, Lakshmann Lehl. 1979. *Indian Sword Strikes in East Pakistan*. New Delhi: Vikas.

———. 1981. *Victory in Bangladesh*. Dehra Dun: Natraj Publishers.

Singh, Sukhwant. 1980. *India's Wars Since Independence: The Liberation of Bangladesh*. Vol. 1. New Delhi: Vikas.

Sisson, R., and L. E. Rose. 1990. *War and Secession: Pakistan, India, and the Creation of Bangladesh*. Berkeley: University of California Press.

Skaria, Ajay. 1999. *Hybrid Histories: Forests, Frontiers, and Wildness in Western India*. Delhi: Oxford University Press.

Smith, Anthony. 1986. *The Ethnic Origin of Nations*. Oxford: Basil Blackwell.

Spivak, Gayatri. 1988. "Can the Subaltern Speak?" In *Marxism and the Interpretation of Culture*, edited by Cary Nelson and Lawrence Grossberg, 271–313. Urbana: University of Illinois Press.

Staub, Ervin. 2000. "Genocide and Mass Killings: Origins, Prevention, Healing and Reconciliation." *Political Psychology* 21, no. 2: 367–82.

Stiglmayer, Alexandra, ed. 1994. *Mass Rape: The War against Women in Bosnia-Herzegovina*. Lincoln: University of Nebraska Press.

Stone, Dan, ed. 2008. *The Historiography of Genocide*. New York: Palgrave Macmillan.

Straus, Scott. 2005. "Darfur and the Genocide Debate." *Foreign Affairs* 84, no. 1 (Jan.–Feb.): 123–33.

Syed, A. H. 1992. *The Discourse and Politics of Zulfiikar Ali Bhutto*. New York: St. Martin's Press.

Tal, Kali. 1996. *Worlds of Hurt: Reading the Literature of Trauma*. Cambridge: Cambridge University Press.

Talbot, Cynthia. 1995. "Inscribing Self, Inscribing Others: Hindu-Muslim Identities in Precolonial India." *Comparative Studies in Society and History* 37, no. 4: 692–722.

Talukder, Muniruzzam. 1980. *The Bangladesh Revolution and Aftermath*. Dhaka: Bangladesh Book International.

Tambiah, Stanley. 1989. "Ethnic Conflict in the World Today." *American Ethnologist* 16, no. 2: 335–49.

———. 1990. "Reflections on Communal Violence in South Asia." Presidential Address. *Journal of Asian Studies* 49, no. 4 (November): 741–60.

Tan, Tai Yong, and Gyanesh Kudaisya. 2000. *The Aftermath of Partition in South Asia*. London: Routledge.

Tarlo, Emma. 2003. *Unsettling Memories: Narratives of the Emergency in Delhi*. London: Hurst.

Taylor, Diane. 1997. *Disappearing Acts: Spectacles of Gender and Nationalism in Argentina's Dirty War*. Durham: Duke University Press.

Thapar, Romila. 1992. *Interpreting Early India*. New York: Oxford University Press.

———. 2002. *Somnatha: The Many Voices of a History*. New Delhi: Penguin, Viking.

———. 2004. *Early India: From the Origins to AD 1300*. Berkeley: University of California Press.

Thomson, Alistair. 1998. "Fifty Years: An International Perspective on Oral History." *American Historical Review* 85, no. 2 (Sept.): 581–95.

Tilak, Bal Gangadhar. 1956. *The Artic Home in the Vedas: Being also a New Key to the Interpretation of Many Vedic Texts and Legends.* Poona: Tilak Bros.

Totten, Samuel, and Stephen Jacobs. 2002. *Pioneers of Genocide Study: Confronting Mass Death in a Century of Genocide.* Wesport: Greenwood Press.

Trouillot, Michel-Ralph. 1995. *Silencing the Past: Power and the Production of History.* New York: Beacon Press.

van der Veer, Peter. 1992. "Playing or Praying: A Sufi Saint's Day in Surat." *Journal of Asian Studies* 51:545–64.

————. 1994. *Religious Nationalism: Hindus and Muslims in India.* Berkeley: University of California Press.

————. 2001. *Imperial Encounters: Religion and Modernity in India and Britain.* Princeton: Princeton University Press.

Vickers, J. 1993. *Women and War.* London: ZED Books.

Waller, Margaret, and Jennifer Rycenga, eds. 2000. *Frontline Feminisms: Women, War, and Resistance.* New York: Garland Publishing.

West, L., ed. 1997. *Feminist Nationalism.* New York: Routledge.

White, Hayden. 1987. *The Content of the Form: Narrative Discourse and Historical Representation.* Baltimore: Johns Hopkins Press.

Wiesenthal, Simon. 1998. *Sunflower: On the Possibilities and Limits of Forgiveness.* New York: Schocken Books.

Wilson, Richard A. 2001. *The Politics of Truth and Reconciliation in South Africa: Legitimising the Post-Apartheid State.* Cambridge: Cambridge University Press.

Wink, Andre. 1990. *Al-Hind: The Making of Indo-Islamic World.* Vol. 1. New Delhi: Oxford University Press.

Withaker, B., Ian Guest, and Rt. Hon. David Ennals. 1975. *The Biharis in Bangladesh: Minority Rights Group.* London: Amnesty International Report no. 11.

Wolf, Richard. 2006. "The Poetics of 'Sufi' Practice: Drumming, Dancing, and Complex Agency at Madho Lal Husain (and Beyond)." *American Ethnologist* 33, no. 2: 246–68.

Wolpert, Stanley. 1993. *Zulfi Bhutto of Pakistan: His Life and Times.* New York: Oxford University Press.

Woolf, Virginia. 1938. *Three Guineas.* New York: Harbinger Books.

Yaeger, Patricia. 1997. "Consuming Trauma; or, The Pleasure of Merely Circulating." *Journal X* 1, no. 2: 226–51.

Zaheer, Hasan. 1997. *The Separation of East Pakistan: The Rise and Realization of Bengali Nationalism.* Karachi: Oxford University Press.

Zamindar, Vazira. 2007. *The Long Partition and the Making of Modern South Asia: Refugees, Histories, and Boundaries.* Columbia: Columbia University Press.

INDEX

abortion program, 52, 59, 78, 83, 143–
44, 168–75, 200, 258 n. 38, 260 n. 46,
268 n. 9

abortions, performing: sense of duty
for, 169–70, 174

accountability: cultural issues with,
277 n. 18; distortion of, 27, 62, 262
n. 59, 266 n. 80; establishing, 14,
54, 226

adoption program for war babies,
58–59, 260 nn. 46–47

agents of change: denying women as,
59; humanism as, 22; reshaping of
partition history as, 18; social service as, 164; understanding of the
Other as, 264 n. 68; women's memories as, 10, 189

Ahmed, Laila: context and research
for, 186–90; story, 190–202

Ahmed, Tajuddin, 204, 209, 275 n. 15

Al-Badr, 3, 40, 46, 51

Al-Shams, 3, 40, 46

American Institute of Bangladesh
Studies (AIBS), 73–74

ashrams, 20, 177–80, 183, 272 nn. 17–18

Assam, India, 24, 159, 245 n. 14, 247
n. 27, 250 n. 42; All Assam Students
Union (AASU) in, 67, 254 n. 20; Bangladeshi refugees in, 42–44, 67–69,
262 nn. 58–59; identity movement
of, 67, 254 n. 20

Awami League (AL), 38–39, 74–75, 160,
204–5, 210, 267 n. 1, 272 n. 15

Bangladesh, 264 n. 67; attitude toward sexual violence in, 53–59, 77–
80, 122, 125, 264 n. 69; construction
of history of, 72, 79; formation of,
3, 15, 44; historical perspectives on,
3, 31, 55, 79; independence movement in, 204–6, 210, 261 n. 53, 272
n. 15; perspective of 1971 war in, 3,
46, 60–62, 72–73, 97; post-1971 in,
163, 204, 253 n. 17, 260 n. 45, 275
nn. 15–16, 278 n. 20 (*see also* abortion
program; discrimination against
women: after liberation); ruling
elite in, 72–73; war criminals and,

Bangladesh (*cont.*)
  50–51, 55, 60, 100, 237, 264 n. 65,
  267 n. 3, 278 n. 20; women's role
  in creation of, 15, 244 n. 9 (*see also*
  Ahmed, Laila; Begum, Mumtaz).
  See also Bangladesh National Party;
  East Pakistan
Bangladeshi refugees in Assam, 42–44,
  67–69, 262 nn. 58–59
Bangladesh National Party (BNP), 32,
  75, 267 n. 1
Beauty (the person): context and research for, 109–13; story, 119–22
Begum, Mumtaz: context and research for, 202–4; story, 204–12
Begum, Nur: context and research
  for, 109–13; story, 114–19
Begum, Nurjahan, and group of Bihari women: context and research
  for, 146–53; story, 153–57
Begum, Sitara, 85, 243 n. 2 (preface),
  273 n. 1
Begum, Taramun (Taramun Bibi), 85,
  243 n. 2 (preface), 273 n. 1
behavior, excuse for inhumane,
  during war: duty as, 47–49, 218–20,
  230–33; fear of India as, 257 n. 31,
  277 n. 8; nationalism as, 10–14, 22,
  92, 98–104, 149, 203, 224–25, 234–35;
  the vulnerable as symbols of enemy
  as, 167–68, 205, 215, 258 n. 36
Bengalis, nationalist, 19, 30–31, 44, 49,
  225, 233; antagonism with Biharis
  by, 3, 46, 151, 168–69, 216–18, 238;
  attitude toward sexual violence
  from, 258 n. 39, 264 n. 69; overcoming antagonism with Biharis by,
  86–87; perspective of 1971 war of,
  61–62, 72, 146–47; role of in East-

West Pakistan tensions, 4, 35;
  secular ethnicity of, 76; violence
  committed by, 41, 50, 86, 96, 103,
  151, 155, 238, 253 nn. 14–15, 255 n. 25,
  256 n. 29, 270 n. 7; violence from
  others and, 40–42, 48, 151, 168
Bhakti, 9, 20, 24
Bharatiya Janata Party (BJP), 18, 30–
  32, 248 n. 32
Bhutto, Zulfikar Ali, 38–39, 63, 251
  nn. 6–7, 277 n. 12
Bibi, Taramun (Taramun Begum), 85,
  243 n. 2 (preface), 273 n. 1
Bihari colony camp, Khulna, Bangladesh, 151–54
Biharis, 243 n. 1, 251 n. 4, 252 n.12, 263
  nn. 61–62; antagonism between
  Bengalis and, 3, 46, 151, 168–69, 216–
  18, 238; immigration to Pakistan of,
  149 (*see also* Hindu: immigration to
  India from East Pakistan); overcoming antagonism between Bengalis and, 86–87; refugee camps and,
  42, 46, 49–50, 70–73, 97, 147–51, 253
  nn. 16–17; research difficulties with,
  147–53; stateless refugees and, 3,
  40–42; violence from Bengalis and,
  40–41, 50, 86, 96, 103, 151, 155, 238,
  253 nn. 14–15, 255 n. 25, 256 n. 29,
  270 n. 7; violence to Bengalis and,
  40–42, 48, 151, 168 (*see also* rajakars);
  women, 61, 146–57, 253 n. 16, 260
  n. 48
Bihari women's stories: Nurjahan
  Begum and group of Bihari women,
  153–57
birangonas, 55–59, 82, 93–94, 99, 168,
  259 n. 44; Nur Begum, 109–19;
  Taslima's mother, 136–46

British colonialism. *See* colonialism in South Asia, British

Camp Geneva, 41, 70, 147–48

Chittagong, Bangladesh, 87, 94–95, 168–69; Jharna Chowdhury and, 176–84; Syed Ahmed Nurjahan and, 167–76

Chowdhury, Jharna: context and research for, 176–78; story, 178–84

civil war between East and West Pakistan, 3, 39–42, 46, 64, 223–25

collective memory. *See* memory, collective

colonialism, West Pakistan's, 3, 31, 243 n. 2 (chapter 1)

colonialism in South Asia, British, 51, 243 n. 2 (chapter 1), 249 n. 40; perspectives of history of, 8–9, 18, 26, 33, 242, 250 n. 42; relationship between Hindu-Muslim conflict and, 9, 26. *See also* partition of 1947

Devi, Suhasini: context and research for, 158–62; story, 162–67

Dhaka, Bangladesh, 69–80, 72, 92, 116–18, 228, 271 n. 6, 277 n. 8; mock trial for violence perpetrators in, 58, 267 n. 3; as site of National Assembly 1971 meeting, 38, 251 n. 6; University of, 39, 221

differences among peoples, 242; acceptance of, 12, 23; categorizations by, 46; nonacceptance of, 12. *See also* enemy, the: identifying and labeling of; Other, the

Dinajpur, Bangladesh, 137–38, 268 n. 7

discrimination against women (in Bangladesh), 56, 93, 186–89, 207; after liberation, 72, 93, 136, 163, 190, 202–4, 209, 212, 243 n. 2 (preface), 244 n. 9

domestic abandonment, 117–18, 253 n. 16; due to rape, 57, 93, 258 n. 9

domestic abuse, 121, 126–29, 132

duty, sense of: in committing violence, 47–49, 218–20, 230–33; for performing abortions, 169–70, 174

East Bengal Regiment, 64, 190, 197, 261 nn. 53–54, 270 n. 8

East Pakistan: cultural inclusion into West Pakistan of, 30; economic issues between West Pakistan and, 31, 35, 40–41; ethnicity issue between West Pakistan and, 19, 35–41, 46, 51, 72; government-in-exile and, 197, 203, 207, 274 n. 9, 275 n. 15; relationship between West Pakistan from 1945–1970 and, 27–31, 34–38, 225–28, 246 n. 19; tensions and civil war between West Pakistan and, 3–4, 38–41, 46, 64, 223–28, 243 n. 3, 251 n. 7, 257 n. 31, 270 n. 7, 275 n. 16; view of, by West Pakistan, 218, 225–28

economic issues: between Bangladesh and India, 266 n. 81; between East and West Pakistan, 31, 35, 40–41; for women victims, 83–85, 93, 126

election, 1970 Pakistan general, 38–39, 251 n. 6

enemy, the, 11, 98–99, 167, 228, 235; East Pakistan as, 37–39; identifying and labeling of, 31–40, 49, 60–61, 92, 100–103, 147, 215, 258 n. 36, 263 n. 61, 267 n. 1; India as, 38, 50, 257; West Pakistan as, 50, 239. *See also* Other, the; perpetrators of violence

ethical humanism, 12–14, 244 n. 10

ethics, 5, 10–14, 17, 20, 26, 67, 100–101, 217–18; as historical need, 9, 105; nationalism and, 93; of oral history and research, 84–85, 123. *See also* insāniyat

ethnicity: Assamese, 68; Bengali secular, 76; role of, in conflict between East and West Pakistan, 19, 35–40, 46, 61, 72, 76, 246 n. 19

forgetting: in construction of history, 4, 7–10, 14, 25, 32, 55, 62–65, 71, 75, 79, 226, 259 n. 44, 260 n. 45; as contrasted to remembering, 5, 7, 11, 16–17, 43, 66, 71; imposition of, through religion and society, 53, 59–62, 91; self, 250 n. 40; by survivors, 32, 53, 85, 90–92, 112

forgiveness, concept and act of, 7, 102–3, 171–73, 217, 231, 234–35, 265 n. 76, 277 n. 18; Islamic, 101–2

Gandhi, Indira, 44, 67, 183, 208, 254 n. 22, 262 n. 57, 274 n. 6

Gandhi, Mahatma, 164–67, 269 n. 3; ashram, Noakhali, Bangladesh, 177–79

gender: communication impacted by, 88; violence and impact on memory, 10–12, 79–80, 96; war and, 3. *See also* discrimination against women; sexual violence, attitude toward; vulnerable, the, as violence target

gender violence. *See* sexual violence, attitude toward

genocide, 47–50; conference in 1971 and, 256 n. 26

Ghatak Dalal Nirmul Committee (GDNC), 123, 267 n. 3

Great Britain. *See* colonialism in South Asia, British

guilt, of perpetrators: Brigadier Aga, 229, 271 n. 14; Colonel Nadir Ali, 227–29; Kader Siddique, 238–39, 257 n. 33; Kajol, 215; Major Faroukh, 239–40, 270 n. 8; Malik, 230–32; Mohammad, 233–35

guilt, of victims, 112, 140

hanadar, 111, 142, 267 n. 1, 268 n. 8

Hindu: antagonism with Muslims, reasons for and development of, 4, 9, 18, 26–31, 37–46, 52, 137, 165, 223–25, 232, 243 n. 3, 250 n. 1; 252 n. 13, 277 n. 8; -Bhakti concepts, 9, 20, 24; concepts and practices of, 180, 245 n. 15, 268 n. 4, 270 n. 6; identity with India and, 37–38, 248 n. 32, 252 n. 13; immigration to India from East Pakistan, 39–44, 167; overcoming antagonisms with Muslims and, 34–35, 156–59; views about sexual violence of, 54, 101; violence against, 63, 151, 162–65, 180–84, 223, 270 n. 8, 272 nn. 17–18

Hindutva history, 27–28, 248 n. 32

historians, Indian: Marxist, 28; secular nationalist, 26–27; subaltern, 28

historians, Pakistani, 27–29, 261 n. 52

history, 25; construction of, 8, 46, 65–66, 260 n. 45; as created by British colonial powers, 8–9, 250 n. 42; ethics and, 9, 105; institutions and, 18–19, 75, 97; people's, 101; state control of, 29–33, 245 n. 15. *See also* Bangladesh: historical perspectives on; history of 1971; history, oral;

India: historical perspectives on;
Pakistan: historical perspectives on
history, oral, 88–89, 245 n. 15; methodology of, 4, 14–16, 215, 265 n. 15;
research ethics and, 84–85, 123;
violence and, 16
history of 1971, 82; Bangladesh
perspective on, 3, 46, 61–62, 72–73,
97; exclusion of women in, 10–11,
54–55, 62, 75–77, 140–41; India
perspective on, 3–4, 46, 64–65, 72;
issues with official, 4, 8, 33, 60–62,
267 n. 1; Pakistan perspective on, 4,
46, 63–64, 225–26
history of 1971, women's memories
and: exclusion of, 4, 10, 77–79;
importance of, 15, 66, 186
Holocaust, 7, 9, 16–17, 256 n. 28, 263
n. 64
honor, women's: destruction of, as
war strategy, 42, 49, 52–53; loss of,
11, 58–59, 78, 97–98; societal and
religious pressure about, 54, 78,
82–83, 143, 150, 168–71, 192, 231, 258
n. 39, 264 n. 69
humanism, 24–25; ethical, 12–14, 244
n. 10; Islamic, 244 n. 11, 245 n. 13;
listening and, 14, 245 n. 14; Sufi and
Bhakti relationship with, 9, 20

immigrants: Bihari, in Pakistan, 253 n.
16; Hindu Bengali, in India, 42–44;
Muslim Bengali, in India, 35, 42–44,
254 n. 20; Urdu-speaking, in Pakistan, 35
immigration: Assamese–Bangladeshi
issue and, 67. See also immigrants;
refugees

India: antagonism between Pakistan
and, 31, 42–44, 63, 105, 252 n. 13, 266
n. 81; historical perspectives on,
8, 17–18, 26–34, 245 n. 15, 246 n. 18
(see also Hindutva history); 1971 war
between Pakistan and, 3–4, 39–50,
64–67, 155–56, 175–78, 195–209, 212,
233, 251 n. 8, 252 n. 11, 255 n. 23,
273 n. 20 (see also Indian Army);
overcoming antagonism between
Pakistan and, 237; perspective of
1971 war and, 3–4, 46, 62–65, 72;
politics of, 34, 159; recent violent
events in, 17–18, 28; relationship
between Bangladesh and, after war,
59, 65, 175, 200, 212, 262 n. 55, 262 n.
59, 266 n. 81; as viewed by Pakistan,
37–38, 225; wars over Kashmir between Pakistan and, 44, 63–64, 266
n. 81. See also Gandhi, Indira
Indian Army, 40, 44, 48, 156, 175,
207–12, 262 n. 56, 276 n. 7
individual stories, women's: Beauty,
119–22; Firdousi Priyabhasani,
126–36; Jharna Chowdhury, 178–84;
Laila Ahmed, 190–202; Mumtaz
Begum, 204–12; Nur Begum,
114–19; Nurjahan Begum, and
group of Bihari women, 153–57;
Suhasini Devi, 162–67; Syed Ahmed
Nurjahan, 172–76; Taslima's
mother, 141–46
Indo-Pak conflict. See war of 1971
inhumane behavior during war,
excuse for: duty as, 47–49, 218–20,
230–33; fear of India as, 257 n. 31,
277 n. 8; nationalism as, 10–14, 22,
92, 98–104, 149, 203, 224–25, 234–35;

inhumane behavior during war, excuses for (*cont.*)
the vulnerable as symbols of enemy as, 167–68, 205, 215, 258 n. 36
insāniyat, 9, 12–13, 24, 98, 216–18, 230–35, 244 n. 8, 248 n. 29. *See also* ethics
institutions, 92, 99; history and, 18–19, 75, 97; role of, in categorization of people, 12. *See also* state, the
Islam, 36–38, 249 n. 35, 251 n. 3; concepts and practices of, 13, 101–2, 234–35, 244 n. 11, 265 n. 77, 266 n. 79, 267 n. 79, 268 n. 4, 268 n. 10, 269 n. 15, 277 n. 18; gender issues and, 54, 59, 77; history of, in South Asia, 27–29, 250 n. 33; humanism and, 244 n. 11, 245 n. 13; role of, in 1971 war, 4, 39, 44, 232, 277 n. 8; views about sexual violence and, 53–54, 77, 101, 200. *See also* insāniyat; Islamic Research Institute; Islamic Socialism; Jama'at-e-Islami; Muslim League; Muslims; Sufis, Sufism
Islamic Research Institute, 29–30, 249 n. 35
Islamic Socialism, 38

Jama'at-e-Islami, 76, 251 n. 6
Jinnah, Mohammad Ali, 34–35, 236 n. 18, 251 n. 2

Kashmir wars between India and Pakistan, 42, 63–64, 266 n. 81
Khan, Ayub, 30–32, 36–38
Khan, Sahabzada Yakub, 225, 277 n. 11
Khan, Yahya, 38–39, 225, 251 n. 7, 277 n. 11
Khulna, Bangladesh, 96, 151; 253 n. 15

Lalon Fakir, 21–25, 217

language, 9, 16, 67, 87; as lost, for the past, 148; about rape, 54, 91, 101; riots and, 19, 35–37, 272 n. 15. *See also* Urdu language
lessons from violence, 12–13, 51, 71–72, 87, 92–94, 98–99, 153, 217, 226–27
Liberation War. *See* war of 1971
listening, role of, 13–14, 33, 71–72, 75, 84–91, 98–100; 245 n. 14, 260 n. 49
location: of emotion, 97; empirical, 263 n. 62; of historical production, 65; of self, 12; of thought beyond/after violence, 105, 216; TRC's, of conflict, 6; of understanding, 245 n. 14
loss: beyond, 98; feeling of, from violence, 125; of humanity, 12–13, 24–25, 100, 217–18, 230–32, 237, 248 n. 29; as leading to speechlessness/silence, 91, 150; of memory, 112, 114–18; of memory for camp refugees, 148–49; shared experiences of, 8, 11, 44–46, 83, 226; of trust, 11, 92
loss of collective memory, 18, 59, 62, 126; of Bangladeshi women, 53

manabata, 9, 24, 247 n. 27
manushyata, 9, 13, 24
memories, specific men's: Alam, 222, 276 n. 6; Amin, 220–22; Brigadier Aga, 229, 271 n. 14; Colonel Nadir Ali, 227–29; Kader Siddique, 238–39, 257 n. 33, Kajol, 215; Major Faroukh, 239–40, 270 n. 8; Malik, 230–32; Mohammad, 233–35
memories, specific women's: Anwara, 93–94; Aparna, 95; Beauty, 119–22; Fatima, 70–71; Firdousi Priyabhasani, 126–36; Jharna Chowdhury, 178–84; Laila Ahmed, 190–202;

Mrs. Jewel, 94–95; Mumtaz, 93; Mumtaz Begum, 204–12; Nur Begum, 114–19; Nurjahan Begum, and group of Bihari women, 153–57; Saji, 68–69; Sakeena, 97–98; Suhasini Devi, 162–67; Syed Ahmed Nurjahan, 172–76; Taslima's mother, 141–46; Zaibunisa, 95–96, 265 nn. 73–75

memory: complexities of, 94, 112–13, 171–72, 240–41; connection with the external, 10–11; gender and, 5, 8–10, 53, 61, 186; iconic, 53, 94, 171, 259 n. 40; impact on history, 4–15, 18–19, 26, 32–33, 242; loss of, 112–18; loss of, for camp refugees, 148–49; methodology involving, 8, 14–15, 89–91; for reclaiming women's humanity, 26, 127; reconstituted childhood, 176–77; and relationship to silence, 7, 224; role of, in understanding violence, 5–7, 12–14, 92–98, 227; suffering from, 227–33, 238–40; women's, 4

memory, collective, 4–5, 8–10, 75–76, 104–5, 226; of Bangladesh's urban elite, 73; colonialism and, 250 n. 42; creation of, 32; effect of partition on, 18–19; ignoring women's experiences in, 6, 47, 260 n. 45; loss of, 18, 59, 62, 126; loss of by Bangladeshi women, 52

men's stories. See stories, men's, Mukti Bahini; stories, men's, Pakistan Army

methodology, 5–6, 14, 81–82, 103–4; multi-sited ethnographic research as, 4, 244 n. 4; oral history and, 4, 14–16, 215, 265 n. 15. See also memory: methodology involving; research: issues with

mock trial against violence perpetrators, 58, 267 n. 3

mothers, destruction of sacred image of, 99

Mukti Bahini(s), 3, 40–42, 44–46, 114, 138, 158, 197; Kader Siddique as, 238–39, 257 n. 33; Major Faroukh as, 239–40, 270 n. 8; reasons for joining with, 79, 224; violence of, 50–51, 137, 238, 256 n. 29, 257 n. 33

mukti jouddhas (freedom fighters), 55, 73, 103, 190, 195; women and, 11, 85, 93, 243 n. 2 (preface), 273 n. 1, 273 n. 5

Mukti Juddho. See war of 1971

Mukti Juddho Jadughar (Liberation War Museum), 62

Muslim League, 30, 34, 159, 246 n. 18, 251 n. 2, 251 n. 6, 253 n. 15, 264 n. 65, 269 n. 1

Muslims: antagonism with Hindus, reasons for and development of, 4, 9, 18, 26–31, 37–46, 52, 137, 165, 223–25, 232, 243 n. 3, 250 n. 1; 252 n. 13, 277 n. 8; East Pakistani, and development of antagonism toward West Pakistan, 41–42, 223–24; Hindu violence against, 17–18, 31; history in South Asia of, 27–31, 34, 67, 149, 159; immigration of, to India from East Pakistan, 42; overcoming antagonisms between Hindus and, 34–35, 156–59. See also Islam; Jama' at-e-Islami; Sufis, Sufism

National Assembly meeting, 1971, Dhaka, 38, 225, 251 n. 6

nationalism: construction of, 61–62, 77, 266 n. 82; ethics and, 93; influence of, on history, 33, 62, 66; religious,

nationalism (*cont.*)
34–35; violence of war and, 10–14,
22, 92, 97–104, 149, 203, 224–25,
234–35
nation-state. *See* state, the
Naxalite movement, 198, 204, 208,
274 n. 6
Noakhali, Bangladesh, 160, 166, 177,
179
nomadic self/subject, 83
noncombatants, violence against, 3,
5, 218, 255 n. 24, 269 n. 12. *See also*
vulnerable, the, as violence target
Nurjahan, Syed Ahmed: context and
research for, 167–72; story, 172–76

oral history. *See* history, oral
Other, the, 5, 12–13, 19, 87, 216, 242,
248 n. 30; Bengalis as, 151; Bihari
women as, 61, 260 n. 48, 263 n. 61;
the East Pakistani enemy as, 219,
237; Hindus as, 35, 39, 219; Muslims
as, 27; Pakistan as, 31; rajakars/
Biharis as, 72–73, 162, 263 n. 61; role
of, in producing biased narratives,
4; women as, 96–98

Pakistan: antagonism between India
and, 31, 42–44, 63, 105, 252 n. 13,
266 n. 81; historical perspectives
on, 17–20, 24, 27–31, 34–35, 251 n.
3; 1970 general election in, 38–39,
251 n. 6; 1971 war between India
and, 3, 39–50, 64–67, 155–56, 175–78,
195–209, 212, 233, 251 n. 8, 252 n. 11,
255 n. 3, 273 n. 20; overcoming antagonism between India and, 237;
perspective of the 1971 war and, 4,
46, 62–64, 225–26, 243 n. 3, 248 n.

29, 277 n. 8; realignment of ethnicity in, 36–38; relationship of East
and West, from 1945–70, 27–31,
34–38, 225–28, 246 n. 19; ruling elite
of, 4, 39, 251 n. 7; tensions and civil
war between East Pakistan and,
3–4, 37–40, 46, 223–28, 243 n. 3, 251
n. 7, 257 n. 31, 270 n. 7, 275 n. 16;
views about sexual violence in, 266
n. 80; wars over Kashmir between
India and, 42, 63–64, 266 n. 81. *See
also* Bhutto, Zulfikar Ali; Islamic
Socialism; Jinnah, Mohammad Ali;
Khan, Ayub; Khan, Yahya; Pakistan Army; Urdu language
Pakistan Army, 38–40, 50, 276 n. 7,
277 n. 8; actions against civilians
by, 42, 44–49, 63, 114, 140, 156, 168,
174, 190–233, 253 n. 15, 278 n. 19;
research with members of, 215–37,
257 n. 30, 257 n. 31; sexual violence
and, 83, 92, 115, 125, 133, 170, 192,
195, 230–34. *See also* Khan,
Sahabzada Yakub
Pakistan Army soldiers' stories:
Alam, 222; Amin, 220–22; Brigadier Aga, 229; Colonel Nadir Ali,
227–29; Kajol, 215; Malik, 230–32;
Mohammad, 233–35
Pakistan general election of 1970,
38–39, 251 n. 6
Pakistan Peoples Party (PPP), 38
partition of 1947, 17–19, 24, 34, 159,
167, 246 n. 19, 247 n. 23, 247 n. 28;
India's perspective of, 3, 246 n. 18.
See also colonialism in South Asia,
British
partition of Pakistan, 3, 277 n. 12

peace committees, 50–51, 86, 162, 269 n. 1

perpetrators' awareness: of guilt, 231; for renewal, 216–17, 234

perpetrators of violence, 51, 97, 152, 162, 258 n. 36; Bengalis as, 40, 50, 86, 96, 103, 151, 155, 238, 253 nn. 14–15, 255 n. 25, 256 n. 29, 270 n. 7; Biharis as, 40–42, 48, 151, 168; Islamic perspective of, 100–102; memories of, 215–26; Mukti Bahini as, 50, 238, 256 n. 29, 257 n. 33; Pakistan Army as, 42, 44–49, 63, 92, 114–15, 125, 133, 140, 156, 168, 170, 174, 190–234, 253 n. 15, 278 n. 19; rajakars, 51, 72–76, 114, 140–43, 252 n. 12, 258 n. 36. See also domestic abuse; sexual violence

politicide, 50

polyversal narratives, 4, 82, 104, 243 n. 1 (preface)

power: exercise of, 14, 38, 77, 93, 99, 260 n. 45, 260 n. 49; history and, 8–9, 16, 33, 65–66, 74, 79–80; language and, 35; as masculine, 12, 52–53, 61, 92, 98, 103; as political, 73, 170, 204, 227, 232–34, 251 n. 6; relationship between the Other and, 26; relationship between survivors and history and, 8, 77; violence and, 218, 223–24

prisoners of war (POWs), 149, 226, 234, 269 n. 12

Priyabhasani, Firdousi, 80; context and research for, 122–26; story, 126–36

Projonmo Committee, 83

Punjabis, role in Pakistan, 4, 19, 35–38, 46

Quran, the, 13, 234

Rahman, Sheikh Mujibur: 38–39, 47, 55, 74–75, 204, 264 n. 67, 270 n. 7, 272 n. 15, 275 nn. 15–16, 275 n. 18; role of, in abortion program, 59

rajakars, 51, 72–76, 114, 140–43, 252 n. 12; 258 n. 36; identification of, for war crimes, 55, 60, 264 n. 65. See also Biharis

Rakhi Bahini, 210, 275 n. 18

Rangpur, Bangladesh, 81–83; Beauty, 119–22; Nur Begum, 114–19

rape. See sexual violence

recognition, lack of, for women in liberation struggle, 85, 93, 209–11, 243 n. 2 (preface), 253 n. 1

Red Cross, International, 46, 70–71, 175–76, 255 n. 25

refugees: Bangladeshi, in Assam, 42–44, 67–69, 262 nn. 58–59; from East Pakistan to India, 40–44, 67, 149, 167; stateless Bihari, 3, 40–42. See also immigrants; immigration

relationship between victims and perpetrators, 6–8

religion: humanism and, 24, 245 n. 13; influence of, on Hindu–Muslim conflict, 19, 31, 37–40, 52, 72; influence of, on history, 29, 33, 248 n. 32; politics and, 252 n. 13; taboos about sexual violence in, 53–54, 57–60, 77–82, 101, 122, 125, 264 n. 69; use of, in creating the enemy, 38–40, 72. See also Hindu; Islam

research, 160, 177, 215; issues with, 52, 54, 73–81; 85–91, 109, 123, 148, 266 n. 80; language and, 87. See also

research (*cont.*)
  Biharis: research difficulties with;
  memory: methodology involving;
  methodology; religion: taboos
  about sexual violence in
responsibility: of historian, 85, 215,
  226; individual sense of, 12–13, 92,
  102, 161, 231–34, 244 n. 10, 247 n. 27,
  277 n. 18; as shared, 93; of state, 103
responsibility for violence, 47, 50–51,
  175, 216–17, 229, 266 n. 80; of Bangladesh, 103; of Pakistan, 103; of
  state and society, 98
riots: Bengalis vs. non-Bengalis, 270
  n. 7; Hindu vs. Muslim/communal,
  17–18, 28, 31, 160, 167, 177–79, 250
  n. 1; language, 35, 179, 272 n. 15
Rumi, Maulana Jalaluddin, 21–25, 217

Saidpur, Bangladesh, 84–85, 97, 136–37
sale of women and children, 93
self: Bengali-, 79; loss of, 217, 250 n. 40;
  and Other, 20–24, 87, 217, 244 n. 8,
  266 n. 82; perspective of, 5, 11, 20,
  95, 243 n. 1; transformation of, 8, 22,
  227; women and, 12, 52, 83, 95, 100,
  113, 126, 188
services stories, women's: Jharna
  Chowdhury, 178–84; Suhasini Devi,
  162–67; Syed Ahmed Nurjahan,
  172–76
sexual violence, 259 n. 41; dehumanization of victim and, 112–13, 155,
  167–68, 257 n. 32; men's perspective
  of, 215; obstacles in research of, 52,
  54, 76–77, 80; as political symbol,
  76, 99; suppression of information
  about, 77–79, 85–86; in war, 42,
  49–54, 60, 79, 89–92, 99, 122, 136,

150, 169, 200. *See also* gender:
  violence and impact on memory;
  sexual violence, attitude toward;
  sexual violence, testimony about
sexual violence, attitude toward: Bangladeshi, 53–59, 122, 125; Bengali,
  258 n. 39, 264 n. 69; Hindu, 54; Islamic, 53, 77, 101–2, 200; Pakistani,
  266 n. 80
sexual violence, testimony about, 89,
  100, 215; Beauty, 119–22; Firdousi
  Priyabhasani, 126–36; Nur Begum,
  114–19; Nurjahan Begum, and
  group of Bihari women's, 153–57;
  Taslima's mother, 141–46
Sikhism, 20
Sikhs, 18, 247 n. 23
silence(s): of Bihari camp refugees,
  148–50; in history, 18, 26, 32–33, 46,
  65–66, 72, 77–79, 101; of nations,
  32–33; about partition, 18; in public
  memory, 46; of society, 1, 4–16, 26,
  32–33, 46, 65, 72, 77–81; soldiers',
  224, 232; Tripura and, 247 n. 20. *See
  also* silence, women's; silenced, the
silence, women's, 150, 243 n. 2; and
  collective memory, 7, 62; and guilt,
  112, 140; importance of, in understanding 1971, 10–15, 65; for protection, 77, 113; of violence survivors,
  7, 10–16, 53, 60–62, 66–67, 72, 77–81,
  90–91, 96–97, 140–41, 146, 162–64,
  171–75, 260 n. 49
silenced, the, 15–16, 33, 67, 109
South Asia: concerns of, 14; cultural
  aspects of, 54, 99–100, 104; gendered memory and, 5; healing of
  differences in, 10–12, 15; postcolonial identities in, 5, 10, 13, 17, 20, 25,

92–93, 217–18, 242; relationship between 1971 violence and, 105, 217–
18, 242
South Asian history: control of, 74;
exclusion of women in, 67, 79; exploration of, 8–10, 15, 26–32, 51,
65–67, 71–74, 104–5; oral, 4, 15–16,
88–89, 109–10, 143, 177, 245 n. 15;
people's, 32, 104, 242; production
of, 8–9, 66, 72–73, 104, 216, 263 n.
63; silencing of, 32–33. See also Bangladesh; India; Pakistan; partition
of 1947
state, the, 6, 28, 73, 78, 98, 102–4, 217–
18, 232, 235, 266 n. 82; control of
history by, 29–33, 245 n. 15. See also
Bangladesh; India; Pakistan
stories, additional women's: Anwara,
93–94; Aparna, 95; Fatima, 70–71;
Mrs. Jewel, 94–95; Mumtaz, 93;
Saji, 68–69; Sakeena, 97–98; Zaibunisa, 95–96, 265 nn. 73–75
stories, individual women's: Beauty,
119–22; Firdousi Priyabhasani, 126–
36; Jharna Chowdhury, 178–84;
Laila Ahmed, 190–202; Mumtaz
Begum, 204–12; Nur Begum, 114–
19; Nurjahan Begum, and group of
Bihari women, 153–57; Suhasini Devi,
162–67; Syed Ahmed Nurjahan,
172–76; Taslima's mother, 141–46
stories, men's, Mukti Bahini: Kader
Siddique, 238–39, 257 n. 33, Major
Faroukh, 239–40, 270 n. 8
stories, men's, Pakistan Army: Alam,
222, 276 n. 6; Amin, 220–22; Brigadier Aga, 229, 271 n. 14; Colonel
Nadir Ali, 227–29; Kajol, 215; Malik, 230–32; Mohammad, 233–35

stories, nonremorseful perpetrators':
Alam, 222; Amin, 220–22
stories, victims': Beauty, 119–22;
Firdousi Priyabhasani, 126–36; Nur
Begum, 114–19; Nurjahan Begum,
and group of Bihari women, 153–57;
Taslima's mother, 141–46
stories, women fighters': Laila Ahmed,
190–202; Mumtaz Begum, 204–12
stories, women's services: Jharna
Chowdhury, 178–84; Suhasini Devi,
162–67; Syed Ahmed Nurjahan,
172–76
student organizations, 39, 74; All Assam Students Union (AASU), 67, 254
n. 20; Students League (SL), 204–6,
210, 275 n. 18
subcontinent, the. See South Asia
survivors, retrieving memories of, 5–8,
14, 263 n. 64; Beauty, 109–13; Firdousi Priyabhasani, 122–26; Jharna
Chowdhury, 176–78; Laila Ahmed,
186–90; Mumtaz Begum, 202–4;
Nur Begum, 109–13; Suhasini Devi,
158–62; Syed Ahmed Nurjahan,
167–72; Taslima's mother, 136–41
Sufis, Sufism, 9, 20, 247 n. 23, 249
n. 33; relationship to language of
insāniyat, 24
Sylhet, Bangladesh, 78, 94, 159–60;
Suhasini Devi in, 162–67
symbolic use of women victims, 76

Taslima's mother: context and research for, 136–41; story, 141–46
trauma, 14, 91–92; Bengali claim to,
62, 146–47; as experienced by children, 176–77; ignoring, in history, 4,
8, 16, 32, 62–66, 71; memory and,

trauma (*cont.*)
10–11, 171, 224–26; partition as, 17–19, 246 n. 19; processing of, 6–8, 15; silence and, 58, 65
trial against violence perpetrators, mock, 58, 267 n. 3
Tripura, India, 246 n. 20
trust, loss of, 11, 92
Truth and Reconciliation Commission of South Africa (TRC), 6–7, 61

Urdu language: speakers of, 251 n. 4; tensions and riots relating to, 19, 35–37, 272 n. 15. *See also* Biharis

victims' stories: Beauty, 119–22; Firdousi Priyabhasani, 126–36; Nur Begum, 114–19; Nurjahan Begum, and group of Bihari women, 153–57; Taslima's mother, 141–46
violence, excuse for: duty as, 47–49, 218–20, 230–33; nationalism as, 10–14, 22, 92, 98–104, 149, 203, 224–25, 234–35; vulnerable as symbols of enemy as, 167–68, 205, 215, 258 n. 36
violence, techniques for victims to survive, 14, 83; as narrative about others, 150, 219–20; as unconsciousness, 90–91, 115, 133, 143
violence after the war: of Bengalis against Biharis, 50, 96; escalation of, 136, 151
violence of 1971, 158, 179, 184, 256 n. 28, 259 n. 41; lessons from, 12–15, 23, 51, 71–72, 87, 92–94, 98–99, 152–53, 217, 226–27; methodology in study of, 25–26; perspective of duty in, 47–49, 218–20, 230–33; processing of, 5, 14, 105; responsibility for, 46–51, 92, 97–98, 103, 229, 253 n. 17, 256

n. 28; women's role in, 93. *See also* perpetrators of violence; sexual violence
violence of 1971, memories of men: Alam, 222, 276 n. 6; Amin, 220–22; Brigadier Aga, 229, 271 n. 14; Kader Siddique, 238–39, 257 n. 33; Kajol, 215; Major Faroukh, 239–40, 270 n. 8; Malik, 230–32; Mohammad, 233–35
violence of 1971, memories of women: Anwara, 93–94; Aparna, 95; Beauty, 119–22; Fatima, 70–71; Firdousi Priyabhasani, 126–36; Jharna Chowdhury, 178–84; Laila Ahmed, 190–202; Mrs. Jewel, 94–95; Mumtaz, 93; Mumtaz Begum, 204–12; Nur Begum, 114–19; Nurjahan Begum, and group of Bihari women, 153–57; Saji, 68–69; Sakeena, 97–98; Suhasini Devi, 162–67; Syed Ahmed Nurjahan, 172–76; Taslima's mother, 141–46; Zaibunisa, 95–96, 265 nn. 73–75
violence targets. *See* vulnerable, the, as violence target
vulnerable, the, as violence target, 3–7, 12, 41, 46–47, 93, 103, 158, 178, 242; Biharis, 40–41, Bengalis, 41, 218; children, 70–71, 176–78, 180–83, 192, 195; religious minorities, 42; women, 41, 52–53, 57, 73, 98–99, 122, 149, 153, 183–84, 188, 195, 262 n. 56. *See also* noncombatants, violence against

war babies, 82–83; adoption program for, 58–59, 260 n. 46, 260 n. 47; Beauty and, 110, 119–22. *See also* abortions, performing

war behavior, excuse for inhumane:
duty as, 47–49, 218–20, 230–33; fear
of India as, 257 n. 31, 277 n. 8; nationalism as, 10–14, 22, 92, 98–104,
149, 203, 224–25, 234–35; the vulnerable as symbols of enemy as,
167–68, 205, 215, 258 n. 36
War Crimes Fact Finding Committee (WCFFC), 50–51
war criminals, 60; Bangladesh and,
50–51, 55, 60, 100, 237, 264 n. 65,
267 n. 3, 278 n. 20
war of 1971: causes of, 4, 9, 19, 39–40,
46, 50–51; opposing factions in, 158
(see also Bengalis, nationalist Biharis; Hindu; India; Muslims; Pakistan); perspectives of, 3–5, 72–76,
86, 162; results of, 3, 95; women's
role in, 93, 190–12; women's
sacrifices for, 85, 141, 159, 163, 202,
209–11
war of 1971 between Bengalis and Bi-
haris/non-Bengalis, 3, 40, 255 n. 25,
270 n. 7
war of 1971 between East and West
Pakistan, 3, 38–41, 46, 64, 225
war of 1971 between Pakistan and
India, 3, 39–50, 64–67, 155–56,
175–78, 195–209, 212, 233, 252 n. 11;
Indian operations, 277 n. 8; prewar
activities, 255 n. 23
West Pakistan. See Pakistan
witness, bearing, 5–17, 62–65, 84–85,
244 n. 12; Suhasini Devi, 162–67
women, dehumanization of, 26, 51–52,
79, 113, 155, 257 n. 32
women fighters' war stories: Laila
Ahmed, 190–202; Mumtaz Begum,
204–12

women's bodies violated, 100–101;
Bangladesh abortion program
and, 52, 59, 78, 83, 143–44, 168–75,
200, 258 n. 38, 260 n. 46, 268 n. 9;
representing the enemy and, 49–52,
98–99, 105, 167–68, 215, 258 n. 36;
and used to vilify the enemy, 60,
76, 99, 168. See also birangonas;
sexual violence
women's honor. See honor, women's
women's rehabilitation centers, 52,
115–16, 141–44, 163
women's services stories: Jharna Chowdhury, 178–84; Suhasini Devi, 162–67;
Syed Ahmed Nurjahan, 172–76
women's silence, 60, 76–77, 146, 150,
243 n. 2; guilt and, 112, 140; collective memory and, 7, 62; importance
of, in understanding 1971, 10–15;
for protection, 77, 113, violence experienced and, 11, 16, 53, 72, 77–81,
90–91, 96–97, 140–41, 162–64,
173–75. See also women's voices,
lack of
women's stories, additional: Anwara,
93–94; Aparna, 95; Fatima, 70–71;
Mrs. Jewel, 94–95; Mumtaz, 93;
Saji, 68–69; Sakeena, 97–98; Zaibunisa, 95–96, 265 nn. 73–75
women's voices, lack of, 260 n. 49; in
1971 history, 10–11, 54–55, 62, 77,
140–41; in Truth and Reconciliation Commission, 6–7
women victims' stories: Beauty, 119–
22; Firdousi Priyabhasani, 126–
36; Nur Begum, 114–19; Nurjahan
Begum, and group of Bihari
women, 153–57; Taslima's mother,
141–46

YASMIN SAIKIA is the Hardt-Nickachos Chair in Peace Studies and professor of history at Arizona State University.

Library of Congress Cataloging-in-Publication Data

Saikia, Yasmin.
Women, war, and the making of Bangladesh : remembering 1971 /
Yasmin Saikia.
p. cm.
Originally published in India in 2011 by Women Unlimited, K-36,
Hauz Khas Enclave, New Delhi-110016, India. Published outside of
the South Asian market by Duke University Press.
Includes bibliographical references and index.
ISBN 978-0-8223-5021-7 (cloth : alk. paper)
ISBN 978-0-8223-5038-5 (pbk. : alk. paper)
1. Women—Political activity—Bangladesh. 2. Women and war—Bangladesh.
3. Women—Violence against—Political aspects—Bangladesh.
4. Bangladesh—History—Revolution, 1971. I. Title.
HQ1236.5.B33S255 2011
954.9205'11082—dc22   2010049742